Developments in Soviet and Post-Soviet Politics

Developments in Soviet and Post-Soviet Politics

Second Edition

Edited by

Stephen White
Alex Pravda
Zvi Gitelman

Duke University Press   Durham 1992

First published 1990 as *Developments in Soviet Politics*
Reprinted 1990, 1991
Second edition, *Developments in Soviet and Post-Soviet Politics*, 1992
Published in the USA by
DUKE UNIVERSITY PRESS
Durham, North Carolina
and in Great Britain by
THE MACMILLAN PRESS LTD
Houndmills, Basingstoke, Hampshire
and London

Printed in Great Britain

Library of Congress Cataloging-in-Publication Data
Developments in Soviet and post-Soviet politics / Stephen White, Alex Pravda, Zvi Gitelman, editors. —2nd ed.
p. cm.
Rev. ed. of: Developments in Soviet politics. 1990.
Includes bibliographical references and index.
ISBN 0–8223–1259–X — ISBN 0–8223–1267–0 (pbk.)
1. Soviet Union—Politics and government—1985–1991. 2. Soviet Union—Economic policy—1986–1991. 3. Soviet Union—Social conditions—1970–1991. 4. Perestroika. I. White, Stephen, 1945– . II. Pravda, Alex, 1947– . III. Gitelman, Zvi Y. IV. Developments in Soviet politics.
DK286. 5. D47 1992
947. 085'4—dc20
92–12050
CIP

Contents

Contents

List of Illustrations and Maps

List of Tables

Preface

In our preface to the first edition of this book we explained that this was above all a guide for students, but hoped it might be considered more than 'just' a textbook. As befitted a volume on developments, we made no attempt to cover every aspect of what could still be described as the Soviet political system; our aim, then and now, was to allow ourselves a little more room in which to concentrate upon the more important changes in a rapidly evolving system, and to deal with the (often controversial) issues of interpretation to which they give rise. We also thought it proper, dealing with issues of this kind, to allow for a diversity of approach within a common framework.

As we wrote in 1990, our assumptions about Soviet politics were 'changing almost daily'. But not even we could claim to have foretold the changes with which we deal in this second edition, with the end of Communist Party rule and of the USSR itself. This is accordingly a very different book: all of the chapters have been rewritten, most of them are entirely different, and several of the contributors as well as the subjects with which they deal are new to this edition. Our aim, however, remains the same: to offer an interpretive framework for what is now a group of political systems whose evolution – in an age of nuclear weapons and telecommunications – matters almost as much to the outside world as to their own citizens.

Once again, for this second edition, we would like to thank our chapter authors for their contributions and for their willingness to provide us with revisions almost to the date of publication so that this book can be as up-to-date as possible. We would like particularly to thank our publisher, Steven Kennedy, whose commitment to this series and to this book in particular has been a great inspiration. We hope that not just our students, but a wider circle of scholars and members of the general public, will find that the outcome justifies the effort that has been invested in it.

Stephen White
Alex Pravda
Zvi Gitelman

Notes on the Contributors

David Wedgwood Benn worked for many years in the BBC World Service, where he eventually became head of its Yugoslav section. He is the author of *Persuasion and Soviet Politics* (1989), an historical study of the Soviet approach to communication, and has also written on Soviet affairs in *The World Today*, *Soviet Studies*, the *Journal of Communist Studies*, *International Affairs* and other journals. He first visited the USSR in 1955 and most recently in 1991.

Mary Buckley is Senior Lecturer in Politics at the University of Edinburgh, Scotland. Her books include *Soviet Social Scientists Talking* (1986), *Women and Ideology in the Soviet Union* (1989) and *Perestroika and Soviet Women* (edited, 1992); her contribution to this volume draws on work supported by the British Academy and the British Council.

William E. Butler is Professor of Comparative Law in the University of London and Director of the Centre for the Study of Socialist Legal Systems. His books include *Russian Law* (1992) and *Basic Legal Documents of the Russian Federation* (1992), and he has acted as adviser to the USSR, Russian and Lithuanian governments, to the European Community and the World Bank.

Alfred B. Evans Jr is Professor of Political Science at California State University, Fresno. His articles have appeared in *Slavic Review*, *Soviet Studies*, *Problems of Communism*, *Studies in Comparative Communism* and elsewhere, and he has coedited *Restructuring Soviet Ideology: Gorbachev's New Thinking* (1991).

Zvi Gitelman is Professor of Political Science and Judaic Studies at the University of Michigan, Ann Arbor. A specialist in Soviet political sociology and ethnic issues, his books include *Jewish Nationality and Soviet Politics* (1972), *Public Opinion in European Socialist Systems* (coedited, 1977), *Becoming Israelis* (1982) and *A Century of Ambivalence: The Jews in Russia and the Soviet Union* (1988).

Jeffrey W. Hahn is Professor of Political Science at Villanova University, Philadelphia. The author of *Soviet Grassroots* (1988) and of contributions to journals and symposia on Soviet elections and local government, he is currently working on a study of the politics of transition in the Russian city of Yaroslavl.

Ronald J. Hill is Professor of Soviet Government at Trinity College, Dublin. His books include *The USSR: Politics, Economics and Society* (1989) and *Communism under the Knife: Surgery or Autopsy?* (1991); he is also the author of numerous contributions to professional journals and symposia, with particular reference to local government and the CPSU.

David Mandel is a member of the Department of Political Science at the Université du Québec à Montréal, Canada. His books include *Petrograd Workers and the Fall of the Old Regime* (1983), *Petrograd Workers and the Soviet Seizure of Power* (1984) and most recently *Perestroika and Soviet Society: Rebirth of the Soviet Labour Movement* (1991). He is also editor of the English edition of *Socialist Alternatives* and a regular contributor to *International Viewpoints* and *Inprecor*.

Alex Pravda is Fellow of St Antony's College and Lecturer in Soviet and East European Politics at Oxford University. He was previously Director of the Soviet foreign policy programme at the Royal Institute of International Affairs (Chatham House). His most recent books include *British–Soviet Relations since the 1970s* (coedited, 1990), *Perestroika: Soviet Domestic and Foreign Policies* (coedited, 1990) and *The End of Soviet Foreign Policy and After* (1992).

Thomas F. Remington is Professor of Political Science at Emory University, Atlanta. His books include *Politics in the USSR* (with Frederick Barghoorn, 1986), *The Truth of Authority: Ideology and Communication in the Soviet Union* (1988) and *Politics and the Soviet System* (edited, 1989); he is also a member of the board of *Russian Review*.

T. H. Rigby is Professor Emeritus and University Fellow in the Research School of Social Sciences, Australian National University, Canberra. His books on Soviet politics include *Communist Party Membership in the USSR 1917–1967* (1968) and *Lenin's Government: Sovnarkom 1917–1922* (1979) as well as two recent collections of essays, *Political Elites in the USSR* (1990) and *The Changing Soviet System: Mono-organisational socialism from its origins to Gorbachev's restructuring* (1990).

Peter Rutland is an Associate Professor of Government at Wesleyan University, Connecticut. He is the author of *The Myth of the Plan* (1985) and *The Politics of Economic Stagnation in the USSR* (1992). In 1991–2 he was a visiting professor at Charles University and an adviser to the Czechoslovak Ministry of Foreign Affairs.

Stephen White is Professor of Politics and a member of the Institute of Soviet and East European Studies at the University of Glasgow, Scotland. His recent books include the third edition of *Communist and Post-Communist Political Systems: An Introduction* (with others, 1990), *New Directions in Soviet History* (edited, 1991) and *Gorbachev and After* (3rd ed, 1992), and he has acted as general editor of the proceedings of the Harrogate World Congress for Soviet and East European Studies.

John P. Willerton, Jr is a member of the Department of Political Science at the University of Arizona, Tucson. His articles have appeared in *Slavic Review, Soviet Studies, Studies in Comparative Communism* and other journals and professional symposia. A specialist on Soviet elite politics and centre–periphery relations, he is the author of *Patronage and Politics in the USSR* (1992).

Glossary of Abbreviations and Terms

Advokatura	Advocacy
Apparat	Party administrative apparatus
Apparatchik	Full-time party official
Arbitrazh	Tribunal system for disputes between state enterprises
Bolshevik	Radical ('majority') faction of Russian Social Democratic Labour (later Communist) Party
CC	Central Committee
CIA	Central Intelligence Agency (USA)
CIS	Commonwealth of Independent States
CPD	Congress of People's Deputies
CPE	Centrally planned economy
CPSU	Communist Party of the Soviet Union
CSCE	Conference on Security and Cooperation in Europe
Glasnost'	Openness, publicity
GNP	Gross national product
Gorkom	City party committee
Gosagroprom	State Agroindustrial Committee
Gosplan	State Planning Committee
Gospriemka	State quality control
Gossnab	State Committee on Supplies
Goszakaz	State order
INF	Intermediate-range nuclear force
Ispolkom	Executive committee of a soviet
Jurisconsult	Legal adviser to ministry, enterprise, etc.
Kadry	Cadres, staff
KGB	Committee of State Security
Khozraschet	Cost accounting
Kolkhoz	Collective farm
Komsomol	Young Communist League

Krai	Territory
Menshevik	Moderate (minority) faction of the Russian Social Democratic Labour (later Communist) Party
NEP	New Economic Policy (1921–8)
Nomenklatura	List of party-controlled posts
Oblast	Region, province
Obshchestvennik	Activist
Okrug	Area, district
Perestroika	Restructuring
Plenum	Full (plenary) meeting
Podmena	Substitution, supplantation
PPO	Primary party organisation
Pravo	Law (in general sense)
Pravo kontrolya	Party's right of supervision
Raikom	District party committee
RSFSR	Russian Soviet Federal Socialist Republic (now Russian Federation)
Sblizhenie	Drawing together (of nationalities)
Sliyanie	Fusion (of nationalities)
USSR	Union of Soviet Socialist Republics
Val	Gross output
WTO	Warsaw Treaty Organisation
Zakon	(Statute) law
Zastoi	Stagnation

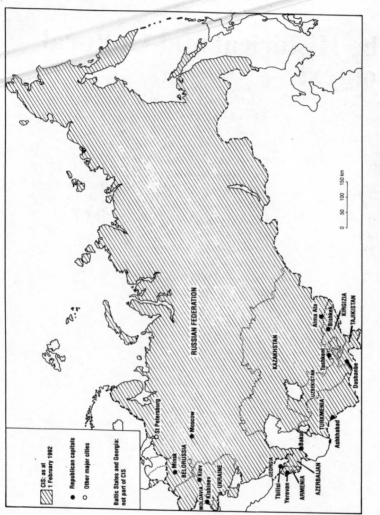

MAP 1 The Commonwealth of Independent States

CIS: as at
1 February 1992

● Republican capitals
○ Other major cities

Baltic States and Georgia:
not part of CIS

RUSSIAN FEDERATION

St Petersburg
Moscow
Minsk
BELORUSSIA
Kiev
Kishinev
MOLDAVIA
UKRAINE
GEORGIA
Tbilisi
Yerevan
ARMENIA
AZERBAIJAN
Baku
TURKMENIA
Ashkhabad
KAZAKHSTAN
UZBEKISTAN
Tashkent
Dushanbe
TAJIKISTAN
KIRGIZIA
Bishkek
Alma Ata

0   50 100 150 km

PART ONE

The Historical and Cultural Context

1

Towards a Post-Soviet Politics?

STEPHEN WHITE

In 1990, when the first edition of this book appeared, the Soviet political system was still one that older generations of students would have recognised. The 1977 Constitution, adopted during the years of Brezhnevite stagnation, was still in force. Article 6, which gave legal force to the Communist Party's political monopoly, had just been reformulated to allow other parties and movements the right to take part in the administration of public life. Yet none of them, in members or influence, could hope to compete with the Communist Party of the Soviet Union (CPSU); and the party, under the leadership of Mikhail Gorbachev, was still insisting that it should play a dominant role in the multiparty politics of the future, winning its majorities through the ballot box rather than imposing them on the basis of its scientific understanding of the laws of social development. There was a working Soviet parliament, elected for the first time on a largely competitive basis; yet a higher proportion of deputies were party members than ever before, and party members still virtually monopolised positions of influence within government and outside it. The economy was still based upon a modified form of planning and state ownership, and political controls were still strong in the armed forces, the courts, the media and associations of all kinds.

By 1992, and the appearance of the second edition of this book, almost all of these features of the traditional Soviet system had been altered beyond recognition. Gone, for a start, was the Communist Party of the Soviet Union, fairly described in the first edition of this book as 'not simply a feature of Soviet political life but its central and defining characteristic'. Gone, too, was Mikhail Gorbachev, the architect of *perestroika*, both as party leader and as Soviet President. Gone, indeed, was the state itself: the union treaty, originally concluded in 1922, was repealed in December 1991, leaving eleven of the fifteen republics to seek their future in a loose and ill-defined 'Commonwealth of Independent States'. There was no Soviet government any more, and no national parliament, although the members of the outgoing Congress of People's Deputies voted to pay themselves their deputies' salaries until their term expired in 1994. A determined start had meanwhile been made on privatising a substantial part of the Soviet economy, and the right to buy and sell land – for the first time since 1917 – had been conceded. In a fitting change of symbols, out went the hammer and sickle and in – or back, perhaps – came the Russian Republic's new version of the imperial double-headed eagle.

This, then, was 'post-Soviet politics'; and yet our volume is also concerned with 'Soviet politics', not just because they shaped the patterns of earlier decades but because they continued to exist in the post-communist era. Indeed in one important sense it was still a 'Soviet' political system, in that power continued to be exercised by the elected councils or soviets that had first been established in 1905, well before the Bolsheviks had taken power. Within those councils, indeed, power was often exercised by the same people, although they no longer called themselves communists. Boris Yeltsin, after all, had been the party's First Secretary in Sverdlovsk for nine years and left its ranks only in 1990. The new Ukrainian President, Leonid Kravchuk, left in 1991; and the influential Kazakh President, Nursultan Nazarbaev, was a member of the Politburo until just after the coup. Some of the changes that took place were largely cosmetic ones: in Kazakhstan and Uzbekistan, for instance, the republican party organisation adopted a new name but continued to operate much as before. The bulk of economic activity remained in the hands of the state, and although the old union had disappeared Russia remained the dominant partner within the territory it had formerly occupied. As compared with Eastern Europe in 1989, this was much less clearly the overthrow of a system and its replacement by multiparty capitalism; not surprisingly, perhaps, because the Soviet system had not originally been an external imposition.

The August Coup

The decisive moment in the transition with which this volume is concerned was the attempted coup of August 1991. August, by a coincidence, was the month in which General Kornilov had attempted to overthrow the Provisional Government in 1917, and it was the month in which Mikhail Gorbachev normally took his family holidays in the Crimea. In 1987, he spent the time writing his best-selling book, *Perestroika*. In 1991, he was working on the text of a speech on 18 August when four emissaries arrived unexpectedly from Moscow. All his telephones had been disconnected, so this was clearly no ordinary visit. Gorbachev refused either to resign or to sign a decree instituting a state of emergency, and was thereupon placed under house arrest and isolated from the outside world. In the early hours of 19 August a self-styled State Emergency Committee informed a startled world that Gorbachev was 'unwell' and unable to perform his duties; his responsibilities would be assumed under these circumstances by his Vice-President, Gennadii Yanaev. The Emergency Committee, it later emerged, had eight members. Apart from Yanaev himself there was the KGB chairman, Vladimir Kryuchkov; the Defence Minister, Dmitrii Yazov; the Interior Minister, Boris Pugo; the Prime Minister, Valentin Pavlov; and three other members of less prominence, Oleg Baklanov, Vasilii Starodubtsev and Alexander Tizyakov.

The Committee, in a series of decrees, suspended the activities of all parties (other than those that supported the emergency), banned the publication of all but a small number of newspapers (including *Pravda*), and prohibited meetings, strikes and demonstrations. The Committee's message was not simply a coercive one; it also promised to cut prices and increase wages, and to place food supplies under strict control with priority being given to schools, hospitals, pensioners and the disabled. In a 'message to the Soviet people', broadcast on the morning of 19 August, the Committee attempted to justify its action. The Soviet people, it explained, were in 'mortal danger'. *Perestroika* had reached an 'impasse'. The country had become 'ungovernable'. Not only this: 'extremist forces' had emerged that were seeking to break up the Soviet state and to seize power for themselves. The economy was in crisis, with the breakdown of central planning, a 'chaotic, ungoverned slide towards a market', and famine a real possibility. Crime and immorality were rampant. The Committee, it promised, would reverse these trends, strengthen public order, arrest the fall in living standards and restore the Soviet Union's international standing. The appeal was less to socialism (which went unmentioned in the statement) and much more to the 'pride and honour of the Soviet people'.

The coup, it soon became clear, had been poorly planned (indeed two of its principal members, Yanaev and Pavlov, appear to have been drunk for most of its duration). The coup was opposed from the outset by Russian President Boris Yeltsin, who made a dramatic call for resistance on 19 August, standing on one of the tanks stationed outside the Russian parliament building. Yeltsin denounced the Committee's action as a 'right-wing, reactionary [and] unconstitutional coup' and called for an indefinite general strike to oppose it. Gorbachev, he insisted, must be restored to office, and a meeting of the Soviet parliament must be convened so that constitutional procedures could be reestablished. Huge demonstrations in front of the Russian parliament the following day were addressed by former Foreign Minister Eduard Shevardnadze, by Andrei Sakharov's widow, Yelena Bonner, and by other democrats. The critical moment was the evening of 20 August when about 50,000 Muscovites defied the curfew and assembled in front of the 'White House' to defend it against an expected attack by pro-coup forces. That night, three men were killed – one shot and two crushed by tanks on the Moscow ring road – but the attack on the building itself did not materialise. It later emerged that substantial sections of the armed forces had declared against the coup, and that the elite KGB 'Alpha' anti-terrorist group had rejected the order they had been given to storm the Russian parliament.

On Wednesday 21 August the coup began to collapse. The Russian parliament met in emergency session and gave Yeltsin their unqualified support. Media restrictions were lifted, and the Ministry of Defence ordered troops to return to their barracks. The USSR Supreme Soviet Presidium declared the actions of the Emergency Committee illegal, and the Procurator General's office announced that criminal proceedings for high treason had been instigated against its members. One of the coup leaders, Boris Pugo, committed suicide; several others went to the Crimea to seek Gorbachev's forgiveness (the Russian parliament sent its own representatives to bring the Soviet President back safely); and still others, such as Foreign Minister Alexander Bessmertykh, tried to explain why they had – in his case – suffered a sudden 'cold' while the emergency had been in force (he was dismissed two days later). The most ambiguous figure of all was the Chairman of the Supreme Soviet, Anatolii Lukyanov, an old college friend of the Soviet President, who had refused to denounce the coup at the time and was accused of being its 'chief ideologist' (by the end of the month he was one of the fourteen people involved in the coup that had been arrested and charged with high treason).

Gorbachev was flown back to Moscow in the early hours of 22 August, where he later addressed a crowded press conference. He thanked Yeltsin personally as well as the Russian parliament for securing his release, and began to describe the difficult conditions under which he had been held. He had refused to accept the conditions his captors had tried to dictate to him, and had been able to rig up a makeshift radio with which he had been able to listen to Western radio broadcasts. There was some surprise that the Soviet leader continued to defend the Communist party, whose role in the attempted coup had been obscure ('I shall fight to the end,' Gorbachev insisted, 'for the renewal of the party'). Later, however, when the complicity of the party leadership became clear, Gorbachev resigned the general secretaryship and called for the Central Committee to take the 'difficult but honourable decision to dissolve itself'. On the night of 22 August, in an act of great symbolic importance, an enormous crane removed the statue of Felix Dzerzhinsky, founder of the KGB, from its place in front of the organisation's Lubyanka headquarters. Yeltsin signed a decree suspending the activity of the Communist Party throughout the Russian Federation the following day, and on 29 August the Supreme Soviet suspended the activities of the party throughout the USSR.

The Soviet state was itself a still greater casualty of the coup. Its organisers had sought to prevent the signature of the latest draft of a new union treaty on 20 August, believing that it gave too much power to the individual republics. In the event, their actions led first to the negotiation in November of a much looser 'Union of Sovereign States', and then (following a Ukrainian referendum in favour of

TABLE 1.1   *The Commonwealth of Independent States, 1992*

State	Population			Chief executive
	mn, 1990	% titular	% Russian	
Armenia	3.3	93.3	1.6	Levon Ter-Petrosyan
Azerbaijan	7.1	82.7	5.6	Ayaz Mutalibov
Belorussia (Bielarus)	10.3	77.9	13.2	Stanislav Shushkevich
Kazakhstan	16.7	39.7	37.8	Nursultan Nazarbaev
Kirgizia (Kyrgyzstan)	4.3	52.4	21.5	Askar Akaev
Moldavia (Moldova)	4.4	64.5	9.4	Mircea Snegur
Russian Federation	148.0	81.5	—	Boris Yeltsin
Tajikistan	5.3	62.3	7.6	Rakhman Nabiev
Turkmenia	3.6	72.0	9.5	Saparmurad Niyazov
Ukraine	51.8	72.7	22.1	Leonid Kravchuk
Uzbekistan	20.3	71.4	8.4	Islam Karimov

independence) to the abolition of the USSR itself. The Ukraine was the first formerly Soviet republic to declare its independence after the coup, on 24 August. By the end of the year all of the republics apart from Russia had adopted declarations of this kind and many had proceeded further, establishing a national army and applying for membership of the United Nations. The Ukrainian vote appears to have convinced Boris Yeltsin that it would be unprofitable to pursue the goal of political union any longer. On 8 December 1991, at a country house in Belorussia, the three Slav leaders met and concluded an agreement establishing an entirely new entity, a 'Commonwealth of Independent States' with its headquarters in Minsk (see Table 1.1). On 21 December, in Alma Ata, a broader agreement was signed by the three Slavic republics and eight more: Armenia, Azerbaijan, Kazakhstan, Kirgizia, Moldavia, Tajikistan, Turkmenia and Uzbekistan. The USSR, they all agreed, had 'ceased to exist'. Gorbachev, denied a place in the new order, resigned as President on 25 December, and the following day the USSR Supreme Soviet formally declared an end to the treaty of union that had originally been concluded in 1922. The post-Soviet era had begun.

The Gorbachev Agenda

A very different atmosphere had prevailed when in March 1985 a vigorous, stocky Politburo member from the south of Russia became General Secretary of what was still a united and ruling party. Gorbachev, according to his wife at least, had not expected the nomination and spent some time deciding whether to accept it; all that was clear was that (in a phrase that later became famous), 'We just can't go on like this.' The advent of a new General Secretary had certainly made a significant difference in the past to the direction of Soviet public policy, although any change of course took some time to establish itself as the new leader marginalised his opponents and coopted his supporters onto the Politburo and Secretariat. At the outset of his administration, however, Gorbachev's objectives, and even his personal background, were still fairly obscure, even at leading levels of the party. He had not addressed a party congress, and had no published collection of writings to his name; and he had made only a couple of important visits abroad, on both occasions as the head of a delegation of Soviet parliamentarians. Only a few important speeches – in particular an address to an ideology conference in December 1984 and an electoral address in February 1985, which mentioned *glasnost'*, social justice and participation – gave some indication of his personal priorities.

The new General Secretary's policy agenda, in fact, took some time to develop. In his acceptance speech Gorbachev paid tribute to his immediate predecessors, Yuri Andropov and Konstantin Chernenko, and pledged himself to continue their policy of 'acceleration of socioeconomic development and the perfection of all aspects of social life'. At the first Central Committee he addressed as leader, in April 1985, he spoke in a fairly orthodox manner about the need for a 'qualitatively new state of society', including modernisation of the economy and the extension of socialist democracy. The key issue, in these early months, was the acceleration of economic growth. This, Gorbachev thought, was quite feasible if the 'human factor' was called more fully into play, and if the reserves that existed throughout the economy were properly utilised. This in turn required a greater degree of decentralisation of economic management, including cost accounting at enterprise level and a closer connection between the work that people did and the payment they received (there was no talk of 'radical reform', still less of a 'market'). The months that followed saw the gradual assembly of a leadership team that could direct these changes and the further extension of what was still a very limited mandate for change.

Of all the policies that were promoted by the Gorbachev leadership, *glasnost'* was perhaps the most distinctive and the one that had been pressed furthest by the early 1990s. *Glasnost'*, usually translated as 'openness' or 'publicity', was not the same as freedom of the press or the right to information; nor was it original to Gorbachev (as David Wedgwood Benn points out in Chapter 9). It did, however, reflect the new General Secretary's belief that without a greater awareness of the real state of affairs and of the considerations that had led to particular decisions there would be no willingness on the part of the Soviet people to commit themselves to his programme of *perestroika*. Existing policies were in any case ineffectual, counterproductive and resented. The newspaper *Sovetskaya Rossiya*, for instance, reported the case of Mr Polyakov of Kaluga, a well-read man who followed the central and local press and never missed the evening news. He knew a lot about what was happening in various African countries, Polyakov complained, but had 'only a very rough idea what was happening in his own city'. In late 1985, another reader complained, there had been a major earthquake in Tajikistan, in Soviet Central Asia, but no details were made known other than that 'lives had been lost'. At about the same time there had been an earthquake in Mexico and a volcanic eruption in Colombia, both covered extensively with on-the-spot reports and full details of the casualties. Was Tajikistan really further from Moscow than Latin America?

Influenced by considerations such as these, the Gorbachev leadership made steady and sometimes dramatic progress in removing taboos from the discussion of public affairs and exposing both the Soviet past and the Soviet present to critical scrutiny. The Brezhnev era was one of the earliest targets. It had been a time, Gorbachev told the 27th Party Congress in 1986, when a 'curious psychology – how to change things without really changing anything' – had been dominant. A number of its leading representatives had been openly corrupt and some (such as Brezhnev's son-in-law, Yuri Churbanov) were brought to trial and imprisoned. More generally, it had been a period of 'stagnation', of wasted opportunities, when party and government leaders had lagged behind the needs of the times. The Stalin question was a still more fundamental one, as for all Soviet reformers. Gorbachev, to begin with, was reluctant even to concede there was a question. Stalinism, he told the French press in 1986, was a 'notion made up by enemies of communism'; the 20th Party Congress in 1956 had condemned Stalin's 'cult of personality' and drawn the necessary conclusions. By early 1987, however, Gorbachev was insisting that there must be 'no forgotten names, no blank spots' in Soviet literature and history, and by November of that year, when he came to give his address on the seventieth anniversary of the revolution, he was ready to condemn the 'wanton repressive measures' of the 1930s, 'real crimes' in which 'many thousands of people inside and outside the party' had suffered.

In the course of his speech Gorbachev announced that a Politburo commission had been set up to investigate the political repression of the Stalinist years, and this led to the rehabilitation of many prominent figures from the party's past (and thousands of others) from 1988 onwards. The most important figure to be restored to full respectability in this way was the former *Pravda* editor Nikolai Bukharin, whose sentence was posthumously quashed in February 1988 (later in the year his expulsions from the party and the Academy of Sciences were both reversed). Two other old Bolsheviks, Grigorii Zinoviev and Lev Kamenev, were rehabilitated in July 1988. Trotsky had not been sentenced by a Soviet court and there was therefore no judgement to be quashed; but his personal qualities began to receive some recognition in the Soviet press, and from 1989 onwards his writings began to appear in mass-circulation as well as scholarly journals. An extended discussion took place about the numbers that Stalin had condemned to death: for some it was about a million by the end of the 1930s, but for others (such as the historian and commentator Roy Medvedev) it was at least 12 million, with a further 38 million repressed in other ways. Perhaps more significant, a number of mass graves of victims of the Stalin period began to be uncovered, the most extensive of which were in the Kuropaty forest near Minsk. The victims, as many as 100,000 or more, had been shot between 1937 and 1941; this, and the other graves that were still being discovered in the early 1990s, was an indictment of Stalinism more powerful than anything the historians and writers could hope to muster.

Glasnost' led to further changes in the quality of Soviet public life, from literature and the arts to statistics and a wide-ranging discussion on the future of Soviet socialism. Public information began to improve, with the publication of statistics on crime, abortions, suicides and infant mortality. Subjects that had been taboo during the Brezhnev years, such as violent crime, drugs and prostitution, began to receive extensive treatment. Many events of the past, such as the devastating earthquake in Ashkhabad in 1948 and the nuclear accident in the Urals in 1957, were belatedly acknowledged. Figures for defence spending and foreign debt were revealed to the Congress of People's Deputies for the first time in 1989; figures for capital punishment followed in 1991. The Congress itself was televised in full and followed avidly throughout the USSR; so too were Central Committee plenums, Supreme Soviet committee hearings and other public occasions. Still more remarkably, the Soviet media were opened up to foreign journalists and politicians, and even (in a few cases) to emigres and unapologetic opponents of Soviet socialism; and the first 'spacebridges' were instituted, linking studio audiences in the USSR and many Western nations. Opinion polls suggested that *glasnost'*, for all its limitations, was the change in Soviet life that was most apparent to ordinary people and the one they most valued.

The 'democratisation' of Soviet political life was an associated change, and was similarly intended to release the human energies that, for Gorbachev, had been choked off by the bureaucratic centralism of the Stalin and Brezhnev years. The Soviet Union, he told the 19th Party Conference in the summer of 1988, had pioneered the idea of a workers' state and of workers' control, the right to work and equality of rights for women and all national groups. The political system established by the October revolution, however, had undergone 'serious deformations', leading to the development of a 'command-administrative system' which had extinguished the democratic potential of the elected soviets. The role of party and state officialdom had increased out of all proportion, and this 'bloated administrative apparatus' had begun to dictate its will in political and economic matters. Nearly a third of the adult population were regularly elected to the soviets and other bodies, but most of them had little influence over the conduct of state and public affairs. Social life as a whole had become unduly governmentalised, and ordinary working people had become 'alienated' from the system that was supposed to represent their interests. It was this 'ossified system of government, with its command-and-pressure mechanism', that was now the main obstacle to *perestroika*.

The Conference duly approved the notion of a 'radical reform' of the political system, and this led to a series of constitutional and other changes from 1988 onwards that are discussed in full in several chapters of this book. An entirely new electoral law, for instance, approved in December 1988, broke new ground in providing for (though not specifically requiring) a choice of candidate at elections to local and national-level authorities. A new state structure was established, incorporating a relatively small working parliament for the first time in modern Soviet political history and (from 1990) a powerful executive presidency. A constitutional review committee, similar to a constitutional court, was set up as part of a move to what Gorbachev called a 'socialist system of checks and balances'. Judges were to be elected for longer periods of time and given greater guarantees of independence in their work. And the CPSU itself was to be 'democratised', although in practice the changes were less dramatic than in other parts of the political system. Leading officials, it was agreed, should be elected by competitive ballot for a maximum of two consecutive terms; members of the Central Committee should be involved much more directly in the work of the leadership; and there should be much more information about all aspects of the party's work, from its finances to the operation of its decision-making bodies.

Together with these changes, for Gorbachev, there must be a 'radical reform' of the Soviet economy (see Chapter 10). Levels of growth had been declining since at least the 1950s. In the late 1970s they reached the lowest levels in Soviet peace time history and may altogether have ceased per head of population. Indeed, as Gorbachev explained in early 1988, if the sale of alcoholic drink and of Soviet oil on foreign markets were excluded, there had been no real growth in the USSR for at least the previous fifteen years. Growth, at least for many reforming economists, could not be an end in itself; what was important was the satisfaction of real social needs. But it was equally apparent that without some improvement in living standards there would be no popular commitment to *perestroika*, and no prospect that socialism would recover its appeal to other nations as a means by which ordinary working people could live their lives in dignity and sufficiency. There was indeed a real danger, in the view of economists like Nikolai Shmelev, that without radical reform the USSR would enter the twenty-first century a 'backward, stagnating state and an example to the rest of the world of how not to conduct its economic affairs'.

Radical reform, as Gorbachev explained to the 27th Party Congress in 1986 and to a Central Committee meeting in the summer of 1987, involved a set of related measures. One of the most important was a greater degree of decentralisation of economic decision making, leaving broad guidance of the economy in the hands of the State Planning Committee (Gosplan) but allowing factories and farms throughout the USSR more freedom to determine their own priorities. They should be guided in making such decisions by a wide range of 'market' indicators, including the orders they received from other enterprises and the profits they made on their production. Retail and wholesale prices would have to reflect costs of production much more closely so that enterprises could be guided by 'economic' rather than 'administrative' regulators, and so that the massive subsidies that held down the cost of basic foodstuffs could be reduced. Under the Law on the State Enterprise, adopted in 1987, enterprises that persistently failed to pay their way under these conditions could be liquidated; some economists were willing to argue that a modest degree of unemployment was not simply a logical but even a desirable feature of changes of this kind. The state sector, more generally, should be gradually reduced in size and cooperative or even private economic activity should be expanded in its place. Gorbachev described these changes, which were gradually brought into effect from 1987 onwards, as the most radical to have taken place in Soviet economic life since the adoption of the New Economic Policy (NEP) in the early 1920s.

There was a still larger objective, discussed by Alfred Evans in Chapter 2: the elaboration of a 'humane and democratic socialism' that would build on Soviet achievements but combine them with the experience of other nations and schools of thought. Khrushchev had promised that the USSR would construct a communist society 'in the main' by 1980 in the party programme that was adopted under his leadership in 1961. His successors swiftly dropped that commitment and began to describe the USSR, from the early 1970s, as a 'developed socialist society', whose evolution into a fully communist society was a matter for the distant future. Brezhnev's successors in turn made it clear that the USSR was at the very beginning of developed socialism, whose proper development would require a 'whole historical epoch'. Gorbachev, for his part, avoided the term 'developed socialism' and opted instead for 'developing socialism', in effect a postponement into the still more distant future of the attainment of a fully communist society. Later still, in 1990, the objective became 'humane, democratic socialism'.

It remained unclear, these generalities apart, how a socialist society of this kind was to be constructed and how its further development was to be assured. Gorbachev resisted calls to set out the way ahead in any detail: did they really want a new *Short Course*, he asked the Party Congress in 1990, referring to the discredited Marxist primer produced in 1938? And what was the point of programmes like railway timetables, with objectives to be achieved by particular dates; surely an authentic socialism must be the achievement of the people themselves, not something they were directed towards by others? Gorbachev's objectives emerged as a set of fairly general propositions: a humane and democratic socialism would assume a variety of forms of property and would not necessarily exclude small-scale capitalism; it would be governed by a broad coalition of 'progressive' forces, not just by communists; it would guarantee freedom of conscience and other liberties; and it would cooperate with other states in an 'interconnected, in many ways interdependent' world. However adequate as an expression of general principle, this could scarcely offer practical guidance to party members and the broader public in their daily life; nor did it necessarily carry conviction at a time of economic difficulty, nationalist discontent and the acknowledgement of mistakes in public policy for which a party that had monopolised political power could hardly avoid responsibility.

An obscurity about objectives was compounded by some uncertainty on the part of the instrument that was supposed to realise those aims, the Communist Party of the Soviet Union. Traditionally, a centralised Marxist–Leninist party exercising a 'leading role' in the society had been taken as the single most important characteristic of a communist system. The role of a party of this kind, however, became more difficult to sustain in a society in which a wide range of political forces had taken advantage of the opportunities of 'socialist pluralism'. Perhaps the most direct challenge to the party's political leadership came from the process of electoral reform, which allowed the return of deputies armed for the first time with a genuine popular mandate. The March 1989 elections, the first exercise of this kind, saw a series of senior party officials defeated at the ballot box in a manner that clearly called into question the party's right to rule; the experience was repeated at local and republican elections in late 1989 and 1990. The decision to abandon the constitutionally guaranteed monopoly of power in March 1990 was, above all, a recognition of these new circumstances: it marked the end of a party that could claim to articulate a unitary national interest, and the beginning of a party that would seek its support through the ballot box from ordinary citizens. But there was no clear break with the Leninist past – Gorbachev himself told the 28th Congress in 1990 that the CPSU must be a vanguard as well as a parliamentary party – and the change into a modern social democratic party had not been completed (if it was ever feasible) by the time of the coup which brought an end to the party's organisational existence.

Gorbachev had hoped, in his speech on political reform to the Central Committee in January 1987, to combine popular control 'from below' with the continued maintenance of political leadership 'from above'. His assumption appears to have been that the Soviet people were basically committed to collectivist values and that they would respond to his call for a more open, pluralist socialism in which a diversity of interests could express themselves. His emphasis upon leadership change equally reflected the view that the Soviet system was fundamentally sound and that it had been 'subjective' causes, above all the 'conservatism' of party officials, that had led it into crisis. The experience of his leadership was that the appointment of his own management team made relatively little difference (within two or three years he was being forced to sack the people he had himself appointed – some of them even led the coup against him). The opportunities that were provided for 'socialist democracy' led to no obvious improvement in economic performance but rather to the open articulation of national and other differences (and to substantial loss of life). And the attempt to construct a presidential system, without the backing of a nationally based party, led to an inability to implement decisions or what began to be called 'powerlessness'. By the early 1990s it was this question of political authority, or more generally of the manageability of the processes of change he had encouraged, that was perhaps the most fundamental of all those the Soviet leader bequeathed to his successors.

Towards a Pluralist Politics?

There were certainly parallels between the transition to post-communist rule in the former Soviet Union and the transition to democratic politics in East Central Europe (see for instance Stepan and Linz, forthcoming). The central reality was a fall in economic growth rates which placed an intolerable strain upon the 'social contract', by which the regimes concerned traded a restricted range of political rights for a secure and steadily improving standard of living. The Soviet authorities had certainly failed to deliver, in this sense, by the early 1990s: there was an unprecedented decline in national income in 1990, and then in 1991 a fall of 15 per cent or more. Inflation, 19 per cent during 1990, had reached 2 per cent a week the year after. Unemployment, an almost entirely new pheno-menon, became official in the Russian Federation in the summer of 1991 and was expected to reach 30 million within a year or so.

Shortages became still more widespread; by the early 1990s there were even shortages of coupons, by which some attempt had been made to allocate basic necessities. Nor, according to the polls, was there any belief that the authorities had a credible programme for extracting the country from its difficulties. By the summer of 1991 only 2 per cent expected a 'considerable improvement' in the economic situation in the near future; 18 per cent thought there would be 'some improvement', but 27 per cent thought there would be worse to come and 36 per cent thought there would be much worse.

In parallel with these developments, and again in line with the experience of Eastern Europe, there was a sharp fall in public support for the regime and its political institutions. During 1990 Gorbachev's rating as President and General Secretary fell from 60 to 12 per cent; by late 1991 it had fallen as low as 4 per cent, in a poll designed to find the Soviet Union's most popular politician. Asked to comment in more detail in the spring of 1991, 28 per cent (the largest group) found the Soviet President 'hypocritical and two-faced'; 20 per cent found him 'flexible and able to manoeuvre', but the same proportion found him 'weak and lacking in self-confidence'; and 18 per cent thought him 'indifferent to human suffering'. Boris Yeltsin, by contrast, was 'open and straightforward' (34 per cent), 'ambitious' (26 per cent) but also 'resolute' (24 per cent). There was a corresponding decline in public support for the Communist Party, the regime's central support for more than 70 years. In 1989, 37 per cent were prepared to trust the party, but by 1990 only 8 per cent were willing to do so, and by September 1991 – just after the coup – the party's level of support was down to 2.3 per cent. The level of support for Marxism–Leninism was lower still, at 2 per cent.

This, at least, appeared to satisfy two of the necessary conditions for transition to a post-communist order: economic decline and a collapse of the legitimacy of the old order. For a stable, self-sustaining pluralist system, however, there are still further requirements. One of these, according to an old but still instructive literature, is an identification with democratic institutions in themselves, quite apart from any material benefits they may provide (see Almond and Verba, 1960). Another, according to a newer literature that has itself been heavily influenced by the experience of communist rule in Eastern Europe, is a civil society: in other words, a network of autonomous and self-regulating civic associations of various kinds, from political clubs to sporting societies and church groups (see for instance Keane, 1988). It was an 'alternative society' of this kind that allowed Solidarity the political space in which to sustain its challenge to the Polish authorities; and it was the framework of the Lutheran church in East Germany, similarly, that allowed a broadly-based coalition of oppositionists to develop into a political movement powerful enough to bring down the regime itself. Civil society helped to undermine totalitarian structures by providing a realm of citizen self-activity that was beyond the reach of government; and it was the parties and movements that matured within civil society that could then provide the basis of a post-communist order.

Viewed from this perspective, there were three features of the political system that emerged after the attempted Soviet coup that suggested a stable pluralist order might still lie some distance in the future. The first of these was the weakness of the party system that emerged in the late 1980s and which was then responsible for providing political leadership in the early 1990s. By the spring of 1991 at least 20 bodies that called themselves parties had been formed at a national level, and 500 more in the republics. Some restored the names of pre-revolutionary parties, like the Constitutional Democrats; others took more obvious labels, such as the Social Democratic Party; and others still were more innovative. There was a Humour Party, for instance, formed in Odessa, and an Idiots' Party of Russia, certain of victory in a 'land of fools', whose slogan was 'Give the people beer and sausage'. The USSR Ministry of Justice, which was responsible for registering the new nationally-based parties, had at least two thousand applications. By August 1991, however, only two parties had completed all the necessary formalities: one of these was the Liberal–Democratic Party headed by Vladimir Zhirinovsky, which openly supported the coup, and the other was the CPSU, whose registration had obviously no practical effect after its suspension. By the early 1990s there was still no sign, in particular, of a 'president's party' that could support the reformist leadership of Boris Yeltsin.

The parties, again, had relatively few members. Some kept no central register of members, and could therefore report no figures; others kept them secret; others still exaggerated them; and in all cases there was double counting. Some were centrally disciplined neo-Bolshevik parties and others were loose confederations that allowed the formation of fractions, even of communists, within their ranks. Taking these various circumstances into account, it was still clear that, by the early 1990s, no grouping of parties had emerged that could take the place of the formerly dominant CPSU. The Democratic Party of Russia, led by people's deputy and former CPSU member Nikolai Travkin, was the largest of the new parties with an estimated 25–30,000 members. The 'left centrist' Republican Party of the Russian Federation was the second largest, with an estimated 20,000 members; Social and Christian Democrats each had about 10,000. Other parties, however, had significantly fewer members than this; some were even called *divannye* or 'sofa parties'. All of this scarcely compared with the 15 million members the CPSU could still command in the summer of 1991, or even the 46,000 that had joined in the first three months of the year.

The new parties, moreover, commanded the support of a very limited proportion of the mass public. Polls at the end of 1990 suggested the CPSU could still count upon the support of 34 per cent of Soviet voters, with the Democratic Party a distant second, with 15 per cent support, and no other party enjoying more than 4 per cent support. Polls in the summer of 1991 found that about 69 per cent of the mass public had no clear party preference at all; but of those that did, the Communist Party still came a clear first, with 19 per cent support. Democratic Russia, a coalition of reformers rather than a party as such, came second with 7 per cent; the Democratic Party had 2 per cent; and then came the Social Democratic, Peasant and other parties with 1 per cent support or less. The new parties lacked a clear identity, they were prone to damaging splits (as when chess player Gary Kasparov left the Democratic Party in the spring of 1991, or when Democratic Russia divided in November 1991) and they proved incapable of forming stable groupings in the Soviet parliament or of sustaining executive leadership. Gorbachev, speaking to American senators in 1990, described the USSR as the 'most politicised society in the contemporary world'; but the elements concerned were still very fluid, and it would clearly be some time before Russia and the other post-Soviet republics developed a system of competing, nationally organised parties that could offer a coherent alternative to the centralised domination of the CPSU (in the view of some Western scholars, a process of this kind could take 70 years or more (Converse, 1969)).

A second major weakness was the lack of a firmly based rule of law, before or even after the attempted coup. A rule of law was essential if any boundary was to be drawn and maintained between the state and civil society; it was the rule of law, again, that was necessary if the 'politicisation of society' that was characteristic of totalitarianism was to be eliminated. The attempted coup was at least nominally legal: the Emergency Committee based their action upon Article 127(7) of the Constitution, which stated that, if the President of the USSR were unable to perform his duties 'for any reason', his functions automatically passed to the Vice-President. (The Constitution was changed in September 1991 to guard against any repetition of these circumstances: if the President were unable to perform his functions for reasons of health, a medical commission appointed by the Supreme Soviet would have to confirm the diagnosis and the newly-formed State Council would then elect a temporary President

from among its own membership.) The defeat of the coup, and the
ostensible triumph of democracy and constitutionality, has for its part
been followed by a series of actions that give little reason to believe
that the new order will be marked by the supremacy of legal process.

One of the earliest actions of this kind was the decree issued by the
Russian President banning a series of newspapers, for the most part
those that the Emergency Committee had allowed to appear. Under
the Law on the Press, however, adopted in June 1990, a newspaper
may be suspended or banned only if it advocates – in this instance –
the forcible overthrow of the government. Whatever their criticisms
of the Gorbachev leadership, *Pravda*, *Sovetskaya Rossiya* and the
other newspapers concerned had hardly been advocating any action
of the kind. In any case, any banning or suspension of a newspaper,
under the Law, must be the result of a court decision, not a
politician's directive, and only after evidence has been produced in
support of the charges and, if necessary, contested. As *Izvestiya*
pointed out, there were many precedents for actions of this kind in
world history; but they had always been associated with seizures of
power, never with democratic transformations. 'The power of government to decide where information in the press is "accurate" and
where it is "false",' the paper argued in words that could have come
straight from John Stuart Mill, 'is the first step to dictatorship.' The
decree, in the event, was soon superseded as the papers concerned
registered themselves again under new auspices, but it showed how
vulnerable were these newly-established liberties. The dismissal of
the heads of state television and of the state news service immediately
after the coup was again an action in excess of the powers that Yeltsin
formally enjoyed as President of Russia.

Nor, it appeared, was there an adequate legal basis for the banning
or suspension of the Communist Party. As a department head at the
Moscow Juridical Institute pointed out in *Pravda*, the party could
properly be suspended only under a state of emergency, which was no
longer in force after the coup had collapsed and the Emergency
Committee's decisions had been repudiated. Similarly the existing
law did not allow the nationalisation of the property of the CPSU or
of any other public organisations. Under the Law on Public Associations, adopted in October 1990, the property of liquidated organisations reverted to the state; but the Communist Party had not been
liquidated, and only the USSR Supreme Court could adopt a decision
to this effect. The Russian parliament went still further in November
1991 when it gave Boris Yeltsin the power to suspend elections and
referenda until December 1992, to form local administrations
throughout the Russian Federation and to appoint their members.
More than this, he was specifically authorised to issue decrees in a

limited number of areas, even if these contradicted existing Russian or Soviet laws. Yeltsin, who had suspended the operations of the Communist Party in Russia just after the coup, banned the party outright in November 1991 on the grounds that the coup had been the 'logical outcome' of its policies; this action was again without judicial foundation.

It was a third and related weakness of the new pluralist order that it appeared to count upon the limited and qualified support of the mass public. There was certainly substantial support, in the abstract, for a multiparty system and for many of the more familiar democratic freedoms. In national surveys conducted in 1990, for instance, 54 per cent agreed that the competition of various parties strengthened the political system, more than half believed that 'the further democratisation of society is impossible without the direct involvement of all citizens in the administration of the country', and about 40 per cent claimed to be 'supporters or sympathisers' of the new parties and movements. Several national polls, at the same time, have found substantial support for a 'firm hand' rather than democracy (about 35 per cent took this view in a survey in the summer of 1991) and, though large majorities saw the attempted coup as illegal, there was relatively little support for the call for a national strike to oppose it. Gorbachev himself suggested, in talks with journalists, that as many as 40 per cent had supported the coup. Polls in Kazakhstan, conducted while the coup was taking place, found it had and indeed continued to have a 'real social base', with half or more of those surveyed supporting the coup or taking an indifferent attitude towards it, and with a tendency for this support to increase over time.

The coup was certainly defeated by the crowds that gathered to support the 'White House' in which the Russian parliament held its meetings. The evidence nonetheless suggests a relatively weak level of attachment to representative institutions as such, and a steady fall in support for the new institutions of state as they argue about procedures while the living standards of ordinary citizens continue to decline. The 'ratings' of newly elected soviets have steadily fallen – in Leningrad (St Petersburg), for instance, from 74 per cent in June 1990 to just 20 per cent by 1991. A relatively small minority (26 per cent) appear to be willing to vote for the same candidate in future elections, and increasing numbers have refused to vote at all, leaving elections invalid and seats vacant. Local elections in Leningrad in late 1990 generated no more than a 20 per cent turn-out; despite the best efforts of the parties, all 45 seats that were up for contention in by-elections to the Moscow and Leningrad Soviets and to the Russian Supreme Soviet had to be left unfilled. Political power, in any case, seemed to lie elsewhere: either with the party authorities (up to the coup, and in some cases after it) or with the mafia; but only 6 per cent, in a poll in Moscow, thought it lay with the city soviet. The main characteristic of public opinion on matters of this kind appeared to be 'political alienation', with 45 per cent believing that the deputies they elected 'soon forget about our interests'. According to another inquiry, there is now a 'general distrust of power structures of all kinds'.

This general decline in support for all soviets, all parties and all leaders (including Yeltsin) has been combined with a relatively low level of attachment to civil rights and a sharply hostile attitude to minorities. Public attitudes tend to be sharply polarised, much more often 'against' than 'for', and inclined to denounce rather than to compromise. The most characteristic attitudes during 1990, according to the polls, were 'hatred and aggression'. Levels of inter-ethnic hostility, perhaps surprisingly, appear to be lower than in other European countries; ethnic and communal tensions, nonetheless, have led to about three thousand deaths since 1988, and about 600,000 have become refugees in their own country. And attitudes towards other minorities are still more intolerant. According to surveys conducted in 1990, a startling 33.7 per cent would 'liquidate' all homosexuals; similar proportions would 'liquidate' all prostitutes (28.4 per cent), drug addicts (28 per cent), hippies (21.2 per cent) and the congenitally abnormal (22.7 per cent). In a separate poll in the summer of 1991, 30 per cent of a national sample repeated the call for homosexuals to be put to death; another 30 per cent favoured imprisonment and a further 30 per cent compulsory medical treatment. In early 1992 there was majority support for the CPSU to be put on trial, and calls for party members or at least its leading officials to be banned from public office.

The states that had made up the Soviet Union accordingly entered the 1990s with their democratic institutions intact but still insecurely founded. The Russian historical inheritance, it has to be remembered, was very different from that of most of Eastern Europe. There was no experience of Roman law (with its conceptions of private property and due process); there had been a very limited experience of independent party activity and competitive elections (just a decade or so before the revolution); and Russia had lacked the articulated class formations that in other European countries had held the monarchy in check and then established representative government in their own interests. Broader theories of modernisation or political transition failed to take account of this national specificity; and 70 years of Soviet rule had scarcely supplied the experience of democratic rule that earlier centuries had not provided.

The party programme that was adopted in draft in July 1991 had spoken of the construction of a 'civil society' in which there would be political pluralism, popular sovereignty and constitutionally guaranteed rights; and Gorbachev, addressing the Supreme Soviet after the coup, had called similarly for the establishment of a civil society based upon economic and political freedoms and the rule of law. Democratic reform pursued through legislation was certainly a part of the new order that began to emerge in the 1990s; but unless it was sustained by corresponding sets of attitudes, practices and institutions its future might once again be undermined by much longer-standing traditions of firm or even authoritarian government as a response to public disorder, economic decline and territorial fragmentation.

2

The Crisis of Marxism–Leninism

ALFRED B. EVANS, JR

One of the paradoxes of Mikhail Gorbachev's leadership was that, while his expressions of dissatisfaction with the performance of the Soviet system had a pragmatic character, he consistently argued that successful reform of that system required a thorough reexamination of the tenets of the official ideology. Another paradox is that, though after becoming the head of the Soviet Communist Party he set out to revitalise the ideology of Marxism–Leninism, the questioning of formerly orthodox assumptions subsequently brought on a crisis of the belief system to which several generations of Soviet leaders had paid homage. That crisis left the ranks of the Soviet Communist Party in disillusionment, confusion and disarray over questions of theory as well as practice, and left few defenders of ideological premises that had long been taken for granted. With the fragmentation of the consensus previously imposed on Soviet society, a spectrum of varied political viewpoints has appeared. Nevertheless most political activists and citizens in the former USSR (and many outside, such as Fukuyama, 1992) now agree on the lack of credibility of the ideological synthesis whose dominance was unchallenged from the 1930s to the early 1980s; and the few who argue for the restoration of the Marxist–Leninist orthodoxy of the past appear to have a very narrow base of support within Russia, or the Commonwealth of Independent States more generally.

The Pillars of Orthodoxy

Before 1985, the dominance of Marxism–Leninism as the officially supported system of belief in the Soviet Union was unquestioned and its central teachings were known to all. The pillars of Soviet Marxist–Leninist orthodoxy, which had rested unshaken for decades, despite certain narrowly focused debates among adherents of the ideology and some gradual changes in specific elements of its content, were the following:

1. Marxism–Leninism is scientifically validated as the sole correct mode of interpretation of the development of human society and indeed of the operation of the entire universe. Dialectical materialism has unlocked the secrets of the movement of all matter, and historical materialism has identified the basis of the evolution of human societies. With the development of humanity's powers of production, societies have progressed through a definite succession of stages; that process eventually leads to a predetermined end, as foreseen by Karl Marx and Friedrich Engels. Within each historical stage, the conflict between social classes grows ever sharper, until the framework of existing society is destroyed, and revolution gives birth to a new stage of development.

2. The present stage of development of Soviet society is socialism, or the first phase of communism. In that society the exploitation of one person by another and the struggle between opposed classes have been abolished by the introduction of public ownership of the means of production. The central features of capitalism, in particular private ownership of productive property and the operation of a free market, are repudiated as antithetical to the values of Soviet society, as necessarily creating exploitation and alienation, and as dooming Western societies to crises which will ultimately bring about their collapse. There is only one true model of socialism, as epitomised, with minor variations, by the Soviet Union and its Eastern European allies. The pretences of Western democratic socialists are dismissed as a facade for capitulation to the capitalist class. 'Socialism' is defined as including, not only the socialisation of the means of production, but also central planning of almost all production, bureaucratic supervision of plan fulfilment and direction of all social and political organisations by a single ruling party.

3. The goal of the Soviet Union is communism, or the higher phase of communist society. By achieving that goal, which will entail a high level of material affluence, the disappearance of class divisions and the withering away of the state, socialism will realise the main condition of its triumph over capitalism. (From Lenin's time on,

Soviet leaders increasingly postponed the realisation of full communism. Continued belief in the inevitability of the achievement of that ultimate goal was necessary, however, in order to maintain the credibility of the entire scheme of interpretation of history which was the basis of the Communist Party's claim to rule.)

4. In the course of movement towards a fully communist system, the Soviet Union will eventually surpass the leading capitalist powers in technological advancement and economic productivity. Though from the 1960s on Soviet leaders also showed a tendency to postpone the time of the achievement of victory in the economic competition with capitalism, they did not openly renounce Stalin's assertion that the superior growth potential of socialism is assured by the correspondence of productive relations (political organisation and economic management) to productive forces (the inputs into the process of production, including land, raw materials, labour and technology). The consistency between the political superstructure and the economic base makes it possible for Soviet society to avoid the crises which inhibit the further development of the economy in capitalism and eventually tear that system apart. The pluralism characteristic of Western political systems ensures anarchy, drift and decline. A crucial advantage of socialism is conscious direction of change by a central leadership, which guides society to the implementation of the goals set by the ideology, by mobilising society's resources for the achievement of collective objectives.

5. There is a fundamental harmony of interests among all groups and classes in Soviet society, since all share in ownership of the means of production and in fulfilment of the obligation of productive labour, and all will ultimately enjoy the benefits of the realisation of full communism. The abolition of economic exploitation, the experience of several decades of life under Soviet rule, and the patriotism of the Soviet people, proven in the searing test of history's costliest war, have forged a basic moral and political unity among the historical community of the Soviet people. With the advance towards the higher phase of communism, differences between groups will decrease, the degree of social homogeneity will grow and the consensus of the community will be consolidated ever more firmly.

6. In international relations the class struggle is waged on the scale of the entire world. While there are many conflicts within the sphere of domination of capitalism, the main source of tension in world politics is the interaction between socialist states, defending the interests of the working class, and capitalist states, protecting the interests of the bourgeoisie. Though peaceful coexistence is imperative to prevent the catastrophe of a major military clash between the principal

socialist and capitalist nations, there is an underlying instability in the relationship between socialism and capitalism. The interrelationship or correlation of forces in the world is gradually but perceptibly shifting in favour of socialism. The influence on international affairs by the Soviet Union and its allies is growing, and capitalism's capacity to preserve the scope of its domination is diminishing, though the continued potential of capitalism for adaptation and growth should not be underestimated. The Soviet Union is the central source of inspiration and encouragement for progressive and revolutionary forces around the entire world.

7. The Communist Party is guiding the Soviet people towards higher and higher attainments. The party plays the leading role in Soviet society, defining the ideological perspective, setting policies and directing other social and political organisations to the achievement of its objectives. It has won the right to its monopoly on electoral activity and policy determination by its faithful service to the Soviet people, which has been rewarded with their near-unanimous acceptance of its authority.

Marxist–Leninist ideology obviously legitimated the power of the Communist Party and the Soviet state, but it also did more than that. It expressed a framework of interpretation of forces and trends in Soviet society and in the world outside. The party set itself the theoretical tasks at any time of describing the most salient features of the current stage of development of Soviet society and showing the relationship of trends in the present period to the movement towards the future state of full communism. Though it was acknowledged that the ideology's specific conclusions should periodically be updated in accordance with changing conditions, the basic assumptions of the belief system were regarded as absolute truths which were never to be subjected to criticism. The claim that the party's leadership was able to interpret and apply the ideology of scientific communism was used to justify the Communist Party's role in guiding and directing all other organisations in Soviet society. From the late 1980s, as all of the teachings of the ideology summarised above were called into question, the Communist Party of the Soviet Union (CPSU) found it necessary to abandon its former claim of a monopoly of guidance of the Soviet system, and after its suspension could obviously offer no guidance at all. However, while the model enshrined in Soviet ideology since Stalin's time has been widely repudiated, it is not clear what new model of social development – if any – will prove a successful replacement.

Efforts at Reform and Revitalisation

During the first few years after his election to the post of General Secretary of the CPSU in March 1985, as Gorbachev sought to stimulate reform in established Soviet political and economic institutions, he also introduced increasingly radical changes in ideological theory with the evident intention, not of discrediting the ideology, but of updating it and infusing it with renewed vitality. Gorbachev bitterly criticised the rigidity and sterility of the ideological tenets inherited from the Stalin period and decried the political consequences of placing those postulates beyond questioning. The persistence and bitterness of Gorbachev's attacks on dogmatism may be explained by the functions which he saw an ossified version of Marxism–Leninism performing for Stalin and his successors. Those functions may be summarised as follows:

1. The dogmatic construction of the belief system assisted in legitimating Stalinist institutional structures, protecting the power of bureaucratic elites and insulating the political system from change, by denying the potential of values other than those enshrined in the official version of Marxism–Leninism, and identifying the existing Soviet institutional pattern as the only way of faithfully realising those values.
2. Insistence on the observance of doctrinal limits on debate inhibited the assimilation of new information, protecting the ideological tenets from testing with reference to factual evidence and preserving perceptions which were increasingly out of touch with reality. In other words, the conservative implications of the function of legitimation were allowed to weaken the ideology's capacity to perform the function of interpretation, as the perpetuation of antiquated myths distorted perceptions of domestic and international conditions.
3. Ideological dogmatism was also used to isolate Soviet society from the 1930s on, by justifying a strategy of economic development based on the principle of autarky, and posing barriers to cultural integration with the West. Marxism–Leninism's tendency towards paranoia was extended to the fullest under Stalin, and even during subsequent periods of improvement in relations with the West the assertion that the fundamental divisions in international relations reflected a conflict between social systems built on mutually incompatible principles justified suspicion of Western cultural and political influence as fundamentally subversive. In Gorbachev's view, the isolation of the Soviet economy from the world market consigned the USSR to the status of a technological backwater, and economic isolation would

persist as long as the Soviet Union was culturally and politically estranged from the West.

The transformation of Marxist–Leninist ideology was intended by Gorbachev to deny opponents of reform in the party-state regime the enjoyment of the benefits of the functions traditionally performed by the established doctrines. The reexamination of the Stalinist model of socialism would undermine the legitimacy of conservative officials by challenging the values for which they stood and the means by which their values were institutionalised. The destruction of dogmatism would open the belief system to the examination of changing facts and bring it into line with contemporary realities. Finally, discarding the assumption of ideologically derived hostility between the Soviet Union and the West would remove the doctrinal basis for the economic, cultural and political isolation of the Soviet system and open the prospect for closer interaction with the most technologically advanced societies.

The depth of Gorbachev's dissatisfaction with established ideological theory and entrenched Soviet institutions was not immediately apparent when he assumed power as General Secretary, however. The radicalism of his aspirations was only gradually revealed as his programme for change progressively unfolded, and it may well have been true that his radicalism intensified as experience taught him the full capacity of the Soviet system to resist change. The tone of Gorbachev's arguments during his first year in power was set by his speech to a meeting of the Communist Party's Central Committee in April 1985, calling for the acceleration (*uskorenie*) of the development of the Soviet economy. It was unusual for a Soviet leader of the post-Stalin decades to be as much of an alarmist as Gorbachev, who openly suggested that the Soviet Union's status as a great power was at risk, but it was well within the limits of conventional discourse for a Soviet leader to advocate the speeding up of technological innovation and economic growth. By the time of the 27th Congress of the CPSU in February and March 1986, however, there were some signs that Gorbachev's intentions touched on more than technological modernisation. The beginning of criticism of the legacy of the Brezhnev years was signalled by Gorbachev's complaint in his report to the Party Congress that during that period a peculiar psychology had taken hold – 'How to improve things without changing anything?'

While under Brezhnev the word 'reform' had given way to the euphemism of 'improving the economic mechanism', Gorbachev spoke of the need for 'radical reform' in the Soviet economy. Most significantly, the conception of 'developed socialism', which had been the central ideological focus of Brezhnev's description of the Soviet system, received only perfunctory mention in a new programme adopted by the 27th Congress, and Gorbachev's summary of the discussion which preceded the framing of the final version of the programme suggested that the connotations of the conception of developed socialism had been allowed to slide from realism to complacency. Though the new party programme retained a substantial influence of the outlook of the pre-Gorbachev regime it still revealed a fundamental shift in perspective, implying that, while Brezhnev had viewed the Soviet system as moving into a more stable equilibrium, Gorbachev saw the system as being increasingly destabilised as need for a systemic transition built up.

The radicalism of Gorbachev's vision began to surface more clearly a few months after the 27th Party Congress, as the slogan of *perestroika* (restructuring) assumed a central role in his prescriptions for change. By 1987 his speeches and his book, *Perestroika*, revealed the reasoning behind his programme of radical reform. Gorbachev noted that the political and administrative institutions of the Soviet Union in the 1980s were still largely those that had taken shape in the 1930s under Stalin 'in extreme conditions'. In 1987, he seemed willing to concede that, under the harsh conditions of the 1930s, the Stalinist regime might have made a positive contribution to economic development. His main thesis, however, was that, as the Soviet economy reached higher levels of development during subsequent decades, the nature of the structures of management became increasingly inconsistent with the needs of the productive base, so that the managerial superstructure acted more and more as a mechanism braking the growth of the economy. The result was the 'period of stagnation' of the economy and society under Brezhnev, which, according to Gorbachev, brought the Soviet Union to the brink of crisis. That analysis had two implications, which were as crucial for Soviet ideological theory as they were radical in their portent for policy. First, Gorbachev's assertion that in the Soviet Union managerial structures had become ever more ill-adjusted to the demands of a growing economy and had therefore acted increasingly to inhibit economic development effectively repudiated Stalin's doctrine that the consistency between productive relations and forces of production was an inherent advantage of socialism which ensured that its growth potential was superior to that of capitalism. Second, the argument that for decades the Soviet system had resisted adaptation led to the conclusion that inconsistency between different elements of the system had built up, to the point where fundamental change would have to be enacted in a short time in order to avert a systemic crisis. Hence Gorbachev's call for radical restructuring to make up the ground lost over generations, which even led him to predict by 1987 that *perestroika* would constitute a genuine revolution. It might be said that he did not anticipate the full truth of that prediction.

During 1988, 1989 and early 1990, Gorbachev's theoretical position became progressively more radical, though his stance in manoeuvring for political support took numerous twists and turns, and the degree of his effort to implement radical reform in Soviet political and economic structures was inconsistent. As might well be imagined, inconsistency between his programmatic declarations and the policies which he endorsed damaged his credibility in the eyes of the Soviet population, with consequences which are spelled out fully in other chapters of this volume. The point which needs to be made here is that Gorbachev's theoretical arguments struck ever more deeply at the intellectual roots of the political, economic and social institutions that had flourished in the Soviet Union over several decades. In its early stages in 1986 and 1987, this radical critique of the Soviet *status quo* had focused on the need to 'activate the human factor' in order to overcome the effects of stagnation and accelerate the growth of the Soviet economy. The complaint voiced by Gorbachev and his supporters was that the motivation and enthusiasm of people in the USSR as workers and as participants in social and political organisations had deteriorated to an alarming degree. Under Gorbachev, such 'deviations from socialist morality' as alcoholism, the shirking of labour, theft, black marketeering and bribe-taking were not only admitted to be growing phenomena, but were ascribed, not to the vestiges of the influence of the pre-revolutionary past, but to defects in the functioning of Soviet socialism.

The main factor restraining the initiative of Soviet citizens, in the opinion of reformers, was the superstructure of control inherited from the Stalin period, which had been highly centralised and bureaucratised in order to achieve the fulfilment of directives from the top down. That regime became routinely characterised as the 'administrative-command system', which Gorbachev later frankly described as authoritarian and still later flatly labelled as totalitarian. The emphasis on the human factor was based on the assumption that the slowing down of the rate of economic growth in the Soviet Union was due not only to technical but also to social causes, and that apathy and disillusionment in the society were fundamentally conditioned by the nature of the established political and economic organisations. The proponents of *perestroika* argued that the authoritarian state's dominance over society had suppressed the independence of citizens' activity and discouraged the display of popular initiative. They insisted that the masses could be reenergised only through the opening of channels for the expression and satisfaction of the interests of individuals and groups in Soviet society. Gorbachev and his supporters called for fuller observation of 'socialist justice' as the principle governing material reward in the Soviet economy, which for those reformers meant making the enjoyment of material benefits more dependent on money wages and making those earnings more dependent on the labourer's productive contribution, even if the result were the growth of inequality between higher and lower-paid workers.

Reformist intellectuals also advocated the airing of a 'socialist pluralism of opinions' to direct attention to problems and promote debate over solutions. In broad terms, what was proposed was a reduction of the sphere of control by the state in order to allow more space for the growth of 'civil society', or the sphere of social autonomy and initiative in which citizens would be free to devote their energy to the pursuit of private and public interests. Such notions implied the abandonment of the traditional Soviet Marxist–Leninist tenet of the growth of the homogeneity of socialist society, and involved the open recognition that the differentiation of society gives rise to diverse, competing interests.

During 1987 and 1988, Gorbachev repeatedly emphasised his conviction that successful economic reform was impossible in the USSR without radical political change. The general title which Gorbachev gave to his programme of restructuring of political institutions was democratisation (*demokratizatsiya*). The premise underlying his conception of democratisation was that, in the highly centralised system established by Stalin, the bureaucratisation of political and economic life exerted a depressing effect on popular activism. While previously Soviet sources had insisted that alienation was a problem confined to economic systems based on private ownership and the exploitation of labour, growing complaints about alienation in the Soviet system were heard under Gorbachev and, by 1989 and 1990, the most authoritative Communist Party sources identified alienation as a fundamental problem in the USSR. Gorbachev came to admit openly that the bureaucratisation of Soviet socialism had deprived the working people of control of the state and economic institutions, instilling feelings of powerlessness and apathy in the masses. Democratisation was intended to overcome the citizens' alienation from political authority by opening opportunities for the expression of popular interests. The breaking down of the bureaucrats' insulation from mass dissatisfaction was to mobilise pressure which would make reform irreversible, and was to restore the dynamism of the Soviet system by building in a process of pluralistic competition of interests. Citizens would feel safe to voice their opinions under a law-governed state (*pravovoe gosudarstvo*) in which personal authority was subordinated to the rule of law. The Stalinist principle of the relation between citizens and the state that 'whatever is not permitted is forbidden' would be replaced by the axiom that 'whatever is not forbidden is permitted'. Officials' observance of legal limitations on their power and citizens' enjoyment of constitutional rights would be protected by checks and balances between different branches of government. Democratisation would unleash popular energy and enthusiasm, smashing conservative resistance to economic reform and revitalising the Soviet state, by debureaucratising the political system.

An analogous process of transformation was to take place in the economic sphere, where bureaucratic direction would give way to market relations. Though previously the market had been regarded as a feature of capitalism which was anathema to socialism, Gorbachev and his supporters declared with increasing frankness that the market had a universalistic character. They denied that the use of market relations had anything to do with the choice between capitalism and socialism, and asserted that there was no alternative to the market for the efficient operation of any developed economy. Marketisation was to introduce more vigorous competition among enterprises and among individual members of the workforce, ensuring that prosperity would be granted to the strong and the eager. In July 1991, Gorbachev even said that the essential contribution of market relations to the implementation of reward according to labour meant that socialism and the market were not only compatible but inseparable. He and his advisers realised that building greater competition into the Soviet economic system was necessary in order to emulate the dynamism of technological innovation in the advanced capitalist economies.

There would be limits to the pluralism in the Soviet political system and the Soviet economy, however, in the new order visualised by Gorbachev. What Gorbachev sought was not the wholesale adoption of Western democracy and capitalism, but the introduction of a system which would synthesise features traditional to the Soviet Union with the advantages of Western pluralism. That was the meaning of Gorbachev's assertion in his book, *Perestroika*, that restructuring was to unite socialism and democracy, and his insistence that the purpose of reform was not to import a foreign model, but to bring more socialism and more democracy to the USSR. He argued that the task of restructuring was to take advantage of the enormous untapped potential of socialism, by which he meant a system of the Soviet type. The competition of interests and opinions was to remain within the limits of 'socialist pluralism', while the marketisation of the economy was to stay within the boundaries of a 'planned market economy'. Gorbachev continued to affirm even in the first several months of 1991 that the choice in favour of socialism, supposedly made by 'the Soviet people' in October 1917, was irrevocable. He had argued in *Perestroika* in 1987 that Lenin was the master source of creative thought about reform, and of the ideal of socialism which Soviet reformers sought to reinstitute. Gorbachev's thesis was that the intellectual task of restructuring was to rediscover the Leninist conception of a flexible, adaptable single-party system with strategic guidance by central planners. As Gorbachev recognised, direction by a theoretically informed political elite and initiative from enthusiastic and energetic masses had both been inherent elements of Lenin's vision of socialism. Gorbachev charged that, over time, the balance between those elements had been tilted, so that the centralist side had predominated overwhelmingly over the democratic side of democratic centralism. Gorbachev's aim was not to abandon democratic centralism, but to revive mass initiative while preserving a proper role for the guiding elite.

Gorbachev believed that allowing the expression of a greater diversity of ideas would contribute to the revitalisation of Soviet socialism, and not threaten the stability of the Leninist foundations of that system, because he assumed that diversity would observe the boundaries of an underlying *loyalist consensus* in Soviet society. What George Breslauer (1976) has observed about Khrushchev's conceptions concerning changes in the relationship between elite and masses in the USSR applies to the thinking of Soviet communist reformers from the 1950s to the early 1990s. The crucial question raised by reformers was that of trust: How much could Soviet society be trusted? If the society was filled with latent hostility towards the political regime, then pervasive, authoritarian control of society was a prerequisite for stability, and detailed bureaucratic direction was necessary to guide the activity of Soviet citizens towards the achievement of desirable goals. But if, as Gorbachev believed even more firmly than Khrushchev, several decades of the experience of a single-party political system and a centrally planned economy had inculcated basic Leninist values in the overwhelming majority of Soviet citizens, then the costs of excessive regimentation of citizens' activities need not be paid. A major reason that *perestroika* was ultimately unsuccessful in realising Gorbachev's aim of revitalising the established institutions of the Soviet system was that his assumption of the presence of a loyalist consensus proved incorrect. He seriously underestimated the depth of unsatisfied grievances among the people of the USSR and failed to sense the extent of their disillusionment with structures of authority. He also made the error of overestimating the potential adaptability of the institutional frame-work protected by the dominant ideology. As a result, the democratisation launched by Gorbachev went beyond his control, aroused the expression of far more diverse interests than he had initially anticipated, and finally not simply failed to revitalise the communist party-state regime but left it in ruins.

Between the Past and the Future

The first cracks in the Soviet official consensus were opened by Gorbachev's assault on the complacency and conservatism of the bureaucratic elite. The tendency of those fissures to widen more rapidly than Gorbachev had wished was indicated by the broadening and deepening of the debate which followed his words focusing attention on the flaws of the Soviet system and drawing attention to its origins under Stalin. In *Perestroika* in 1987, Gorbachev had indicted Stalinist institutions for resisting adaptation to changing circumstances in the decades subsequent to the 1930s. But more radical advocates of democracy began openly to raise the question of whether the Stalinist model had been a bad choice from the very start. Gorbachev was gradually prodded towards a more fundamental repudiation of Stalinist authoritarianism, so that by 1988 spokesmen for the Gorbachev leadership concluded that the nature of the system adopted in the Soviet Union in the 1930s had been conditioned not only by 'objective' factors such as a low level of industrialisation and a hostile international environment but also, and perhaps decisively, by 'subjective' factors, or the attitudes and decisions of political leaders. Vadim Medvedev and others associated with Gorbachev's position began to sound the theme later endorsed explicitly by the General Secretary himself, describing the construction of the Stalinist theory and structures as a distortion of Lenin's principles and a deformation of socialism. Such pronouncements naturally raised the question of the sources of Stalinist authoritarianism. Within a few years the discussion of that question had ranged very widely and had included sharply differing interpretations, including one critical of the centralising proclivities of the Bolsheviks at the time of War Communism from 1918 to 1921, another which dwelt on Lenin's own authoritarian preferences, another which emphasised the dangerous implications of a strain of thought among European revolutionaries form 1789 to 1917 embracing the forcible transformation of society to fit the vision of a small elite of utopian intellectuals, and another which traced the roots of Soviet authoritarianism to the pre-revolutionary Russian autocratic tradition. Some interpretations combined all of these factors to varying degrees.

A critical survey of the origins and development of the institutional framework which had persisted in the USSR for several decades also invited discussions over the accomplishments and prospects of that system. Gorbachev and his supporters came openly to characterise Brezhnev's conception of developed socialism as a self-congratulatory facade hiding the growing defects of established institutions, and to describe the existing reality in Soviet society as 'developing socialism', implying that the society had yet to reach a high stage of development. The new programme accepted by the 27th Congress of the CPSU in 1986 had foretold a period of restructuring of political, economic and social institutions in the USSR leading to the attainment of a 'qualitatively higher condition of socialism', without spelling out the way in which the achievement of that state or condition of society would mark progress towards full communism. What was even more disturbing for the defenders of ideological orthodoxy was that the exploration of flaws in Soviet institutions raised the question of whether the essential values of socialism had been realised in the USSR.

By the time of the 19th Conference of the CPSU in the summer of 1988, Gorbachev's rejection of the Stalinist heritage had led him to encourage the search for a 'new model of socialism' in the USSR. To fill in the content of the new image of socialism and guide the drafting of a new interim platform for the party, Gorbachev issued a theoretical statement in November 1989 on 'The Socialist Idea and Revolutionary Restructuring', which on the one hand warned that the people of the USSR could not renounce their history, but on the other hand described the objective of restructuring as the building of 'humane socialism'. The programmatic declaration which was adopted by the 28th Party Congress in July 1990 conceded that the Soviet Union was in a deep crisis, whose causes that document attributed not to 'the idea of socialism itself' but to 'those deformations to which it was subjected in the past'. An indication of the frankness of official sources was the programmatic statement's admission that the dictatorship which had ruled the USSR was not that of the proletariat but that of the party-state elite, which had given birth to 'new forms of alienation of the person from property and power' and had permitted 'arbitrariness and lawlessness' on the part of the authorities. The declaration provided a general orientation for the future by asserting that the 'essence of *perestroika* consists of the transition from the authoritarian–bureaucratic order to a society of humane, democratic socialism'. The document gave barely a passing nod to the prospect of eventually reaching full communism, which was mentioned only in a reference to the CPSU as 'a party of the socialist choice and communist perspective'. One could have searched in vain in the text of the declaration for a suggestion of the contribution which the realisation of 'humane, democratic socialism' would make towards preparation for the transition to a communist society.

By early 1991, a special commission of the party was charged with the responsibility of writing a draft of a new programme for the CPSU, since the programme adopted in 1986 was said already to be out of date, as a mixture of old and new thinking. Disagreements were to raise difficulties for those who attempted to shape a new programme, however, as contending drafts were advanced by various sources. One proposed text, which reportedly was forwarded from the Programme Commission to union republic party organisations around the USSR in June 1991, took a relatively conservative position, counselling patience for the population of the country, who were urged to view *perestroika* as encompassing an 'entire historical period', and stressing the need for continuity in policy, and for normalisation and stabilisation of the political situation. Apparently Gorbachev was so dissatisfied with the results of the Programme Commission's work that he rejected its draft altogether and called on an *ad hoc* group, headed by Georgii Shakhnazarov, a prominent political scientist and adviser to the General Secretary, to compose an alternative proposal, which Gorbachev presented to a plenary meeting of the Party's Central Committee in July 1991. That proposed programme adopted a distinctly more radical stance than the document put together by the Programme Commission (while still failing to satisfy the demands of the most radical proponents of democratic reform), not only accusing the Soviet regime in past decades of 'mistakes, arbitrariness and crude distortions of the principles of socialism and popular sovereignty', but saying that the Soviet leadership in Stalin's time had made a choice in favour of 'the totalitarian system'. This programme also reaffirmed the goal of Soviet society as 'humane, democratic socialism', while only vaguely referring to the prospect of communism by asserting that the future belongs to a society 'in which the free development of each is the condition of the free development of all'. That draft was to be exposed to widespread public discussion before the adoption of a final version of the new programme at the 29th Congress of the CPSU, which might have been held in late 1991 if not for the intervening events in August of that year.

Before the deepening of the internal crisis which led to the attempted coup of August 1991, and before the beginning of a phase of post-communist politics which apparently was ushered in by the failure of the machinations of those conspiring at the seizure of power, Gorbachev had introduced alterations in the outlook of the Soviet political elite whose significance has proved to be fundamental. He encouraged a rethinking of the sources of the principal problems of Soviet society. Traditional Soviet Marxist–Leninist theory had ascribed problems in the system chiefly to the vestiges of cultural patterns carried over from pre-revolutionary Russian history, the baleful influence of Western capitalism and its agents, and the still incomplete maturity of socialism in the USSR. As we have seen, Gorbachev's indictment of the Soviet system for failing to adapt to changing economic and social conditions and a changing international environment discredited the Stalinist doctrine that in socialism there was an automatic correspondence between productive relations and productive forces. The result was a tendency to reason that the most serious problems in the society were generated by conflicts inherent in the logic of development of a system of the Soviet type.

Leonid Abalkin, for instance, who served for a time as one of Gorbachev's main economic advisers, admitted in the economics journal *Voprosy ekonomiki* in May 1987 that its principal conflicts 'are not introduced into a socialist economy from without, and they are not rudimentary remnants of the past or the result of mistakes or delusions. Contradictions are immanent to a socialist economy, as to any living, developing organism.' In the theoretical journal *Kommunist* in November 1987, Abalkin even argued that the basic principle of socialisation of the means of production contained the potential of authoritarianism: 'Historical experience testifies that the very system of socialised property and state leadership of the economy potentially contain in themselves the danger of extreme centralisation of management which will become a reality in the absence of corresponding counterbalances.' Other Soviet scholars have subsequently emphasised that the authoritarian, statist tendency was fully expressed in the institutionalisation of socialism in the USSR and they have contended that such a tendency must be countered by those who strive to build democratic socialism.

Another trend of thought associated with the Gorbachev leadership which seems likely to have a lasting effect has been the infusion of greater realism into the vision of the future of Soviet (and now post-Soviet) society. By the time of discussion of the draft of the Programmatic Declaration adopted by the 28th Party Congress in 1990, key advisers to Gorbachev were openly advocating the virtual abandonment of the dream of full communism. Georgii Shakhnazarov, in writings in *Kommunist* and in the weekly paper *Literaturnaya gazeta* in March and April of 1990, referred to the idea of communism as a 'hypothesis' and a 'utopia', while arguing that utopian consciousness was the 'main source of negative phenomena' in Soviet history. Alexander Yakovlev, a member of the party Politburo who was thought to be one of the main architects of *perestroika*, wrote that it was difficult to convince people of the possibility of a classless society from which the market and money would be absent. Yakovlev added that the notion of distribution of material benefits according to need was vulgar and utopian. That thinking was reflected in the neglect of the prospect of a communist future by the Programmatic Declaration of 1990 and by the draft of the new party programme presented by Gorbachev in July 1991. In his address to the Central Committee on the proposed new programme, Gorbachev maintained that the 'communist idea' of a society in which the free development of each was the condition for the free development of all remained 'an attractive orientation for humanity'. Though that aphorism was drawn from Marx, it might be recalled that for Marx and Engels, as for Soviet leaders from Lenin to Chernenko, communism was not merely an ideal but a goal, whose eventual achievement was said to be historically inevitable. While earlier Marxist–Leninists expected Soviet society fully to implement the features of the goal of communism, Gorbachev regarded the communist idea as a source of values which could be put into practice only to a degree, and which had to be balanced against other values. As Shakhnazarov made clear in an article in *Kommunist* in March 1991, that change in thinking necessitated a reassessment of the linear theory of progress, bringing an admission of scepticism towards the Marxist depiction of history as moving deterministically through a series of stages, each one of which was higher than the preceding one. The abandonment of Marx's conviction that communism would prove to be the end towards which history was moving led Shakhnazarov to advocate directing greater attention to the implementation of the principles of socialism in the shorter term.

For Gorbachev and his supporters to shift emphasis from communism to socialism was to dilute the distinctiveness of the values for which Soviet communists stood. With the abandonment of the goal of a classless and stateless society, the proponents of *perestroika* fell back on the reassertion of the values of nineteenth-century European socialism. In 1989 and 1990, the rediscovery of the original 'socialist idea' of a society of social justice and shared well-being was linked with open appeals by Soviet communist ideologists for rapprochement with the democratic socialists who had been previously dismissed by the communists as accomplices of the capitalist class. Gorbachev's speeches and the 1990 Programmatic Declaration foresaw the overcoming of the historic split in international socialism which dated back to the time of the First World War, the Bolshevik Revolution and the founding of the Comintern. Even more broadly, the ideal of socialism was said to be drawn from common human values, and the effort to realise the democratic potential of that ideal was described as an inseparable part of the development of human civilisation. The stress on 'humane, democratic socialism' was linked to Gorbachev's hope to break down Soviet society's ideological insulation from the political culture of the West, a subject discussed elsewhere in this volume (pp. 254–7).

Divisive Issues

The degree to which Soviet society should assimilate features characteristic of Western capitalism and democracy aroused intense controversy as Gorbachev's programme of change took shape. Paradoxically, though Gorbachev's position became increasingly radical from 1985 to 1989, he found himself in the centre of the spectrum of thought among political influentials at the end of that period. In fact, after late 1987, it became ever more apparent that, while Gorbachev was drawing fire from those who wished to protect essential elements of the traditional Soviet administrative-command system and feared that his reforms were so radical as to undermine the pillars of support for the old order, his efforts to conciliate the critics of reform stimulated the impatience of those who were becoming outspoken in urging more fundamental changes than those he was willing to endorse. One of the issues which caused alarm for the opponents of reform, and split centrist reformers from radical reformers, was the question of the revision of forms of property ownership in the USSR. By 1986, Gorbachev advocated the legislation of private ownership of small enterprises, mainly to fill gaps in the availability of retail trade and services. Soon afterwards he supported the introduction of leasing contracts, which would permit the reemergence of family farming within the framework of collective farms which would have been transformed into producers' cooperatives. In 1989 and 1990, Gorbachev, his advisers and authoritative party documents spoke of the desired society of humane, democratic socialism as including a mixed economy with a variety of forms of property ownership.

The goal of change in property relations, according to Gorbachev, was to overcome the labourer's sense of alienation from the means of production, and to make it possible for each worker to have the feeling of being a proprietor (*khozyain*) of the enterprise. From the start, the opponents of reform were suspicious of the reintroduction of private enterprise in the USSR. As more radical proposals for changes in ownership were unveiled, however, divisions appeared even among proponents of reform. Some, like the jurist Boris Kurashvili, had been early advocates of radical decentralisation of economic administration, and later indicated that they were prepared to allow the introduction of private ownership in limited spheres. But those scholars were shocked by the willingness of others, like Vladimir Tikhonov, to contemplate not only the debureaucratisation of the economy but also the privatisation of large-scale enterprises. That position was attacked by moderate reformers as implying nothing less than the wholesale readmission of capitalism into the Soviet economy, with the attendant consequences of the exploitation of labour and extreme inequality. Radical reformers replied that it would be impossible to realise the advantages of a competitive market without the drive to maximise profit which is instilled by private ownership, and added that private enterprise was an indispensable condition for civil society's independence in relation to the state.

Another issue that touched on the limits of socialist pluralism – and ultimately the most crucial one – was that of the role of the Communist Party in the Soviet political system. When he began to campaign for democratisation, Gorbachev insisted that the CPSU was uniquely qualified to guide the process of restructuring, since it was the only organisation capable of directing change in other institutions and managing the diversity of interests that would be asserted more openly with the growth of pluralism. Gorbachev argued that the Communist Party could play the role of the chief agent of change only if it were subjected to internal restructuring by democratising the relationship between party members and the party apparatus. Even in late 1989, he continued to stress that a pluralism of interests could thrive within the boundaries of a single-party system. Gorbachev finally abandoned that position in February 1990, sacrificing the doctrine of the 'leading role' of the CPSU, as the Soviet constitution was amended to legalise competition between multiple political parties. He was left in the ambiguous position of maintaining that, although the Communist Party could not claim to play the 'guiding and directing role' in the political system, it had not been reduced to the status of a parliamentary party, but still played the 'vanguard role' in the system. Evidently Gorbachev believed that, even though the CPSU had been forced to relinquish its formal monopoly on party activity, it could still dominate politics in most of the republics of the USSR by making use of its unique advantages, including its organisational base in workplaces and its influence on the careers of upwardly mobile workers and professionals. As officials in the party apparatus in most regions of the country successfully fended off attempts to infuse more democracy into the operation of the organisations which they headed, and as a growing number of supporters of reform criticised the CPSU either from within or without, Gorbachev found himself in the ambiguous stance of one who defended the power of a conservative institution while he espoused a radical programme of change.

Gorbachev's ambivalence towards the consequences of changes which had gone farther than he had wished and the build-up of contradictory pressures on him from entrenched conservatives and radical democratisers was reflected in the manoeuvring and compromises in which he engaged in 1990 and 1991. In the autumn of 1990, he attempted to make peace with the opponents of reform, but, in the spring of 1991, he again reached out to the radicals in an effort to rediscover a common cause among those seeking further change. Throughout both periods he endeavoured to portray himself as the leader of centrist forces and called for the formation of a coalition of all groups that were committed to the health and prosperity of the whole society. In his conservative phase of late 1990 and early 1991 his emphasis shifted from restructuring to stabilisation, and from the expansion of *glasnost'* to the attainment of *soglasie* (civil harmony or concord). In that period he explicitly affirmed that his overriding objective was to prevent the disintegration of the ties among the constituent republics of the USSR. Since he had come to office as the head of the Communist Party in 1985 vigorously asserting the need to protect the status of the USSR as a great power he could not cheerfully acquiesce in the dissolution of the Union, which would undermine the country's stature in the international arena. As Gorbachev told the Supreme Soviet of the USSR in November 1990, 'the USSR's role in the world and its responsibility for the course of international development are exceptionally great. We cannot tolerate attempts by separatists to turn the Union into a flimsy formation without a unified will, or even to dismember it.'

Later, between April and August 1991, after apparently recognising the inevitability of changes which would remove some republics from the USSR and radically decentralise the remaining Union, Gorbachev renewed his emphasis on further democratisation and decentralisation. He consistently reproached his main opposition at any time, whether on the left or the right, with selfishly putting its narrow interests ahead of the interests of the entire society. His emphasis on the objective of civil harmony led to a retrogression from his earlier tendency to acknowledge the legitimacy of competing interests in Soviet politics, as he argued that stability depended on the subordination of particular interests to the interests of the community. In July 1991 he declared to a meeting of the Central Committee of the CPSU that 'strong executive power . . . necessarily demands the concord of basic political forces, their readiness to act mutually in the name of national interests'. Gorbachev continued until the eve of the attempted coup to persist in expressing the hope that the Communist Party could undergo renewal and revitalisation to enable it to lead a coalition uniting all the patriotic forces dedicated to saving the USSR from chaos and fragmentation. In the final analysis, his hope that a coalition of centrist forces could be rallied around the Communist Party proved to be an illusion. The crisis of the old order had led to a degree of polarisation of political forces which made it impossible to bridge the gulf between opponents and supporters of fundamental change. Gorbachev's tenure as President of the USSR did not survive the resulting confrontation, nor did the reign of Marxist–Leninist ideology.

Conclusion

After assuming power as head of the Communist Party of the Soviet Union, Mikhail Gorbachev challenged many established dogmas of Marxism–Leninism in an attempt to breach the intellectual barriers to change and undermine the theoretical defences of opponents of reform. Within a few years, a whole series of doctrines which for generations had been regarded in the USSR as settled articles of faith were left in a shambles. His objective was to revitalise the ideology by opening it to the assimilation of new information and restoring its effectiveness as a framework for the interpretation of evolving social and political conditions. He professed the intention of eliminating Stalinist distortions in order to restore the genuine, Leninist conception of socialism. Ideological revisionism was to show the way in which the Soviet system could be reenergised by competition among diverse interests and was to guide the Soviet Union towards a breakout from the economic, cultural and political isolation which Stalin had imposed on it. Socialist pluralism in the USSR was to combine the dynamism of pluralistic market systems with the stability provided by a single-party political order and central economic planning.

Contrary to Gorbachev's expectations, the effect of the changes which he introduced was not the revitalisation of Marxist–Leninist ideology but the collapse of that belief system. His assumption that an underlying consensus of support for the central values of the ideology would guard against major threats to the survival of single-party rule proved to be incorrect. It is now evident that the credibility of the ideology was already seriously damaged before Gorbachev came to power, and that the potential for the renewal of the ideology and the reform of the political system was not as great as Gorbachev

supposed. The bankruptcy of the system of beliefs which had legitimised the authority of the Soviet regime since 1917 was apparent
during the days of August 1991, when neither the self-styled
Emergency Committee, attempting to grasp the levers of power, nor
its opponents, repudiating its claim to rule, made any pretence of
appealing to Marxist–Leninist doctrines or invoking the authority of
the CPSU in order to win support for their actions.

During the months before the attempted coup Gorbachev, who
had long since failed to convince most Soviet citizens that he had a
coherent vision of the future, had presented himself not as the
proponent of a distinctive ideological position as much as the defen-
der of law and order. The conspirators who formed the Emergency
Committee attempted to replace Gorbachev in that role, but were
defeated quickly by a diverse collection of forces who were able to
reach a consensus on their hostility towards the old order in the
Soviet Union as epitomised by the institution of the Communist Party
and the ideas of Marxism–Leninism. In July 1991, Gorbachev had
conceded that 'the previous theoretical and practical model of socialism, which in the course of many decades was foisted on the party,
turned out to be inadequate'. The collapse of the formerly dominant
official ideology in turn hastened the end of a period in which the
political spectrum had been defined in relation to a *status quo*
structured by the communist party-state regime, and has opened the
way for the gradual emergence of a political spectrum in which
positions are taken in response to the principal features of the new
system that is currently taking shape in Russia and the other post-
Soviet republics.

PART TWO

The Contemporary Political System

3

Executive Power and Political Leadership

JOHN P. WILLERTON, JR

Democratising and decentralising forces are driving the political agenda and institutional restructuring now under way in the states that constitute the former USSR. Decades of mounting economic pressures, exacerbated by below-the-surface political and ethnic tensions, led to the dramatic policy changes of the latter 1980s and 1990s. The policies of *perestroika*, *glasnost'* and democratisation all fuelled the momentum for root-and-branch political, economic and societal changes that have been shaking the Soviet polity and society. These developments put a severe strain on the complex, developed and once well-entrenched Soviet political system. By 1991, the long-dominant *nomenklatura* elite was scrambling to retain at least a part of its traditional privileged status through 'golden parachute' opportunities in cooperatives, academic institutes and even elected parliamentary bodies. Once unchallenged Communist Party (CPSU) and state apparatus posts were rapidly succumbing to the pressures of democratisation and open political competition; later the party posts disappeared entirely.

Gorbachevian reforms and consequent societal pressures have transformed the basic notions of political leadership that evolved over the nearly 75-year history of the USSR. Principles of public accountability and the rule of law have become increasingly influential in the conduct of political life. Meanwhile, an ongoing series of institutional reforms have fundamentally altered the Soviet political landscape, leaving the CPSU without a legal existence and state bureaucracies less able to administer policy directives in the vast periphery. Political reforms resulted in a shifting of power and authority to parliamentary bodies – and at both the Union and the republic levels. A viable parliamentary system was created in May 1989, followed in less than a year by the creation of a new presidential system (March 1990). By the end of 1990, the new Union executive had been overhauled, with the presidency given enhanced decision-making powers, a vice-presidency created, the Council (renamed Cabinet) of Ministers downgraded, and the newly created Council of the Federation – composed of the USSR President and leaders of the fifteen Soviet republics – upgraded to a policy-making body. Taken together, these institutional reforms reflected the ongoing transfer of Union-level authority to non-party executive bodies, with Gorbachev and reform-oriented forces in a strong, but not dominant, policy-making position.

Concomitant with these reforms was a power shift from the political centre, Moscow, to the diverse periphery. Decentralisation signified that the authority of regional and local officials was increasingly rooted in bottom-up pressures, with regional and local constituencies – rather than Union authorities – driving those leaders' career interests. Subnational officials became assertive in addressing not just regional, but Union, problems. With the regions and districts subject to institutional reforms comparable in nature and scope to those at the Union level, major policy changes were to be anticipated. Centrifugal forces throughout the USSR were of such a magnitude that, by the end of 1990, all fifteen Soviet republics had already declared their sovereignty or outright independence from Moscow; by the end of 1991 the USSR itself had ceased to exist.

All of these changes have been conducive to the transformation of Union and regional leaderships during the 1980s and early 1990s. Among Union-level leaders, only Mikhail Gorbachev survived this tumultuous decade, to retain power at the highest level from 1985 until his resignation in December 1991. Several sets of 'reformist' Union-level leaders had risen and fallen since Brezhnev's death in November 1982. The breaking of the CPSU apparatus's power hold over the decision-making process left elements outside the traditional power establishment in a growing position to influence the policy agenda. Iconoclastic politicians such as Russian President Boris Yeltsin and Leningrad (later St Petersburg) Mayor Anatolii Sobchak were increasingly able to use public forums to press for radical economic and political change. Patterns of elite behaviour were changing, as elite mobility channels opened. Up-and-coming politicians – at the centre and in the periphery – were less needy of apparatus experience and more in need of coalition-building and negotiating skills in advancing their policy interests. The skills that had led a faceless *apparatchik* such as Konstantin Chernenko to ascend to the highest decision-making posts were no longer critical to effective career building. Indeed they were increasingly a liability. Notions of public accountability, consensus building and observance of laws, among other qualities, were more and more important to officials' career futures. Rising stars such as Sobchak or Moscow Deputy Mayor Sergei Stankevich relied upon personal charisma, effective oratory and careful parliamentary manoeuvring to advance their causes – and their political careers.

The traditional Soviet system had relied upon strong political executives, well ensconced within the party apparatus, to direct the massive state bureaucracy. Upon consolidation of power, a process that required upwards of five years, forceful leaders such as Stalin, Khrushchev and Brezhnev were able to initiate major programmatic reforms (Breslauer, 1980). Gorbachevian reforms altered notions of a strong executive and, in the end, left the country devoid of such an executive at the Union level. Strong executives increasingly emerged at the republic level, particularly in Russia, with the mounting authority and power of republic chief executives coming at the expense of Union (and local) officials. But those reforms, and the powerful centrifugal tendencies they unleashed, have not removed the country's need for some broader form of policy coordination. The Union presidency, established in 1990, was intended to provide such institutionalised leadership, with the President serving as an arbiter among openly competing interests, as a policy coordinator and as the top official overseeing the country's sociopolitical and economic transformation. The Union President was thought to be in the best position to balance the conflicting interests and perspectives of rival independent political actors in Moscow and the republics. The President's constitutional powers and public authority (through competitive nationwide election) would help to offset the lost bureaucratic prerogatives that once permitted the top Union-level leader (that is, the CPSU General Secretary) to rule by *diktat*.

By the early 1990s a new form of political leadership had emerged which reflected a developing system of checks and balances. The informal politics of patron–client networks and hidden bureaucratic bargaining were giving way to an institutionalised politics of competition, debate and open consensus building. Union and republic-level leaders were compelled to bring together officials and groups with ever more diverse and even opposing views. Effective governance in the country necessitated the simultaneous balancing of rival interests at the Union level, at the sub-Union level, and (after 1991) between the Commonwealth and its constituent units. The broad contours, not to mention specific institutional arrangements, of this nascent institutionalised checks and balances system had still not been established at the time of writing; and the division of political responsibilities as between Commonwealth, republic and local actors has still to be determined. It is clear, at least, that central authority has largely been replaced by a system based upon the republics, most of which have established their own elective presidencies. Subnational leaderships are now struggling to organise their new responsibilities and to fashion coherent policy programmes. The current strong centrifugal push, and concomitant political and economic chaos, could serve to revive formerly strong central political institutions, and some kind of presidency and Commonwealth assembly could still become important elements in a post-Soviet decision-making process. But the complex push–pull of the new democratic politics makes it difficult to see beyond today's chaos to the particular arrangements of an orderly political future; and in the immediate post-Communist period it was not entirely clear that even republican leaders would be able to establish a stable form of authority in what had now become independent states.

The Traditional Soviet System

An Authoritarian Political Legacy

Contemporary dramatic changes in the USSR must be considered against the backdrop of an authoritarian political legacy. Were one to describe the essential characteristics of the traditional (Stalinist) Soviet political system, one would note its centralised, hierarchical nature and its massive set of interconnected bureaucracies linking all institutions and interests to an apparatus ruled by a small and relatively homogeneous cohort of Slavic and Russian elites. The political system was moulded by Lenin's thinking and the CPSU's early experiences, with important rules such as the principle of democratic centralism in place by the early 1920s. The set of CPSU and state apparatuses, and the norms governing their operation, were more fully developed during the Stalin period (1928–53). Each Union regime attempted to leave its mark on the Soviet political process, with frequent reorganisations of selected *apparats* or sectors characterising the Stalin, Khrushchev and Brezhnev periods. One Western scholar described the traditional Soviet political system as one of 'bureaucratic shapelessness', with the various party and state *apparats* lacking clear domains of responsibility or definite lines separating the organisational obligations of competing bureaucracies (Bialer, 1980). Each regime attempted to harness the massive party-state apparatus through its own set of institutional reforms and personnel rotation. But even with these changes, it was continuity, and not change, that characterised the Soviet system from the 1930s to the early 1980s.

In the traditional system, party bodies enjoyed supremacy over state bodies in the making of policy. This was true at the Union level as well as in the regions and districts. It was the CPSU General Secretary who set out the broad political agenda directing the polity and society. As the leading member of the top decision-making body – the Politburo – he guided the policy process. As the 'general' secretary within the CPSU Secretariat, the party's primary administrative organ, he possessed broad supervisory power over all other secretaries and all subordinate departments of the party apparatus. The General Secretary's access to information and his ability to comment on all policy matters made him the most formidable actor in the highly bureaucratised Soviet system. Moreover he was also in a decisive position to influence personnel recruitment. All general secretaries, from Stalin to Gorbachev, played critical roles in the mobility of cadres and the formation of ruling coalitions at both the Union and regional levels. In the post-Stalin period, Leonid Brezhnev was especially effective in this regard, drawing upon a large patronage network and an effective coalition-building strategy ('stability of cadres' policy) to govern for nearly two decades.

In this traditional Soviet system, broad policy-making and supervisory powers were vested in the party Politburo and Secretariat: their 25 or so members were the *crème de la crème* of the political establishment. The Central Committee (CC), with its apparatus of about 20 departments and thousands of professional party workers, constituted the nerve centre of the political system. Among the CC's 350 or so members were the top officials drawn from all central and lower-level institutions. As the party's top representational body, the CC legitimated the policy line set by the top leadership, with its members – as the heads of all major institutions and organised interests in the country – transmitting that line to subordinate officials in Moscow and in local areas. CC *apparatchiki* assisted top decision makers in supervising state and subordinate party organisations, coordinating those organisations' activities and transmitting information up and down the institutional hierarchies.

In the traditional system, matters of policy implementation and administration were left to state bureaucracies, led by the Council of Ministers, its governing council (or Presidium) and the Prime Minister. The 'popularly elected' Supreme Soviet, with deputies selected through single-candidate elections, provided the *post hoc* legitimation needed for the party leadership's initiatives. Taken together, these bodies unified the policy-making, implementing and legitimating functions in a single interconnected hierarchy. The system ensured the concentration of real power and authority while increasing the institutional mechanisms linking the governing elite to the diversity of interests found within Soviet society.

The Nomenklatura Elite

The term *nomenklatura* symbolised the hegemonic and conservative elite which for so long directed this political system and dominated the country's political life. It was derived from the system of lists of both official positions and politicians aspiring to those positions: lists controlled by party leaders and used at every level of authority in the recruitment and mobility of subordinate officials. The long-ruling *nomenklatura* proved to be stable and predictable in its composition and behavioural proclivities. Its members were ideologically committed to the system; their careers were primarily in the party-state apparatus. Often of working-class backgrounds, the *nomenklatura* elite – up to three million in the 1980s – brought technical educations and bureaucratic expertise to their career aspirations.

After the Stalinist purges, and particularly in the post-1953 period, there was considerable continuity in the *nomenklatura*'s ranks and in its commitment to the basic Stalinist system, norms and issue agenda. This continuity contributed to a discernible political and societal stability which continued into the 1980s. The *nomenklatura* system structured the career aspirations of upwardly-mobile officials throughout the USSR. Especially dominant was the cohort of officials whose careers began in the 1930s and 1940s. This so-called 'Stalin generation' of politicians included Khrushchev, Brezhnev, Andropov and Chernenko, and it governed the polity for nearly 40 years. It was only in the Brezhnev period (1964–82) that the negative consequences of this *nomenklatura* stability became evident. Under Brezhnev there emerged a political lethargy and policy stagnation that exacerbated economic and political problems deeply rooted in the Stalinist system. The *nomenklatura* elite – and Stalinist political system – proved unwilling and unable to address these rapidly mounting policy dilemmas. With the brief Andropov–Chernenko interregnum (1982–5) entailing few corrective measures, the stage was set for far-reaching changes under a dynamic and eventually anti-*nomenklatura* Gorbachev leadership.

Momentum for Change

Reorganisations and Personnel Changes

The March 1985 succession which brought Mikhail Gorbachev to power occurred against the backdrop of simmering domestic and foreign policy dilemmas which required the Union leadership's immediate attention. Most high-level officials were agreed on the need to address these problems with new policy solutions, but after a decade of weak and indecisive regimes there was a felt need for strong central leadership. The *perestroika* programme that became the hallmark of the reformist Gorbachev leadership took shape only after several years of regime consolidation (1985–9). Gorbachev used authoritative settings such as the January 1987 CC plenum to press for political reforms (including secret and multicandidate election for state and party officials), but considerable *nomenklatura* resistance slowed the pace of institutional and policy change. Many Stalin-generation officials and remnants of the old Brezhnev regime needed to be removed from the ruling elite. Several years of intricate political manoeuvring by Gorbachev and other reformers were required before a governing team was in place which was committed to a comprehensive reform programme.

Important institutional and personnel changes first emerged within the party apparatus, though government bureaucracies proved equally vulnerable to reorganisation and 'cadre renewal'. During the first five years of the Gorbachev regime, party and government agencies were streamlined and significant numbers of positions abolished (upwards of one-third of the personnel in a typical CC department or government ministry). An ongoing series of institutional changes throughout the 1985–9 period weakened the organisational might of the CC apparatus while strengthening the position of high-level party reformers (Sakwa, 1990). The November 1988 CC plenum entailed an especially important set of organisational reforms which redistributed power and responsibilities among top-level party organs. The Politburo's policy-making preeminence was temporarily reinforced with the downgrading of the Secretariat, creation of six Central Committee commissions and consolidation of CC departments. Gorbachev was able to oversee the advance of a number of influential reform-oriented allies into the ranks of the top leadership, but these politicians confronted subordinates who resisted more comprehensive political and economic reform.

Institutional changes within the CPSU helped remove many of those resistant incumbents: during the late 1980s, most CC members were retired, with the April 1989 ouster of 100 CC members an especially dramatic indicator of the momentum for personnel change. Organisational slots were opened to permit politicians more inclined towards system change to advance themselves and their policy positions (Willerton, 1992). Personnel turnover was quite high in the CC apparatus, as well as in the Politburo and Secretariat. There were comparable changes in the government apparatus, with institutional reorganisations and personnel turnover used in an effort to counter conservative resistance. Streamlining efforts, as, for instance, in the priority agricultural sector, were used to heighten the political leadership's hold over the key administrative agencies. Yet the creation of entities such as *Gosagroprom*, the agricultural supra-ministry formed out of a half-dozen government agencies, did not make the apparatus more efficient or ensure the adoption of radical reform measures. Indeed *Gosagroprom*'s head, Vsevolod Murakhovsky, a Gorbachev protege, proved to be cautious and hesitant about profound agricultural policy changes. Within a few years his supra-ministry was abolished and he was retired.

Bureaucratic reorganisations and personnel changes were standard approaches to addressing institutional resistance and they were widely used during the early years of the Gorbachev regime. They could not ensure the immediate formation of a new governing coalition of politicians genuinely committed to fundamental system reform – Union leaders, including the party secretary for cadres, Georgii Razumovsky, acknowledged the dearth of reform-oriented officials and the need for educational training programmes to cultivate them – but institutional and personnel changes did alter the balance of power among elite elements within the political establishment, allowing for the emergence of a cautiously reform-oriented Soviet regime. Officials emerged who were not members of past regimes and who were not tainted by associations with now-discredited former leaders. Some of these new leaders were, to judge by reputation, past action and public profiling, conservative, while others were reformist. By the late 1980s the Soviet national leadership included a diversity of conflicting policy perspectives that portended serious and public struggles over power and policy. The traditional norms of cautious debate and elite consensus would rapidly give way to open argument and even hostile confrontation.

Gorbachev promoted politicians such as Viktor Chebrikov (KGB), Yegor Ligachev (CPSU apparatus), Nikolai Ryzhkov (central planning) and Lev Zaikov (military–industrial establishment), who favoured limited economic reforms while championing traditional party and government bureaucratic interests. But he also sponsored other officials, such as Aleksandr Yakovlev (CPSU apparatus), Eduard Shevardnadze (Georgia) and Boris Yeltsin (Sverdlovsk), who articulated increasingly reformist stances. Differences within the ranks of this governing elite became increasingly evident as the *glasnost'* campaign led to more wide-ranging policy debates. The well-publicised Ligachev–Yeltsin confrontations of 1987–8 proved to be a harbinger of other intense polemical battles which came to engulf all politicians. By the July 1989 CC plenum, a number of top leaders (including Prime Minister Ryzhkov and Party Secretary Ligachev) openly challenged Gorbachev and reformers to alter major policy initiatives; there was increased public wrangling over goals and tactics. Within a year, officials would be emboldened enough to challenge Gorbachev's power base, even openly calling for his ouster. The most fundamental norms of the traditional Soviet system were rapidly disappearing. A political free-for-all now engulfed the political leadership.

Fundamental System Restructuring

Institutional and personnel changes of the 1985–8 period clearly weakened the traditional system and prepared it for root-and-branch structural and policy reforms. But it was only from 1989 that non-traditional elements, operating outside the political establishment, came to influence directly the content and direction of that reform. Fundamental system restructuring shifted power and authority to new organisations and different sets of officials. Revitalised, popularly elected parliamentary bodies were upgraded to help stimulate bottom-up pressures and to form and legitimate reform measures. New executive agencies were created to generate and supervise a reform programme, while the party apparatus was displaced as the fulcrum of power. Meanwhile bottom-up reform urges were reinforced by decentralised structural changes that increasingly favoured regional interests over those of conservative national-level bodies.

Policy initiative was shifted to a reworked system of popularly elected soviets and a new Soviet executive branch. The years 1989 and 1990 witnessed the creation of a new parliamentary system – with a larger representative body (Congress of People's Deputies, CPD) and smaller deliberative body (Supreme Soviet) – and a new executive presidency. Contested secret ballot elections gave non-traditional and reformist interests mounting influence in the selection of legislators and in the setting of the national parliament's agenda. These elections also gave the new parliamentary bodies an authority unmatched by any party or government bodies. The first sessions of these bodies (see pp. 98–103) revealed a contentiousness and political dynamism that would challenge the efforts of anyone – including

Gorbachev – to channel the reform process. Gorbachev used first the chairmanship of the CPD and subsequently a new executive presidency to direct the actions of the parliamentary bodies as well as the government (Council of Ministers). We will examine his leadership efforts shortly, but suffice it to say that he was challenged at every turn by parliamentary members of both conservative and reformist persuasion. For its part, the Council of Ministers was freed from the stifling interference of party bodies, but it became increasingly dependent on the new presidency and parliamentary bodies. Ministries were made accountable to the parliament, with ministers now confirmed in occasionally stormy nomination proceedings and made to account regularly before legislative standing committees.

Perhaps of even greater importance, the CPSU lost its preeminent political position and the CPSU apparatus lost its monopoly control over the decision-making process. The March 1990 revision of the USSR Constitution which permitted other parties to compete for power initiated the formal institutional decline of the CPSU: a decline which culminated in its implication in the failed August 1991 coup attempt and the consequent suspension of its activity. But the 28th CPSU Congress (July 1990) had altered a number of fundamental rules by which the party leadership had operated. In particular the General Secretary's organisational preeminence was weakened: he was made reponsible to the party congress and not to the CC, thus ending the so-called 'circular flow of power' which had given the General Secretary clout through his ability to structure the membership of the very body to which he was supposedly responsible. Meanwhile the overlap in the membership of the Politburo, Secretariat, Central Committee and government Council of Ministers was ended, removing the high concentration of power within a relatively small top elite. The Politburo was directed to oversee the 'democratisation' of the party. With its membership increased to 24, the Politburo was hardly the small, homogenous decision-making body which had ruled the Soviet polity for decades. And Politburo and Secretariat members were made to account to the full party congress for their actions during the five-year interval between party congresses. Bottom-up pressures and top-down notions of accountability were emerging even within this bastion of Soviet conservatism. The 1990 creation of a Russian Republic Communist Party and apparatus only served to further divide the CPSU elite, with conservatives rallying to the new Russian party and reformers turning to nascent rival parties and anti-communist politicians such as Yeltsin. With the Politburo and Secretariat meeting less and less frequently in 1989 and 1990, the policy-making initiative was clearly moving elsewhere.

The Soviet political landscape was fundamentally transformed by the early 1990s. New and reconstituted institutions were groping for the means and processes by which to direct an accelerating reform programme. There were considerable uncertainties among those institutions regarding their relative responsibilities and the formal and informal means by which they would share power. Traditional power-brokers watched their influence wane, even as their authority all but disappeared through the earlier revelations of *glasnost'*. But all of these institutional and personnel changes did not amount to a coherent new policy process. To the contrary, old norms and patterns broke down but were not replaced by new working arrangements. A political log-jam ensued. Several years of policy impasse would leave the conditions in place for a major showdown among competing conservative and reform elements within the ruling elite. Even Mikhail Gorbachev's impressive efforts at balancing those contrasting elements would ultimately collapse as the country descended towards system chaos.

The Divided Political Elite

Uncontrolled reform and emergent socioeconomic chaos naturally left the governing political elite divided and uncertain as to the appropriateness of the *perestroika* programme. In a general sense, all top leaders diverged from their predecessors in their rejection of past orthodoxies and their willingness to countenance some level of policy and even system change. But the differences in overall goals, in broad strategies and in particular tactics were considerable. These differences became increasingly evident as elite behavioural norms changed and public debate heated up.

Although there were numerous competing perspectives and programmatic preferences, we can identify three basic groupings of union and regional officials who articulated relatively distinct sets of orientations on an orthodoxy-to-reform policy continuum: (1) conservatives; (2) establishment reformers; and (3) radical reformers. Each of these groupings of politicians had different but significant political resources at its command, and each influenced the decision-making process. But none was able to secure a dominant political position, at least not before the failed August 1991 coup.

Conservatives, who were better thought of as party technocrats and not as Stalinists or Brezhnevites, championed a modest reform programme similar to the pre-1989 *perestroika* policies. That is, they favoured cautious and carefully regulated market reforms without the market as a desired end. Rather than privatise industries, conservatives were interested in transforming them into large public enterprises or joint-stock companies. These politicians were uncomfortable with the accelerating political changes of the post-1988 period, and they increasingly articulated that discomfort in public settings. They had opposed the CPSU's abandonment of its leading role and were sceptical of the role assumed by emergent interest groups and nascent rival parties. Long dominant in the party-state apparatus, these officials appeared to have the most influence over the control of power, yet they lacked a strong and effective leader who could rally their interests. Several prominent politicians – Party Secretary Ligachev, Prime Minister Ryzhkov and Russian First Secretary Ivan Polozkov among them – attempted to assume that role, but all proved unsuccessful.

Establishment reformers, guided by President Gorbachev, were committed to policy change and system reform, but without a repudiation of Marxism–Leninism and the traditional Soviet system. They directed the *perestroika, glasnost'*, and democratisation initiatives throughout the late 1980s, but they were increasingly cautious in the light of post-1988 developments. Politically, establishment reformers championed a more open political process which permitted a diversity of organised interests and parties to operate. They reluctantly supported the withdrawal of the CPSU's privileged position, but they reasoned that its tradition and organisational prowess would still enable it to dominate the coming political free-for-all. In the economic realm, establishment reformers cautiously supported privatisation, entrepreneurial activities and market relations. They were, at heart, uncomfortable with the movement towards capitalist economic structures, and attempted to moderate or stifle more extreme reform measures. Establishment reformers tried to balance the policy initiatives of both conservatives and more radical reformers, but in the process carefully resisted the root-and-branch reform efforts of radical reformers.

Radical reformers, generally operating on the fringes of political power, rejected a discredited Soviet Stalinist system while promoting economic liberalisation and political democratisation. They pressed for the complete opening up of the political process, with a legalised multiparty system, legally protected independent interest groups and wholesale removal of the CPSU's institutional privileges in all settings (including the workplace and the military). Economically radical reformers promoted massive privatisation, Western-style regulated market relations and policy changes permitting relatively unrestrained entrepreneurship. These reformers found little of utility in the traditional Soviet system; they looked to the experience of other countries, as well as pre-Bolshevik Russia, for ideas and inspiration. Considered together, radical reformers constituted the most diverse of the three groupings, bridging elements from within the CPSU and strongly anti-communist elements on the extreme left.

By the early 1990s there was a precarious power balance among these elite groupings. Conservatives were arguably the strongest, being well ensconced in the party and state bureaucracies. They were certainly the dominant element in the early years of the Gorbachev regime (1985–8), as they assumed a centrist position between Brezhnev-period incumbents and more committed reformers. But the emergence of increasingly influential bottom-up pressures came to favour reformers, and especially radical reformers with whom authority and legitimacy came to rest in time. In the latter 1980s, Gorbachev's own political manoeuvrings strengthened the position of reformers as he attempted to offset the weight of the conservative bureaucracy with high-level officials committed to his reform measures. The rise of establishment reformers such as Yakovlev, Shevardnadze and Razumovsky was important in bringing top-down pressures within the party apparatus itself. The power balance within top party and government bodies had clearly shifted towards establishment reformers as the decade came to an end.

But by the early 1990s the accelerated pace of change and increased divisions within the elite had left Gorbachev more and more wary of 'extremist' reformers and he attempted to fashion a governing coalition with a balance of reform and conservative elements. His selection of members of the advisory Presidential Council, formed in March 1990, was illustrative: conservatives, establishment reformers and radical reformers were all included in its membership (see Table 3.1). Gorbachev tapped leading representatives of the conservative and establishment reformist groupings, turning to individuals outside of the party-state bureaucratic establishment (such as the Russian nationalist writer, Valentin Rasputin). With the presidency and Presidential Council displacing the Politburo and Secretariat as the top decision-making actors, powerful institutional leaders (from the Ministries of Defence and Interior, Gosplan, KGB and elsewhere) spanning the ideological spectrum were included in the new Council. In his own statements and profiling, the Soviet President communicated a strong preference for establishment reformers, while distancing himself from the more radical elements. But in fact he vacillated between conservative and reform elements, maintaining a centrist position but alienating many once-loyal allies.

In the spring of 1990, Gorbachev appeared to be forging a better working relationship with Russian Republic Chairman and later President Boris Yeltsin. Both politicians appeared to be trying to give momentum to serious economic reform efforts as their specialists were encouraged to work out a comprehensive reform programme

TABLE 3.1 *Composition of leading advisory and policy-setting councils to USSR President, 1990–1*

Presidential Council (March 1990)

Name		Position
Chingiz Aitmatov	E*	Kirghiz writer
Vadim Bakatin	E	USSR Min. of Interior
Valerii Boldin	C	Head, CC General Dept.
Albert Kauls	R	Chm., Latvian Agroindustrial Enterprise
Vladimir Kryuchkov	C	Chm., USSR KGB
Yurii Maslyukov	C	Chm., USSR Gosplan
Yurii Osipyan	R	Vice-Pres., USSR Acad. of Sciences
Yevgenii Primakov	E	Director, IMEMO
Valentin Rasputin	C	Russian writer
Grigorii Revenko	E	1st Sec., Kiev Oblast
Nikolai Ryzhkov	C	USSR Prime Minister
Stanislav Shatalin	R	Economist
Eduard Shevardnadze	E	USSR Min. of Foreign Affairs
Alexander Yakovlev	E	CPSU secretary
Venyamin Yarin	C	Russian worker
Dmitrii Yazov	C	USSR Min. of Defence

Political Consultative Council (September 1991)

Name		Position
Vadim Bakatin	E*	Chm., USSR KGB
Nikolai Petrakov	R	Consultant (economy)
Gavriil Popov	R	Mayor, Moscow
Yurii Ryzhkov	E	Consultant (military)
Eduard Shevardnadze	E	Consultant (general)
Anatolii Sobchak	R	Mayor, Leningrad
Yevgenii Velikhov	E	Vice-Pres., USSR Acad. of Sciences
Alexander Yakovlev	E	Consultant (general)
Yegor Yakovlev	R	Chm., Gosteleradio

Notes: *Political orientation: C = conservative; E = establishment reformer; R = radical reformer.

(the Shatalin–Yavlinsky group). By late 1990, however, the Soviet President was inclining in a conservative direction. He rejected the Shatalin '500 Days' economic plan, permitted the setting of limits on the *glasnost'* policy, forged an alliance with military and internal police officials, and permitted the use of force in the Baltic (early 1991). Leading establishment reformers (such as Interior Minister Vadim Bakatin and Foreign Minister Shevardnadze) left the Gorbachev team, while reform-oriented advisers turned to Yeltsin as the leader now on the cutting edge of institutional and policy change.

Meanwhile Gorbachev was cultivating nondescript *nomenklatura* party-state officials such as the new Prime Minister, Valentin Pavlov, the new USSR Vice-President, Gennadii Yanaev, and the USSR Supreme Soviet Chair, Anatolii Lukyanov. Pavlov and Yanaev were little-known Gosplan and trade union officials who had risen through traditional organisational ranks. Both were to be seen as Gorbachev aides; neither had independent bases of political power. One observer commented that Pavlov was selected as USSR Prime Minister because of his 'obedience to instructions from above'. Lukyanov was a friend and confidant of Gorbachev, having studied with him at Moscow State University in the early 1950s, and having risen as Gorbachev's career took off in the 1980s. These and similar Gorbachev proteges articulated increasingly anti-reform stances in 1990–1. Indeed Lukyanov, in chairing the contentious and often reform-oriented Supreme Soviet, proved especially deft at obstructing reform measures and at favouring conservative elements (such as the Soyuz group) within the body's membership.

Given that these officials were assuming increasingly anti-*perestroika* stances (and would be among the ringleaders in the August 1991 coup effort), Gorbachev's active cultivation might appear inexplicable. By early 1991, he seemed to be institutionally quite powerful: he was CPSU General Secretary, USSR President, the chair of leading government councils and overseer of the revamped Cabinet of Ministers. But in fact he was politically vulnerable. Officials on either side of his centrist stance were becoming more critical of his programme and his leadership. One well-informed adviser, Georgii Shakhnazarov, commented early that year that, had Gorbachev not moved towards the conservatives, he might have been ousted (*Der Spiegel*, 21 January 1991). Even the conservative Prime Minister Pavlov publicly observed that Gorbachev's cautious political manoeuvring was necessary and that to have done otherwise would have been to 'commit political suicide' (*Izvestiya*, 15 June 1991). Gorbachev struggled to control the party-state apparatus, even while labouring not to be coopted by that apparatus to assume hard-line policy stances.

Longer-term political momentum, however, was with reformers, as subsequent events revealed. Ever stronger reformist impulses were rising in the republics – and even among officials who had once been linked with the traditional party-state establishment. Powerful republic chief executives adopted more reformist policy lines, challenging the central authorities at every turn. By spring 1991, Gorbachev saw national conservatives as increasingly out of touch with Soviet society. In reaching out to subnational leaders, and in addressing the rising pressures for increased republic autonomy, the Soviet President initiated a series of Union–republic negotiations that would yield a new centre–republic alliance. Negotiations between Gorbachev and the republic leaders, held in the Moscow suburb of Novo-Ogarevo in the spring and summer 1991, yielded a Union ('nine-plus-one') Treaty. A new Gorbachev–Yeltsin alliance seemed to bridge the political interests of establishment and radical reformers. Gorbachev lessened his dependence on the traditional bureaucratic power-holders, which included many of his own proteges, and linked the success of his programme and his political future to rising subnational reform forces.

In being a party to the new Union Treaty, Gorbachev agreed to cede important responsibilities to subnational officials, but he and other establishment reformers had been weakened by the slow pace of reform and the high expectations of an increasingly impatient elite and populace. The once-dominant central bureaucracies would be gutted, but the executive presidency and associated bodies would remain as important supervisory and coordinating agents. The new centre–republic working relationship, combined with Gorbachev's institutionalised role as President, bolstered him in his efforts to protect *perestroika* initiatives; they arguably saved him when he fell victim to the political machinations of proteges during the August 1991 attempted coup.

Gorbachev and the New Union Presidency

Pre-coup Institutional Arrangements

The magnitude of the reform effort and the speed with which polity and society changed made Mikhail Gorbachev's leadership role important to the fate of *perestroika*. By the standards of past Soviet leaders, he had consolidated his power position quickly. Regardless of the particular policy inclinations of his subordinates, he had overseen the reconstitution of the country's leadership in fewer than five years. Yet power realities and programmatic needs necessitated a major overhaul of top executive institutions. The logic of the radical reform period, which commenced in 1989 with the emergence of an independent national parliament and the ascent of powerful reform-oriented subnational leaders, required a reconstituting of the national executive to give Gorbachev a more authoritative, legitimate and flexible power base. He needed to be able to circumvent traditional bureaucracies while meeting popular challenges from below. He also needed to be able to take swift action in addressing the country's economic and ethnic crises. The USSR presidency and related set of executive bodies were the institutional outcome.

Gorbachev had assumed the head of state position as USSR Supreme Soviet Chairman in 1988, but a new executive presidency was created in early 1990, with Gorbachev elected by the Congress of People's Deputies and sworn in on 15 March. The new presidency's powers were considerable: they included many of the formal chief of state functions assumed by the traditional USSR Supreme Soviet Presidium and Chairman (such as approving treaties and declaring war) while encompassing numerous new functions. The USSR President was granted extensive powers in issuing decrees, in influencing the work of parliamentary bodies and in appointing government personnel. He would not only nominate the country's Prime Minister, but also the Chairman of the USSR People's Control Committee, the Supreme Court Chairman and the USSR Procurator-General. He would be able to dismiss these officials (excepting the Supreme Court Chairman) and he was additionally empowered to dissolve the USSR Supreme Soviet. He was nominally accountable to the Supreme Soviet – and its parent CPD – but he was actually in a strong position to dominate these parliamentary bodies, where he could use his talents as an orator and presiding officer to pressure parliamentarians to accept his policy preferences.

Only six months into his presidency, Gorbachev sought and received additional executive powers for the presidency, at least formally making him more powerful than any of his political predecessors had been. He was granted the power to issue decrees that would have the force of law; and he was given the ability to bypass the Prime Minister to nominate all members of the Council (renamed Cabinet) of Ministers. The President's position was not unchecked – the Supreme Soviet and the Cabinet of Ministers would have to implement his decisions and the Supreme Soviet would have to confirm his Cabinet nominees – but it was the USSR President who would be in the best position to initiate policies.

Beyond the office of President, a number of other executive bodies were created which would help in setting the country's policy programme. These bodies needed to function outside the traditional party-state apparatus and they needed to be independent of the increasingly powerful national parliament. Beginning in early 1990, and continuing through 1991, a series of institutional reforms resulted in the emergence of a national executive branch which displaced the party apparatus as the fulcrum of decision-making power. Beginning with the Presidential Council, and continuing with the Council of the Federation, the Security Council and the Political Consultative Council, executive bodies were formed which were to advise the executive President. Their memberships included some of the most influential officials within the political establishment. Over time they came to include more and more non-traditional elite elements, drawn not just from Moscow but from the regions.

The Presidential Council was originally conceived of as an advisory body to the President, who selected all its members, with only the Prime Minister included *ex officio*. The Presidential Council's areas of purview were to be set by the President, but given Gorbachev's interest in upgrading new non-party executive bodies and the political standing of the Presidential Council's members, it had considerable potential as a policy-setting body. As Table 3.1 indicates, its membership was institutionally and ideologically varied. Included were some of Gorbachev's most trusted advisers (such as Valerii Boldin and Yevgenii Primakov). In fact the Council proved to be a transitional body, as the decision-making initiative shifted from central authorities to republic leaders. The growing importance of republic chief executives such as Russian Republic leader Yeltsin and Kazakh President Nursultan Nazarbaev, who worked with Gorbachev in another new executive body, the Federation Council (also created in March 1990), made the Presidential Council of less utility to the USSR President. It was abolished in December 1990, with its powers simply transferred to the Federation Council.

The upgrading of the Federation Council was more than a mere reorganisation; the Federation Council was more independent of the USSR President's institutional prerogatives. It had functioned during its early months as a consultative body under the President's guidance, but the growing importance of republics as active decision-making entities transformed it into the critical arena where centre–periphery issues were addressed. Its 37 members, who included the President, the newly-created Vice-President, the fifteen republic chief executives and the chief executives of the 21 autonomous republics (including the new Crimean Autonomous Republic), were all *ex officio* members. Unlike the Presidential Council, the USSR President had no powers of selection here. The Federation Council was intended to bridge the increasingly fractious division between central and republic-level authorities. Its decision-making power was not clear at the time, especially since a two-thirds majority was needed for the body to enact a decision, and the presiding President had but one vote. But its potential as a powerful executive institution was evident: it was to monitor the observance of a new Union Treaty, it was to address nationality issues and deal with ethnic disputes, and it was to coordinate the activities of the USSR President and the republic chief executives. Its regularised 1991 meetings in Novo-Ogarevo culminated in the April 'nine-plus-one' Treaty, the treaty that would fundamentally alter the power balance between Moscow and the republics and that would help instigate the August 1991 coup attempt by conservative opponents. Subsequent events, especially after the failed coup, would underscore the important organisational precedent set by the Federation Council, as genuine institutionalised executive power sharing between central and republic officials commenced; it may even have had some influence, after December 1991, on the institutions of the new Commonwealth.

A third executive body, the Security Council, was formed in December 1990 and was intended to absorb certain of the executive functions of the Presidential Council. In particular it would deal with Union-level issues such as defence, security and inter-ethnic relations, and it would be free of the direct control of the republic leaders. The Security Council was to have a permanent staff – as had the party Secretariat – and it would advise the USSR President. But, in essence, Gorbachev would be able to supervise the country's military–industrial complex without interference from subnational officials. There were no radical reform elements in this body; it was dominated by conservatives and included KGB head Kryuchkov, Prime Minister Pavlov, Interior Minister Pugo, Vice-President Yanaev and Defence Minister Yazov.

All these institutional changes were intended to balance Union and republic interests while enabling Gorbachev to maintain a supervisory position over a decentralising decision-making process. The reorganisation of the traditional Council of Ministers into a Cabinet in December 1990 was yet another effort designed to enhance Gorbachev's institutional standing while weakening a resistant bureaucracy. The post of Prime Minister was downgraded; the Prime Minister became little more than an aide to the President, coordinating the day-to-day functions of the government rather than directing them. This reorganisation did serve to shift certain responsibilities (such as construction, machine building and trade) to the republics it also heightened the President's direct control over the government bureaucracy.

The series of institutional reforms undertaken in 1990–1 weakened the position of long-time party-state bureaucracies, entailed the creation of a new non-party union executive and made the USSR presidency the top decision-making body in the USSR. Yet beyond *de jure* institutional prerogatives, all of these changes occurred as the overall power of Union-level bodies was receding. In fact the USSR President had to balance a growing number of diverse political interests in Moscow and the republics. Political power was increasingly deconcentrated and shared among rival institutions, whether in the Union-level executive (for example, between the Federation and Security Councils) or below (for instance, between the USSR and republic parliamentary bodies).

Even with his new prerogatives, the USSR President was accountable to rival and subordinate bodies. He was required to make an annual account of his activities to the Congress of People's Deputies and he could be removed by a two-thirds vote of that body. His Cabinet nominees needed the approval of the Supreme Soviet and, as from January 1990, a Committee for Constitutional Supervision could review and void his decrees. That Committee was an independent organ, legally mandated to review laws and actions by executive bodies to ensure that they conformed to the USSR Constitution. The Committee's September 1990 decision to void a presidential decree that attempted to transfer control over all demonstrations and public events in Moscow from the local soviet to the USSR Council (Cabinet) of Ministers was graphic evidence of its emerging independence. The USSR President, operating under the pressures of conservatives and reformers, from this point began to experience new constraints associated with the 'rule of law'.

The August 1991 Coup and its Aftermath

The abortive August 1991 coup would bring yet another institutional reconfiguration in late 1991, but the underlying logic of these organisational changes rested on the earlier 1990–1 reforms already discussed here. The failed coup, engineered by conservatives and many associates of Gorbachev, further discredited the standing of most Union-level bodies and officials. The CPSU apparatus was directly implicated in the coup, as were many central ministry officials. The USSR Supreme Soviet, under Anatolii Lukyanov's leadership, failed to resist the coup attempt and was compromised. Many trusted advisers of the USSR President were also implicated. As a result, Union-level executive bodies were weakened, their remaining power and authority shifting almost immediately to republic leaderships. A new State Council, formed out of the membership of the Federation Council and including the USSR President and the chief executives of the republics, became the new top policy-setting body. Its initial actions revealed that the policy preferences of central authorities, including the USSR President, were now subject to the approval of republic leaderships. The State Council assumed the lead role in directing the activities of the USSR Cabinet of Ministers. Indeed, within months of the coup, most of the central ministries comprising the USSR Cabinet would be abolished by the State Council, their functions shifted to republic agencies. An Economic Management Committee, established to supervise the economic revitalisation of the country and charged to formulate an appropriate reform package, now assumed the directing role in the country's economic life. Its leading members (such as Grigorii Yavlinsky) were associated with republic leaderships (as in the Russian Republic and Kazakhstan) and articulated radical reform perspectives.

Gorbachev, betrayed by his conservative proteges, formed yet another advisory body, the Political Consultative Council, which was to provide an institutional bridge to reform elements. As Table 3.1 reveals, the Council's membership was entirely reformist, including politicians who now championed the complete overhaul of the country's political and economic systems. Throughout the period 1989–91 Gorbachev had been behind the times in appreciating the need for fundamental system and policy reform. He had alienated many of those very politicians on whom he now relied in attempting to shore up his political position. Now the USSR President turned to reformers as he confronted a myriad of problems that were pulling the country apart. He approached Shevardnadze, Sobchak and Yakovlev to negotiate the terms of independence and withdrawal of Soviet troops from Lithuania, Estonia and Latvia respectively. He appointed the radical reformer, Yegor Yakovlev, to head the Gosteleradio complex and turned to his reform-oriented press secretary, Vitalii Ignatenko, to direct TASS. Yet by late 1991 these institutional and personnel changes were of marginal importance, for the political momentum had already turned dramatically to republic-level forces and radical reformers. The executive presidency may have saved Gorbachev's *de jure* standing, at least temporarily, but his *de facto* powers were more limited than ever. In December 1991, these developments were brought to their logical conclusion with his own resignation and the abolition of the USSR presidency.

Political Log-jam and a Society in Transition

Nearly a year before the ill-fated coup effort, the radical Leningrad (St Petersburg) Mayor Anatolii Sobchak surveyed the Soviet political scene and commented: 'There is a President who cannot put anything into effect and a Council of Ministers that cannot do anything' (*New York Times*, 25 September 1990). The conservative USSR Prime Minister Nikolai Ryzhkov – a staunch opponent of Sobchak and like-minded radical reformers – offered this characterisation of the political process to a session of the USSR Supreme Soviet in November 1990:

> Control has been totally lost at all levels of the state structure. Authority has been paralysed ... Universal destructiveness is basically becoming the norm. One can say with sufficient conviction and grounds that, throughout the greater part of the country's territory, a situation has been created in which no one is in charge, and that this has led to a complete or partial deterioration of all systems of administration.

Whether at the Union, republic, or local level, a political log-jam had overwhelmed the Soviet policy process by the early 1990s. In many urban settings, popularly elected reformers faced conservative party and state bureaucrats. The failed coup attempt compromised the party apparatus and further weakened many traditional power centres. The CPSU lost four million members within a month of the coup, with its properties and resources seized. Yet the country was devoid of other influential political parties. Many had been formed, but they had few members or resources. It was not clear in the wake of the failed coup whether sufficient momentum would at last emerge for reform-oriented executives and parliamentary members to construct a consensus economic reform programme. Once-privileged Union, regional and local political elites were abandoning their old bureaucratic settings, but their connections and clout enabled many to move into the private sector. They struggled to maintain influence in their old bailiwicks as part of a new post-Soviet bourgeoisie. They might yet pose serious obstacles to effective future reform efforts.

Perhaps the failed coup would serve finally to bridge the gap that had arisen between actors holding power and authority in the political system. As we noted, power and authority had been divided among competing sets of elected and bureaucratic officials: this had been true in Moscow and in the republics. Elected USSR parliamentarians with considerable authority had come up against powerful central ministries, just as popular reformist mayors such as Sobchak and Moscow Mayor Gavriil Popov came up against influential and well-entrenched city party organisations. New momentum for fundamental policy change emerged in late 1991 as power shifted to elected and republic-level reformist elements. The State Council's November

1991 decision to abolish most central ministries increased the potential now before reformers actually to claim institutional power; their powers increased further with the ending of the USSR itself and the transfer of political authority to republics and lower-level bodies.

Would reformers be able to coalesce and bridge radical and establishment elements to carve out a cohesive programme? The Movement for Democratic Reform, established in July 1991 by such leading reformers as Shevardnadze, Yakovlev, Sobchak and Popov, held out the potential to unify reformers. But could this movement draw democratic parties to its ranks? A number of its founding members were in Gorbachev's Political Consultative Council. Could they finally move the Soviet President in a radical reform direction? And after Gorbachev's resignation, would movements of this kind be able to work with the now powerful reform-oriented republic leaders such as Yeltsin and Ukrainian President Leonid Kravchuk in a new Commonwealth of Independent States?

There were certainly important incentives driving the republics to work together and with Moscow in a new union – Commonwealth arrangement. The economic and political viability of many republics was highly suspect. Extreme ethnic tensions reinforced the need for a neutral arbiter. But could Moscow, or any central institutions, play that role? Many strong republic leaders had to contend with factionalism and disarray in their own governing coalitions. The Yeltsin group, for instance, had grown quite powerful through 1991, and especially after the failed coup, but in the early 1990s it was racked by divisions between those who favoured a rapid transition to the market and those (such as Vice-President Alexander Rutskoi) who favoured a more gradual approach with greater compensation for the poor and elderly. The survival of the Russian Federation was itself in some doubt as Tatars, Bashkirs and others pressed for local sovereignty on even independence. Could Yeltsin and other leaders bring some semblance of stability to political life in their own republics and at the same time fashion a new relationship with other Commonwealth members?

As the former Soviet Union evolves through a dynamic political and economic transition period, we must be wary in not overreacting to the subtle manoevrings of republican and local actors as they stake out their claims and attempt to solidify their institutional prerogatives. Assuming the new Commonwealth survives there will be a pressing need for a new type of Union-level executive. That executive – perhaps, once again, in the post of Union President – will need an ability to engage in consensus politics: an ability to bridge divergent interests and use moral suasion. That executive would operate in a system where competing actors, with independent bases of power and authority, could resist his policy preferences. That executive, of whatever ethnic identity, would need to look beyond the needs of one republic to consider the integrated needs of a diverse grouping of nations.

A post-Soviet political system is now being forged, with new governing elites driving each of the republics towards fundamental system and policy change. The Soviet Union has always had need of strong political leadership. Perhaps this has never been truer than today, despite the collapse of the central institutions of the old Union. Chaos and political paralysis have gripped the society for several years. As we have seen, numerous institutional reforms and the constant elite turnover of the past years have already profoundly altered the decision-making process, with the Russian government, under Boris Yeltsin, taking over most of the governmental functions of the old Union by the early 1990s, and the leaders of other republics becoming the heads of independent states with their seats, alongside Russia, in the United Nations. But much remains to be accomplished before a system is established that will be capable of leading the post-Soviet republics towards a stable political and economic relationship with each other, and still more so with the wider international community.

4

The Communist Party and After

RONALD J. HILL

The first two years of the 1990s witnessed the collapse of communist rule in the country of its creation. After almost three-quarters of a century of unchallenged political monopoly, the party of Lenin, Stalin, Khrushchev, Brezhnev and Gorbachev was removed from power as a result of changes introduced by itself. It may continue some kind of shadowy existence – or several existences, in the form of revived splinter organisations that may even enjoy some electoral support – but the effect is to remove the principal pillar of the traditional system of communist rule, and it is virtually inconceivable that the old system can ever be restored. In order to assess the significance of the change, we shall consider briefly the party's position in the Soviet system in recent decades.

The CPSU Before Gorbachev

Until the spring of 1990, the Communist Party of the Soviet Union (CPSU) was, according to its own claim and by common consent, the central political institution in the Soviet political system. As the USSR Constitution of 1977 (Article 6) accurately expressed it, the Communist Party of the Soviet Union was 'the leading and guiding force of Soviet society and the nucleus of its political system, of all state organs and public organs'. The same source outlined the party's principal functions: determining the general perspectives of the development of society and the course of the home and foreign policy of the USSR, directing 'the great constructive work of the Soviet

people', and imparting 'a planned, systematic and theoretically sub-
stantiated character to their struggle for the victory of communism'.

One of the most powerful political and social organisations any-
where in the world, the CPSU was the inheritor of a revolutionary
tradition that went back way into the nineteenth century. Its status as
the ruling party dated from the revolutionary seizure of power in
October 1917. In the early 1920s the dominance of the party (which
changed its name to Communist Party of the Soviet Union in 1952)
was made real, and until the present decade it never showed any
inclination to forfeit that privileged position. Its relative strength as
an institution fluctuated and its precise role varied alongside that of
other institutions, notably the Soviet state; but it never so much as
hinted that it performed any role other than that of directing the
general course of Soviet development. Under Stalin the country may
have been ruled mainly through the powerful ministerial empires,
and the dictator himself undoubtedly wielded massive personal
power; hundreds of thousands of loyal party members were expelled
and put to death in the purges of the 1930s, yet the party as an
institution maintained continuity with its revolutionary origins, which
served to inspire, especially in times of leadership change.

By the time of Gorbachev's accession in 1985, following some
eighteen years under Leonid Brezhnev's indulgent leadership, the
CPSU had become a major social and economic institution, as well as
a ruling force. From 1961 it saw itself as the party of the whole Soviet
people and went out to recruit 'the best' representatives of all social
categories – workers, peasants, members of the intelligentsia and a
multiplicity of national and ethnic groups. By 1989, at its peak, its
membership embraced almost 10 per cent of the adult population,
standing at 19,487,822 on 1 January. Of these, 45.4 per cent were
classified as workers, 11.4 per cent as collective farm peasants and the
remaining 43.2 per cent as white-collar employees, including the
intelligentsia, drawn from a wide variety of specific occupations and
professions. It had become an institution of the best-educated Soviet
citizens, with higher education increasingly common among members: some 34.3 per cent enjoyed that status in 1989, while 81.3 per
cent had completed secondary education or beyond. It had representatives of 'over 100' nationalities, with members in virtually all
workplaces.

As an institution, the party had developed a complex set of offices
and committees, intertwining with those of the state, economic
management and the trade unions, which together offered a career
structure that appeared increasingly attractive under the Brezhnev
leadership's policy of trusting cadres (personnel). Party membership
was, indeed, the *sine qua non* for a successful career in administra-

tion, and millions of Soviet citizens had grown dependent on the party in their working life; many depended on it for their very livelihood. A massive organisation that functioned through thousands of local offices, the party was an important employer in its own right, offering jobs to politicians at all levels and to various auxiliary staff: secretaries, typists and general office staff, janitors, chauffeurs and (increasingly) information processors – computer operators, office managers and even social scientists (employed to conduct public opinion research and to rationalise administration).

The CPSU also played a significant economic role. It owned or used (probably rent-free from the state) significant amounts of office space and other property, which had to be heated, lit, cleaned, maintained and repaired. It possessed fleets of vehicles and could call on those of other organisations: these used fuel and needed maintenance. It ran publishing houses, hotels and vacation homes; and its normal functioning as a political organisation meant that it used large quantities of office furniture and equipment, and consumed vast amounts of paper, ink, typewriter ribbons, floppy disks and other office stationery. Thus the CPSU contributed significantly to the creation of work for the Soviet population; or, seen from a different perspective in an economy characterised by shortages, it consumed significant quantities of the products of the Soviet economy. Hence the CPSU as an institution not only charted the course of the Soviet economy, but was an economic actor in its own right.

Moreover its members' entrance fees and subscriptions (a percentage of their monthly earnings, so that, as earnings rose, so did their party dues) plus the profits of its eleven publishing houses and other subsidiary enterprises permitted the party to dispose of funds to the tune of about one-tenth of the official defence budget (admittedly an artificial figure). Its expenditure went mainly on the salaries of party officers and employees and the upkeep of various party facilities. In 1988, running the Central Committee apparatus alone devoured 50.4 million rubles, or 3 per cent of expenditures. Quite apart from its political power, therefore, the CPSU also possessed a substantial amount of economic power. It was, nevertheless, principally a *political* institution, and the remainder of this chapter will focus on that role.

The Party's Political Role

The CPSU had three different identities, which it is important to distinguish in attempting to understand its former position in the system and to assess its likely future. It was, first, a *collection of members* (nearly twenty million at its peak in 1989) who gave it a complex social identity; they shared little except adherence to a particular set of values associated with the building of a communist society, to which they declared their commitment (although it is far from certain that their understanding of those values was identical). The CPSU was also an *institution*: a set of roles, offices and organs that functioned as a unit to devise policy for implementing the prescriptions of the ideology (that is, for 'building communism') and to lead and supervise the application of those policies. Thirdly, the party was a *hierarchy* of professional officers who directed those organs and at any one time spoke in the party's name: they determined the official 'line' of the party as an institution, to which the party as a collection of members was formally committed. When we speak of the party it is important to distinguish which identity we have in mind, for there are certain tensions among them, which are significant for an understanding of the nature of the collapse of party rule.

Ideology and the Party

The CPSU claimed the right and responsibility to rule the Soviet Union on the basis of a 'special' relationship with the ideology of Marxism–Leninism. This 'scientific' body of doctrine, mediated by the 'party line' (the official position on a given problem at a given time) supposedly permitted the party as an institution to devise 'correct' policies. Ideology is frequently seen as being something immutable, carved on tablets of stone, and, indeed, it was sometimes treated in such a dogmatic fashion. In practice, neither the party line nor the ideology was unchanging: the line was adapted to changing circumstances and the ideology, too, became modified as new phenomena demanded fresh interpretation, sometimes with the use of new concepts, such as 'developed socialism', introduced in the Brezhnev era, or Gorbachev's notion of *perestroika*. Developments in the ideology were signalled in the speeches of politicians, notably the party leader, and especially in the party's basic documents, such as the party programme, the third and (as it turned out) last of which was revised at the 27th Party Congress in 1986. This constant reinterpretation and development of the ideology gave the party some flexibility in its search for policies to solve the country's problems. The ideology may have served to rule out certain policy options, even if it did not prescribe specific policies, but even that may not be an accurate perception. The most that can reliably be said is that the ideology made it somewhat more difficult for the party to defend some policies than others. Moreover, as party rule headed towards collapse, clear ideological distinctions destroyed its claimed monolithic unity: in part, these arguments concerned the continuing utility of a world view derived from the experience of nineteenth-century Europe and of the Soviet Union at the early stages of industrialisation. (For further detailed elaboration of the nature and role of the ideology, see Chapter 2.)

The Party and the State

The CPSU's role as a 'permanently' ruling party placed it in a dominant position *vis-à-vis* the representative and administrative organs of the state, although the relationship was quite complex, partly because the CPSU presented confusing versions. Sometimes it asserted its 'leading and guiding' role in such a way as to suggest that the state was subordinate to the party. Yet spokesmen insisted that the party ruled not by giving orders to the state, but by the political method of persuasion: by placing its members in key positions and using them to convince non-members of the correctness of the party's policy. In practice the party exploited various political conventions to ensure that its policy was given the force of law; subsequently, the party monitored the administration of the policy.

The Soviet state thus never enjoyed independence. It was politically beholden to the Communist Party, which used its effective monopoly to devise policy and select, or at least approve, those whose function was to give legal force to party policy, and it dutifully carried out that policy. Many Western observers have seen the relationship as one of party dictatorship, and in Soviet commentary the problem of *podmena* (literally 'substitution' or 'supplantation', referring to undue party interference in the work of state and other bodies) has long been identified as something that prevented both the party and the state from performing their functions effectively. From that practice derived much of the power of the *apparatchiki*, and it is clear why they resisted attempts to change the system. Indeed it was the persistence of this tendency on the part of entrenched party officials, despite Gorbachev's attempts to curtail it, that led directly to the eventual collapse of Communist Party rule.

Party Structures

In order to perform its role, the CPSU had a complex network of structures, from the five-yearly congress down through conferences and committees at the levels of the republic, province, city and district, and ultimately to the primary party organisations (PPOs) in virtually every place of work in the country (see Figure 4.1). Every party member belonged to such a primary organisation (of which there were approaching 450,000 in the late 1980s) and it is in these organisations that party policies were implemented, through the allocation of specific 'party assignments' to individual communists. Monthly PPO meetings discussed various party concerns, including the allocation of assignments and the admission of new members. The organisation was headed by a secretary and, if large, it elected a bureau and was subdivided into groups according to workshop or shift. Election to such a local office at the autumn 'accounting and election' meeting was frequently the start of a political career, which depended on impressing one's superiors, who controlled further advance. District or city party conferences elected the district or city party committee and delegates to the next higher conference, at the province or republic level, and so on up the hierarchy to the all-Union party congress; this discussed broader policy matters and elected the Central Committee, which formally elected the Politburo and the General Secretary, the highest party ofice.

This indirect system of election deprived rank-and-file members of any say in the selection of the party leadership, a process that in any case was subject to further constraints, principally the appointment system known as *nomenklatura*. In practice, places on party committees were virtually 'reserved' for the occupants of specific posts in the party and state hierarchies and, in this way, steadily moving up the hierarchy, individuals pursued political careers, frequently gaining experience of direct administration by interspersed office-holding in the state apparatus. Whatever their identity, and whatever the pretext on which they were elected, more than five million party members were chosen to serve on party committees in the autumn and winter of 1985–6 – over a quarter of the total membership.

At the local level, various party organs discussed and interpreted central edicts and made arrangements for their implementation. Records were kept of the personal details of all party members, who in a real sense subordinated themselves to the needs of the party, as determined by their superiors. The party's financial affairs were scrutinised by the Central Auditing Commission (whose chairman frequently reported on financial indiscipline, occasionally on a massive scale). Infringements of party regulations were punished through the Party Control Committee.

As a large and relatively complex organisation, the CPSU required a substantial apparatus to handle its affairs. Each committee elected a bureau from among its voting members, headed by a first secretary and two or more secretaries. The first secretary was the most power-

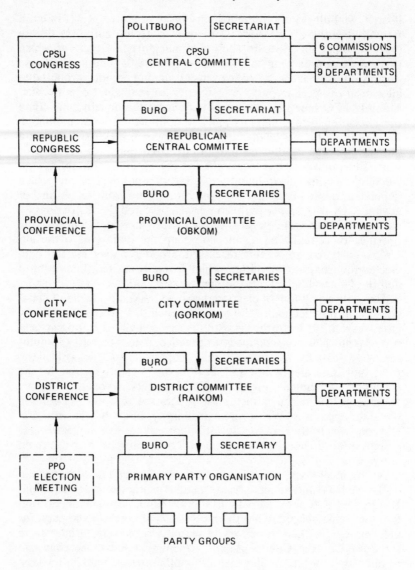

Indicates election (subject to nomenklatura)
Indicates lines of authority (subject to democratic centralism)

FIGURE 4.1 *The structure of the CPSU (to 1991)*

ful politician in the locality, and his deputy was usually in charge of recruitment: this post frequently went to a Russian in the republican organisations – a source of irritation that acquired political relevance in the era of *perestroika*. The work of the party organisation was administered through the *apparat* (apparatus) – hence the designation *apparatchik* for a worker in the party administration – which had a number of administrative departments, including some that dealt with internal party matters, and others that effectively paralleled those of the state. Attempts in the late 1980s to simplify the structure and define the party's role more precisely achieved little success, primarily because of the resistance of those whose power lay in controlling such appointments, with their accompanying privileges and perquisites.

This brief description indicates the scope of the CPSU's involvement in the country's political life. Furthermore party membership was for life. Joining was a major step and depended on more than simply the will of the person concerned; once a member, extreme devotion to the party and its cause was required, on pain of party punishment and, in extreme cases, expulsion (tantamount to exclusion from legitimate participation in political life). The CPSU created the system and directed it, using its own officers and members to ensure the compliance of other institutions, including the political security agencies, through which the population was kept under control.

The Apparatchiki

The people who ran the apparatus, the *apparatchiki* (also known in Russian as *kadry*, or cadres), appointed through *nomenklatura*, in a real sense dominated the system, linking various institutions through this common leadership appointment system. Members of this group were responsible to their superiors through patronage links and *nomenklatura* allowed them in turn to dispense patronage by arranging appointments for associates. The opportunities for corruption, nepotism, cronyism and a host of other anti-democratic practices can easily be imagined, and evidence revealed in the Gorbachev era showed that the apparatus had become riddled with corrupt 'leaders' under Brezhnev's policy of 'trusting cadres'. From the Uzbekistan of Sharaf Rashidov and Kazakhstan under Dinmukhamed Kunaev right up to the capital city Moscow under Viktor Grishin, and from local foodstore managers to deputy ministers of foreign trade (including members of Brezhnev's own family), corruption became endemic, but was hidden from the public record by the veil of official party and state secrecy.

The *apparatchiki* performed vital functions, nevertheless, in using their authority as party officials to unblock bottlenecks in the economy: the power of the telephone call from the local party committee office has long been an important form of lubricant for the administrative wheels of Soviet society. As a recent Soviet source put it, 'everyone knew that if you wanted to resolve this or that major question you had to go to the district or city party committee, to the provincial or Central Committee. There it would be reviewed and they would give the word which, before all else, would be final' (V. S. Lipitsky, writing in Zhuravlev *et al.*, 1990, p. 439). The party administrators' prestige and power were thereby enhanced.

In a very real sense, these important individuals set the tone of the whole system, and their understanding of the way society was actually run, plus self-defensive networks among themselves, proved an extremely effective hindrance to the reforms initiated by Gorbachev. The image of the faceless bureaucrat as typical of the *apparat* proved depressingly accurate, and those who led the abortive coup in August 1991 were precisely individuals drawn from such a background who stood for the maintenance of the system of rule based on administrative and command methods, for which a privileged and comfortable lifestyle was a highly desirable reward.

Party Discipline and Indiscipline

The corruption among 'leaders' indicates the failure of a basic element in intra-party relations: *democratic centralism* (defined in Party Rule 19), which meant in principle that ultimate authority lay at the centre, and that lower party bodies were subject to firm guidance by their superiors. Although it prescribed the elective principle and accountability, accompanied by strict discipline and the binding nature of decisions by higher bodies on inferior organs, those in the apparatus were clearly prepared to ignore reformist decisions in order to protect their own status. In fact, in more senses than this, party discipline was not as effective as the strict centralist image would hold. The policy of *glasnost'* revealed that in many parts of the country the party had, as it were, turned into a benefit society for bestowing privileges on the elite at all levels. The top central and republican leaders lived in luxury while living standards for the masses stagnated and declined, and at lower levels party members sought to use their connections to enhance their position. The slogan adopted at the 1986 Congress, that a communist must be 'pure and honest' (*chistyi i chestnyi*), allowed the reformers to remove many of the more blatantly corrupt from positions of influence and in some cases put them on trial, following a change in Party Rule 12 to allow this without prior expulsion from the party. Others, however, simply used their ingenuity to evade responsibility and fought a rearguard action to discredit Gorbachev and the reformers. The final attempt was that of the coup plotters of August 1991, whose ill-conceived, ill-prepared and botched actions led to the final collapse of Communist Party rule – the very opposite of their intention.

The Party in Decline

Well before that traumatic and liberating event, however, there were many signs that the Communist Party was in a state of increasing disarray. Its membership had begun to decline, for a variety of reasons, so that a quarter of its peak membership returned their membership cards or simply ceased to attend meetings and pay their subscription. Its financial position deteriorated sharply and morale collapsed as the country's problems failed to respond to the party's prescriptions. The rise of new state institutions offered alternative routes to political self-expression and the party found it had to modify its own identity if it was to survive. This in turn led to polarisation and variety of opinion within the party's ranks, culminating in splits and the establishment of distinct platforms in advance of the 28th Party Congress in the summer of 1990. That event appeared almost an irrelevance in the face of the mounting chaos in the economy, in inter-ethnic relations and in the Soviet Union's relations with her former allies in Eastern Europe, most of which had abandoned monopoly communist rule in 1989.

Membership

As indicated above, membership of the CPSU was not open. Rather individuals were selected according to criteria determined by the party, which carefully balanced sociological characteristics and sup-posed political merits, so as to create a membership body that served symbolic as well as activist functions. With an aspiration to embrace identities as a party of the working class, a ruling party, a means of imposing discipline on key groups of society, a party of the whole people and a vanguard, the party managers had a complex task in controlling the membership profile. In the Khrushchev and Brezhnev eras, particular efforts were made to recruit more women, more working class (but increasingly the highly-trained, skilled workers in modern industry) and representatives of minority ethnic groups, while the expulsion of 'passive' members was deployed to assist in the task of membership management as the size of the party was stabilised at some 10 per cent of the workforce.

The complex admissions procedure involved application forms, references from party members in good standing and discussions in several forums before an individual became a candidate (probationary) member. During the year's probation, the candidate had to fulfil party assignments and attend ideological study courses before repeating the same application procedure. Some 70 per cent of new recruits came from the Komsomol (Young Communist League), for whose members joining the party was held up as the highest aspiration. Members were subject to party discipline and had to accept assignments at the party's behest and seek the party's permission to make basic life decisions, such as changing employment; even when travelling away for more than a few days, they became temporarily attached to an organisation at their destination. In principle, therefore, the party saw its members as troops to be deployed wherever the cause of building communism demanded it. It placed high demands on them and the greatest sin was to be passive: 'losing contact with one's organisation' was a principal ground for expulsion from the party.

By 1989, the apparently inexorable growth of the party's membership was halted: after steady expansion of around 2 per cent a year in the 1970s, a decline began, which became precipitate in 1990 and accelerated further in 1991. Following the abolition of quotas that favoured certain groups, the number of blue-collar workers among new recruits slipped, and even the number of women candidates for membership fell in 1988 (as did, surprisingly, the proportion of women holding official party positions). The crisis of confidence at the revelations of corruption of party officials under Brezhnev led to resignations, a trend that was accelerated following the bloody intervention in Latvia and Lithuania in January 1991. Reports in the daily newspaper *Pravda* of new recruits in the spring of 1991 were not convincing.

Finances

In part a consequence of the falling membership, but also associated with a sharp decline in the profitability of its newspaper and other publishing ventures and with heavy investment in modernising its central administration and raising the salaries of its paid officials (partly in order to reduce the temptation to corruption), the party's current financial position deteriorated sharply. It suffered a deficit of over 200 million rubles in 1990, and all party organisations and institutions were instructed to exercise stringent financial discipline, to economise and seek additional sources of income in the following year as the party faced a deficit of 1,100 million rubles, which would entail a massive depletion of its reserves.

Already by that stage, with the break-up of the CPSU as major blocs of members (notably the adherents of the 'Democratic Platform') left to form separate organisations, the question of the party's property had become a political issue. And in the wake of the failed coup, which resulted in the freezing of the party's assets, controversy raged over an alleged cache of 200 million rubles (some of it in hard currency) given to front organisations and foreign banks in order to cushion the enforced 'retirement' of its officers and to enable it to run competitive election campaigns more effectively than its rivals. In an example of the former use, it was reported that the retired Central Committee Secretary, Aleksandra Biryukova, was allowed to purchase for about 17,000 rubles a residence worth 200,000–300,000 rubles on the market. Clearly, even as it faced catastrophe, the CPSU was prepared to treat its loyal servants with extreme generosity.

Party Prestige

The reports of such actions, in the wake of the banning of the party, confirmed the erosion of confidence in the party that had been gaining momentum for some time. By 1991, there had been an obvious change in the public's perception of the party. Membership was no longer seen as a desirable enhancement to the individual's status which would accompany higher education and facilitate career advancement. For one thing, the expressed intention of promoting non-members to positions of responsibility had removed the necessity of party membership as a qualification for a high-flying career. An additional factor was the creation of alternative vehicles for political expression. The most significant cause of the disenchantment, however, was the dismal failure of the party to produce policies that could stabilise the failing economic situation or resolve the mounting crisis in ethnic relations.

By the summer of 1990, on the eve of the 28th congress, an opinion poll published in the radical weekly *Moscow News* revealed that fewer than half of the respondents believed that the party could solve the country's problems. Half believed that the Party Congress would have no significant influence on the country's destiny; 74 per cent felt the CPSU should be held responsible for its errors over the past 70 years; and 64 per cent did not see the CPSU as the only force capable of extricating the country from its crisis; opinions on the creation of the Russian republic's own party shortly before the All-Union Party Congress betrayed indifference (*Moscow News*, 1990, no. 30, p. 4). A survey in Siberia a few months earlier showed that 86 per cent felt that the official platform contained no concrete programme to resolve the country's crisis, while 85 per cent believed party policy promoted the interests of party functionaries; only 27 per cent of communists would join the party a second time (*Moscow News*, 1990, no. 24, pp. 8–9). By then there were alternative vehicles for political expression and the party itself was divided and splitting.

All these developments resulted from the policy of *perestroika*, or restructuring, introduced and adopted as official party policy in 1987.

The Party and Restructuring

Under the influence of its General Secretary, Mikhail Gorbachev, particularly following the 19th Party Conference in the summer of 1988, the CPSU embraced a policy of political reform. This entailed modification of the party's own structures and other changes affecting both internal party affairs and the party's relations with other institutions, notably the state. In brief, *perestroika* required a reinterpretation of the party's role.

Intra-party Democratisation

Gorbachev's attempt to regain respect for the CPSU involved efforts to exorcise the nepotism, venality and corruption of the Brezhnev era and to bring the practice of intra-party life into closer correspondence with its long-enunciated democratic principles and the principles of 'communist morality' set out in the Party Rules. The policy was launched at the January 1987 Central Committee plenum, in a devastating attack on the way the party had been run. The principle of contested elections for party office was subsequently incorporated into the conventions of intra-party behaviour and the practice was extended steadily (although not made mandatory). Rule changes restricted the number of terms a single party officer might serve – a measure reminiscent of a similar restriction adopted under Khrushchev in 1961; and the party began to publish far more information about its internal functioning, including detailed financial statements and personal information about leading officers, mainly in the monthly *Izvestiya TsK KPSS* (CPSU Central Committee News) from January 1989 onwards. A restructuring of the central apparatus in

1988, abolishing departments and replacing them with a smaller number of commissions, was also accompanied by a reduction in the size of the *apparat* over subsequent months.

However, other tendencies undermined the effectiveness of these measures in stabilising the party's position. In particular the freeing of public life to more or less open expression and organisation allowed the public new opportunities to play an active political role and, inevitably, by the end of the 1980s a number of 'proto-parties' were in existence. The range of opinions, diagnoses and prescriptions in society at large multiplied rapidly in response to the party-led policy of *glasnost'* and, as the turmoil of opinion grew, so the party itself became affected. By the end of 1989, the party had several identifiable tendencies within its ranks. In December the party in Lithuania split from the CPSU (leaving a rump of pro-Moscow communists), an example that was followed elsewhere over the following months. And, in advance of the 28th Congress, two 'platforms' were published in addition to the official platform – a development that came dangerously close to infringing the ban on fractions that had been a rule of party life since 1921.

By that stage a further constitutional development had destroyed the CPSU's political monopoly. Following a campaign lasting several months, during which Gorbachev as party leader had initially resisted the move, on 7 February 1990 a Central Committee plenum formally recommended the amendment of Article 6, which since 1977 had identified the CPSU as the leading force of the Soviet system. The new wording, approved by the Congress of People's Deputies in March, referred to 'political parties' and the way was thereby opened for the establishment of alternative parties, to compete with the CPSU for popular support – or for disaffected members of the CPSU to break away. The 28th Congress, in July 1990, debated issues relating to the party's future and was marked by public indifference or hostility. The party's prestige was dealt a further blow by the dramatic resignation of leading figures, led by former Politburo candidate member Boris Yeltsin, who had used the new political opportunities to secure the 'rehabilitation' denied by the party in 1988.

Power was already being transferred from the party to state institutions. A new Congress of People's Deputies, which in turn elected a professional Supreme Soviet, had been inaugurated in the late spring of 1989, and it quickly became apparent that it was no longer prepared to play the role of the party's dutiful handmaiden: leading party figures had failed to secure election to the new body, whose deputies were now willing to challenge and reject the party's nominations to ministerial office. In March 1990, a new post of President of the USSR had been created, flanked by a Presidential Council and a Council of the Federation, and this state presidency – headed by Gorbachev, who remained party General Secretary – steadily expanded its role, at the expense of the Politburo and Central Committee secretariat. As the party approached its 28th Congress, its position was already quite different from what it had been in advance of the 1986 Congress, before *perestroika* had even been thought of.

The 28th Congress

This event, advanced from the spring of 1991 to July 1990, attracted little of the attention of previous congresses, and none of the excitement of the 19th Conference held just two years previously. Taking place at a time of mounting crisis both within the party and in the country at large, it was preoccupied with its internal affairs and with trying to secure its role within the broader political system. It was probably much too late for that, however, and in the event its modest reforms and promises for the future simply appeared to accelerate its decline.

The downgrading of the Politburo was continued, with its expansion to include *ex officio* the first secretaries of the republican party organisations. Its members were thus widely dispersed, its meetings became still less frequent and it became quite impossible for it to continue its former role as supervisor of day-to-day policy making. Moreover, under pressure to devote more time to his role as General Secretary, Gorbachev proposed the creation of the new post of Deputy General Secretary, in the election to which the traditionalists' spokesman, Yegor Ligachev, lost to Gorbachev's own nominee. Indeed Ligachev failed to secure election to the Politburo or even the Central Committee, as did other former colleagues of Gorbachev, in the first genuine elections to such positions for decades. The new rules redefined 'democratic centralism', simplified the structures of party committees and codified the democratising principles adopted by the 19th Conference, and the Congress also authorised the preparation of a new programme, based on the official 'platform' and entitled 'Socialism, Democracy, Progress'. A draft of this was approved in July 1991 and published for discussion in advance of the projected extraordinary 29th Congress, scheduled for November–December 1991, but never held.

In contrast to the carefully orchestrated and controlled forums of previous decades, the 1990 Party Congress was characterised by the very spontaneity that had always been rejected, and that had made the 1988 Conference such an exciting political event. But, rather than saving the CPSU as a political institution, in 1990 the experience exacerbated the polarisation of opinion. It precipitated the departure of the 'Democratic Platform', whose members saw the CPSU as incapable of genuinely reforming itself, and stimulated the formation of traditionalist bodies, such as 'Unity', set up by the formidable Nina Andreeva, whose letter extolling Stalinist principles had been published in the newspaper *Sovetskaya Rossiya* in March 1988, and whose supporters considered that the CPSU had become hopelessly compromised by its flirtation with reform. It was out of broad sympathy for such a stance that the coup of August 1991 was mounted.

The Congress failed to address the serious issues facing the country, being more concerned with avoiding the very split that it provoked. Over the following year, the economic and political state of the country continued to decline and the Communist Party appeared quite incapable of coming to grips with the situation. The initiative passed to other bodies, notably the elected councils at republican and local level. Controlled in a number of significant cases by non-communists, former communists and anti-communists, the party as an institution found itself under attack. Symbols of its power, such as statues and portraits of Lenin and the familiar republican flags, were removed from view and replaced by icons of pre-communist nationhood; party organisations were made to rent office space away from places of work, and in other ways its traditional functioning was undermined. This tendency came to a head when, on 20 July 1991, Boris Yeltsin, following a sweeping victory in an election for the post of President of the Russian Republic, issued an edict banning political activity in state-owned factories and other places of employment – a move that was aimed directly at the CPSU's capacity to function.

The party was already severely split, other parties were vying for recognition and some were calling for the banning of the CPSU as an organisation that, through its actions over seven decades of monopoly rule, had brought the country to ruin. Given its own experience, it was somewhat disingenuous of party spokesmen to accuse the CPSU's rivals of behaving undemocratically. The struggle for the heart of the CPSU continued between rival factions and the attempted coup, with the support and connivance, if not the direct involvement, of senior conservative figures in the party hierarchy, gave radicals outside the party the opportunity to eliminate it from active political life, a development with which Gorbachev had little option but to concur. After several republics (including the largest, Russia) had introduced such measures by decree, on Saturday 24 August Gorbachev resigned as General Secretary, nationalised the party's property, invited the Central Committee to dissolve itself and banned party organisations in the various security forces. In November Boris Yeltsin, who had already suspended the operations of the CPSU in the Russian Federation, banned it altogether. While the party has not been formally disbanded, it has certainly been destroyed as an effective political force.

In the light of the party's centrality to Soviet life, the effects have been both liberating and devastating. Its property, worth some 4,000 million rubles, is being confiscated and reallocated. The suspension of its activities removed the livelihood of some 150,000 direct employees of party committees. Moreover, given the commitment and devotion required of members, the void in many millions of individuals' lives can be imagined. It is not surprising, therefore, that former party members are taking the lead in the newly emerging party system.

The Emerging Party System

From the very start, the strategy of radical reform carried considerable risks, since the system traditionally functioned according to certain well-understood rules of the game, one of which was the notion that the party knew best, because of its understanding of the ideology, and that it therefore had the right to intervene to guide other institutions and correct mistakes. As Gorbachev noted, 'it seems such a well-trodden path: exert party pressure and the plan is fulfilled!' Once the pressure was removed, and the party accepted that mistakes would be made, chaos might ensue.

Such, at least, was the fear of many so-called conservatives within the party, who saw editors' eagerness to publish information about 'negative' features of Soviet reality as licence to slander the form of 'socialism' developed under the party's benevolent guidance over the past half-century. This 'licence' also includes pointed questions about the party's own role in the system, which eventually led to the party's disavowal of its need for a constitutional buttress for its monopoly. For some time, well-argued assessments had been made by leading reformist thinkers within the party as well as outside it, which persuaded Gorbachev to argue that the party had to earn the right to rule. Speaking at the opening of the 1989 Soviet election campaign, he pointed out that the party now had to present a programme in competition with those of other organisations.

The proliferation of such organisations developed rapidly in the following two years. Movements, particularly those such as Sajudis in Lithuania and Rukh in Ukraine, calling for political independence of Moscow, joined the thousands of political discussion groups and clubs and embryonic parties to challenge the narrow orthodoxy of the CPSU. Legitimised in principle from March 1990, political parties were given the right to form and to register with the Ministry of Justice by a law on public associations adopted in October 1990; the CPSU formally registered on 4 April 1991. Shortly after the 28th Congress, the CPSU's monthly *News of the CPSU Central Committee* published a brief rundown of fifteen parties with claims to national status. They ranged from the Social-Democratic Party of the Russian Federation, the Socialist Party and the Liberal-Democratic Party, through the Democratic Party and the Democratic Party of Russia, to the Russian Christian Democratic Movement, the Orthodox Monarchist Union and the Confederation of Anarcho-Syndicalists. Moreover it became clear that the CPSU was contemplating coalition government with one or more of these rivals, and debated which ones it might be prepared to collaborate with.

By the time of the suspension of the CPSU in August 1991, scores of parties and party-type institutions were in existence, representing a broad spectrum of interests and opinions in what had long been a complex and relatively sophisticated modern society. One analysis published after the coup (Slavin and Davydov, 1991) identified three broad blocs of parties. The 'conservative–dogmatic' political forces, including the neo-Stalinist 'Unity' organisation associated with Nina Andreeva, the supporters of the 1990 founding congress of the Russian Communist Party, and other 'defenders of socialist principles'. They base their approach on a 'vulgarised class approach', seek a renewed form of socialism – in reality a monolithic, totalitarian type of party monopoly – and denounce reformers from Khrushchev to Gorbachev as traitors to the cause whose aim is a 'bourgeois restoration' and whose policies betray generations of workers who strove to build socialism against the odds. Given the economic decline that contrasts so markedly with the feverish construction of the 1930s, such a position finds some resonance in society at large.

A second bloc comprises democratic socialists, including progressive forces from the CPSU, left social-democrats, anarcho-syndicalists and those of similar views. They pitch their appeal towards the masses of workers, recognising that the working class of today is very different from the ex-peasants who were the mainstay of the Bolshevik party under Stalin. This group of parties, itself quite heterogeneous, favours pluralist democracy, but is concerned for the interests of the workers in the difficult period of transition from a command to a market economy, and consequently they enjoy widespread support.

A third bloc, which draws most of its support from the intelligentsia, looks westwards for its inspiration, believing broadly that the salvation of what was the Soviet Union lies in the thoroughgoing assimilation into the mainstream of Western civilisation. Generally liberal in orientation, they favour the market, parliamentary democracy, ideological pluralism and minimal state intervention in the affairs of society.

A further tendency in Russia is neo-Slavophilism, which has absorbed some of the ideas of Alexander Solzhenitsyn, but also includes monarchists and is the Russian parallel of the nationalistically-oriented movements of the Baltic republics, Georgia, Ukraine and elsewhere. The broad aims are a resurgence of Russia on the basis of a return to traditional values such as Orthodoxy, Russian state power and a rekindled sense of pride in national identity.

Some of these parties have clearly been formed by 'refugees' from the Communist Party and may bear the marks in terms of organisational structures and internal practices; others look to the West for inspiration and guidance. It is by no means clear, in this early stage of democratisation, that they will all succeed in behaving with proper regard for the conventions of pluralist democracy. It is equally unclear that the electors to whom they appeal for support appreciate the role of representative or parliamentary institutions. The economic circumstances are so dire that the pressures on the fledgling parties, inside or outside government, may be such as to delay the attainment of full democracy. Either emergency measures will need to be introduced by government and implemented by force, or shifting multiparty coalitions will lead to instability and political drift. In either case a reversion to authoritarian rule cannot be excluded.

More positively the various coalitions of parties within the tendencies may form united organisations in the wake of elections over the next several years, so that by the end of the decade a broadly conventional democratic spectrum will exist, with extreme parties that command little electoral support pushed to the margins of political life. Much depends on the type of electoral system that is introduced, the laws covering campaigning, the access to the public through the mass media and many other factors that have been excluded from political life for practically the whole of this century – indeed that have never been part of the living experience of the population. The way ahead is therefore fraught with obstacles of various kinds: but it does seem that the peoples of the Soviet Union have been matured politically by their experience since the mid-1980s and are unlikely to tolerate a reversion to dogmatic orthodoxy. The experience of seven decades of communist rule, negative in so many ways, has had a politically formative effect that appears, on balance, to be positive. The past few years have shown the Soviet people to be able to identify their interests and to act upon them. The next few years will see whether they are now capable of channelling them through a new party system.

5

State Institutions in Transition

JEFFREY W. HAHN

The Background to Reform

The first two years of Mikhail Gorbachev's tenure as General Secretary of the CPSU gave little indication of the dramatic changes to come in the Soviet state system. In his speech to the 27th Congress in February 1986 his remarks on the subject contained few new initiatives, and these lacked specifics. Thus he promised 'the development of socialist self-government for the people', but noted that the party was to be the 'leading force and chief guarantor' of that development. He announced that new proposals were being developed to enhance the authority of local councils – called soviets – in economic affairs and spoke of the need to 'strengthen the prestige' of the deputies who were elected to these councils, but offered no details. He hinted at 'necessary adjustments' in Soviet electoral practice. Finally he alluded to the problem of the dominance of administrative personnel in political life and the need to hold them more accountable before the people's elected representatives. But such proposals had been heard before. As far as Soviet parliamentary institutions and practices were concerned, it was a speech that Brezhnev or Chernenko could have made.

In the light of subsequent reforms, Gorbachev's comments on state institutions at the 27th Congress seem limited and cautious; in retrospect they may one day be seen as tentative first steps in the revival of democratic aspirations reaching back to the time of the Russian Revolution of 1917 and before. In origin the term 'soviets' (from the Russian word meaning 'advice' or 'council') was used with reference to workers' councils which began to be elected in Russian factories at the start of the century. Intended as a means for workers to communicate economic grievances to management, the soviets took on a political character at the time of the 1905 Revolution. The most significant of these was the Soviet of Workers' Deputies in St Petersburg led by Leon Trotsky, then a Menshevik. In 1917, the emergence of the Petrograd Soviet of Workers' and Soldiers' deputies as a political force with *de facto* veto power over decisions by the Provisional Government contributed greatly to the downfall of that government and to the Bolshevik victory in the October revolution.

Lenin's attitude towards the soviet was essentially instrumental: they were the means for making a revolution. It was with this in mind that he declared in his 'April Theses' that Bolsheviks would not support the Provisional Government; he insisted instead on the slogan 'all power to the soviets'. The political problem for Lenin was that, at the time, the Petrograd Soviet was dominated by Mensheviks. It was only in September, when the Bolsheviks gained majority control of the Executive Committee, that Lenin explicitly identified the soviets as the 'new state apparatus', and used them to overthrow the Provisional Government. When he did assume power on 7 November 1917, he did so in the name of the All-Russian Congress of Soviets of Workers' and Soldiers' Deputies.

Lenin's designation of the soviets as institutions of state power may have been motivated by pragmatic considerations, but their role was justified on ideological grounds. In his conceptualisation of the state in socialist society Lenin drew on contradictory elements found in the writings of Karl Marx: Marx's analysis of the Paris Commune of 1871 with its emphasis on proletarian self-rule and direct democracy from below, and his view of the state as a 'dictatorship of the proletariat' necessary during the transition to the social ownership of the means of production. While the view of the state as a dictatorship of the proletariat is elaborated by Lenin in his *State and Revolution* (1917), in other writings Lenin clearly saw the soviets as the embodiment of the communal form of government described by Marx as the prototype of proletarian democracy. After all, the soviets were the political expression of the industrial working class. Moreover in Lenin's conception those elected to the soviets would retain their status as workers while serving in government. In this way the creation of a professional class of politicians as found in bourgeois parliamentary systems would be avoided. Executive and legislative powers would be fused with those making decisions simultaneously responsible for implementing them. In this conception there is a strong emphasis on active political participation from below; most

decisions would be made locally, not centrally, although all the
soviets were organically linked by common class interests in a
'unified' system.

In understanding the current efforts to 'democratise' the Soviet
state system, it is important to recognise the ideological ambiguity in
Lenin's thinking on the state. Gorbachev himself repeatedly justified
his political reforms as a return to the 'spirit of Leninism'. But what
did this mean? It is arguable that the state system that emerged in
April 1918 (after Lenin's brief fling with pluralism in the Constituent
Assembly ended in the abolition of that body on 19 January 1918)
moved inexorably in a 'dictatorial' direction in response to the
exigencies of survival during the civil war (1918–20). The centralisation of state institutions and their strict subordination to the will of
the party, both of which took place during this time, created the
conditions for Stalin's rise to power. In this view, the state system as
it developed during the early years of 'war communism' and under
Stalin and his successors was an aberration, and it was time to
'reconstruct' the state along the lines that Lenin originally intended.
What Lenin really intended is, of course, an open question. What
seems clear is that the legitimacy of later efforts at 'democratisation'
rested on a conception of the soviets as representative institutions
based on mass political participation with those elected accountable
to the electorate.

Certainly the state system Gorbachev inherited was the antithesis
of the participatory self-government from below implicit in the original conception of the soviets. The problem is both structural and
functional. The structure of the Soviet state, until December 1991,
was defined by the 1977 USSR Constitution. Until amended on 1
December 1988, it remained essentially unchanged from Stalin's
Constitution of 1936. The state system was subdivided into a complicated network of administrative–territorial units arranged hierarchically. At the top a national parliament was established known as the
Supreme Soviet. It was made up of 1,500 directly elected deputies
holding five-year terms, from among whom was chosen a government, called the Council of Ministers, and a collegial head of state,
named the Presidium. One level below the USSR Supreme Soviet,
and reflecting the federal character of the state system, were the
Supreme Soviets of the fifteen union republics and 20 autonomous
republics. The organisation of executive agencies at this level replicated that of the national body.

Below the national and republican level, all soviets are called local
soviets. There were 52,568 of them in 1987, subdivided administratively into six *krais* or territories, 123 *oblasts* or regions, eight
autonomous regions, 3,127 districts, 2,164 cities, 667 city districts (or

boroughs), 3,864 settlements and 42,599 rural soviets. In 1987, 2,322,421 deputies were elected to these soviets, ranging in size from about 32 deputies per rural soviet to 800 members of the Moscow city council. Terms of office at this level were two and a half years. Day-to-day affairs in the local district were run by executive committees (*ispolkomy*) whose dozen or so members were elected from among the deputies. Within this highly centralised structure all lower units were subordinated to the centre by the principle of 'democratic centralism'.

But the real problem with the soviets had less to do with their centralised structure than with how they came to function in practice. Constitutionally guaranteed the exclusive right to make laws and take decisions, the soviets at all levels had become legislative councils in name only by the time of Stalin's death. Nor had matters changed much by 1985, when Gorbachev took over, despite resolutions and legislation advocated by Khrushchev, Brezhnev and even Chernenko aimed at reviving the soviets and strengthening the role of the deputy. Why did these efforts fail?

In theory the executive organs of the soviets were elected by and accountable to the deputies; in reality, the executive branch came to dominate the legislative. The pattern for this was established under Stalin, but it continued under his successors. The executive body, frequently chaired by the corresponding party secretary, was chosen unanimously from a single slate of candidates. The determination of who was nominated fell within the *nomenklatura* or patronage of the party secretary. Sessions of the council as a whole were held only infrequently during the year, and then for short periods of time. At a typical city council meeting perhaps 200 deputies would meet for two to three hours four times a year. At these sessions deputies would unanimously approve legislation drafted by the executive body. The executive committee was also responsible for determining the agenda, the list of speakers, the amount of time each item would receive and even the content of the speakers' remarks during carefully staged 'debates'.

As a result the deputies' legislative role was largely reduced to a ritualistic confirmation of what had already been decided in advance by members of the bureaucracy and party apparatus. Candidates for deputy who might have challenged this system were simply not nominated; control of the single slate belonged, ultimately, to the local party secretary. Suffice it to say that from 1937 to 1988 all decisions by the 1,500 members of the Supreme Soviet were made unanimously in two sessions a year, each lasting only a few days. Obviously one had to look for real political power elsewhere; it certainly did not belong to the soviets.

It is against this background that Gorbachev's proposals to 'restructure' or 'reconstruct' the Soviet state must be seen. Broadly speaking, the most pressing overall goal of his reforms was the modernisation of the Soviet economy. But by 1987 it had become increasingly clear that a major obstacle to economic reform was the resistance of those in the state bureaucracy, from top to bottom, whose personal interests were served by preserving the *status quo*, not by changing it. How to undermine this entrenched resistance? What Gorbachev needed was a way to replace those within the state bureaucracy and party apparatus who were opposed to his programme of *perestroika* with those who supported it. He appeared to have found the key in the reintroduction of a degree of competition in elections to party, state and economic institutions, an approach he outlined in his watershed speech to the Central Committee in January 1987.

With respect to the soviets, a cautious experiment with competition was carried out in connection with elections to the local soviets held in June 1987. Less than 5 per cent of the deputies elected were chosen from multimember districts in which there were more candidates than seats. What made this experiment interesting, apart from offering the voters a choice which they had not enjoyed since the early days of the revolution, was that in many of the multimember districts the candidates who lost, or were reduced to 'reserve' status, were those in executive positions, especially among those regarded as part of the old leadership. These results were not lost on Gorbachev. A year later he proposed to the extraordinary 19th Conference of the CPSU, apparently with the support of the Politburo, that competitive elections become the norm, starting with elections to a new Congress of People's Deputies to be convened in the spring of 1989. In making this proposal he explicitly praised the 1987 experimental elections for having 'increased the deputies' sense of responsiblity'.

Competitive elections were only one element, though a critical one, in the comprehensive set of proposals on political reform introduced by Gorbachev at the 19th Conference, which began on 28 June 1988. With respect to the institutions of the Soviet state, he proposed to increase the decision-making authority of the local soviet and their budgetary discretion; he called for a restructuring of executive–legislative relations within the soviets to ensure greater executive accountability; he outlined a major reorganisation of the parliamentary system at the national level; and he sought the creation of a Constitutional Review Committee as part of a broader effort to establish a more genuine rule of law. Perhaps most significantly, he insisted on ending the substitution (*podmena*) of the authority of the party for that of the state, calling for, in his words, 'the demarcation of the functions of party and state agencies'.

In scope Gorbachev's proposals were breathtaking and they engendered lively debate and open criticism at the Conference, itself a major change from past practice. In the end Gorbachev's proposals, essentially unchanged, received CPSU approval in a series of resolutions adopted by the Central Committee in July 1988. Draft legislation on national elections and on amendments to the 1977 Constitution to implement the proposals was forthcoming in late October. After a month of 'public discussion' which resulted in comparatively minor, but important, revisions, the draft legislation was adopted as law by the old Supreme Soviet in December 1988. But, for the first time in at least 50 years, the vote, while overwhelmingly favourable, was not unanimous. In what follows the major changes introduced into the Soviet state system will be examined in greater detail, starting with the new electoral process, then moving to changes in the national parliament and local government, and ending with an assessment of the implications of these changes for what is now a post-Soviet system.

Elections

The purpose of elections in democratic societies is to provide citizens with a mechanism for changing elites. The fulfilment of this purpose presupposes an element of choice; elections lacking choice serve only to perpetuate elites in power. The inertia which had gripped the Soviet system when Chernenko died in 1985 in no small way reflected the effects of a lack of choice over a long period of time. The introduction of a competitive element in the elections to the USSR Congress of People's Deputies held on 26 March 1989 was almost certainly aimed at breaking this inertia by replacing, or at least threatening, those in positions of power who opposed Gorbachev's programme of reform. In the light of this, two questions would seem to follow: (1) how much of a choice did the voters have and (2) who won?

The elections to the USSR Congress of People's Deputies (hereafter the Congress) were undertaken in three stages: preliminary nominations, or primaries, were held from 26 December 1988 to 24 January 1989; district pre-election meetings to determine the final list of candidates took place from 25 January to 23 February; and campaigns were conducted from 24 February to 25 March, with elections held on Sunday 26 March 1989. In two important respects, however, the outcomes in each stage were conditioned by decisions reflected in the Law on Elections adopted in December 1988. First, in addition to the 1,500 seats in the Congress to be filled by election in 750 territorial and 750 national–territorial districts, 750 additional seats were allocated to public organisations specified in Article 1 of the Law on Elections, including 100 to be chosen by the CPSU. Secondly, the elections were to be conducted in accordance with the decisions of a 35-member Central Election Commission and 1,500 district election commissions comprised of eleven to seventeen members each. In all cases, appointments to these commissions ultimately depended on those already in power. The commissions were in place and functioning prior to the opening up of nominations on 26 December.

The nomination process (26 December to 24 January) was quite remarkable by previous Soviet standards. Candidates could be nominated, as before, at places of work or from military units, but now this right was extended to public organisations and to residents at meetings attended by at least 500 of those living in the district. The number of those nominated was 'unlimited', a choice of words which allowed for single, as well as multiple, candidacies. At nomination meetings, anyone in attendance was free to propose (or oppose) any nominee, including themselves. Individuals were nominated if 50 per cent of those present voted for them. In a significant departure from past practice those holding positions in government were excluded from running, with the exception of the Chairman of the Council of Ministers. This rule ultimately resulted in a sharp reduction in the number of those in the administrative apparatus simultaneously holding elective office.

The results of the nomination process, completed on 24 January, offer a mixed picture with respect to the issue of public choice and involvement. On the one hand, there is a good deal of evidence to suggest that in many cases people took part in the selection of candidates to an unprecedented degree. This was especially the case in nominations for the 1,500 district seats, where 6,132 candidates were put forward and many more were discussed. The average of better than four nominees per seat is misleading, however; in some districts there were many more nominees than four, while in others the absence of a requirement that more than one candidate be nominated resulted in a single candidate running as before. Moreover the existence of a numerical requirement (500) for nomination from residences, but not from labour collectives, worked to the advantage of those who ran the nomination meetings in the workplace. There a decision to nominate by a show of hands rather than by a secret ballot could be an inhibiting factor for voters whose well being depended on voting the 'right' way.

The element of choice is even more limited when it is remembered that 750 seats were reserved for public organisations with national constituencies. Here nominations were made at plenary sessions convened by their central bodies. Although it was possible for these meetings to produce a list with more nominees than the number of spaces allotted to them, many did not, including the CPSU whose plenary session approved 100 nominees for their 100 seats. Overall the public organisations nominated only 880 candidates for the 750 seats reserved for them in the Congress.

During the next stage of the elections (25 January to 23 February) pre-election meetings were held in those districts where more than two candidates were nominated. The delegates to these meetings were chosen by those groups which had nominated the candidates, according to norms established by the district election commission which was also responsible for calling and running the meeting. At the meetings the nominees presented their programmes, which, according to Article 45 of the Law on Elections, could not be 'in contradiction to the USSR Constitution, or to Soviet laws'. Nominees receiving a majority vote – by open vote or secret ballot – from those present were then registered as candidates.

Pre-election meetings were held in 836 of the 1,500 districts. Nearly 400,000 delegates took part in their proceedings – an average of about 450 delegates per meeting. Out of the 4,875 nominees considered in these district meetings, 1,720 survived and were registered as candidates; 3,155 were rejected. The large drop-out rate must be attributed, at least in part, to two undemocratic features of the pre-election meetings. First, the fact that individuals could be nominated by an unlimited number of groups meant that those nominated in several different places could pack the meeting. For example, Konstantin Masik, the party first secretary in Kiev, was nominated by 30 different groups, ensuring him a majority of delegates. Not surprisingly he alone survived among five nominees. Secondly, the meetings were open to manipulation by the district election commission. There is a good deal of evidence in the Soviet press to indicate that, in some cases, these commissions interfered on behalf of one or another nominee, or pressured others to withdraw.

When the four-week campaign finally got under way on 24 February a total of 2,895 candidates were registered to run for 1,500 seats, a competitive situtation unknown in Soviet history. However in 383 of the 1,500 seats only one candidate was registered. In 953 districts there were two candidates and in 149 there were three or more (in the Gagarin district of Moscow, twelve contenders vied for one seat). If one includes the 750 seats assigned to the public organisations it could be argued that the possibility for truly competitive campaigns existed for fewer than half of the 2,250 seats in the new Congress.

Where the opportunity for the voters to choose existed, however, the campaigns were vigorous and public interest appears to have been intense as large numbers of voters attended meetings at which the candidates debated their positions and answered questions from the voters. Campaign staffs were limited to ten people and although the law was silent on campaign finance, except to guarantee equal access to the media, it was clear from the widely varying quality (and quantity) of the campaign literature that some candidates, or their supporters, had spent more than others, despite a ruling by the Central Election Commission that fund-raising was impermissible.

In past years election day had been a dull affair. On paper, 99 per cent of the electorate turned out to vote for the single candidate in their district, but only because of an army of party 'agitators' who noted with displeasure those who refused to vote, or owing simply to false reporting in the interest of closing the polls early. The election of 26 March 1989 was different. Some 89 per cent of the electorate turned out, but without prodding. When they received their ballots, in all but 399 cases offering a choice of candidates, they were required to vote privately in an area secured for that purpose. There they crossed off the names of those against whom they wished to vote, leaving one name or none to be deposited in the ballot box. On the whole the elections appear to have been run honestly. The presence of foreign observers and journalists, as well as the participation of competing campaign staffs in the vote count, helped to ensure this.

One unexpected result of the elections was the large number of seats not decided on election day. To win, candidates needed to receive more than 50 per cent of the ballots cast. However, because of the negative voting procedure and because in 149 districts there were more than two candidates to split the vote, the possibility that none would receive the necessary majority was increased. In the 149 districts with three or more candidates, 76 run-off elections were held on 9 April between the top two vote-winners. In 199 of the 1,424 districts where one or two candidates were nominated, none received the necessary majority and new nominations as well as new elections had to be held. One conspicuous example was that of Yuri Solovev, head of the Leningrad regional party organisation and a candidate member of the Politburo, who was defeated in an uncontested election. The first round was held on 14 May, with final run-offs scheduled for 21 May, only four days before the Congress was convened. Even more surprising, perhaps, was that, in some cases, those nominated by the plenary sessions of the public organisations failed to receive the necessary 50 per cent from those members of their organisations who were able to vote. Although these candidates were presented as a list, those voting could cross off individual names. The most dramatic case was that involving the Academy of Sciences, in which only eight of the 20 proposed were elected. Repeat elections yielded seats for a number of prominent critics, including Andrei Sakharov (who died the following December).

What about the results of the elections? Who won? Demographically speaking, the freest elections in Soviet history yielded a Congress whose composition was less representative than the Supreme Soviet elected in 1984 under the old system. The percentage of women declined from 32 to 17 per cent, workers from 16 to 11 per cent, and collective farm workers from 16 to 11 per cent. Youth (representatives under 30) also lost. Among the 'winners', two groups stood out statistically: the percentage of party members increased, from 71 to 87 per cent, and so did the proportion of specialists, especially among the scientific and creative intelligentsia, whose share increased from 1.8 to over 12 per cent. These data are misleading, however. In previous elections certain groups would receive a more or less fixed share of seats in accordance with an informal 'quota system' determined in advance by the CPSU. It is possible to do this when only one candidate is nominated for each seat; in genuinely competitive elections it is extremely difficult.

Looked at qualitatively, the elections appeared to have resulted in a stunning victory for reformers both in and out of the party, and an embarrassing defeat for party regulars. Probably the most dramatic evidence of this was the election of Boris Yeltsin to the Moscow national–territorial seat. Only a year earlier Yeltsin had been ousted from his position as Moscow party secretary by those in the party who found his support for reform too radical. He was also dropped from the Politburo. Still a member of the party, he beat the organisation-backed party candidate by garnering 89 per cent of the vote. During the campaign, the Central Committee's attempt to discredit Yeltsin by initiating a formal inquiry into his political views appears to have actually increased his popularity among Moscow voters. Other well-known critics elected included Andrei Sakharov, Nikolai Shmelev, Tatyana Zaslavskaya and Gavriil Popov. Equally indicative of the strength of the new opposition was the success, especially in the Baltic republics, of the 'popular front' movements whose candidates campaigned for greater autonomy from central control. In Lithuania, the popular front movement (Sajudis) won 32 of 42 possible seats outright and were favoured to win eight more in run-offs.

On the other side, many party organisation candidates fared poorly. Out of approximately 160 regional and city party secretaries nominated, about 40 lost. What makes this figure remarkable is that only 25 of the seats were contested. All of these were lost, along with another fifteen or so in which there was no opposition (in other words, their names were crossed out by more than 50 per cent of those voting). It seems clear that, if the party organisation's candidates had not been protected by inclusion in the single candidate lists drawn up by public organisations with guaranteed seats, their losses would have been even greater.

Still the results of the 26 March elections to the Congress need to be put into perspective. The real organ of legislative power under the new system was not the Congress, but the Supreme Soviet elected by the Congress at its first session. And here, as will be shown in the next section, the reformers' euphoria turned to frustration, leaving the question of 'who won?' much less clear than it seemed at first.

The Reformed State System: National Level

When the 2,249 newly elected deputies met for the first session of the Congress of People's Deputies on 26 May 1989 there was a great deal of uncertainty about what was going to happen. According to the amendments to the Constitution adopted in December 1988, some items of business were clear. The Congress was responsible for electing 542 of its members to a continuously functioning USSR Supreme Soviet; deputies were to choose a Chairman and First Vice-Chairman of the Supreme Soviet, and a Constitutional Review Committee; they had to confirm (or reject) the appointment of a Prime Minister, the Chairman of the People's Control Committee, the Chairman of the Supreme Court, the Prosecutor General and the USSR Chief Arbiter. In addition to these items the proposed agenda included reports by the newly elected chairman of the Supreme Soviet and the Chairman of the Council of Ministers on their foreign and domestic programme for the country. The Constitution, however, also granted the Congress the right to examine and resolve any issue it wished, including amending the Constitution. Moreover, given the widely divergent points of view known to be held by many members of the Congress and the absence of clear procedures as to how contentious issues would be handled, no one could predict the outcome of this first meeting.

It became clear within minutes after the Congress was called to order at 10 a.m. by V.P. Orlov, Chairman of the Central Election Commission and presiding officer, just how different this legislative body was going to be, compared with the old Supreme Soviet. The first speaker to take the rostrum was a deputy from Latvia who promptly asked for a moment of silence for those killed by police in anti-government demonstrations in Tbilisi, Georgia, on 9 April 1989, and then demanded the names of those responsible. Even the two main items of business, the approval of the Credentials Committee report and the election of the Supreme Soviet Chairman, proved contentious and provided deputies with opportunities to raise whatever issues were on their minds, no matter how tangential. It was late in the evening before Gorbachev was elected Chairman of the Supreme Soviet, and not before one candidate had compared him to Napoleon and another insisted that he first resign as General Secretary of the CPSU. Although Gorbachev eventually won in an uncontested race, 87 deputies (out of 2,210 voting) voted against him. Most remarkable, perhaps, was an unknown design engineer from Kola named A.M. Obolensky, who proposed himself as a non-party candidate to run against Gorbachev; 795 deputies, more than a third of those voting, supported the idea of adding Obolensky's name to the ballot!

The election of deputies to the Supreme Soviet which took place very late on the second day of the Congress was also a struggle, but one which served to confirm the minority status of those considered anti-establishment reformers. The process by which the 542 members of the Supreme Soviet were selected proved cumbersome and somewhat complicated. The new Supreme Soviet, like the old one, was divided into two chambers, the Council of the Union and the Council of Nationalities (see Figure 5.1). Each chamber was comprised of 271 deputies who met in continuous session to consider and adopt legislation. One-fifth of these members were to be replaced annually

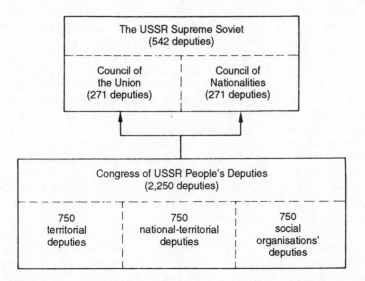

FIGURE 5.1 *The USSR Congress of People's Deputies and Supreme Soviet (1989–91)*

at meetings of the Congress. Members of the Council of the Union were elected from among the 1,500 deputies representing territorial districts and public organisations. As with the US House of Representatives, seats were apportioned by population. Members of the Council of Nationalities came from among the deputies elected from national–territorial districts and public organisations according to the following norms: eleven deputies from each of fifteen union republics; four deputies from each of 20 autonomous republics; two deputies from each of eight autonomous regions; one deputy from each of ten *okrugs* (areas). Deputies to the Congress decided who the 542 members of the Supreme Soviet would be by crossing off the names of those against whom they wished to vote. Those who received less than 50 per cent of the votes cast were defeated. If necessary, repeat or run-off elections would be held.

At this first Congress, 600 deputies were nominated for the 542 seats. But how were these deputies nominated? With what results? Nominations to the Council of the Union took place in regional caucuses based on population. Thus the Moscow regional caucus was allotted 29 seats; they chose to nominate 55 candidates. This was probably a tactical mistake since it gave the more conservative majority a chance to reject those it did not like. In the Council of Nationalities nominations were by republican caucuses. The Russian Republic, like the other republics, had eleven seats. It chose to nominate twelve, including Boris Yeltsin, who was the one defeated when 964 of the 1,500 cast votes against him. However he was appointed later as a result of a vacancy in the Russian delegation.

On the whole, the results proved disappointing for those advocating a faster pace of reform. A series of procedural votes prior to the election to the Supreme Soviet indicated that a decided majority – perhaps 70–80 per cent – of the deputies of the Congress were comparatively more conservative. The composition of the Supreme Soviet reflected this, even though the social and professional profile of those elected had changed considerably from the one elected in 1984 (see Table 5.1). According to one of the deputies considered a progressive, Yuri Afanasev, the Director of the Institute of Historical Archives, 'an aggressively obedient majority' had elected a Supreme Soviet so much like its predecessor in attitude that he labelled it a 'Brezhnevite–Stalinist' Supreme Soviet.

Although the major functions of the Congress – the elections of the Supreme Soviet and its chairman – were accomplished in its first three days of work, the Congress remained in session longer than anticipated. When the final session ended on 9 June 1989, those in attendance and those watching the proceedings on television – it set a record for the number of viewers – knew they had observed events

TABLE 5.1 *Social composition of the USSR Supreme Soviet (1984), Congress of People's Deputies (1989) and the USSR Supreme Soviet (1989)*

	Supreme Soviet, 1984 (%)	Congress 1989 (%)	Supreme Soviet, 1989 (%)	No.
Top political leadership	1.5	0.7	0.2	1
Top and middle-level managerial personnel*	40.0	39.8	32.8	178
Lower echelon managerial personnel**	6.6	25.3	35.3	191
Workers, collective farmers, non-professional office employees	45.9	22.1	18.3	99
Highly professional intellectuals	6.0	10.2	12.5	68
Priests	–	0.3	–	0
Pensioners	–	1.6	0.9	5
Total	100	100	100	542

Source: Moskovskie novosti, no. 24 (1989).
Notes:
  *Republican, regional and territorial-level party leaders, responsible employees of the CPSU Central Committee, leaders of the Supreme Soviets of the USSR and the union republics, government ministers, top military leaders, directors of research and educational institutions, etc.
  **Chiefs of workshops, departments, work teams, laboratories, collective and state farms, etc.

unique in Soviet history. Each day seemed to outdo the day before it. On one day, Yuri Vlasov, a former Olympic weight-lifter, condemned the KGB as 'an underground empire' which was incompatible with a democratic society. On the next, KGB Chairman, Vladimir Kryuchkov, called for the creation of an intelligence oversight commission, citing 'the experience of the Americans'. On 8 June, a large number of the delegates from the Baltic republics walked out to protest against the election of the Constitutional Review Committee, only to return after Gorbachev promised to meet them and to respond to their concerns that such a Committee would encroach on Baltic independence. The day before, Valentin Rasputin, a writer sympathetic to Russian nationalism, argued that Russia should secede from the USSR at an organisational session of the Council of Nationalities. Andrei Sakharov was booed and vilified as a traitor when he demanded a criminal investigation into the actions of the Soviet Army in Afghanistan. In the meantime, Anatolii Lukyanov was elected First Vice-Chairman of the Supreme Soviet, albeit with 179 voting against and 137 abstaining; and Nikolai Ryzhkov was nominated to be Chairman of the Council of Ministers at the first session of the Supreme Soviet held on 7 June 1989, with nine opposed and 31 abstaining.

As indicated above, the work of the Supreme Soviet actually got under way while the Congress was still in session. The constitutional changes introduced in December 1988 created a potentially more powerful parliamentary body than the previous one. Those powers, as specified in Articles 113–17, included the right to confirm (or reject) long- and short-range economic plans and to change the state budget; to initiate and pass legislation on any issue related to government which was not exclusively within the jurisdiction of the Congress; to reverse edicts of the Presidium of the Supreme Soviet, decrees of the Chairman of the Supreme Soviet and resolutions and decrees of the Council of Ministers; to ensure the uniformity of the law for all areas of the USSR and to interpret the laws; and to supervise national security issues, including mobilising troops and declaring war. The differing jurisdiction of the two chambers was spelled out in greater detail in Article 116. Each chamber had to approve the legislation proposed by the other; any differences in proposed legislation were to be resolved in a joint committee or, failing that, by the Congress of People's Deputies.

One of the main reasons for the greater potential impact of the reformed Supreme Soviet was that it was to meet in two continuing sessions in the spring and in the autumn, each of them lasting three to four months. At least some of the deputies would be freed from other professional work, although efforts to extend this to all deputies of the Supreme Soviet were rejected. Among truly 'full-time' deputies, the chairmen of the standing committees soon became focal points of legislative activity. While the Council of Nationalities had four additional commissions to deal with specific ethnic issues, there were fourteen joint committees: Agriculture and food; Construction and architecture; Defence; Ecology; Economic reform; *Glasnost'* and citizens' rights; Health; International affairs; Legislation and legality; Science, education and culture; Local government; Veterans' affairs; Women; and Youth. In order to involve deputies elected to the Congress, but not to the Supreme Soviet, in the work of the new parliament, 50 per cent of the membership of the standing committees was to be drawn from deputies not chosen for the Supreme Soviet. They could participate in discussion, but did not have voting rights.

In the event this reformed legislative system lasted for just over three years, from the spring of 1989 (when it was elected) to September 1991, just after the attempted coup. The Supreme Soviet had played no direct part in the negotiations that had led to successive drafts of a new Union treaty and (deputies complained) the President took less and less interest in their proceedings. As with many other institutions of the Soviet era, the attempted coup proved a fatal blow. Gorbachev himself was disappointed that the Supreme Soviet had not rallied more vigorously in defence of democracy and the constitution; but it was the collapse of the USSR itself that brought about the end of the all-Union legislature. The Congress of People's Deputies met in Moscow in late August and early September 1991 for its final, fifth session. On 5 September it approved a set of procedures for the transitional period until a new constitution had been approved; during this period 'supreme legislature power' was to be in the hands of a new Supreme Soviet, formed by the individual republics rather than by direct election. A new State Council was formed, consisting of the President and representatives of the republics, and an interrepublican committee was set up to manage the economy. The post of President, and an interrepublican parliament, were both preserved in the draft Union treaty that was finally initialled in November 1991; but it was overtaken by the Ukrainian referendum and the formation of the Commonwealth of Independent States (CIS). The new Commonwealth, in turn, made it clear that it would not sustain executive or legislative institutions that exercised authority beyond the borders of each of its member states.

Republican and Local Government

The collapse of all-Union institutions meant that republican and local government became the loci of power in each of the member states of the new Commonwealth. Gorbachev's reform proposals, introduced in June 1988, had included four main elements: competitive elections; the assertion of legislative control over executive agencies; the diminution of the party's role in governing; and the decentralisation of decision making to local bodies. So far as the last of these was concerned, the thrust of Gorbachev's proposals was to enable locally-elected officials to resolve issues of primarily local significance. These would include questions such as land-use planning, urban renewal, retail trade, local transportation, housing, the environment, public works and so forth, problems which it was argued could better be dealt with locally than by Moscow. Along with increased authority to make decisions in these areas, local government was to be given greater control over its financial affairs. Originally this was to involve a reduction in federal subsidies and a substantially broadened tax base.

The first reforms of local government to be introduced were those pertaining to competitive elections. Because of widespread criticism of the electoral law that had been in place during the national elections of 1989, constitutional amendments were approved by the USSR Supreme Soviet on 25 October 1989 and adopted by the Congress of People's Deputies on 22 December 1989. The most significant changes included abolishing provisions of the old law by which a certain number of seats had been reserved for the CPSU and affiliated public organisations. It also eliminated the requirement that pre-election meetings be held to approve nominations. All of those properly nominated would appear on the ballot. Each republic was to decide for itself when, for what offices, and in what manner to conduct elections. As a result, parliamentary elections and elections to local government varied greatly among republics. The elections that took place in February and March 1990 in the three Baltic republics led to nationalist majorities and, eventually, to fully independent status. In the Russian Federation and in the other predominantly Slavic republics the elections that were held on 4 March resulted in dramatic victories for the democratic opposition in Moscow and St Petersburg, where Gavriil Popov and Anatolii Sobchak, respectively, were elected to head the new urban councils. In the Russian Federation as a whole about 350 of the 1,068 seats available went to radical candidates and they in turn elected Boris Yeltsin their parliamentary chairman in May 1990.

Throughout the Russian Federation in April and May 1990 the first sessions of the newly-elected soviets met to organise their local governments; some important changes from the old system were introduced. Proposed by Gorbachev, they were designed to enhance the power and authority of the legislative branch of government relative to the executive. Most of his proposals, in the event, were adopted and reflected in constitutional amendments in December 1989 and in the law 'On general principles of local self-government and local economy in the USSR' which was adopted on 9 April 1990. Among the significant organisational changes introduced at the first sessions of the soviet were: (1) the separate election of a full-time chairman of the legislature and for the executive committee; (2) the election of a Presidium from among the deputies to oversee the work of executive committees and to organise the legislative agenda; (3) the separation of legislative and executive personnel (only the chairman of the executive committee can still hold a deputy's seat); and (4) the election by the deputies of members of the executive committees and department heads.

As originally proposed, the restructuring of local government was intended to reverse the long-standing dominance of the executive branch over the legislative, and to make its members accountable before the popularly elected deputies. This was to be done by introducing a degree of separation of powers and through the creation of a deputies' Presidium. In the words of one Soviet analyst, 'The presidium will exercise oversight (*kontrol*) over the implementation of the soviets' decisions by the *ispolkom*; it will be a counterweight to the *ispolkom*' (Tsabriya, 1990, p. 150). By the early 1990s, however, it had become clear that in practice the division of powers between the soviet, the Presidium and the executive committees was far from settled. This created what another Soviet specialist, B. N. Gabrichidze, has referred to as an 'unhealthy competition in the battle for "real" power between the presidiums and the executives of the local soviets'. Gabrichidze argued that the presidiums were themselves guilty of exceeding their authority with respect to the soviets and executives and that, acting as a sort of 'mini-soviet', they were improperly interfering with the work of the executive branch (he gave several examples). This 'confusion of functions' between the two branches he attributed to a lack of clarity in the legislation governing the work of the local soviets (Gabrichidze, 1991, pp. 77, 82–4). A close examination of at least one local soviet, in the Russian town of Yaroslavl, suggests that the decisive factor in the dominance of executive agencies may simply be experience: in the early stages of reform executive positions have been filled, as a rule, by those (including party officials) who were able to acquire the necessary expertise under the former system.

One further objective of the reforms in local government was to strengthen local legislative authority in those areas that most affected local life. An important corollary of this was that local government would assume greater fiscal control. Legislation introduced in the USSR Supreme Soviet in 1989 was intended to achieve precisely this; it was adopted on 9 April 1990 after a good deal of controversy. This law, along with the amendments to the USSR constitution that were adopted in December 1989 and March 1990, was supposed to establish a basis of power for all 'local bodies of state authority'. According to Article 46 of the Constitution (now superseded) local soviets were required to 'deal with all matters of local significance . . . within their territory', while Article 147 (also superseded) placed within their jurisdiction all 'activity as regards land use, environmental protection, construction, manpower, consumer protection and social, cultural, communal and other amenities and services for the public'.

The law of April 1990 defined the rights and obligations of the local soviets in greater detail and embodied an important distinction. Local self-rule (*mestnoe samoupravlenie*) was a term reserved for city,

district and village soviets, while regional-level soviets and above
were to be considered bodies of state authority (*gosudarstvennaya
vlast'*) and were part of the federal administrative system. Within
their defined areas of competence, the former were supposed to have
a degree of independence that might be compared to limited 'home
rule'. Thus one of the 'basic principles' of local self-rule is the
'independence and sovereignty of local soviets in deciding questions
of local significance' (Article 4). The implementation of such a
distinction would mark a real departure from former practice and
severely limit the ability of the state at higher administrative levels to
control local affairs. This tension was pointed out by the Soviet jurist
G. V. Barabashev in a round-table in *Pravda* (29 June 1990):

> The republics and regions have nothing to gain by this municipal
> revolution, you understand. People have something to gain. Cities
> and districts do. Deputies do. But not all republican and regional
> structures do. They don't understand – how can they not direct a
> city? How can a region not direct a district?

This potential limit on republican and regional authority was
undoubtedly a source of much of the controversy.

By the time the Law on Local Self-Rule was adopted, however, it
proved to be too little and too late to have as much impact as it might
have had. Too little, because by the time it was passed many of its
tougher provisions had been weakened, especially those relating to
finance, and also because provisions were too general to be enforce-
able. Too late, because two months later, to the day, the Russian
parliament, at Yeltsin's urging, adopted a declaration of sovereignty
which asserted the priority of its own laws over those of the USSR, to
which it was previously subordinate. Russia's lead was followed
within months by the remaining republics, setting in motion what
became known as the 'war of laws' (or, in another formulation, the
'parade of sovereignties'). As far as local government was concerned,
the legislative definition of its competence was not a matter for each
republic to decide. The effect of the 'law of wars' was devastating: it
resulted in a paralysis of power which has lasted well into the 1990s.
More generally it exposed a complex struggle for power, vertically,
between city and region, region and republic, and horizontally
between the executive and legislative branches. The outcome of that
struggle would in turn determine the future shape of post-Soviet
politics: centralised and authoritarian (as Yeltsin's nomination of
local representatives and suspension of elections until the end of 1992
suggested) or democratic and participatory, much more in line with
the original objectives of the reforms and, indeed, with the original
conception of soviet rule.

6

The Rule of Law and the Legal System

WILLIAM E. BUTLER

Law and the legal system were at the very heart of *perestroika* and *glasnost'* in two respects during the period 1986–91: as objects of reform themselves and as vehicles of reform in all realms of political, socioeconomic and cultural life. The same will be true of the Commonwealth-building era, whatever directions it ultimately takes. No reform of consequence fails to affect the legal system or to rely upon law for its ultimate success and even implementation. A principal objective of *perestroika* was the creation of, initially, a 'socialist rule-of-law state' (*sotsialisticheskoe pravovoe gosudarstvo*); the reference to 'socialist' was dropped by 1989, but devotion to the rule-of-law state was reaffirmed by the leaders of the Commonwealth in their foundation documents confirmed in December 1991. This signals the continuation of a momentous debate about the role of law within the members of the Commonwealth and about the nature of Commonwealth law itself that will affect the structure, powers and role of the legal profession, the courts and law enforcement agencies.

Towards the Rule of Law

What are the Russians talking about when they advocate a 'rule-of-law state'? Partly it depends upon what sort of 'law' they have in view. The classics of Marxism–Leninism were construed by many as predicting that law would play a minimal role after a socialist revolution occurred and in due course would die away under communism. Lenin was widely quoted as saying, 'law is policy', which was interpreted to mean that it had no eternal value as a restraint upon the state. But what kind of 'law' did he have in mind?

The Russian language has two principal terms for law: *pravo* and *zakon*. The former is basically the equivalent of *droit* (French), *Recht* (German), *derecho* (Spanish), *diritto* (Italian) and the like. The second, *zakon*, refers to statutory law of the highest parliamentary type: enactments of the supreme soviets or their functional equivalents. *Pravo* carried with it connotations of right and justice, and consistency with moral principles, that prevail always and everywhere, that may not be transgressed by citizen or state – a species of natural law originating in the community, nature, divine will, or some other source. *Zakon* suggests man-made law, positive law, which may or may not be consistent with *pravo*.

No special knowledge of the Russian language is required to see that it matters enormously which rule of 'law' one has in view. If *zakon* is meant, then the rule of law means whatever the majority as the highest parliamentary body should decree, irrespective of whether the substance conforms to deeply-rooted community rules or values; and even if the state is expected to behave in accordance with its own laws, there is no higher authority or standard to evaluate its degree of compliance. Referendums may be a partial antidote, but in practice they are an expensive, time-consuming and clumsy institution.

Translating *pravovoe gosudarstvo* as the 'rule-of-law state' gives the benefit of the doubt to those who advocate the broader and more fundamental concept of law. Other translations widely used include 'legal state', 'law-governed state'; 'law-ruled state', 'law-based state' and '*Rechtsstaat*'. These tend to accept the '*zakon*-minded' approach, but the key point for the Western student is to be aware of a vital dimension within the dialogue about the nature of law in the Commonwealth and its members which turns on these terminological distinctions difficult to draw sharply in the English tongue.

Towards the Improvement of Legislation

To say that the Commonwealth and its members are seeking to introduce a rule-of-law state is not to suggest that, even in the darkest days of Stalinist terror, they lacked laws or legislation. *Zakon* was plentiful, especially at the level of subordinate legislation issued by ministries, state committees and local levels of government. Precise figures are not available, but one is speaking of literally millions of enactments issued at all levels of the state apparatus, mostly unpublished and limited in circulation. 'Knowledge of the law' became physically impossible and the opportunities for arbitrary behaviour boundless. This was the most tangible symptom of what in the Gorbachev era came to be called the 'administrative-command' system and it operated both within the normal state apparatus and within those portions charged with exercising repressive functions on behalf of the leadership.

The antidote pursued under *perestroika* was diverse in response. The bodies of state democratically elected – the congresses of people's deputies and the supreme soviets – were in more or less permanent session and made laws more frequently; in doing so they displaced the need for so much subordinate legislation and were able to hold local agencies of government more accountable. The courts were enjoined to be more rigorous in their evaluation of state behaviour. In certain situations collegial decisions taken by officials could be appealed to a court. The USSR Constitutional Supervision Committee, although it enjoyed a limited life and role, actively used its powers to review the constitutionality of subordinate legislation. And a variety of other legal institutions were reshaped or reinvigorated to become responsive to the challenges of *perestroika*. The economic reforms buttressed the politico-legal measures, for by decentralising or eliminating state responsibility for enterprise management they reduced the need to rely on 'administrative-command' methods and use law rather to 'regulate' relations among parties enjoying equal legal status – which is much the same way that law is used in the Western tradition. The Commonwealth and its members have committed themselves to the market economy more explicitly than was true under *perestroika* and accordingly one may anticipate substantial efforts to continue to improve legislation by consciously adapting European and Anglo-American legal models to their circumstances. However the 'administrative-command' approach is one with deep roots in Russian behavioural patterns and will not be easily supplanted.

Legislative reform in the domain of human rights, which achieved some notable successes in the *perestroika* era, is scheduled to continue. The Russian Federation on 22 November 1991 adopted a Declaration of the Rights and Freedoms of Man and Citizen which incorporated more explicitly international human rights standards into Russian law and expressly noted the need 'to bring legislation of the RSFSR into conformity with the standards of human rights and freedoms generally recognised by the international community'. Crucial to the success of the legal strategy of *perestroika* and the Commonwealth-building era are the legal profession and legal institutions.

The Legal Profession

The October 1917 revolution abolished Imperial Russian legal institutions and recast those deemed essential in a proletarian guise. But the principle that individuals should have a right to representation in court and should be able to retain and pay a professional if they wished was continued. Lawyers who specialise in representing the interests of individual clients, what in the Western tradition would be classified as a private practitioner, are called 'advocates'. They practise law, as a rule, as members of the *Advokatura* in each Commonwealth member or large city or region (Moscow, St Petersburg, Kiev, and others) and are usually grouped into law offices in urban and rural areas sited to serve population catchment areas. Their fees are fixed or guided to some extent by the ministry of justice or its equivalent. A few advocates have registered to offer their services as entrepreneurs or have formed cooperatives, limited responsibility societies or joint-stock societies for this purpose.

In the pre-*perestroika* era the advocate was often portrayed as an unavoidable anachronism whose private income, paid directly to the law office by the client, was contrasted sharply with the socialisation of other walks of life. The anachronism was rationalised on the grounds that to require an individual client to employ a state-salaried advocate in a case where the investigator, judge, procurator and people's assessors were also civil servants or possibly so would be unjust with respect to the client. And in certain areas – alimony, dismissal from work and others – the advocate was required to render services without a fee.

In the *perestroika* and post-*perestroika* eras the advocate, together with other segments of the legal profession, has been called upon to perform an enhanced role. Rather than an anachronism, the advocate's economic independence is viewed as a positive factor to be emulated in other social domains. Ceilings on monthly earnings 'voluntarily' accepted in the Brezhnev era by advocates have been eliminated, enabling the most gifted to offer their services as demand requires. Advocates are at liberty to negotiate 'contract prices' with clients, including foreign clients, for most legal services. As foreign investment increases in the Commonwealth members, advocates will be in increasing demand to advise, and this represents a fundamental reorientation of their traditional areas of practice.

Criminal procedure reforms give the advocate an earlier and more active role in defending client interests at the stage of preliminary investigation. Normally excluded in the past from this vital stage of any serious criminal case, the republic codes of criminal procedure as amended in 1989–90 allow, and sometimes even require, the presence of defence counsel.

The role and prestige of the profession has been enhanced through a body founded in February 1989, the Union of Advocates, and through advocates' membership in the largest legal social organisation, the Union of Jurists, formed in June 1989. There are about 26,000 advocates in the Commonwealth members, and in excess of 300,000 'jurists' – the general term for people holding a degree in law or employed or otherwise engaged in jobs that fall within the rubric of the legal profession. The formation of the Union of Advocates and of the Union of Jurists has contributed to a sense of professional identity amongst those legally trained. In pre-revolutionary Russia the emergence of a law-trained elite during the nineteenth century contributed significantly to the limitation of tsarist absolutism and the emergence in 1905 of a constitutional monarchy. Destalinisation from 1953 accentuated the restoration of socialist legality and economic reforms since 1965 required a massive expansion of the legal profession, principally the jurisconsults (see below). Gorbachev was the first Soviet leader since Lenin to bring legal skills to that position. The rising *perestroika* generation is in part the product of the gradual rehabilitation of law as a positive and desirable force in society. That jurists should feel a sense of professional community, an awareness of values and principles which have enduring implications for the well-being of society, is a natural outgrowth of factors and forces gestating during the past almost four decades and potentially a powerful element driving policies towards the rule-of-law state.

The jurisconsults, perhaps 150,000 more in number, are the other type of legal practitioner who serves clients. They act as legal advisers to ministries, departments, parliamentary bodies and committees, local government, enterprises, cooperatives, joint ventures, farms and the like. Unlike advocates, they are salaried employees and are not dependent upon fee income for their livelihood. Their numbers increased dramatically from 1970 as a direct result of the 1965 economic reforms: a certain decentralisation in economic management and greater autonomy to state enterprises disciplined by contracts among the enterprises and larger numbers of legal advisers to assist enterprise managers. The jurisconsult was positioned to help the manager, but also to verify whether the manager acted in accordance with law. Accordingly the jurisconsult may refuse to sign or 'visa' documents which in his view are contrary to law. The expansion of the private sector in the Commonwealth may reduce the role of jurisconsults as a check on management, but in those areas of government and state-managed enterprises this role may be preserved. Increasingly the role of the jurisconsult is likely to approximate that of a company legal adviser in the West.

The Courts

The elimination of the USSR in late 1991 created a certain confusion with respect to court organisation. Under the USSR Constitution there existed two types of courts: the courts of the USSR (the USSR Supreme Court, the Supreme Arbitrazh Court of the USSR, and the system of military tribunals) and Union republic courts (all other courts in the Soviet Union, which varied in importance depending upon the hierarchy of administrative–territorial subdivisions within each Union republic). The foundation documents of the Commonwealth created no judicial institutions, whereas those of the Economic Community made provision for the formation of the Arbitrazh of the Economic Community in order to ensure the uniform application of the Treaty on the community throughout the entire territory of member states.

Substantial differences in court organisation within the republics are likely to emerge in the mid-1990s as they reshape their judicial structures and move away from the unitary model associated with the former Union. The debate has already commenced over whether the ordinary people's courts, which traditionally decided 95 per cent of all criminal cases and civil cases between citizens, should have jurisdiction over economic disputes between enterprises. Voices are heard favouring special courts for family, patent and labour cases. The Russian Federation has created a Constitutional Court with powers of juridical review over the constitutionality of legislation. Since 1989 a jury system has been possible in the republics, but few have moved to introduce it, apparently preferring the long-established system of people's assessors who have the full rights of a judge.

The Judges

The judiciary was a major object of reform in 1988–9 under *perestroika*. Judges were accused of being too passive, of being subject to local external influences of various kinds, or of being too easily disposed to accept the procurator's version of the law. At the Union level, in December 1988, constitutional amendments sought to give the judiciary greater independence by extending their terms of office from five to ten years and by doing away with the popular election of people's judges at all inferior levels and passing this responsibility to local soviets immediately superior to each level of court. This procedure removed judicial selection away from the levels of government at which the judges serve. Judges may be recalled by the agency which elected them.

Although Soviet constitutions provided for decades that 'judges ... shall be independent and subordinate only to law', the 1988 constitutional amendments sought to add substance to the phrase by stipulating that conditions must exist for the 'unhindered and efficient exercise of their rights and duties'. Further 'any interference whatever' in the activities of judges was declared to be 'inadmissible' and punishable. In a law enacted in August 1989, 'On the Status of Judges in the USSR', the legislator attempted a more precise answer by prohibiting: (1) interference in the activities of judges when they are 'effectuating justice'; (2) pressure in any form whatever with a view to obstructing the 'comprehensive, full and objective consideration' of a specific case or to obtaining an illegal judicial decision, prejudgement by the mass media when reporting the proceedings in a case, or otherwise pressuring a court before its judgement had entered into legal force. The sanctions for violations were set out in special legislation adopted in November 1989 and replicated in many republics.

The qualifications for judicial office were strengthened under *perestroika*. All judges must have a higher legal education, be 25 years of age on election day, have at least two years' work experience in law, and have passed a qualifying examination. All of these except the age limit were new, although by the 1970s and 1980s most Soviet judges did have a degree in law. Judges of superior courts must have at least five years' work experience in law, including two as a rule as a judge.

In a fascinating departure from earlier practice, where Soviet judges wore ordinary dress while sitting on the bench, the 1989 reforms authorised the republics to determine models of judicial dress. This was a formal reintroduction of the symbolism of judicial power – the first such since the October 1917 revolution. Although introduced at Union level, the 1988–9 judicial reforms were well received by the republics and are likely to be strengthened rather than discarded.

People's Assessors

While *perestroika* led to further professionalisation of the judiciary, the lay element in dispensing justice was preserved through the people's assessors. These are laymen who have reached 25 years of age and have been elected by meetings of citizens at their places of residence and work for a term of five years to serve on a people's court. Each assessor gives two weeks each year to the service, with paid time off from his or her regular job. Thus each people's court will have 50–75 people's assessors per judge, and in 1987 more than 850,000 people's assessors were elected to this position. The superior courts also have people's assessors available wherever the courts sit at first instance; in this event the assessors are elected by the respective local soviet at the same level.

The people's assessors have equal rights and an equal vote with the judge and, in theory, and sometimes in practice, can outvote the judge. In most cases it is likely that the expertise and experience of the judge dominates the assessors. As a result, since 1989, Union legislation has allowed the replacement of people's assessors in selected situations by a jury containing more people's assessors or jurors. Whether and how the lay element is to be preserved in the administration of justice will be a major concern in the debate over judicial reform in the 1990s.

Guiding Explanations

Soviet law never recognised the doctrine of judicial precedent. Although some court decisions were published to help guide the legal profession, those decisions were not binding upon other courts. The USSR and republic supreme courts issued 'guiding explanations' which interpreted difficult or controversial legislative provisions in the light of judicial practice. These guiding explanations were binding upon all lower courts, were published and amended when necessary and comprised an extremely important adjunct to the legislation. They also served as a mechanism for promoting uniformity in the application of Union and republic legislation. The debates over judicial reform have raised the question of whether judicial precedent should be introduced.

The Procuracy

Very much a Russian institution, with roots dating back to Peter the Great, the modern procuracy has long been the most prestigious component of the Soviet legal profession. There were more than 18,000 of them in the early 1990s. Highly unified and centralised, the procuracy has sometimes been called the 'fourth estate'. The Procurator General of the USSR was appointed by the USSR Supreme Soviet for a term of five years and in turn either appointed or confirmed, depending upon the tier of government involved, all inferior procurators.

In the early years of *perestroika* the four basic functions performed by the procuracy were strengthened. The most important of these was the exercise of 'general supervision' by the procuracy over the execution of laws by ministries, state committees, enterprises, local government on the executive and administrative sides, collective farms, social organisations, officials, citizens and others. 'Execution' for these purposes encompassed the enactments adopted by those entities and officials and their implementation. If the procurator considers that a ministry has issued a decree whose provisions violated superior legislation, the procuracy files a 'protest', giving reasons, and demands that the illegal decree be repealed or altered to remove the offending formulation. In some cases the act was suspended for ten days while the agency receiving the protest considered the matter. It is important to note that the procuracy could not itself repeal or change the legislation it considered to be illegal; through the protest, the matter was drawn to the attention of the issuing agency, which was to consider the protest within a particular time period, and either concur with the protest (and rectify the matter) or decline to do so. If the procuracy disagreed with the rejection of the protest, the superior procurator would submit it to the next higher agency and seek satisfaction there. Theoretically protests and rejections could reach the highest level of government, whose decision would be final.

Where the procuracy encountered behaviour by an agency or official which was in clear violation of the law, under 1987 amendments it could issue a written instruction to eliminate the violation. The instruction must cite the provision of law being violated and suggest corrective steps. The instruction could be appealed by the recipient within ten days to the superior procurator, whose decision was final; an appeal did not suspend the instruction in the meantime. The concept even extended to unlawful acts at a preparatory stage on the part of an official or a citizen; in this event a written caution was issued. Prosecution could follow if the warning was not heeded. If a violation caused financial harm to the state, the procuracy could initiate a civil suit for recovery of damages.

The other branches of supervision exercised by the procuracy concerned the execution of laws by agencies of inquiry and preliminary investigation, the conformity of judicial decisions to law, and the administration of correctional labour institutions. In the case of court decisions, although the procuracy acts as prosecutor on behalf of the state, it is nonetheless required to ensure that the court has considered the case thoroughly and objectively and that all court decisions, in whatever form, are in conformity with law, well-founded and executed in a timely way. This is merely one illustration of a plurality of roles which on the face of it would seem to involve the procuracy in conflicts of interest. These are minimised to some extent by depersonalising the conflict through the distribution of responsibilities: prosecutions are brought by the section concerned with such activities, whereas protests against judicial decisions are filed by the procuracy section specially charged with reviewing criminal or civil cases.

Although the procuracy is said to enjoy a high success rate when bringing protests, the courts, state agencies and officials can and do reject protests if they do not concur with the reasons adduced to support the protest. In this event the procurator must either acquiesce or carry the protest to the next higher level. The essence of 'supervision' is to persuade agencies to rectify their own errors; except in certain aspects of inquiries and preliminary investigations of criminal cases, the procuracy has no power to change the state of affairs by itself. Aptly the procuracy has been called the 'eye of the state', but its vision is limited to the executive and judicial branches of government below the highest agencies of state power and administration. It also seems to have been the case that the procuracy, amongst all the agencies involved in the administration of socialist legality, was most responsive to Communist Party guidance.

Fundamental reform of the procuracy has been mooted for some years, but the legislation never emerged in the *perestroika* era. In his last months of power, Gorbachev appointed a new Procurator General who publicly favoured abolishing the procuracy's powers of general supervision. In the republics seeking independence there occurred in 1988–91 a considerable struggle between the central and republican authorities over the republic procuracies, and key elements of the USSR procuracy sided with the leaders of the coup against Gorbachev in August 1991. Those republics which introduce constitutional reforms based on the separation of powers will encounter considerable conceptual obstacles to continuing the role of the procuracy in its classical Soviet form.

Police and Investigative Agencies

With the ratification of the Agreement on the Creation of the Commonwealth of Independent States of December 1991 and the elimination of the Union, responsibility for police and security matters passed chiefly to the republics. The only policing matter expressly reserved to the Commonwealth in the foundation treaty was the 'struggle against organised criminality' (Article 7).

On 19 December 1991 the Russian Federation formed its own Ministry of Security and Internal Affairs, which took over the functions and property of the former USSR Ministry of Internal Affairs, the former Russian Soviet Federal Socialist Republic (RSFSR) Ministry of Internal Affairs, the Inter-Republic Security Service (which had replaced the former KGB) and the Federal Security Agency of the RSFSR. This scheme was declared unconstitutional in January 1992 by the Russian Constitutional Court.

It will be some time before the reorganisation of policing and investigative functions is completed. The Russian Ministry would seem to combine all crime prevention functions, including those formerly delegated to the KGB, but whether intelligence functions will be performed there remains to be determined.

In the meantime crime prevention is a priority issue. The crime rates in 1989–91 showed large increases in most categories, although they remained below recorded levels for certain years in the early 1980s. The criminal law reforms contemplated during *perestroika*, which emphasised the 'humanisation' and 'decriminalisation' of criminal legislation, were finally adopted in the 1991 Fundamental Principles of Criminal Legislation, which, however, were not to enter into force until 1 July 1992. That enactment will have died with the Union, although its influence doubtless will be felt in the republic criminal codes to come.

Other Law Enforcement Bodies

The Soviet Union had a vast range of other entities, both state and non-state, which were involved in the 'administration' of justice. Many of these were novel and had no precise equivalent in the Anglo-American legal system. Whether and how these are retained or modified will give considerable insight into whether and to what extent the Commonwealth and its member states depart from the socialist legal model.

State Arbitrazh

Throughout virtually all of Soviet history economic contract disputes between state-owned enterprises were excluded from the ordinary courts. A special system of tribunals whose origins date from 1922 had jurisdiction over such disputes. At present called state *arbitrazh*, it is not to be confused with voluntary 'arbitration' widely used in international commercial disputes, including those in the Commonwealth.

Under *perestroika* the state *arbitrazh* system became more centralised and elevated in status. In the twilight days of the Union a Supreme Arbitrazh Court was created and a chairman appointed, but it never achieved operational status. The demise of the Union left the republics with their own *arbitrazh* systems, the long-term future of which must be in doubt. State *arbitrazh* was essentially a creature of the planned economy, an instrument through which contract discipline pursuant to planning directives was enforced in a highly expeditious and expert way. As market relations develop and the state sector gives way to privatised industry and entrepreneurship, the case for maintaining the *arbitrazh* system diminishes. If there is a case for its continuing to exist, it is likely to be in the form of a special economic court rather than an entity with the mentality of the planned economy.

Administrative Commissions

The Anglo-American legal system has traditionally distinguished between criminal and lawful behaviour, with nothing in between. Illegal behaviour is a criminal offence to be punished accordingly. In the Commonwealth member states certain anti-social behaviour may not be criminal at all, or may be criminal only if previously punished administratively. It may nonetheless be punishable as an 'administrative offence' under the republic codes on administrative responsibility adopted in 1982–8. The administrative sanctions can be quite serious, ranging from a warning to administrative arrest for a term of as long as fifteen days. An enormous number of agencies have the right to impose administrative sanctions. Amongst them are the district and city people's courts or judges, state inspectorates, internal affairs agencies and other officials or agencies specially empowered by law.

Although certain administrative cases are dealt with by judges sitting alone in 'administrative session', a large number, perhaps the majority, come before administrative commissions attached to local soviets. Special systems of administrative commissions deal with juveniles, alcoholics and drug addicts.

People's Guards and Comrades' Courts

From the earliest days of the October 1917 revolution volunteer citizen groups exercised auxiliary police functions and created informal social courts. Under Khrushchev the people's guards and comrades' courts were revived and reconstituted as part of the communist doctrine of the 'withering away of state and law'. During the Brezhnev era both institutions were modified in the direction of greater procedural formality and due process, but the voluntary lay element was retained intact.

The administrative commissions, people's guards and comrades' courts did not figure in law reform proposals under *perestroika*. Whether this means they are peripheral or are performing satisfactorily on the whole is difficult to assess in the absence of empirical data on their respective caseloads and other activities. The collective awareness and discipline needed to make people's guards and comrades' courts effective may come under pressure as the market economy accentuates factors of differentiation based on skill, attainment and individuality.

Citizen Initiative

The Soviet system traditionally made considerable use of citizen complaint, or 'whistle-blowing'. Individuals were expected to serve as guardians of legality against abuse by state agencies and officials on the basis of a 1968 Edict on the Procedure for Considering Proposals, Applications and Appeals of Citizens, as amended in 1980.

The procedures are straightforward: citizens may make proposals, applications and appeals orally or in writing to all state or social agencies, criticise shortcomings, or complain against the actions of officials. The appeal is, first, directly to the immediate superior of the object of the appeal, provided that the superior has direct jurisdiction over the matter in question, or, if there is no superior, to a court or to the executive or administrative body of the agency. Regular office hours must be kept to receive complainants and reasoned decisions issued, usually within a specified time period. Since 1988 anonymous complaints are no longer considered.

Although extensively used, the system was widely criticised as inadequate. In November 1989, legislation was enacted, following much resistance from bureaucratic quarters, allowing citizens access to the courts in order to appeal against the unlawful individual or collegial actions of state officials or agencies. The number of cases reportedly brought under the legislation has been comparatively small.

Commonwealth, Community and Republic Law

The demise of the Union has removed a central lawmaking authority whose actions were felt from top to bottom in the Soviet system. The departure of that authority, however, is not so traumatic as may first appear. First, in key branches of law the Union adopted fundamental principles of legislation which were elaborated in republic codes of laws. The removal of Union legislation leaves the republic codes in place and the latter incorporated verbatim the respective Union enactments. Further, for all the talk of independence and autonomy – proclaimed in various declarations adopted by all of the republics – the republics did not disengage entirely from Union legislation. The basic formula was that Union legislation would continue to be applied on the territory of a republic insofar as it was not expressly repealed or otherwise contrary to the republic's constitution and laws. In effect Union legislation was in this manner incorporated into republic legislation. The sole exception, so long as the Union existed, was Union legislation in areas of competence expressly ceded by the republics to the Union.

In place of the Union, the republics have created two umbrellas of authority whose precise competence, functions and authority will require some time to unfold. Both umbrellas are founded on international treaties concluded amongst the republics: the first the Treaty on an Economic Community opened for signature on 18 October 1991 and the second, the Agreement on the Commonwealth of Independent States, opened for signature on 8 December 1991. Although the October Treaty was not ratified before the December Agreement was concluded, the organs provided for by the October Treaty were set up and commenced operations.

However the two documents and their collateral agreements and protocols are reconciled in the future, both contemplate the creation of institutions which will generate legally binding rules for their members. And, as noted above, the Economic Community makes provision for the formation of an *arbitrazh* to settle disputes arising out of the Treaty. The embryo of some form of Commonwealth or Community law and, perhaps, legal system has been created and, where such law exists, it will have priority over republic legislation.

Moreover the republics will all have to enact new constitutions in order to introduce and consolidate the massive restructurings taking place; the Russian Federation, by far the largest, began to consider new arrangements of this kind in April 1992, with some tension between supporters of a strong executive presidency and proponents of a more limited parliamentary form of government. How community building and the rule of law are to be accorded constitutional expression will be among the salient issues for the 1990s.

7

Nations, Republics and Commonwealth

ZVI GITELMAN

Writing just as the Second World War was ending, the distinguished analyst and historian of Russia, E. H. Carr, asserted: 'In Europe some of the small units of the past may continue for a few generations longer to eke out a precarious, independent existence . . . But their military and economic insecurity has been demonstrated beyond recall. They can survive only as an anomaly and an anachronism in a world which has moved on to other forms of organization.' He reasoned that, 'just as the movement for religious toleration followed the devastating religious wars of the 16th and 17th centuries, so the movement for national toleration will spring . . . from the destructive 20th century wars of nationalism' (1945, pp. 37, 66).

Some 45 years later, the USSR, a state which claimed to have solved the 'national problem' and to have created a new type of harmonious multi-ethnic society, began to disintegrate, largely because of the emergence of militant nationalisms and demands for independent existence, no matter how politically and economically 'precarious' that existence might be. By the end of 1991, power had oozed away from the centre of what had been considered one of the most powerful states in the world. Three of fifteen Soviet republics had opted out successfully from the Union; all the others had declared sovereignty, meaning that their laws took precedence over federal laws; and following the failed coup attempt in August, all of the republics except Russia at least nominally declared independence and eleven of them established a new Commonwealth of Independent States. How did this highly integrated state, which maintained a facade of ethnic peace, fall apart so rapidly? And what explains the resurgence of nationalism so long after both Soviet and Western observers had concluded that acculturation and assimilation had advanced so far that the Russians had succeeded in denationalising, politically and even culturally, large numbers of peoples?

The Soviet 'National Question'

The general collapse of the economic and political systems in the USSR enabled national disintegration as well, though the latter was also a cause, not just a result, of that collapse. Not only did the three Baltic republics leave the federation, and others denounce the original treaty of union and establish a post-Soviet Commonwealth; even within republics peoples began to demand autonomy or even independence from the titular nationality. Thus Abkhazians and Ossetians are protesting against Georgian rule and Chechen-Ingushetia declared a republic independent of the Russian Federation in November 1991. Westerners finally learned not to say 'Russia' when they meant the Soviet Union, and politicians and publics alike are learning to deal separately with many entities which formerly could be dealt with through Moscow alone.

One of the people who has had to learn much about national feelings is Mikhail Gorbachev. In the late 1980s he was forced to become painfully aware that the country over which he presided is a multinational one and that many people are acutely conscious and proud of their nationality, to use the Soviet term, or ethnicity, a roughly equivalent term more often used in the West. The 'nationalities problem' emerged as one of the greatest challenges to Gorbachev's own position and to the political stability and viability of the Soviet Union.

In 1926, when the first Soviet census was taken, there were 178 officially recognised nationalities. By 1979, their number had declined to 101, but the 1989 census enumerated 128 nationalities. Thus the number of nationalities at any given time is a function both of their own shifting demographics as well of government decisions about how to classify peoples. In 1989 there were 22 ethnic groups with populations over one million. Fifteen of them had Soviet republics named after them, and they were the majority of the population in all of those republics. The Union of Soviet Socialist Republics, reflecting these nationality differences, was a federal state. In addition to the fifteen republics, reduced to twelve in September 1991 when Estonia, Latvia and Lithuania gained independence, the USSR comprised 20 'autonomous republics', smaller units within four of the larger republics (sixteen of the 20 'autonomous republics' are in the largest republic, the Russian Federation). Unlike the Union republics, the autonomous republics did not have the legal right to secede from the USSR, but their official languages were those of the majority indigenous nationality. Smaller nationalities had autonomous national regions (*oblasti*). There were eight of these regions. The smallest nationality unit was the national district (*okrug*), of which there were ten. The numbers of these units, including the republics, has fluctuated over the years, reflecting changes in borders and in Soviet nationality policy.

Russians constitute barely half of the Soviet population (50.8 per cent in 1989) and their proportion has been slowly declining. Some observers have concluded that, once the Russians slip below 50 per cent, as they are likely to do before the end of the century, their unquestionable political, economic and cultural dominance will be threatened. But there is no magic about being slightly more or slightly less than half the population. It should be remembered that in 1897, the year of the first comprehensive Russian census, in the period when Russians ruled over all other nationalities with no pretence at sharing power, they constituted only 44 per cent of the population. Nevertheless some Russians are apprehensive about the prospect of their becoming a statistical minority in the country, though they will long remain the single largest nationality within what is now a Commonwealth of Independent States. Russian nationalists debate amongst themselves whether it is better to be an imperial power, dominating other peoples, or to be rid of those peoples and form a more 'purely' Russian state. In any case, together with the Belorussians and Ukrainians, the other two major Slavic nationalities, Russians constituted almost 70 per cent of the population of the USSR and they represent 52 per cent of the population of the new Commonwealth.

Between 1979 and 1989, while the Russian population was growing by 5.6 per cent, the Belorussians by 6 per cent and the Ukrainians by only 4.2 per cent respectively, four Central Asian nationalities were growing by between 33 and 46 per cent (see Table 7.1). Another major Asian nationality, the Kazakhs, grew by a more modest 24 per cent, still four times the Russian rate. These differential growth rates meant that, by the year 2000, 20 per cent or more of the Soviet population, already the fifth largest Muslim population in the world, was likely to be of Muslim background. Later in this chapter we shall explore some of the political, economic, cultural and military implications of these ethnically differentiated growth rates.

The ethnic heterogeneity of the USSR and now the Commonwealth naturally brings with it cultural diversity. There are significant numbers of people whose traditions, if not their current practices, are

TABLE 7.1   *The major Soviet nationalities, 1989*

	Census population, 1989 (millions)	*% of USSR total*	*Linguistic group*	*Traditional religion*
The Slavs				
Russians	145.1	50.8	East Slavic	Russian Orthodox
Ukrainians	44.1	15.5	East Slavic	Russian Orthodox*
Belorussians	10.0	3.5	East Slavic	Russian Orthodox
The Balts				
Latvians	1.5	0.5	Baltic	Protestant
Lithuanians	3.1	1.1	Baltic	Roman Catholic
Estonians	1.0	0.4	Finno-Ugrian	Protestant
The Caucasian Peoples				
Georgians	4.0	1.4	Kartvelian	Georgian Orthodox
Armenians	4.6	1.6	Indo-European	Armenian Orthodox
Azerbaijanis	6.8	2.4	Turkic	Muslim (Shi'ite)
The Central Asians				
Uzbeks	16.7	5.8	Turkic	Muslim (Sunni)
Kazakhs	8.1	2.9	Turkic	Muslim (Sunni)
Tajiks	4.2	1.5	Iranian	Muslim (Sunni)
Turkmenis	2.7	1.0	Turkic	Mulsim (Sunni)
Kirgiz	2.5	0.9	Turkic	Muslim (Sunni)
Others				
Moldavians	3.4	1.2	Romance	Romanian Orthodox

Source: Soviet census data and standard reference works.
Note:
*There is a substantial Roman Catholic (Uniate) minority in the Western Ukraine.

Russian Orthodox, Uniate, Protestant, Catholic, Muslim, Jewish and Buddhist, among others. Georgians and Armenians have ancient and independent Christian churches. There are five alphabets in current use – Cyrillic, Latin, Hebrew, Georgian and Armenian – and there used to be more. About 130 languages are officially recognised by the state. They range across a wide variety of linguistic groups and some are unique to the former USSR. Some of the nationalities have been historic enemies, others historic allies, and still others have had little contact with each other. The lifestyles of Soviet peoples range from nomadic peoples of the far north-east of the country, related and similar to North American Eskimos, to the Turkic peoples of Central Asia, to the Northern European types found in Karelia, and many others. Perhaps it is almost inevitable that in such a diverse country ethnic issues should play a major role in politics, as nationalities vie for recognition, resources and representation.

Until the late 1980s Soviet politicians and scholars claimed that nationality conflicts had diminished to the point that the 'nationalities question' had been definitely solved, and the ethnic diversity of the country was yielding to a unity which would approach and eventually reach homogeneity. Like other dogmas long proclaimed as scientific truth, this one was called into question both by policies of *glasnost'* and by dramatic events which seemed to contradict official beliefs. In fact the nationality question is currently one of the most sensitive and troublesome in each of the states of the new Commonwealth. How it is handled will play a major role in determining not only future relations between these states but also the character of the political systems within the Commonwealth's component parts. The nationalities are testing the viability of the Soviet and now post-Soviet system; its future may depend to a considerable extent on whether or not the non-Russians feel themselves accommodated in a reformed system and a reconstructed state.

The Ethnic Map of the Former USSR

There are several families and groups of nations and nationalities in the former USSR. The three large Slavic nations inhabit the European, western part of the country, though members of all three have migrated eastwards and southwards over the centuries. The Russian Republic, by far the largest of the members of the old Union and new Commonwealth, stretches from Europe across Siberia and out to the Pacific Ocean, just across the water from Japan. Over 82 per cent of the 145 million Russians (1989 census) live in the republic. Ukraine is about one and a half times as large as neighbouring Poland, the largest country in Eastern Europe, and with its more than 50 million people it is comparable to some of the largest countries of Western Europe. Ukraine is an important centre of both industry and agriculture. About 85 per cent of the 44 million Ukrainians live in the newly independent Ukrainian republic, the western part of which was annexed from Poland in 1939. Apart from Ukrainians, Russians and Jews constitute significant proportions of the urban population. Belorussia is considerably smaller than Ukraine, with a population of just over ten million. Historically Belorussian national consciousness and literature were not as developed as their Ukrainian counterparts. Western Belorussia, which used to have a mixed population of Russians, Poles, Belorussians, Jews and others, was also annexed from Poland in 1939.

The three Baltic republics, Latvia, Lithuania and Estonia, now independent, were also 'latecomers' to the Soviet Union, assigned to it in secret protocols of the Nazi–Soviet treaty of 23 August 1939. Red Army troops moved into these countries and ensured that the 'elections' held shortly thereafter would show the great majority of the local populations asking to join the USSR. Exactly 50 years later, on 23 August 1989, two million people in the three republics joined hands in a human chain symbolising their protest at being forced to join the USSR, an act that would have been unthinkable twenty, ten or even five years before. Estonia has less than two million inhabitants, ethnic Estonians constituting 65 per cent of the population. The Estonian language is related to Finnish. This, together with Estonia's location and Protestant heritage, have made that republic more attuned to Western culture than perhaps any other.

Latvia also has a Protestant heritage and a language that is unrelated to any other Soviet language save Lithuanian. About 54 per cent of the republic's population of some 2.6 million are ethnic Latvians. Here, too, a militant movement to wrest autonomy or even independence from the USSR surfaced in the 1980s and culminated in independence in 1991.

Unlike the other two Baltic states, Lithuania has a Catholic background and was historically associated with Poland, though the two nations fought over possession of the present capital of Lithuania, Vilnius. The result was that the city was in Poland, where it was called Wilno, between the two world wars. A higher proportion of the population than in the other two Baltic states – about four-fifths – belongs to the indigenous nationality and the rate of population growth is higher. Religion plays a greater role in Lithuania and buttresses national sentiment. Until the Holocaust, Lithuania was one of the most important Jewish cultural centres. Like the Latvians and Estonians, Lithuanians organised a national movement, called

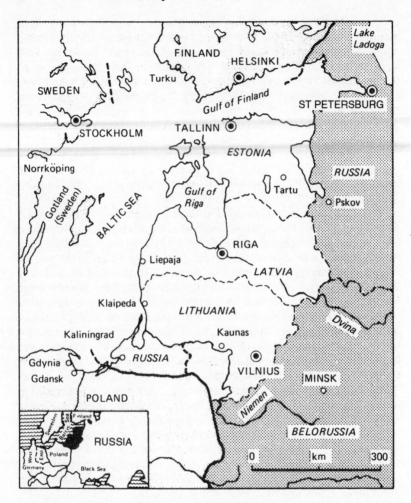

MAP 2   The Baltic States

Sajudis, in 1988. It led the fight to gain autonomy from Moscow and managed to elect three-quarters of the delegates from Lithuania to the national Congress of People's Deputies which began to meet in May 1989. The Lithuanian Communist Party was the first to declare itself independent of the national party, and Lithuania, along with the other Baltic republics, formally recognised political parties other than the communists before this was done elsewhere in the USSR. Now that the Baltic states are independent, Russians, Ukrainians and, in Lithuania, Poles, are worried that they will be discriminated against. Indeed the republics have passed legislation on citizenship which asserts residency and language requirements for those who wish to be citizens of the new republics. The aim is obviously to disenfranchise those who came to the Baltic after Soviet annexation and/or those who refuse to learn the languages of the titular nationalities.

The Caucasus mountains are inhabited by a great variety of nationalities with different religious and cultural traditions. The major nationalities, each of whom has a republic, are Armenians, Azerbaijanis and Georgians. The Armenian and Georgian languages are old and unique, as are their Christian churches. Azerbaijanis are Muslim and related to peoples in Iran and Turkey. The Armenian republic serves as a magnet for the large Armenian diaspora. Of all the republics, Armenia has the highest percentage of its population (90) made up of the titular nationality. It is ethnically the most homogeneous republic, although nearly two million Armenians live outside Armenia, where 2.8 million reside. Georgia has a larger population, over 5 million, and nearly 70 per cent of the population is Georgian. This republic has long had the reputation of being economically more independent and enterprising than the others. Armenians and Georgians, who have not always enjoyed the friendliest relations, have long been among the most educated nationalities and hence well represented in the national intelligentsia and in the economic and, at times, the political elites.

Nearly six million of the seven million inhabitants of Azerbaijan are Azeris. In 1988–9 Armenians living in the Nagorno-Karabakh region of Azerbaijan protested against what they viewed as cultural deprivation and Azeri discrimination against them. Armenians in the home republic supported them, violence broke out, the two republican legislatures passed opposing resolutions about the proper jurisdiction under which Nagorno-Karabakh should fall, and a major ethnic, constitutional and political crisis ensued. The central leadership temporised by placing Nagorno-Karabakh under the direct jurisdiction of the federal government in Moscow, thus avoiding a decision as to which republic had the stronger claim to the region. The issue is far from settled, and in early 1990 further violence between Azeris and Armenians erupted, this time in the Azerbaijani capital of Baku, where about 40 Armenians were killed. At the same time, Azeris tore down parts of the border with Iran and demanded closer contacts with Azeris living there. By early 1992 over 3,000 Armenians and Azeris had been killed in the dispute, despite several attempts at mediation.

There are five republics in Central Asia: Uzbekistan, Turkmenia,

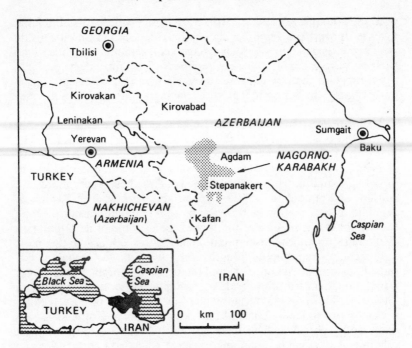

MAP 3   The Caucasian Republics

Kirgizia, Tajikstan and Kazakhstan. The titular nationalities are all of Muslim background, and all the peoples but the Tajiks, who are of Persian stock, are Turkic. Some were nomads until forcibly settled by the Soviets. Nearly all were illiterate at the time of the revolution. Their alphabets and literacy were given to these peoples by the Soviets, partly out of a desire to socialise them politically through written media. Like the Caucasus, these areas had come under Russian rule before the revolution as a result of tsarist imperialism and wars that Russia had fought with her neighbours. All these peoples have high fertility rates: for example, in recent years, when fertility among Slavs was thirteen per thousand, among Tajiks and Uzbeks it was 45 per thousand. Despite migration to their republics by Europeans, the proportion of indigenous nationalities in the population grows because of this high birth rate. The implications of the region's demography will be discussed later in the chapter.

There is a diversity of other territorial groups. The Moldavians, living in the south-eastern part of the former USSR, are very closely related to the neighbouring Romanians, though, in order to justify their annexation of the area from Romania in 1940, the Soviet authorities insisted that the Moldavians were a distinct nationality.

To widen the differences, the Soviets changed the Moldavian alpha-bet from Latin (Romanian and Moldavian are Romance languages) to Cyrillic, a decision that was reversed, at least in principle, in 1989. The Moldavians have since renamed their republic 'Moldova' and declared their independence from the USSR. The Buriats and Kal-myks are Mongolian by language and culture and Buddhist and Shamanist by religion. Yakuts and Chukchi are Siberian peoples, while the Turkic-speaking Tatars are Muslims by tradition.

Finally, non-territorial nationalities include Germans, Jews and Poles, as well as smaller groups of Magyars (Hungarians), Greeks, Bulgars, Kurds and others. The two million Germans, some of whose ancestors came at the invitation of Catherine the Great to improve Russian agriculture, used to have an autonomous republic in the Volga River region but were deprived of it and forcibly exiled at the beginning of the Second World War, when Joseph Stalin presumed they would collaborate with the Nazis. Germans were settled mostly in Kazakhstan and other parts of Central Asia, as well as in the Baltic. In the 1970s and 1980s over 100,000 Germans emigrated, almost all to the Federal Republics of Germany. Only in 1989 did articles begin to appear in the Soviet press which exonerated the Germans of the false accusations Stalin had made and which spoke sympathetically of their cultural and political demands, and moves began to restore their earlier statehood.

The 1.4 million Jews counted in the 1989 census are the most urbanised and educated nationality, but, whereas they were once overrepresented in the government, party and military, for the last 40 years they have been systematically excluded from the higher eche-lons of those hierarchies as well as from other positions where political loyalty or ideological considerations are important. Jews are the only nationality of any significant size who did not have a single school of their own until 1989, when two schools were opened in the Baltic. Since the late 1960s over 700,000 have emigrated, mainly to Israel and the United States. In 1990, a record 184,300 Soviet Jews emigrated to Israel, and another 145,000 did so by the end of 1991. The Poles live mostly in Belorussia and Lithuania. Their linguistic assimilation is almost as complete as that of the Jews: only 14 per cent of the Jews and 29 per cent of the Poles listed their national language as their native one in the 1979 census. Some movement of Soviet Poles to Poland was observed in 1990–1.

Nationalities Policy: Ideology and History

Marx and Engels provided little guidance to their followers on how to deal with ethnic issues. The ideological forefathers of the Soviet state assumed that the fundamental cleavage in modern society was that of class, not ethnicity. They assumed that nations were the artificial construct of the capitalist epoch and that national sentiments were exploited by the bourgeoisie to pit one segment of the proletariat against another, thereby diverting workers from venting their spleen against the exploiting capitalists. It followed that the classless society to be established after the socialist revolution nations would disappear as they no longer served any useful social and economic purpose. This theory did not prevent Marx and Engels from taking sides in the national disputes of their day, or even exhibiting personal prejudices in regard to races and nationalities.

Lenin began thinking about nationalities issues from an orthodox Marxist point of view. He severely criticised the Jewish Labour Bund in the Russian Empire which had borrowed the concept of 'national–cultural autonomy' from Marxists in another multinational empire, the Austro–Hungarian one. This provided for the right of nationalities to administer their own cultural institutions and make independent decisions in the cultural sphere even after the advent of socialism. Lenin rejected even more decisively the Bund's proposal that the Russian Social-Democratic Labour Party, from which the Bolsheviks emerged, allow the formation of national groupings within it which would deal with the cultural affairs of the respective nationalities. The Bolshevik leader felt that such concessions to the nationalities would divert attention from the overall objective, the overthrow of tsarism.

In the years before the revolution Lenin came to appreciate how sensitive and important the nationalities issue was in the tsarist empire, sometimes called the 'prison-house of nations'. He realised that ethnic issues were among the major grievances many people felt against the tsarist system, and was flexible enough to modify his earlier positions in order to make tactical use of these grievances. Thus he conceded that geographically compact and distinct national groups might be granted territorial autonomy within a socialist structure. After the revolution he agreed to the establishment of a Commissariat of Nationalities, headed by Joseph Stalin, himself a Georgian, and even to the creation of nationality sections within the Bolshevik Party. Once the Bolsheviks reconciled themselves to at least the temporary existence of a state – ultimately, it was supposed to 'wither away' – they agreed to organise it along federal lines in order to meet the demands of the nationalities. In the course of the revolution and the civil war, several areas that had been wholly or partly in the Russian empire – Poland, Finland and the Baltic states – managed to break away from the Russian-dominated state. Others which attempted to do so – Ukraine, Georgia and Armenia, for example – were forcibly reincorporated into the USSR, the successor state to the Russian empire.

In the 1920s the Soviet leadership declared that Russian chauvinism was the main problem in nationality relations and that the non-Russians, having been discriminated against for so long, should be assisted in developing their cultures. This would not contradict the ultimate Marxist–Leninist goal of the disappearance and amalgamation of nations, because if one thought 'dialectically' one would appreciate that oppressed nationalities needed to have their cultures flourish first in order to realise that this was not the main purpose of their existence. Once having maximised their cultural freedom the nationalities could then move on to mutual assimilation. The concrete application of this paradoxical idea came in the policy of *korenizatsiya*, 'nativisation' or indigenisation. That meant that members of the non-Russian nationalities were encouraged to take government and party posts; schools in their languages were set up and vigorously promoted; courts, trade unions and even party cells were encouraged to operate in the local languages; and the press, theatre, research institutes and other cultural organisations operating in the local languages were supported by the state. It was during this period of the 'flowering of the nationalities' that the peoples of Central Asia, many of whom were organised in tribes and clans, were given national status and written languages. This was the heyday of ethnic pluralism and cultural development.

When Stalin began his drive to modernise and industrialise the country as quickly as possible, he tried to shift all energies towards that goal. By the early 1930s the goal of promoting national cultures yielded to the overarching aim of rapid industrial development at any cost. What had been laudable efforts to develop national cultures just a few years before now became 'petit bourgeois nationalist deviations'. Cultural and political leaders of the nationalities were arrested and often killed. Cultural institutions were purged, closed down or allowed to disappear by attrition. Parents became fearful of sending their children to national schools and many hesitated even to speak in their native languages. Stalin declared that the cultures of the USSR were to be 'national in form, socialist in content'. That meant that ideological uniformity was to be imposed on all cultures, and only the linguistic and other forms of culture were to be preserved. Indeed all of Soviet culture became subject to a deadly uniformity and conformity. At the same time, there were many who genuinely believed that the epoch of flourishing national cultures had passed and that it was time to move on to a more 'internationalist' mode. Marriages among peoples of different nationalities became more common. As people streamed from the countryside to the city, driven both by the horrors of collectivisation and by the lure of modernity, they began to lose their traditional ways of life, native languages, distinctive dress, foods and lifestyles. Russian was the common language of the cities; housing and food became more uniform; and many began to abandon their former cultures.

As early as the 1930s, and more so in the following decade, Stalin stressed the historical and contemporary virtuosity of the Russian people and made it clear that they were to be regarded as the 'elder brother' of all other peoples. During the war the Russian Orthodox church, severely persecuted in the two preceding decades, was revived. Historic Russian heroes like Alexander Nevsky and General Suvorov were lauded, and the message was sent that the war was being fought to defend historic Russia as much as it was to safeguard the Soviet system. Simultaneously several peoples, among them the Germans, Crimean Tatars, Chechen and Ingush, were deported *en masse* on the grounds that they had intended to collaborate with the German invaders or had actually done so. Collective punishment was meted out for what were often individual crimes.

In his victory toast in the Kremlin in 1945, Stalin singled out the *Russian* people for especial praise, and in the following years Russians were given credit for all kinds of inventions and achievements that properly belonged to people of other nations. This was part of a militant anti-Western and 'anti-cosmopolitan' campaign which sought to isolate the Soviet population from the world outside and which singled out the Jews, especially, as aliens and potential or actual traitors. The 'flowering of the nationalities' seemed long forgotten.

In his 'secret speech' to the 20th Party Congress in 1956, Nikita Khrushchev criticised Stalin for many crimes, including some – but not all – that had been perpetrated against the nationalities. Though Khrushchev curtailed some of Stalin's excesses in regard to the nationalities and opened up the elite to Ukrainians and some others he was not especially sympathetic to ethnic claims, having been Stalin's party secretary in Ukraine at the height of the purges. Khrushchev launched a vigorous campaign against religions, which indirectly impinged on several nationalities associated strongly with certain faiths. In 1958, he initiated an educational reform which eliminated the required study of the native language in the non-Russian regions. His plan to divide the country into economic regions, known as *sovnarkhozy*, threatened to diminish the importance of the national republics.

Under Khrushchev's successor, Brezhnev, dissident nationality movements, among others, began to be more visible. Crimean Tatars demanded to return to their ancestral homeland in the USSR, while Jews and Germans demanded to return to theirs outside it. Lithuanian Catholics pressed for religious and cultural concessions, as did Ukrainians. Brezhnev doggedly asserted, however, that the nationalities question had been solved definitively and that the protestors were deviants and criminals who should be punished accordingly – and many were. During the period of detente in the 1970s, in order to improve relations with Germany and the United States, relatively large numbers of Germans and Jews, and later Armenians, were permitted to emigrate. However many were denied permission to leave the country and were imprisoned or harassed for their efforts to do so. In the 1970s also the concept of a 'Soviet people' was developed and widely promoted. According to one Soviet scholar, Academician P. N. Fedoseev, this was not a nation or an ethnic entity but 'a new historical form of social and international unity of people of different nations' which eliminated antagonistic relations between classes and nations and was based on 'the flowering and drawing together of nations'. It remained unclear whether this 'Soviet nation' was ultimately to replace the peoples of the Soviet Union, though this was presumably the intention.

The official doctrine explaining the present and future of the nationalities was for a long time and until recently encapsulated in the two terms, *sblizhenie* and *sliyanie*. The former means the 'drawing together', or rapprochement, of peoples, while the latter means their fusion into each other, or amalgamation. The two were presumed to exist in a sequential and causal relationship. That is, over time *sblizhenie* would lead to *sliyanie*, because as nations mingled with each other they would lose their specific characteristics and assimilate into one another. The prospect of fusion and loss of identity frightened those who cherished their particular cultures, but they were reassured that *sliyanie* was a rather distant prospect. Both components of the formula came under empirical scrutiny and serious questioning in recent years, and the emergence of militant nationalisms has in any case rendered them largely irrelevant.

Regarding *sblizhenie*, in the late 1980s Soviet commentators began to admit that nationalism and ethnic prejudices and tensions existed in Soviet society. These evils were usually dismissed as 'survivals of the past', but, as one high official of an autonomous republic put it, the great majority of Soviet citizens today were born after the revolution, so how can the fiction of 'survivals' be maintained? It was suggested that nationalism existed because peoples' consciousness changed more slowly than the reality in which they lived and because some peoples entered the USSR relatively recently and had not been fully resocialised. Moreover religion survived and reinforced national exclusivity, and 'bourgeois elements' outside the country tried to fan ethnic tensions. Furthermore 'subjective' factors must be taken into account: insensitive bureaucrats who insulted people on an ethnic basis or attempted to hasten assimilation 'artificially'.

Soviet ethnographers discovered several years ago that national consciousness was not fading, as the theory had predicted, but was growing. Indeed, Gorbachev told the All-Union Party Conference in 1988 that 'The development of our multinational state is, naturally [sic], accompanied by growth in national consciousness. This is a positive phenomenon.' As for *sliyanie*, the 1986 party programme said that the 'complete unity of nations' would take place 'in the remote historical future'. In a speech to scientists and 'cultural figures' in January 1989, Gorbachev stated: 'Of course, we cannot permit even the smallest people to vanish or the language of the smallest people to be lost, nor can we permit nihilism with respect to the culture, traditions and history of both large and small peoples.' In theory, at least, this was a far cry from Lenin and Stalin's assimilationism. The judgement that national consciousness had not faded, and had even grown among some peoples, has been borne out by recent events in the former USSR and by several surveys of recent emigres from that country.

Soviet Nationality Policy

The Soviet Union brought dramatically higher standards of living to many of the peoples of the Caucasus and Central Asia. Industry and modern agriculture were brought to these areas by the Soviet government, along with higher standards of health and education. Still, it has recently been revealed by the Minister of Health that nearly half the hospitals in Turkmenia have no running water. Infant mortality is shockingly high in parts of Soviet Central Asia, and the USSR as a whole ranks fiftieth in the world, behind Barbados and Mauritius, in this respect. For many nationalities there have been trade-offs between higher standards of living and improved economies, on the one hand, and the loss of some or even much of their traditional cultures and religion, on the other. Jews are perhaps an extreme example of this trade-off: the revolution liberated them from the Pale of Settlement, allowing them to live where they chose, and opened educational and vocational opportunities to them that had been denied them by the tsars. At the same time their religious institutions were almost completely destroyed, they were denied the opportunity to study Hebrew, and later they were discriminated against in education, employment and culture. Ukrainians are an example of a nationality whose very existence was denied by the tsars but who received republic status from the Soviets, though they were denied full independence. Great economic progress has been made and Ukrainian cultural institutions have flourished. However there has been steady pressure for Russification within the republic, and few opportunities in their native culture for Ukrainians living elsewhere. Like most multinational countries, the USSR tried to balance the perceived needs of centre and periphery, though ever since the 1930s the centre's interests took precedence.

How did the central authorities control this heterogeneous and potentially fractious population? This was accomplished by a mix of normative and coercive incentives and structural devices. First, the spread of Marxist–Leninist ideology throughout the country imbued the ideologically committed or conforming with the conviction that 'all-Union' interests and those of the party took precedence over the 'narrow, parochial' interests of this or that nationality. They were also taught to believe that nationalism was an evil and that 'internationalist' attitudes and actions were the only ones admissible under socialism. Nations were, in any case, transient. Thus political elites of the nationalities were generally chosen for their 'internationalist' outlooks in addition to any other attributes they might have possessed. As the power of ideology faded rapidly, and with the devolution of power away from the centre, some republican leaders in the late 1980s became more responsive to their constituencies than to the central authorities.

Second, the Communist Party, already in great disarray and now suspended following the failed coup of 1991, was organised as a hierarchical, disciplined organisation in which orders flowed from the top down and must be obeyed. This was the device which effectively weakened Soviet federalism and made inoperative the constitutional right of the republics to secede. The logic of this device was the following: since the nation was represented by its leading class, and since the leading class of all Soviet nations was the proletariat, and since, furthermore, the party was the only authentic representative of that class, ultimately it was the party that decided whether a particular nation could secede or not. Because the party was centralised and hierarchical, no republic-level party organisation could unilaterally recommend secession. By 1990 the Union Treaty that was proposed as a replacement for the overcentralised association established in 1922 implicitly rejected this doctrine and conceded the right of republics to secede with no reference to the party.

A third control mechanism was the cooptation of native elites. Promising people were recruited into the party and imbued with an 'internationalist' world view. Those who aspired to higher education, in almost all cases, had to have an excellent command of Russian, the language of most higher educational institutions. The peoples of the

USSR were given the impression that, at least on the republic and lower levels, they were being ruled by people of the indigenous ethnic groups. Of the 44 republican party first secretaries in 1954–76, over 86 per cent were non-Russians. In 1990, the first secretaries of all republics were members of the titular nationality of that republic. As we shall see, political mobility of non-Russians seemed to stop at the republic level, but most non-Russians did not aspire to run the country as a whole and were more concerned with running the affairs of their respective regions. During the eighteen years of the Brezhnev period, now labelled in the Soviet media the 'era of stagnation', republic leaders, particularly in Central Asia, were given considerable latitude in running republican affairs, apparently in return for their acquiescence to national policy as formulated by the Slavic leadership in Moscow. This resulted in the creation of fiefdoms in which the local leaders' power was enormous. That power was used, according to the Soviet press today, to discriminate against national minorities, mainly Russians, in the republics. It also resulted in enormous corruption and nepotism, with several of the republics looking like the personal possessions of local bosses.

On the other hand, traditionally the second party secretary in the republics was not of the indigenous nationality and was usually dispatched from the central apparatus in Moscow. He was assumed by many to be the 'eyes and ears' of the centre. About two-thirds of the second secretaries from the mid-1950s up to 1976 were Russians or other Slavs. While the second secretary probably did not run things in the republic, he may at least have exercised some influence over his superior.

The centre was also able to exercise great economic leverage on the republics. Investment and trade decisions were, like most economic decisions in the country, highly centralised. It was Moscow which decided, though not always unilaterally, what was to be built where and how much was to be invested around the country. There is considerable debate about whether the centre equalised the distribution of wealth through its policies, or whether some regions, and hence peoples, were favoured over others. Gorbachev's reforms promised that the republics would have greater say in economic decisions, but that was not enough to assuage feelings of exploitation or to stem the tide of nationalism and autonomism.

A sixth instrument of central control was coercion exercised through the militia (police), KGB and armed forces. The KGB played a major role in the repression of nationality dissent in the 1970s and early 1980s. The police were used to break up ethnic and other demonstrations, and in especially serious instances the armed forces were called in. When large-scale violence broke out between

Armenians and Azerbaijanis or between Uzbeks and Meskhetis, several thousand troops of the regular army were introduced. On quite a few occasions the threat of army intervention has been used to head off nationality demonstrations.

Finally there were policies whose obvious aim was to hasten *sblizhenie*, or more concretely, to nudge the nationalities in the direction of Russianisation. The Russian language was clearly the favoured one. Though official doctrine spoke of the 'mutual enrichment of languages', in practice the other languages took much of their scientific, technological and political vocabulary from Russian, while the latter borrowed little from them. As has been pointed out, the educational system was heavily slanted towards Russian. The armed forces operate exclusively in Russian and they are supposed to have a role in the teaching of Russian to those of other nationalities. As a greater and greater proportion of recruits came from Central Asia, and since large numbers of rural Central Asians have only a rudimentary command of Russian, the army's role in teaching Russian gradually increased.

Perhaps the dominance of Russian is the only practical arrangement in such a multilingual country, but non-Russians in the former Soviet Union complained that the media and publications were disproportionately weighted towards Russian. Publication data seem to bear them out. About 41 per cent of the Soviet people considered their native language to be one other than Russian, but in 1983 only 23 per cent of the titles and 16 per cent of the total runs of books and brochures were in non-Russian languages. Still among most nationalities there was little erosion of native-language loyalty; that is, the proportions of people declaring the language of their people to be their 'mother tongue' (*rodnoi yazyk*) have changed very little over the decades, though this is not the case for the non-territorial nationalities. Over 90 per cent of most nationalities consider the language of their people to be their native or mother tongues. At the same time there has been an impressive growth in the Russian-language facility of all peoples, though a leading Soviet ethnographer has recently complained that in some republics the older generation is more conversant with Russian than the younger. There is some debate over the extent to which bilingualism has been achieved, or is even desirable, but on the whole citizens of all nationalities were and still are able to communicate with each other through Russian.

Russianisation was also promoted by the migration of Slavs to non-Slavic areas. Not only the Russians, but Ukrainians and Belorussians also, tend not to learn the local languages and use Russian as the common language of Europeans as well as with indigenous nationalities. Caucasians are quite mobile, but Central Asians tend to stick to their own republics, even eschewing movement from the countryside to the city. Thus they can afford to remain basically monolingual, since the countryside has few Slavs. Baltic peoples complained about the migration of Slavs to their republics as a result of industrialisation. Factories brought Slavic workers and managers, thereby diluting both the ethnic and linguistic character of the countries. For this reason the national fronts in the Baltic in the late 1980s demanded that the republics be given the right to limit migration into the republics. Now independent, they are demanding that the indigenous languages be learned by all non-native speakers and that all official business be transacted in the indigenous languages.

Compared to many other multinational countries, irrespective of political system, the Soviet Union was quite tranquil until a relatively late date. Certainly, when one thinks of Yugoslavia, Lebanon, Iraq, Nigeria, or even Canada and Belgium, the Soviet record in granting opportunities to nationalities and maintaining peace among them looks quite good. It might fairly be asked, however, whether this was the result more of actual and implied coercion or repression rather than of genuine harmony and cooperation. Once the reins had been loosened, at any event, Soviet nationality policy began to be severely tested and the results indicated that the policy, if it ever was as successful as it appeared, had ceased to be effective.

Current Issues and Developments

In line with his effort to make people work more efficiently and thereby improve the economy, Gorbachev attacked the 'affirmative action' practices of his predecessors whereby indigenous peoples in the republics, especially in Asia and the Caucasus, were favoured for jobs, promotions, political appointments and places in higher educational institutions. Gorbachev argued that, while 'affirmative action' might have been justified when some of the nationalities were culturally and economically behind the others, this was no longer the case and therefore a system of proportional representation of nationalities was unnecessary and harmful. Merit, not ethnicity, should be the criterion for employment, promotion and education. The abuses of 'affirmative action' must be reversed.

Gorbachev's first attempt to implement these principles aroused violent opposition. In December 1986, he removed from office the First Secretary of the Kazakh Communist Party, Dinmuhammed Kunaev. Kunaev was old, notoriously corrupt, and a close ally of Leonid Brezhnev. It was not his removal but his replacement that aroused controversy. Instead of appointing a Kazakh to the post the party named a Russian, Gennadii Kolbin. Mass demonstrations broke out in Alma Ata, the Kazakh capital, and there were casualties and arrests. In a break with the tradition of not reporting such embarrassing occurrences, the events received national media exposure. Gorbachev stuck to his guns and the media soon launched a general campaign against 'affirmative action' and corruption.

Pushing the campaign along, Gorbachev replaced all five first secretaries in the Asian republics, and later was to do the same in the other republics. A massive purge was set off in Uzbekistan. Thousands of officials lost their jobs on charges of corruption and incompetence. Leonid Brezhnev's son-in-law, a Russian, was implicated in Asian corruption, tried and convicted in December 1988. Thus, the anti-corruption campaign was linked explicitly to the Brezhnev regime, whose practices were now repudiated.

A different kind of challenge was presented by the Baltic states. In the course of 1988, organisations calling themselves popular fronts were formed. They became the spokesmen for Estonian, Latvian and Lithuanian national interests. They demanded the right to regulate migration, to issue their own currency and establish representation abroad. They also demanded that the indigenous languages be made state languages and that all residents of the respective republics be required to learn them. The prewar national anthems and flags of the republics, previously banned, were restored to public use. In Lithuania two cathedrals seized by the state in the 1940s were returned to the church. The Estonian legislature passed a law giving itself the right to veto legislation emanating from Moscow. Moscow rejected this law but chose not to make it a *cause célèbre*. In early 1991, Soviet troops were sent to Vilnius, capital of Lithuania, and Riga, the Latvian capital, in violent attempts to curb nationalist actions. Within the year, however, the Baltic republics had gained their independence.

In Belorussia and Moldavia more narrowly cultural demands were heard. Though Belorussians were long considered the most Russianised nationality, the Belorussian intelligentsia began to press for schools teaching in the Belorussian language, especially in the cities, and other measures to strengthen their language and culture. Moldavians protested in less peaceful ways, organising several mass demonstrations in the capital republic, Kishinev. They won from the party the concession that in time their language would be transferred back to Latin script. Russians, Ukrainians and Gagauz living in Moldavia have opposed plans for Moldavian independence and have tried to form their own independent entities.

In February 1988, the ancient historical dispute between Christian Armenians and Muslim Azerbaijanis, who had territorial claims on each other, flared into violence in the Nagorno-Karabakh enclave of Azerbaijan. The claims of the local, overwhelmingly Armenian population that they were being discriminated against and denied cultural facilities were supported in the Armenian republic. Thousands were killed in Armenian–Azerbaijani clashes over the next few years and several hundred thousand people became refugees from the conflict, a major portion of some one million internal refugees who have been displaced by ethnic conflict in the southern areas of the country.

In April 1989, Abkhazians living in an autonomous republic of Georgia demanded a republic of their own and Georgians, in turn, demanded independence from the USSR in a series of mass demonstrations and hunger strikes. Troops called in to restore order killed 20 Georgians and the events became a subject of heated discussion in the Congress of People's Deputies. Later in the year fourteen people were killed in Abkhazian–Georgian clashes, and about a hundred were killed in attacks by Uzbeks on Meskhetis, a Turkic minority who had been exiled by Stalin from Georgia to Central Asia. All told, by late 1991 there had been at least three thousand casualties from ethnic clashes.

One issue which emerged and is likely to sharpen in the future is the linkage between ecological and national concerns. As publics grow more concerned with environmental deterioration and dangers, they begin to feel that decision makers in Moscow are locating industries or mines or making use of natural resources in the non-Russian areas without regard to the ecological consequences, partly out of indifference to the environmental impacts outside the Russian lands. Baltic, Caucasian and Central Asian peoples said, in effect, 'It is *our* land that *you* are ruining.' There were protests in the Baltic against mining operations which left the countryside scarred; in Central Asia against the excessive pumping of the Aral Sea for irrigation, excessive spraying of pesticides, and successive plantings of cotton with no crop rotation or letting the land lie fallow; and demands in Ukraine and in the Caucasus that, following the Chernobyl nuclear plant disaster, no further nuclear stations should be built. A plan to irrigate the parched lands of Central Asia by diverting Siberian rivers was shelved, in part because Russians protested against the violation of the Siberian landscape, which plays an important part in Russian nationalist mythology.

Demographic trends have put at least two further issues on the agenda. Present and future population growth is concentrated in Central Asia, whereas industry is concentrated in the European republics. There is considerable migration within the country, mostly of the rural-to-urban kind, but relatively little among the Asians who (as we have noted) are reluctant to leave their own republics and even to move from the countryside to the cities within those republics. So the Soviet and now Russian authorities cannot count on recruiting significant labour reserves to work in the European industries, though attempts in this direction are being made. Of course, if they were successful, another issue would arise: would the state be prepared to depart from its traditional policy and allow schools and other cultural institutions for Asians (and other non-indigenous peoples) outside their republics? This would be an expensive and complicated undertaking.

The logical alternative to moving Asians to Europe is to move industry to Asia. But the lack of water, usually thought of as a barrier to agriculture, is also a hindrance to the development of industry. The terrible depletion of Asian water sources and the cancellation of the Siberian river diversion seem to indicate that industrial development in Asia will be insufficient to absorb the large numbers of Asians seeking to enter the workforce in coming decades. Moreover Soviet social scientists point out that many young Asians do not aspire to employment in industry.

The expansion of the Asian population also has implications for the military. An increasing proportion of draftees in the Russian and Commonwealth joint forces will be of Asian origin. Since they generally have lower educational levels than Europeans, and since their Russian is often rudimentary, they cannot be assigned to the more technologically advanced forces (rocketry, the air force or the navy). They already form a disproportionate number of those assigned to labour battalions, often not trained for combat and used as cheap labour on both military and civilian construction projects. The leadership of the armed forces has made it very clear that it does not want to see those forces stratified by nationality: Slavs overrepresented among the officers and non-commissioned officers and Asians disproportionately in the lower ranks. The military is now discussing going over to an all-volunteer force or to forces that are composed of a higher proportion of professional, long-term soldiers, and several former republics are establishing their own conventional forces. These options, if adopted, may go some way to avoiding the ethnic differentiation of the post-Soviet military.

Having spent his entire career in his native Stavropol province, in the south of the Russian Federation, and in Moscow, Gorbachev had little direct experience in nationalities issues. In his first year or so in office he paid little attention to them. But *glasnost'* allowed people to express national sentiments and grievances and to criticise the cliches and shibboleths that had marked Soviet rhetoric about ethnic issues. *Perestroika* showed them the possibilities of institutional and policy change. The two together led to the explosion of national sentiment and demands that we have described. On the one hand, Gorbachev acknowledged that there was a much higher national consciousness among the Soviet peoples than his predecessors were willing to admit, and that not all was well in relations among nationalities; he tolerated actions and rhetoric in the Baltic that none of his predecessors would have countenanced. On the other hand, his personnel policies indicated a stronger inclination to promote Russian and Slavic dominance than that shown by any of his four predecessors. Nearly all government ministers were replaced by Gorbachev, yet only two of them were not Slavs. It is as if Gorbachev was telling the non-Slavs that, while they could continue to wield some power in their republics, they would not have any share in running the country as a whole.

In his search for a new formula to guide nationalities policy and a new programme to implement it, Gorbachev proposed a new 'Union Treaty' which would restructure the USSR, now to be understood as the 'Union of Soviet *Sovereign* Republics'. It was presented to the Congress of People's Deputies in December 1990, was revised in March and June 1991, and was due to be signed on 20 August by ten republics. The treaty defined each republic as a sovereign state and gave the republics the right to appoint one house of the legislature, which could veto new laws. Republics would have a vote in the cabinet and could block amendments to the Treaty. Republics were given ownership of their lands, water and other natural resources. They would collect taxes and give a share to the centre, reversing traditional arrangements. The nuclear power and arms industries, rail, sea and air transport would be controlled by the centre, as would fuel and energy policy. Foreign policy and the military would also be controlled by the centre.

One aim of those who mounted the coup on 19 August 1991 was to block the signing of this treaty, on the grounds that it would destroy the Soviet Union by giving too much power to the republics. Ironically the coup's failure led to great losses of central power and to declarations of independence by the republics. The Baltic republics, either having declared independence earlier (Lithuania), or having declared the intention to become independent (Estonia and Latvia) now seized the opportunity to implement their declarations forthwith. Georgia, Armenia, Azerbaijan and Moldavia also moved purposefully towards independence. Ukraine scheduled a national referendum on independence for 1 December, where it was supported by over 90 per cent of those who voted. In more politically conservative republics such as Belorussia or Uzbekistan, declarations of independence seemed designed to save the Communist Party from suspension or abolition, since the decree suspending it in the Russian Republic could not be applied to other republics if they were independent.

By the end of 1991 the reconstitution of at least part of the former USSR, albeit on a different basis, had begun to evolve slowly. Russia, Belorussia, Armenia and the five Central Asian republics signed an agreement to create a free market economic community. The signers committed themselves to an economy rooted in private property, a single banking system and measures designed to implement the free flow of goods among them. Ukraine refused to sign on the grounds that the republic's sovereignty would be infringed, but later acceded. At the same time Ukraine announced plans to create a 400,000-man army and a 30,000-man militia, but it was not clear that the republic could afford such forces. Thus a weakened centre found it very difficult to put together some sort of looser union of at least some of the republics of the former USSR, though several of them found it in their economic interest to agree to cooperate closely. That cooperation broadened still further with the conclusion, in December 1991, of the agreement that established a Commonwealth of Independent States (see pp. 6–7).

Conclusion

As the Soviet and now Commonwealth leaders search for new formulas and programmes to deal with their nationalities, they can find little inspiration in other East European countries. Yugoslavia has all but dissolved in a violent and tragic manner. It serves as a warning to the formerly Soviet peoples of the dangers inhering in intolerant nationalism. In Czechoslovakia, Slovaks threaten to secede. Bulgaria and Romania have dealt with their national minorities through combinations of emigration (in the Bulgarian case, deportation) and repression; but a reformist Commonwealth of Independent States is unlikely to find repression either attractive or wholly feasible. Clearly the nationalities question is complex and differentiated. Some Jews, Germans and others might prefer emigration, but others of the same nationality would like to have greater cultural opportunities and experience less discrimination in a larger union. Other nationalities are not at all interested in emigration. Some stress cultural issues, others economic or political concerns, and some have a broad agenda of changes they would like to see. Extremist forms of Russian nationalism have also surfaced. For example, an organisation calling itself *Pamyat*, or memory, has urged that Russians be given more control of the country, and they have adopted explicitly anti-semitic platforms. They view the current system as conceding too much to non-Russians. Apart from these cases, presumably, there are nationalities most of whose members are content with the *status quo*.

It will not be easy to address all these issues, to decide which demands can be met and which must be rejected, all of this with an eye to keeping at least some of the territorial integrity of the former USSR. The Russian, Belorussian and Central Asian republics are likely to remain associated in a looser union, but many of the other republics will distance themselves from that union in one form or other. Russia may take the lead in reshaping a union, but by the same token it may arouse suspicions of imperialist designs; this was particularly the case in a dispute with Ukraine about control of the Black Sea fleet, but it was also implicit in a series of territorial disputes and expressions of concern about fellow nationals elsewhere. Equally, there were increasing pressures for sovereignty or even independence within the boundaries of the Commonwealth member states, particularly in Russia. The nationalities issue, for these and other reasons, remains as formidable a challenge to the republics that have succeeded the USSR as to the state that had originally sought to establish a 'new community of nations' in an area that still encompasses a sixth of the world's land surface.

8

Towards a Participatory Politics?

THOMAS F. REMINGTON

'People Power' and the Collapse of the Soviet Union

On 19 August 1991, the Soviet population and the world were shocked to learn that President Gorbachev had been deposed by a self-formed 'state committee on the state of emergency' which claimed extraordinary powers and declared a state of emergency throughout the USSR. Since the heads of the armed forces, KGB and Interior Ministry were all members of the committee, many observers expected the plotters to demonstrate the resolve to succeed. As we have seen, however (pp. 3–7), the coup collapsed on the third day in the face of an outpouring of popular outrage, defections among military and KGB units charged with suppressing resistance and near-unanimous condemnation of the coup by world public opinion.

The August coup was the catalyst in a chain of events that culminated in the dissolution of the Union in December 1991 as the constituent republics declared independence and the union government became a hollow shell, lacking territory or resources of its own. That which the coup's plotters had acted to save – the integrity of the Union state – was instead the final victim of their desperate act. In place of the Union, an agreement of 21 December 1991, among all of the former Union republics save the Baltic states and Georgia, created a new loose coordinating framework to succeed the union, called the 'Commonwealth of Independent States' (see pp. 6–7, 144–6). On 25 December, Mikhail Gorbachev resigned and Boris Yeltsin took over his office in the Kremlin.

147

Historians will discuss these dramatic events for many years to come. One crucial reason the coup failed was that members of the KGB's elite 'Alpha Team', formed for counter-terrorist strikes, refused orders to storm the 'White House' of the Russian Republic – the large, white building on the embankment of the Moscow river in which both the Supreme Soviet of the Russian Federation and the Council of Ministers of the republic were headquartered. Moreover units of the army went over to the side of the opposition, raising the fear that an attempt to seize the White House by force could plunge the army into fratricidal bloodshed. A decisive factor in both cases was the fact that popular, democratically elected leaders stood up against the coup and rallied widespread support among the population. In Moscow, well-known groups such as Democratic Russia and Memorial organised rallies to oppose the coup, above all by calling on people to form a protective ring around the White House. Here the crowds hastily built tank-stopping barricades out of the concrete blocks and iron rods amply available at nearby construction sites. Many spent the nights of 19–20 and 20–21 August at the barricades, fearing a sudden attack by the army and security troops. On the second night, three young men lost their lives in a confrontation with a tank not far from the White House. Evidently the willingness of thousands of people to risk their lives to defend the symbolic centre of Russian national statehood and democracy raised the costs of suppression to the coup's enforcers beyond a tolerable level.

After the coup, Gorbachev worked doggedly to find some new formula for preserving the political unity of the republics. The disparity in size and power between Russia – comprising three quarters of the territory of the former Union – and the other republics made it virtually impossible to alleviate the fears on the part of Russia's neighbours that Russia would dominate any future union unless Ukraine joined it. But the 1 December popular referendum in the Ukraine on independence, where more than 90 per cent voted in support, made it clear that the Ukrainian republic would refuse to join any new federal state. The most its leaders accepted was a loose structure to coordinate military and economic relations.

Much of the world's attention focused on the crucial role played by Boris Yeltsin, popularly elected President of the Russian Federation, in rallying resistance to the coup. Yeltsin's position was reinforced, however, by many other leaders and institutions throughout Russia and other republics, proving the remarkable shift in the distribution of power in the Soviet (and now post-Soviet) system that had occurred in only two years. Among other leaders of opposition to the coup were the elected mayors of Moscow and St Petersburg (Gavriil Popov and Anatolii Sobchak) as well as the leadership of regional, city and district soviets in Vilnius, Kiev, Lviv, Kemerovo, Tomsk, Sverdlovsk and other areas, who refused to accept the authority of the 'state committee' and instead followed the lead of the Russian Republic's president and parliament. In St Petersburg, Mayor Sobchak won from the commander of the local army garrison an agreement not to use force to carry out the 'state committee's' orders. The leadership of Rukh, the popular front in the Ukraine, together with all the other political parties besides the communist party, adopted a statement rejecting the coup, supporting the position taken by the Russian republic, and preparing for a wave of strikes. The workers' committees in the coalfields of Vorkuta and Kemerovo launched strikes. In Tomsk, the presidiums of the city and regional soviets adopted a motion calling the seizure of power by the 'state committee' unconstitutional. Had the coup lasted longer, it is possible that there would have been massive protests and strikes in several republics.

As in the collapse of dictatorships in other parts of the world in the 1980s and 1990s, 'people power', as widespread popular participation in the anti-Marcos movement in the Philippines was called, proved stronger than the tanks. The four focal points of opposition to the old regime that we have noted – the personal authority of leaders such as Boris Yeltsin, newly elected soviets and mayors, organised civic associations such as Rukh, Democratic Russia and Memorial, and national referenda – all represent new forms of popular participation in Soviet politics. In the short span of a few years they have brought about the end of the Soviet communist regime and of the Soviet Union itself; and it is these forces that are now constructing a post-Soviet politics in Russia and the other states of the new Commonwealth.

Participation and Recruitment before *Perestroika*

For much of the communist regime's history, Soviet citizens were subjected to contradictory messages about the proper role they were expected to fulfil as participants in the state. They were to play the parts prescribed for them in public and private life without opposing the basic principles and structures of the regime, yet at the same time their enthusiasm and initiative were regularly invoked. The regime relied upon a large stratum of activists to generate feelings of identification with the party-state and serve as channels of feedback between public and rulers. But citizens who took it upon themselves to be activists in opposition to the regime were quickly repressed. The authorities acted to maximise participation in the familiar channels established by the regime, as if the pageantry and forms of popular participation were important in themselves but its substance was a threat to the regime's security. Frederick C. Barghoorn (1966) called this contradictory pattern of political culture 'participatory-subject' and in the first edition of this volume, Nicholas Lampert (1990) described it as 'mobilised participation,' observing that:

> In such a setting participation becomes a matter of 'organized enthusiasm', mobilising the population in support of policies determined by the leadership. There is little room for *voluntary* political commitment. Where there is no political choice, party membership and political activism tend to become social duties, and to leave the party becomes an act of political defiance. Behind this regimented participation is an extreme fear of social spontaneity, an unwillingness to countenance any political activity that is not closely managed by the ruling party.

Why did the communist regime place such emphasis on ceremonies of mass participation, the meetings, marches, membership drives, voting days and other conspicuous displays of popular support? One answer lies in the close relationship between participation and the processes by which political elites were recruited to positions of political and administrative responsibility. Elective committees and councils in many spheres of state and society were points of contact between activists and elites in different sectors. For example, the party committee of a city typically included the ranking heads of the city government, the chairman of the trade union council, the first secretary of the Komsomol organisation, directors of major enterprises, the editor of the local newspaper and other notables. Serving as the hub from which a series of membership ties extended into a locality's organised institutions, the party committee at each level of the hierarchy was a vehicle for the *horizontal integration* of elites by offering a common channel for the political participation of leaders at the same level of responsibility. At the same time such channels provided for the *vertical integration* of elites through the inclusion of heads of subordinate organisations on nominally elective collective bodies at higher levels. A good example would be the membership of the first secretaries of the most important regional party committees on the Central Committee of the Communist Party of the Soviet Union.

At the level of mass organisations, such as the trade unions, whose membership encompassed virtually every employed citizen, and the Komsomol, or Communist Youth League, which, at its height, registered some 40 million young people between the ages of 14 and 28, participation in membership organisations for most members was largely nominal, a matter of attending required meetings, paying the monthly dues and voting in favour of proposed motions. For some, however, especially those keen on furthering their careers, mass organisations were an essential rung on a career ladder through which energetic activism, coupled with political reliability, could bring the ambitious to the attention of the party's personnel managers, who in turn could ensure that the individual received the right combination of political education, volunteer assignments and job opportunities to allow him or her to rise up the ladder of power.

The Komsomol, for example, was the principal recruiting ground for the Communist Party. By the mid-1980s, three-quarters of new party members entered directly from the Komsomol, so that a good record as Komsomol member was a prerequisite to admission to the party. For many other people, however, to be put up for membership in various boards, councils, committees and other elective and appointed posts was a largely honorific consequence of achieving a certain status in society. It was understood by all concerned that real power in mass organisations was wielded by their staff rather than their elective governing bodies: the collective and oligarchical forms hardly masked the dominance of the *apparat* over the organisation it supposedly served. This was perhaps most glaringly evident in the case of the country's soviets, considered the centre of governing power at each rung of the state. With only rare exceptions, soviets were a form of ceremonial power with no meaningful decision-making power in themselves.

Power in the Soviet political system, therefore, was not pluralistic, but combined corporatist and bureaucratic–authoritarian tendencies in a framework inherited from the mobilisation, totalitarian party-state shaped under Stalin. To be sure, in the post-Stalin era, the system moved haltingly to rationalise some of its structural features. More attention was given to observing proper juridical forms in relations between the state and citizens. The leadership sought to provide appropriate forms of political and economic education to activists and executives in government and economic sectors. Party executives became specialists, some focusing on industrial adminis-tration, others on agriculture, still others on ideology. The party itself attempted to systematise its work with citizen letters and appeals, even creating a new department of the Central Committee Secretar-iat to process and analyse mail received from the public. At the local level, ordinary citizens had some opportunity to influence govern-ment administration, pushing for improvements in the condition and availability of housing, for example, or for better provision of stores and cultural amenities. But these demands were generally non-political in nature, not aimed at influencing basic policy or challenging the incumbents' right to rule. Often this kind of contact between citizen and state generated a pattern of individualised, parochial participation, in which individuals became adept at 'working the system' for their own private benefit rather than changing the allocation of resources for whole classes of people (see Di Franciesco and Gitelman, 1984).

As is now amply clear, the growth of repressed popular grievances far exceeded the slow and grudging growth of opportunities for Soviet citizens to voice their demands. As a result the gap between approved gestures of participation and the actual realities of power widened. Those new public organisations which were formed with official approval, such as the Rodina Society (the full name of which is the All-Russian Society for the Preservation of Historical and Cultural Monuments), which was dedicated to defending Russia's cultural heritage, quickly grew into branches of the state rather than autonomous expressions of a public interest. Even the Russian Orthodox Church bore an official relationship to the state, despite the constitution's declared separation of church and state, by the Communist Party's rule that senior ecclesiastical officials could only be named with the approval of the party. The party, in short, claimed a 'licensing' power over organised social bodies through which it ensured control over their choice of leaders and the direction of their activity. Because of the statification of public (*obshchestvennye* – meaning formally non-state) organisations, the boundary lines between state and society were never distinct.

Some non-state organisations operated outside the limits of regime approval, of course, and incurred repression. Beginning in the mid-1960s, various groups pressed the regime to respect the civic and political rights that were granted by the Soviet constitution but were denied whenever the authorities found that a particular act violated the limits of permitted expression. The movements for democratic, national and religious rights established alternative normative frameworks to those propagandised by the regime and generated counter-elites whose prestige and authority drew on their willingness to risk arrest and prosecution for their beliefs. Some of the prominent figures of dissent became leaders of new political movements in the late 1980s – such as Andrei Sakharov, the most famous of the democratic dissidents, who became the moral leader of the democratic group of USSR deputies elected in 1989. Others include Father Gleb Yakunin, arrested for dissent in 1979 but who became a leader of the group of democratic deputies in the Russian republic parliament in 1990; Zviad Gamsakhurdia, who was arrested as a dissident in the 1970s, but who became the acclaimed popular leader of the Georgian national movement in 1990 and 1991, until he turned in a clearly authoritarian direction; Vyacheslav Chornovil, imprisoned for his advocacy of Ukrainian national rights and in 1990 elected chairman of the city soviet of Lviv; and Sergei Kovalev, a close friend and collaborator of Sakharov's in the democratic movement who became chairman of the human rights committee of the Russian Republic's parliament in 1990. Thus, in many cases, it was past participation in political movements *outside* and *in opposition to* the regime that lent legitimacy to the new leaders of the democratisation period under Gorbachev.

The formalistic, ritualised nature of most mass participation in the past creates a serious dilemma for the process of transition today to a more democratic system. Since most new movements that are legitimate in the eyes of society have arisen *outside* the regime's established public organisations and often in opposition to them, how can society avoid a debilitating confrontation between the declining structures of the old system and the rising infrastructure of opposition? This dilemma – the weakness of the middle ground – complicates two fundamental processes: one, the transition from a communist party-state to a democratic and market-directed society; the other, the reconstruction of relations between the centre and the nations making up the new Commonwealth. In both cases, the middle ground is disappearing as the polarisation of positions intensifies. Moreover these are two different processes: there is no necessary correlation between support for democratisation and support for national independence. The more that power in Union-wide political structures was subject to democratisation, the stronger independence movements in national republics became, although they were primarily focused upon acquiring full political independence for their republics rather than on democratising a discredited Union. As Robert Dahl observed of authoritarian ('hegemonic', in his terminology) regimes with substantial ethnic minorities, 'the price of polyarchy [democracy] may be a breakup of the country. And the price of territorial unity may be a hegemonic regime' (Dahl, 1971, p. 121).

The legacy of the post-totalitarian patterns of mass participation, therefore, is the severe weakness of civil society, which social scientists understand to mean the infrastructure of mediating institutions that link the multiple interests of citizens with the political regime. In the case of non-communist regimes that make the transition from authoritarian rule, these include associations of labour, farmworkers and business, professional societies and religious communities, as well as parties and interest groups. In the Soviet Union, the effect of the elimination of most forms of private property, the suppression of political and ideological opposition and the spread of state control over social organisations was to leave a vacuum of non-state structures that both the regime and the populace considered legitimate. This vacuum in turn created opportunities for radical nationalist movements, because of the destruction of class and other cleavages that cut across national passions (see Brzezinski, 1989–90).

This factor helps to explain the rapidity with which the old structures of authority have broken down without yielding power to new, democratic institutions. It belies the optimism of observers such as Moshe Lewin, who predicted that the modernisation of Soviet society would allow enlightened communist reformers to democratise the political system while retaining ultimate control over the state on the grounds that 'the party is the main stabilizer of the political system. ... The party, especially if it refurbishes its image, is the only institution that can preside over the overhaul of the system without endangering the polity itself in the process' (1988, p. 113). In reality the only communist societies in which the breakdown of the old regime has given way to a newly adapted communist party hegemony are those, such as in Central Asia and the Balkans, which have remained predominantly peasant societies.

Traditional Forms of Mass Participation

Of the traditional forms of mass participation in the Soviet regime, we shall single out three for mention: public membership organisations, voting and soviets. A fourth category of participation we shall touch on is individual-level contacting of officials.

Since the Bolshevik Revolution the regime has sought to maximise mass membership in a variety of public organisations. Among these were the Communist Youth League (Komsomol), the trade unions, the All-Union Society for Inventors and Rationalisers, the Scientific–Technical Society, the Red Cross and Red Crescent, the Committees of People's Control (in Russian, *kontrol*, meaning auditing or oversight), the Voluntary Society for Assistance to the Armed Forces, the Book-Lovers' Society and the Society for the Struggle for Sobriety, to name only a few. A special case among the country's public organisations is the Communist Party of the Soviet Union (CPSU) which, unlike the other public bodies, deliberately restricted its intake of new members in order to ensure the desired mix of workers, women and other social categories, and to preserve its special role as a 'vanguard' of society. Still, at its peak, the Communist Party enrolled nearly 20 million members before membership began declining in 1990 and 1991.

Stalin called the great, hierarchically structured Soviet public organisations 'transmission belts', because they were called on to connect the masses to the policy decisions emanating from the Kremlin. With time they developed massive staffs and considerable bureaucratic self-interest. The Rodina Society, for example, which was formed in 1965, had by the early 1980s generated a central apparatus comprising 65 subdivisions, and was spending more money on personnel than on preserving monuments. Little wonder that rank-and-file members generally felt indifferent to the organisations of which they were nominally members and to which they contributed little more than their dues. Generally each public organisation enjoyed a monopoly in its field – rival trade unions were simply suppressed, for example, as were rival political parties and youth associations – as well as the benefits of the state's recognition. Given the severe scarcity of resources, including buildings and meeting places, and paper and printing presses, official recognition was virtually essential to an organisation that sought to build a large-scale membership. In contrast dissident movements relied on the close-knit social ties of family and friends to maintain the cohesiveness of their groups and to communicate messages to their followings. The unequal distribution of physical resources, a function of the regime's concern to monopolise control over social organisations, made it extremely difficult for extra-systemic associations to challenge the regime's power, at least until Gorbachev introduced *glasnost'* and democratisation.

In addition to the elimination of competitors to the officially 'licensed' public organisations, the regime monitored their activity to prevent it from taking an anti-system direction. For example, the KGB regularly assigned officers to serve on the staff of public organisations. Ranking leaders of the organisation were approved through the Communist Party's *nomenklatura* system. The organisations' magazines and newspapers were overseen by the party's ideological watchdogs, who oversaw all public communications and prevented unwanted messages from being disseminated. These methods of control prevented public organisations from turning into instruments of opposition or challenging the basic policy direction of the state.

A second form of mass participation, voting for deputies to the soviets, was treated by the regime as a show of civic unity. The authorities went to enormous lengths to ensure maximum turn-out through agitation before and on election day. Despite the fact that in the vast majority of races only one candidate was registered, the regime treated the massive turn-out and near unanimous endorsement of the candidate as a sign of the unshakeable unity of regime and people. The campaign emphasised the ideological solidarity of society – there was no room for an 'opposition platform' – but voters were encouraged to see the deputies they elected as go-betweens who could intercede with the bureaucracy for their particular needs.

Serving as a deputy was a third widespread form of popular participation. The soviets, or councils, were considered the principal vehicle through which the democratic spirit of the October revolution was preserved. In every territorial subdivsion of the state – every town, village, rural district, city, province, ethno-territory and republic – there was a corresponding soviet. (In the case of the Union and autonomous republics, and at the level of the Union government itself, it was called Supreme Soviet.) Soviets tended to be quite large: in 1987, 2.3 million deputies were elected to 52,000 soviets in all. Some of these served in soviets at two different levels, but a deputy could not be elected to more than two soviets at the same time. A deputy's calling was not full-time; soviets usually met on a quarterly or biannual basis, for a day or two at a time, hearing reports and approving the proposed budget and plan. Soviets were not deliberative, policy-making bodies, but were means of acquainting deputies and citizens with the policies and priorities of the regime at each level of the state, of giving deputies a feeling of personal responsibility for the well-being of the system, and of showcasing the democratic character of the state.

This last function is particularly evident in the care taken to ensure a high level of participation by women, blue-collar workers, youth, non-party members and other categories of the populace who were severely under-represented in more powerful organs. For this reason, the party employed a quota system to select candidates to run, controlling the outcome of the nomination process to obtain the desired mix of social characteristics among the elected deputies. Generally speaking, the party tried to select as candidates people who could serve as role models to society, leading citizens from all walks of life who were politically reliable and thought to enjoy a measure of popular esteem. Virtually all prominent Soviet citizens were deputies to soviets at one level or another, often running from districts far from their place of work or residence.

In addition to service as deputies, Soviet citizens were brought into the work of local government and administration in other ways as well. Many served as volunteer members of the standing committees of local soviets monitoring government's performance in housing, education, trade, catering, public amenities and other sectors of community life. Still others joined residential committees and neighbourhood self-help groups. These activities were not entirely ceremonial. Often they gave public-spirited citizens an outlet for their involvement in the community.

Consistent with Lenin's theory of the soviets as bodies concentrating all forms of state power rather than dividing power among separate but equal branches, as in American constitutional theory, the USSR treated the soviets as the final source of state power. This theory is contradicted, however, by two long-standing features of the system. First, and most glaringly obvious, the soviets were never autonomous in their policy-making power, but had to ratify and execute decisions made elsewhere, often by the very executive organs they were supposed to direct. Second, deputies came to take on an intercessory role on behalf of their voters rather than that of law-maker. In the course of the nominations process, voters went through a ritual of presenting *nakazy*, or mandates, to deputies, and deputies in turn solemnly pledged to fulfil their constituents' requests. These might include seeing to it that a new school or apartment building was built. Often such commitments had already been included as part of the local plan before being adopted formally as a deputy's mandate. But the process of proposing *nakazy* and pressing them upon deputies gave voters some opportunity to lobby for particular needs.

The habit of turning to deputies for help with private problems is characteristic of a larger pattern of 'parochial contacting', which might be categorised as a fourth kind of traditional citizen participation. The Soviet authorities had long encouraged citizens to transmit their ideas, grievances, hopes and petitions to a wide range of official institutions, including soviets, newspapers and broadcast media, party committees, the procuracy, the KGB and individual notables. The volume of such mail and personal visits was huge. For 1983 alone, it was estimated that Central Television received about 1.7 million letters; all-Union radio over 600,000; Moscow radio, over 170,000; the central newspapers, around half a million each; provincial news-papers, 30–35,000 letters each; the trade unions, two million letters and personal visits; party organisations, 3.3 million letters and visits (Remington, 1988, pp. 123–4). It should be remembered that some people bombarded many different targets with the same appeal for help, hoping that somewhere, someone could solve their particular problem.

The immense volume of personal contacts with officials through letters and audiences, like other established practices in Soviet and now post-Soviet politics, has multiple explanations. The mass media, much more than in European or American systems, depend upon contributions by the public and encourage active public participation in media production. Another reason is the continuing strength of patrimonial elements in the political culture, which encourages officials to see rank-and-file citizens as 'subjects' and discourages lower officials from taking responsibility for decisions in their given spheres of authority. And perhaps the most important reason is the chronic difficulty of solving even simple material problems of daily life without invoking high-level *ad hoc* intervention. As a result policy makers face a constant stream of SOS calls, requests for favours and other appeals for individual attention to which they can only respond by invoking their personal relations with those who can solve the problem. The ability of the policy process to provide solutions to general problems is undermined by the routinisation of particularistic exceptions to each rule. Moreover, in the late Brezhnev era, the endemic problem of corruption corroded the system's ability to respond even to ordinary appeals for intervention except by invoking favouritism, 'pull' and bribes.

Gorbachev and Democratisation

Like earlier Soviet leaders, especially Khrushchev, Mikhail Gorbachev tried to generate grass-roots pressure for his policy reforms by infusing new life into traditional forms of mass participation. With increasingly forceful rhetoric, Gorbachev called for the 'democratisation' of state and social organisations. As Joel Moses observes (1989, p. 240):

> In Gorbachev's vision, the rigidly administered economy through all-powerful and unaccountable ministries and bureaucracies is the symptom of the real problem. The economic structure merely reflects the core attributes and authority relationships prevalent throughout the Soviet political culture and institutions of society. Democratic changes are thus absolutely essential to spark and unleash the qualities of trust, initiative, assertiveness and power-sharing between leader and led universally needed to revitalize the economy. Democracy is the 'human factor' catalyst to complement and implement wide-scale economic reforms.

Moses points out that, although these themes were articulated only in muffled ways in Gorbachev's initial statements as General Secretary, from late 1986 Gorbachev called for a general 'restructuring' of Soviet society that would eliminate its authoritarian and bureaucratic features and replace them with a newly democratised model of socialism in which the populace would identify with the system and its goals. This programme of restructuring, *perestroika*, would overcome the alienation that he believed deadened people's initiative by bringing about a new feeling of identification between Soviet people and their workplaces, their government and the Communist Party. In his vision of reform, meaningful forms of participation through the democratisation of social life would make people feel committed to the goals of economic revitalisation of the country. By 1988, he was calling for a 'social revolution' that would upset the old bureaucratised relationships in economic and political life, and would unlock the creative potential of the population.

A characteristic element of Gorbachev's reform programme in the 1986–8 period was his advocacy of workplace democracy. This idea had been put forward in cautious ways over the years by reform-minded scholars who sought to liberate enterprises from the stifling control of the central ministries and find incentives to raise worker productivity. The provision for worker election of enterprise managers that was included in the 1987 Law on the State Enterprise was intended to have precisely this effect: without altering the structure of state ownership of industry, the power to elect their managers was intended to give workers a sense that they were co-managers and hence responsible for the enterprise's performance. Another Gorbachev innovation, the creation of 'councils of the labour collective' in each enterprise, through which the entire workforce was to thrash out problems affecting production and work conditions, had a similar intent. But, illustrating the impossibility of finding some organisational middle ground between the old regime and its opponents, these innovations failed either to improve productivity in the workplace or to give workers legitimate new channels for voicing their demands. The 'councils of the labour collectives' were simply irrelevant to the workers' movement when massive strikes broke out in the coalfields in 1989; workers evidently treated these as simply another of the for-show ceremonies in which the state exercised authority over workers. Neither the official trade union structures nor the newer workplace councils represented the workers, who instead formed independent strike committees.

Another of the exercises in managed democratisation, already noted above (p. 92), was the experiment with contested elections of deputies to local soviets held in 1987. In some districts, around 1 per cent of the total, smaller districts were combined into multiseat districts, for which a larger number of candidates ran than there were seats. Fewer than 5 per cent of all deputies were elected in these quasi-competitive races, but even so the experience sufficed to give voters an opportunity to defeat unwanted candidates. Party and government officials, as well as women and youth, tended to do worse than other candidates, foreshadowing the patterns that resulted two years later, when electoral competition became the norm throughout the country. Gorbachev and his advisors evidently considered the 1987 experiment successful, since in his address to the 19th Party Conference in June 1988, Gorbachev called for a sweeping reform of the political system in which contested elections would be the cornerstone of real Soviet power.

Perhaps the most effective means of expanding the freedom available to Soviet people to voice their hopes and demands was *glasnost'*, the policy of official encouragement for freer and franker discussion of public affairs in the press, in the arts, and in public forums. *Glasnost'*, discussed more fully in the next chapter, narrowed the power wielded by Communist Party ideological arbiters over public expression. Once journalists, writers and public figures could voice their opinions more openly, they began to attract followings. In some cases public and state organisations became the sites of struggles between conservatives and reformers, as reformers sought to turn their creative unions, research institutes, academies, professional associations, newspapers, journals, film studios and other organisations into platforms to promote democratisation, economic reform and national rights. In creative unions such as the unions of theatre workers and cinematographers, reform-minded factions succeeded in pushing out conservative old guard officials. In the mass media, certain publications, such as the weeklies, *Ogonek*, *Moscow News* and *Argumenty i fakty*, became the voices of liberal-democratic reformers, while others, such as the paper *Sovetskaya Rossiya* and the literary journal *Nash sovremennik*, became forums for conservative and Russian-nationalist sentiment. New informal associations of all kinds sprang up during 1987 and 1988. Sometimes these overlapped and in other cases they were formed independently of the recognised channels of public life. Many were non-political, but some organised to press the authorities for action on urgent social problems.

The articulation of strong and unorthodox views in the media and the spread of informal associations stimulated one another, a natural consequence of the close link between ideology and organisation in Soviet society. Not only were *glasnost'* and the rise of informal associations (*neformaly*) mutually-reinforcing phenomena, but each also had a powerful demonstration effect of its own. As people responded to the shock of hearing and reading previously taboo positions in the media, they were often prompted to contribute their own still more searching or sensational ideas, leading to a progressive deepening and radicalisation of public debate. Similarly the same types of political associations – popular fronts, environmental action groups, independent workers' committees and the like – spread quickly from region to region and proliferated as factions split away to form their own groups. The standard figures cited by Soviet sources for the numbers of such informal associations can serve as little more than informed guesses as to the correct order of magnitude, but the 30,000 organisations said to exist in 1988 and the 60,000 by 1989 were, in the vast majority of cases, quite small. A few, however, were capable of mobilising extraordinary turn-outs for demonstrations of popular solidarity. On 23 August 1989, for example, to commemorate the fiftieth anniversary of the signing of the Soviet–German non-aggression treaty that enabled Stalin to annex the Baltic republics, the leaders of the popular fronts of Lithuania, Latvia and Estonia organised a continuous human chain along the Baltic coast, when over a million people joined hands.

To explain this new, widespread, politically potent, informal participation we need to understand the nature of the underlying social and political cleavages in Soviet society that gave rise to the new political movements. To what extent did the causes that generated protest converge in a common platform, and to what extent were they distinct and competitive? It is clear now that certain issues were bundled together symbiotically, so that they fed a common sense of collective injury among a population. Others were cross-cutting, meaning that the followings of different movements were independent of one another. The clearest example of a cluster of symbiotic issues is the set of those fostering demands for ethnic–national sovereignty: environmentalism, cultural autonomy, regional autonomy, religious freedom and control of immigration. Another is the cluster of labour demands for decent living and working conditions, desires for workplace and regional autonomy, and resentment at the privilege and power of the ruling elite. The great national and labour protest movements that erupted on a massive scale in 1989, therefore, were each the products of several converging streams of grievances. Moreover labour and environmental protest also converged to some extent. Large-scale strike activity began in 1988 with the use of strikes as a vehicle of ethnic–national protest in Transcaucasia and the Baltic republics. In the Baltic republics and Moldavia enclaves of Russian workers, alarmed at the breakdown of ties to Moscow brought about as part of the republics' drive for independence, organised backlash strikes, such as the strikes in the summer of 1989 at over a hundred enterprises in Moldavia, and the strikes of 13,000 Russian workers at 21 industrial plants in Estonia. Some of the leaders of these anti-independence, pro-union 'Interfront' movements, such as Yuri Blokhin from Moldavia, Viktor Alksnis of Latvia and Yevgenii Kogan from Estonia, became leaders of the Soyuz (union) faction of deputies in the USSR Supreme Soviet in 1990 and 1991.

Thus both ethnic and labour causes contributed to widespread strikes in 1989. The largest labour action was the strike by coalminers in July 1989, when, at its peak, the strike was joined by 300–400,000 workers. The strikes ended when the government promised to make substantial concessions to the workers' demands for better living and working conditions and greater economic control over their mines and cities. In turn the miners' frustration with the government's failure to fulfil these promises led to a new, smaller, but far more politically-directed strike wave in November, centred in the minefields of Vorkuta, in the far north of the Russian republic. There were further strikes in 1991, and in response to the price rises that were introduced in early 1992.

Broadly speaking, it appears that national causes have mobilised more protest than has the labour movement. The evidence from the count of workdays lost to strikes and protest in 1989 indicates that far more downtime was caused by ethnically-related than by economically-inspired protest. Elizabeth Teague notes that around 1.2 million man-days were lost to strikes in 1989 in the Russian Republic, the vast majority of them, one million days, caused by the coalminers' strikes in Kemerovo; nearly a million more were due to the coalminers' strikes in the Donetsk Basin. But the days lost to strikes in *each* of the much smaller republics of Azerbaijan, Moldavia and Georgia in 1989 exceeded the total for the RSFSR! Half of Azerbaijan's total of two million days is accounted for by protest over the issue of the Armenian enclave of Nagorno-Karabakh (Teague, 1990, pp. 13–17).

An important effect of both the labour and national protest movements was to generate new structures of decision making and new leaders, both independent of the old party-state. In the coalfields, the strike movement of 1989 generated a new cadre of working-class leadership as spontaneously created strike committees turned into institutionalised workers' committees. In turn, in May 1990, these workers' committees created an independent confederation of labour, based in Novokuznetsk, to compete with the official trade union structure for the loyalty of workers. However it failed to rally the workers of other industries to its fold. Soon afterwards, coalminers created an independent trade union which departed from the old Soviet habit of organising trade unions vertically to include managers, technical personnel and workers within a given industry, and instead excluded managers and service personnel. These were not the only workers' organisations formed out of the great strike wave of 1989. In addition to efforts by the regime to coopt the movement, there also emerged regional organisations, such as the Union of Kuzbass Workers, which sought to unite workers with peasants and intellectuals, as well as purely local workers' organisations.

The leadership and structure of the workers' committees in the coalfields remained the strongest of the new workers' organisations, as the renewed coalminers' strikes of 1991 showed. The lower total number of workers out in 1991 may have been due to the 'rolling wave' strategy of the workers, intended to ensure that some production continued at all times. At its height, however, the leadership of the strike movement estimated that around a third of the mines were closed. Coordination across regions was managed by a council formed of representatives of the major region strike committees (called the Interregional Council of Strike Committees) and it was this Interregional Council that drafted a list of demands supported by all the striking workers. Besides the demands for a general wage agreement and meaningful improvements in living conditions, the programme included radical political points, including demands for the resignation of the entire structure of central power, including Gorbachev's resignation as President, the dissolution of the USSR Congress of People's Deputies, the resignation of the USSR Cabinet of Ministers and the transfer of power to the republics. Smaller-scale work actions in other industries suggested that workers outside the coal industry were sympathetic to the miners and unwilling to be used by the government to oppose them. The strikes ended only after the Russian Republic government agreed in early May with the Union government on the transfer of the coalmines to the Russian Republic's jurisdiction.

Similarly the waves of ethnic–national mobilisation that swept across the Soviet Union from 1987 spawned new organisational forms, symbols and leaders. Perhaps the most common form large-scale national movements took was that of the 'popular front'. Popular fronts seeking to promote national independence arose first in the Baltic republics, then spread to over 50 other regions. As Paul Goble (1991, p. 169) points out, activists from the Baltic states often helped organise other popular fronts in the belief that only in this way could they achieve independence. Each national movement in the republics had specific grievances, yet certain features of their position were shared by most: almost universal was the conviction that Moscow's centralised rule, and the corresponding instruments of Soviet power such as the party, KGB, army and government bureaucracy, must be eliminated in order to allow the nation to enjoy free economic and cultural development. In contrast, the movements of minorities *within* national republics, 'encapsulated' or 'enclave' nationalities whose security was threatened by the prospect of independence of the surrounding nation from the Soviet Union, often bitterly opposed the republican drives to break up the union. Moreover not all ethnic protest by the national movements of republics was directed primarily at Moscow. Some movements are primarily directed against other nationalities, residing either within the republic or in adjacent republics. Some inter-ethnic grievances were so intense that they spilled over into violence, especially in the Transcaucasian region where Armenia, Azerbaijan and Georgia are located. Undoubtedly the bloodiest is the still continuing dispute between Armenians and Azerbaijani over Nagorno-Karabakh. Of all the issues we have discussed, this has brought out by far the largest share of the affected populations in protest, and has cost the most lives.

Nagorno-Karabakh, as noted in Chapter 7, is a region located within the territory of Azerbaijan, to which the status of 'autonomous *oblast* (province)' was given in view of the fact that it is an Armenian enclave; Armenians constitute approximately three-quarters of its population. For years Armenians both in Karabakh and in neighbouring – but not contiguous – Armenia complained of the discriminatory policy practised by Azerbaijan against Armenians in Karabakh. The complaints centred on the lack of economic development and cultural rights, as well as on the basic position that Karabakh's subordination to Azerbaijan was illegitimate, a product of Stalin's arbitrary remaking of the boundaries of Transcaucasia in the 1920s. On 20 February 1988, the soviet of Karabakh adopted a resolution calling for the transfer of Karabakh to Armenian jurisdiction. In response Armenians in Erevan, capital of Armenia, and in Karabakh, voiced their support for the demand through massive demonstrations: day after day, the numbers of demonstrators in Erevan grew, until on Thursday and Friday of the week following the resolution's enactment, as many as a million people turned out in peaceful solidarity with their compatriots in Karabakh. For Azerbaijan, however, the prospect of losing Karabakh was regarded as a direct blow to its fundamental national interest. As tensions grew between Armenians and Azerbäijani in Azerbaijan over the issue, violence broke out. News of the deaths of two Azerbaijan youths in Karabakh was received by the Azerbaijani population of Sumgait, a city near Baku, with an outburst of anti-Armenian hatred: with no intervention by the civil or military authorities, the Armenian minority of the city was subjected to a horrific two-day massacre. Although the official figure of the toll – 32 dead and 100 injured – was widely thought to be a gross undercount, the true number of victims of killings and atrocities may never be known.

Since then the focal point for both Armenian and Azerbaijani national protest has been the Karabakh issue, although the hatred and fear between the two peoples is the legacy of hundreds of years of antagonism. This deep mutual antipathy, and incompatible claims over Karabakh, have led to thousands of deaths and the flight of hundreds of thousands of people from their homes, Armenians fleeing Azerbaijan and Azerbaijani fleeing Armenia. Military operations in 1991 conducted by Azerbaijani interior ministry troops in cooperation with Soviet army units depopulated, and in some cases destroyed, entire Armenian villages in and around Karabakh as part of an operation to eliminate armed Armenian guerrilla forces. It was not too much, in the early 1990s, to speak of a continuing civil war between Armenia and Azerbaijan.

Elsewhere peaceful mass demonstrations have been suppressed with violence, further inflaming national sentiment in the republics. One such example, regrettably not unique, was the massacre of April 1989 in Tbilisi, Georgia, which deepened the gulf between the old party-state system and popular aspirations for national independence. The Georgian republic is home to a number of ethnic minorities, and is also the object of a powerful drive among the republic's Georgian population for the restoration of Georgian national independence. Hundreds of thousands of people demonstrated in Georgia in 1988 and 1989 for freedom and autonomy. The Georgian independence movement, in turn, provoked counter-demonstrations in the minority enclave of Abkhazia, whose titular nationality, the Abkhaz, make up only 17 per cent of the autonomous republic but dominate it politically. When some of the Abkhaz leaders called for secession from Georgia their demands provoked massive demonstrations in Tbilisi among Georgians, who contested Abkhazia's claims and demanded national sovereignty for Georgia. On 9 April 1989, with massive strikes shutting down industry in Tbilisi and some hundred hunger strikes encamped in the central square of the city, the authorities panicked and called on armed forces from the Union Interior Ministry and Defence Ministry to suppress the protesters. (Who in fact gave the relevant orders is still in dispute.) The attack occurred in the early hours of the morning, when the crowd in the central square had diminished somewhat. In the operation, which employed chemical gas and entrenching tools, among other weapons, nineteen unarmed demonstrators were killed, of whom sixteen were women; more than 4,000 people were injured. Shock and horror at the event united Georgian opinion around the demand for full independence.

Throughout the former Soviet Union, movements of popular opposition focused on national independence over the 1988–90 period, seeing in independence the necessary condition for the improvement of social and political life. As in other revolutionary periods, the initiative passed to the extremes. As a result, what opportunity there might have been to preserve the Union, had the Soviet leadership under Gorbachev tried to find a new formula for a more decentralised Union in 1985–6 rather than in 1991, was lost. In the Baltic republics, Moldavia and Georgia leaders espousing middle-of-the-road positions were rejected by groups demanding a total break with Moscow.

The New Electoral Politics

Gorbachev's strategy of channelling grass-roots political activity into forms that would strengthen socialism rather than destroy it, accordingly faced a severe test as mass labour and national movements developed coherent organisations and legitimate leaders. The compromise Gorbachev hoped to strike between free political debate through *glasnost'* and preservation of the socialist structure of the state – a compromise that he expressed in the 1987–8 formula of 'a socialist pluralism of opinions' – gave way to the need to choose between restoration of traditional party controls over political life and a further expansion of the political space in which groups could compete for power. Gorbachev opted to deepen democratisation rather than to retreat, but adopted a strategy that he hoped would focus the energies of the newly awakened social movements on winning power in the soviets.

In his dramatic speech to the 19th Party Conference in 1988 he outlined a conception of a thoroughly renewed system of soviet power (see Chapter 5): soviets would be filled through contested and open elections, and would make basic policy decisions free of unwarranted Communist Party interference. At the centre, a new two-tiered parliament would assume responsibility for lawmaking. In contrast to its purely ceremonial role in the past, Gorbachev proposed a Supreme Soviet that would debate and decide national policy. In the proposal he outlined the new Supreme Soviet would, however, be elected from among a larger body of USSR deputies who would constitute a Congress of People's Deputies. The latter's role would be broadly representational and it would itself be formed by three different kinds of election: one corporatist, under which one-third of the deputies would be sent by the country's major recognised social organisations, including the Communist Party; one national–territorial, under which a third would be elected in districts apportioned equally among the country's national–territorial subdivisions; and one strictly popular, where the final third would be elected from districts equal in voter numbers. The Congress would be given the power to amend the Constitution and set basic lines of policy while its smaller but quasi-professional offspring, the Supreme Soviet, was charged with the task of adopting most legislation.

Following a hasty, stage-managed national airing of the proposal, constitutional amendments embodying Gorbachev's ideas were adopted at the end of the year by the outgoing Supreme Soviet, paving the way for elections of USSR deputies less than four months later. Notwithstanding the fact that the accelerated time frame in which the electoral campaign had to occur gave endless opportunities to local authorities to rig the process of nominations and voting, the elections of 26 March 1989 proved to be a watershed in Soviet history: for the first time since the period of War Communism just after the revolution significant numbers of Soviet citizens had an opportunity to compete for the right to control the government of the state. Although the election resulted in victory for three or four hundred deputies, out of a total of 2,250, who identified themselves with the democratic cause, the greatest effect of the election was to spur a large number of political organisations to take advantage of the new opportunities for political struggle.

The cumbersome electoral arrangements and the blurring of authority between the Congress and Supreme Soviet clearly represented another of Gorbachev's efforts to bridge the widening gap between the forces of radical change and the powerful vested interests of the old order. The most obvious indication of Gorbachev's desire to placate the conservatives was the provision that deputies from the country's established public organisations, nearly all of which were securely controlled by the Communist Party, would occupy one-third of the seats to the new Congress. Indeed the Communist Party would itself fill 100 of these seats, the trade unions another 100, and the Komsomol 75 more. What is more, none of the country's new informal public organisations were allowed any seats. Another of the concessions to the *apparat*, as we have seen (pp. 93–8), was the multistaged way in which candidates were to be nominated and registered. The complicated system of electoral meetings held to approve candidates before they were entitled to run gave local party and government officials numerous opportunities to weed out undesired outsiders.

Still, although both the electoral process and the new parliamentary system were designed to mollify hard-line old guard elements while appealing to the new informal movements to channel their demands into reform of the existing system of soviet power, Gorbachev had put regional party and government officials in an exposed position. By urging them to run for election, Gorbachev was forcing them to subject themselves to the test of popular approval and therefore to stop depending for their power on the support of higher-ups in the party hierarchy. Local officials were being cast upon their own political resources, much as Eastern Europe's Communist Party leaders were being told to find their own independent bases for rule instead of depending on Moscow's fraternal aid. The results were similar. In republics with active social movements, those leaders who tightened their grip upon their regions in the short run simply delayed the moment when the forces of popular opposition mobilised against them. Those who calculated that they could best survive by opening up the system to limited popular participation enabled groups organised around nationalist and other causes to seize the initiative and thus control the political agenda. In republics and regions with a less politically active populace, local bosses strengthened their power at the expense both of Moscow and of their own populations.

Not surprisingly the electoral process of 1989 reflected the diverse configurations of political forces in the republics. In the Baltic republics, well-organised opposition movements mobilised voters to defeat figures from the old party-state establishment and to elect representatives of the popular fronts. These races resembled parliamentary elections in the West, in that the opposition put forward its own candidates, identified them with a platform and rallied the electorate by using many of the campaign tactics of Western political parties. The result was a resounding victory by the popular fronts in the vast majority of the races they contested and defeats for many of the most prominent members of the ruling apparatus.

The Baltic republics were exceptional, to be sure. Elsewhere most local bosses found ways to win. The races of the first secretaries of the party committees of *oblasts* and *krais* illustrate the point (see Table 8.1). Many of the party and government officials who ran adopted one of three strategies: they succeeded in preventing an opposition candidate from running, ran in a rural district where they were able to persuade a vulnerable electorate to support them, or arranged for unknown shadow opponents to provide the semblance of a contest. Yet, even so, some of the defeats had a resonance far beyond their own regions since they occurred in major cities, especially regional and republican capitals. In what was then Leningrad, the first secretary of the regional party committee ran unopposed, and lost; he was the target of an organised campaign mounted by a group of political activists who appealed to voters to strike out the name of a candidate who symbolised so clearly the party apparatus's disdain for democratic politics. (Soviet elections at the time required that a candidate receive a majority of votes cast to be elected and that a majority of eligible voters cast ballots. Therefore even an unopposed candidate could be defeated if a majority of voters took the trouble to strike out his name on the ballot.) In Ukraine, the chairman of the city executive committee and the first secretary of the party committee of Kiev, both running without an opponent, were defeated. In Belorussia, two provincial party first secretaries and the first secretary of the city party committee of Minsk lost. Upsets did not only occur in the western republics, however. The first secretary of the city party committee in Alma Ata, Kazakhstan, lost, as did his counterpart in Samarkand, in Uzbekistan. The single most important cleavage revealed by the elections was that between urban and rural districts: cities favoured electoral activism by opposition groups. As the authors of a seminal Soviet study of the 1989 elections observe (Berezkin *et al.*, 1990, p. 75): 'The habitats where first secretaries were defeated are not areas of particular social–economic–ecological misfortune, but are areas and spots (let us remember capital cities) of heightened social activism.'

Perhaps the most publicised of the David-and-Goliath matches was that involving Boris Yeltsin in Moscow. Although he had reached the pinnacle of party power as Moscow's city party first secretary and member of the party Politburo, his expulsion from power in 1987 and his vehement denunciations of the power and privileges of the *apparat* made him the most celebrated representative of the populist mood in Russia. His opponent, moreover, was the director of the automotive works in Moscow that produced, among other vehicles, the posh ZIL limousine favoured by the senior echelon of the political elite. The clumsy efforts by the party establishment to muzzle Yeltsin backfired as massive popular rallies supported his underdog challenge to the apparatus. On election day he won in an astonishing landslide, gaining nearly 90 per cent of the vote to his opponent's 7 per cent. Yeltsin drew support from virtually all sections of the Moscow electorate, since his district included the entire metropolitan area.

Still most races were far closer in style to the old party-controlled system than to the dramatic contests of the big cities in the west and

TABLE 8.1   *Electoral performance of* obkom *and* kraikom first secretaries in the 1989 elections of USSR Deputies

Republic	No. running	Victories	Defeats
RSFSR	55	33	22
Ukraine	25	21	4
Belorussia	6	4	2
Kazakhstan	17	17	0
Turkmenia	3	3	0
Uzbekistan	10	10	0
Tajikistan	3	3	0

Source: Author's data.

in the industrial heartland. In Turkmenia it was boasted, for example, that 'all candidates from among party and state leaders were elected', and Azerbaijan's electoral authorities not only claimed that 'all state and party candidates won' but even provided a breakdown of the social make-up of the winners, among whom 30 per cent were workers, 14 per cent peasants, and 33 per cent women. Given that, overall, only 18.6 per cent of the victors were workers, 11.2 per cent peasant and 17.1 per cent women, Azerbaijan's success in adhering to the spirit of the old quota-rigged electoral system is all the more impressive.

With the elections of 1989, the regional heterogeneity of Soviet politics began to increase; north and west of the country, and in urban centres, popular participation began gradually to take on the familiar outlines of party and interest group activity characteristic of liberal democracies, while to the south and east, in predominantly rural areas and in the Muslim republics, the old party–bureaucrat dominance of the political arena continued, albeit weakened by the breakdown of the Communist Party's unity. Increasingly the party found it impossible to maintain that it represented the leading force in Soviet state and public life: the strike movement demonstrated its inability to speak for the class whose vanguard it ostensibly was, and the formation of a parliamentary faction of deputies of a liberal-democratic orientation, led by individuals of such stature as the Nobel Peace Prize Laureate Andrei Sakharov and the redoubtable Boris Yeltsin, was the first step towards a system of multiparty politics. Moreover the fact that 87 per cent of the deputies elected in 1989 were party members was far less significant than the evident intensity of the popular zeal to vote against anyone identified with the party *apparat*.

Not surprisingly, therefore, Gorbachev responded by shifting his own political base from the party to the state, pushing through a set of constitutional amendments in March 1990 that simultaneously dropped the old provision on the party's 'leading role' from the constitution and created a new state presidency whose occupant he quickly became. The great problem for Gorbachev, however, was that the new politics of mass participation that had begun to arise mobilised far more political activity around national causes than on the restructuring of socialism within the Union. The wider the opportunities for democratic participation, the stronger became the forces seeking sovereignty and independence of the constituent republics and the weaker the forces for moderate reform at the centre. This fact was a simple consequence of the state-centred character of Soviet society: there was very little substance to the theory of a trans-ethnic 'Soviet nation' and a great deal to the memory of or aspiration for ethnic national sovereignty over the national territories that Soviet federalism had given them. The consolidation of national societies in the Union had created strong movements for national statehood in the republics and autonomous republics, not least in the republic that had virtually no structures of nominal statehood itself, the Russian Republic. As a result, the further the democratisation of politics at the union level proceeded, the more demands for self-government in the republics were stimulated. Inescapably, therefore, the next wave of elections in the following year, to the Supreme Soviets of the republics and to the soviets of regions, cities and districts within them, reinforced the movements for republican sovereignty at the expense of central authority.

In the 1990 republican elections, the pattern of popular political mobilisation across the republics followed that of the 1989 campaign: opposition movements captured majorities of the seats in the republican parliaments in the Baltic republics and Georgia, whereas, in Central Asia, equivalent movements won fewer than 10 per cent of the seats. In the Slavic core, democratic movements took strong pluralities. In the Russian republic, the democratic opposition group, Democratic Russia, a coalition of democratically-oriented candidates, won between 30 and 40 per cent of the seats in the republican Congress of People's Deputies. (A similar number of seats went to deputies supporting the Communist Party.) In Ukraine, around a quarter of the republican parliament's seats were won by the democratic opposition, and in Belorussia around one-third. As had been the case in the 1989 elections, however, candidates opposing party domination swept the races to republican parliaments in urban and especially capital city areas and gained majorities in regional and city soviets in the most heavily urbanised areas. In Kiev, for example, eighteen of the 22 seats to the republican legislature went to the opposition coalition, while in Western Ukraine, where nationalist sentiment is powerful, the opposition took around 90 per cent of the seats in Lviv's regional soviet. Democratic forces took majorities in the city soviets of Moscow, Leningrad and Sverdlovsk, and pluralities in a number of other industrial cities in the Russian republic.

The republican elections were soon followed by what Soviet observers termed the 'parade of sovereignties'. In each republic, legislatures adopted resolutions declaring their republics sovereign over the natural resources and economies of the republics. In March 1990, shortly after its landslide victory, the Lithuanian Popular Front, Sajudis, won passage of a declaration of independence for Lithuania, which was immediately declared invalid by the All-Union Congress of People's Deputies. Nonetheless Lithuania's example was soon followed by Estonia and Latvia. In the summer, after Boris Yeltsin had been elected chairman of the Russian Supreme Soviet and thus chief of state of the Russian Republic, Russia's congress also declared sovereignty by an overwhelming margin (907 for, 13 against and 9 abstaining). There followed a succession of similar declarations, suggesting that sovereignty had become a valence issue – vague in meaning, popular among the voters, and gladly embraced by both democrats and conservatives. Indeed the drive for sovereignty often played into the hands of entrenched bureaucratic elements who used sovereignty to tighten their grip. In the case of Georgia, the indepence cause was used by President Gamsakhurdia in his turn towards authoritarian rule, as he denounced any opponent as 'an agent of the Kremlin'. Eventually his heavy-handed and divisive rule drove Georgia to the brink of civil war as his opponents joined with many of his former supporters to drive him from office by massive armed force.

The cause of popular sovereignty became embodied in forms such as popular referenda and presidential elections in the republics as the drive for democratically elected legislatures in 1989–90 gave way to a wave of plebiscitarian elections of national presidents in 1990 and 1991, many of whom (including Boris Yeltsin) obtained emergency powers to rule by decree and began to replace local councils with their own nominees. As in other political systems, the use of the referendum and creation of plebiscitarian presidencies in the republics has tended to weaken representative institutions, particularly legislatures.

The drive for national sovereignty also eliminated the middle ground between nationalist movements in the republics and the desire of reformers and conservatives at the centre to preserve some meaningful form of union. As Gorbachev sought to find a new basis for relations with the republics through the 'nine-plus-one' negotiation process in the spring and summer of 1991, he aroused deep opposition on the part of the conservative elements based in the party apparatus, the army, the economic bureaucracy and the security establishment. It was the leaders of these structures who struck in August 1991 in order to forestall the signing of the proposed Union Treaty, which would have laid the constitutional foundation for a greatly decentralised Union. Their ill-conceived and botched act, far from restoring the authority of the centre, struck a mortal blow to the old Union. In November, the Russian Republic absorbed the budget of the Union government. On 8 December, following the Ukrainian independence referendum and election of Leonid Kravchuk as President, the leaders of Russia, Ukraine and Belorussia agreed to form a new Commonwealth of Independent States, declaring the Union dissolved (see pp. 6–7, 144–6). Shortly after, eight more republics –

the Central Asian republics, Armenia and Azerbaijan – declared their agreement to join the new Commonwealth; and Georgia, after the ousting of President Gamsakhurdia, became increasingly associated with its activities.

Whether the Commonwealth will become a viable structure or not remains to be seen. The extraordinary sequence of developments over the last seven years demonstrates clearly, however, that the democratising reforms initiated under Mikhail Gorbachev encouraged the release of new popular energies that mounted with time into a revolution sweeping away centralised communist rule, and ultimately the union of national republics born of the October revolution of 1917. It was in turn those popular energies, still loosely associated with parties, associations and electoral politics, that would determine the nature of the political systems that in Russia and the other republics had replaced the centralised and authoritarian forms that had for so long been associated with Soviet socialism.

9

Glasnost' and the Media

DAVID WEDGWOOD BENN

The demise of the USSR in December 1991 marked the end of a political revolution. It was, however, preceded by an intellectual revolution which had begun soon after Mikhail Gorbachev's accession to power in 1985, and which had been crucially associated with what came to be known as *glasnost'* or 'openness' in the Soviet media. Today the term *glasnost'* has become anachronistic and has been superseded by the more familiar term 'free speech'. The advent of *glasnost'* did not produce much gratitude among the mass of Soviet citizens because it was overshadowed by a period of political disintegration, economic crisis, falling living standards and declining public morale. Yet in spite of this, the new openness was of lasting importance. Although by no means the only element in the Soviet reforms of the 1980s, it was nevertheless one of their essential ingredients. It is indeed highly doubtful whether, in the absence of *glasnost'*, any of the other reforms of the Gorbachev era – or indeed any of the subsequent changes in Russia – could even have begun. The present chapter makes no attempt to carry the story of the media in the former USSR beyond the end of 1991. But the media reforms of the Gorbachev era remain highly relevant to an understanding of the present – because they helped to prepare the ground for all that was to follow.

It is difficult to find any one term to describe the reforms in the USSR in the late 1980s, if only because of all the disagreement and uncertainty as to their exact goal. But one comparison may serve to highlight the extent of the change. In 1985 the USSR was, in some ways, more of a closed society than Nazi Germany had been in the 1930s. Germans, up to the outbreak of the Second World War, were free to make private trips abroad, to stay in private homes when

174

abroad and to subscribe to foreign newspapers. (For example, it was perfectly possible until 1939 in Germany to subscribe to *The Times*.) Foreign visitors to Nazi Germany were also able, if they wished, to stay in private homes. None of these things was generally true of Soviet Russia prior to 1985. However, by the summer of 1991, on the eve of the failed coup, all this had radically changed. The Soviet Union had ceased, in any credible sense, to be a 'totalitarian' state. Even though not fully democratic, it was certainly a far more open society than either Franco's Spain or Tito's Yugoslavia – both of which had often been favourably compared with the Soviet Union in the past because of their 'non-totalitarian' systems of rule. One of the main surviving restrictions on the rights of Soviet citizens – the restriction on the right to travel abroad or emigrate – had been removed in principle by a new Soviet law adopted in May 1991. In the following month genuinely contested presidential elections had been held in Russia; and it had already become perfectly possible to use the media to demand the resignation of the head of state, Mikhail Gorbachev. Nothing like this would have been conceivable under Franco or Tito. Such was the magnitude of the change brought about under the umbrella term of *glasnost'*.

It would be impossible within a single chapter to recount all the changes in the Soviet media since 1985: many of them are in any case well known. The approach in what follows will be more selective and will be addressed to the following questions: What was the pre-1985 media system which the Gorbachev leadership inherited? How did the term *glasnost'* originate and why was it important after 1985? What was its impact on the Soviet media? What were the main legislative and other changes affecting media freedom which came about between 1985 and 1991? And how did the reforms operate in practice?

Before dealing with these questions, it should be pointed out that the Soviet media revolution was not only the result of politics. It was, in an important sense, the result both of better education and of technological progress. The preceding decades had seen a worldwide revolution in communications technology, which had, in particular, meant a vast expansion of radio and television. Consequently the freedom of speech which Russians began to enjoy under Gorbachev was something much more potent than the freedom which they had briefly enjoyed in the months after February 1917, following the overthrow of the Tsar. In 1917, the media in Russia had been extremely undeveloped and illiteracy among the population had been widespread. Radio (except in the form of morse-code signals) and television had not yet come into being; and there were somewhat less than two copies of newspapers per 100 inhabitants. In 1920, when

Bertrand Russell visited the Russian countryside, he found that the peasants were mostly unaware of the Allied blockade against the Bolsheviks which was then in force, and that they had never even heard of Great Britain. All that has, of course, long since changed; indeed the rate of change rapidly accelerated from the 1960s onwards. Thus, whereas in 1960 no more than 5 per cent of the Soviet population were able to watch television, by the late 1980s at least 93 per cent were able to do so. Furthermore listening to Western broadcasts was gradually becoming widespread. According to an American estimate made in 1979, as many as 67.3 million Soviet adults over the age of 16 listened to Western broadcasts in the course of a year – which would have been equivalent to roughly 37 per cent of the Soviet population at the time. Clearly then, even during the Brezhnev era, the Soviet Union was becoming in practice less of a closed society. Its population was becoming far better informed; and of course news was travelling much faster than it had done even a few decades earlier.

The Media and Propaganda System Prior to 1985

Soviet media controls have often been associated in the public mind with censorship. In actual fact, the traditional system of controls was much wider. It involved not just negative prohibitions but a whole range of positive directives issued by a vast and highly-organised apparatus which was itself ultimately controlled by the Communist Party. The mechanisms of this apparatus (whose functions effectively ended in 1990 when the party lost its 'leading role' under the Soviet Constitution) were largely kept secret. But its underlying principles, very far from being denied or played down, were repeatedly and emphatically proclaimed. In 1974, for example, Viktor Afanasev (who was editor-in-chief of *Pravda* from 1976 until 1989) made the following very forthright statements about the party's control of the media:

Our enemies not infrequently criticise the Communist Party for monopolizing the guidance of the political information system . . . However, the guidance of this important sphere of public life is both the party's right and its obligation . . . Our party is the ruling party: and it is therefore called upon to carry out the guidance of all spheres of life in a socialist society, including the ideological sphere . . . the defence of the party's policy and ideology is at the same time also the defence of the most sacred ideas and interests of the people.

Soviet citizens could therefore have been in no doubt as to the party's control over information. And the frequently proclaimed purpose of its propaganda effort was not merely to neutralise opposition but to generate active and enthusiastic popular commitment to the implementation of the regime's goals in building a future communist society. The theoretical justification for the vast propaganda effort smacked very much of what might be called 'the schoolmaster state'. The eventual aim, according to the 1961 Communist party programme, was 'to educate *all* working people in a spirit of ideological integrity and devotion to communism' (Part II, section V, emphasis added). Nor was this commitment to education by any means empty of meaning. Soviet achievements in the educational field were in many ways impressive: ten-year schooling became compulsory in the 1970s; and between 1959 and 1982 the number of people with a completed higher education rose from 3.8 million to 17 million, a more than fourfold increase. It is, of course, open to doubt whether the then Soviet leadership actually believed in the feasibility of universal indoctrination. Nevertheless enormous amounts of time and resources were expended *as if* this was the aim.

The most striking case in point was the existence of a vast system of so-called 'oral propaganda' whose ramifications were constantly being extended. It involved not only a system of *ad hoc* political lectures in factories and other places of work; it also involved a network of semi-obligatory political study courses (usually convened at least once a month) which, by 1986–7, was said to have embraced some 66.4 million people (that is, about 37 per cent of the Soviet adult population at the time). Even in the Brezhnev era there was considerable evidence that these study courses were unpopular and were doing little to strengthen the regime's domestic credibility. Yet the propaganda network continued to be expanded. The reasons for this may be less than totally clear. But at all events the propaganda effort was far from an empty ritual.

This ostensible goal of achieving mass conversion to communist ideas (with the implication that even outright opponents had to be converted) was, of course, ambitious by any standards. It may be noted, incidentally, that in this respect Soviet propaganda differed radically from that of the Nazis, who had no comparable educational aims and were quite avowedly cynical. The Nazi ideology was intended only for a racial *elite*; and certainly not for Germany's subject peoples. Indeed Hitler, when discussing his long-term plans for the colonisation of the Soviet Union, was quoted as saying in 1942 that 'we don't want a horde of schoolmasters to descend suddenly on these territories and force education down the throats of the subject races. To teach the Russians, Ukrainians and Kirghizs to read and write will eventually be to our own disadvantage.' By contrast, the Soviet rulers did undertake an enormous effort for the indoctrination of those under their control – with no very visible long-term success. By the end of the Brezhnev era, the official ideology was, for a whole number of reasons, becoming more and more at odds with the observed reality of Soviet society. To an increasing extent Soviet citizens were required to profess allegiance to a set of ideas in which they did not believe, or to which they had no firm commitment. With the benefit of hindsight it is easy to see why the traditional propaganda system contained the seeds of its own failure.

Negative censorship (as distinct from the principle of positive party control over the media) was rarely mentioned in public in the USSR after the 1930s. The very first Soviet law authorising censorship was issued two days after the Bolshevik Revolution, on 9 November 1917, and was stated to be temporary. Censorship was, nevertheless, put on a permanent footing by a government decree of 1922 which set up a so-called 'Main directorate on matters of literature and publishing', known by the acronym *Glavlit*. The last known law on censorship appeared in 1931. No detailed reference to the subject subsequently appeared until 3 November 1988, when the then head of *Glavlit*, Vladimir Boldyrev, was interviewed in the Soviet newspaper *Izvestiya*; he then stated that the list of forbidden subjects had recently been cut by nearly a third.

The system of censorship which the post-1985 Soviet leaders inherited included the following:

1. The *Glavlit* organisation (by then known as 'The State Committee for the Preservation of Secrets in the Press') whose formal sanction was required before anything appeared in print or in the media. *Glavlit* kept a permanent, and regularly updated, list of forbidden topics which almost to the end had prohibited any reference to itself. In theory its function was not censorship but simply the protection of secrets. In practice it exercised its powers far more widely: for example, even certain quotations from Lenin were said to have been banned. Its powers of preliminary censorship were formally abolished as of 1 August 1990. (It was on that day that *Izvestiya* divulged the information just quoted.) But its functions had been reduced largely to a formality for some time prior to that.

2. A ban on the unauthorised use of photocopying or other duplicating machinery. The ban (so this writer was recently told at the Institute of State and Law in Moscow) had been imposed by an unpublished decree of the USSR Council of Ministers. However it was ruled in 1990 by the Committee for Constitutional Oversight (a body set up under Gorbachev to ensure that Soviet laws complied

with the country's Constitution) that all enactments affecting the rights and duties of members of the public were automatically invalidated unless published.

3. A system of so-called 'closed sections' (*spetskhrany*) in libraries. In July 1990, the Moscow literary journal, *Novyi mir*, published an article on the 'closed section' of the Lenin Library in Moscow and reported that 'inaccessible' publications had broadly fallen into four groups: (1) anti-communist books or newspapers published in Russia during the civil war of 1917–20; (2) material legally published in the USSR between 1918 and 1936, which referred to leaders who had been arrested during Stalin's purges; (3) Russian-language books and newspapers published abroad; and (4) foreign books and newspapers. From the mid-1970s, the 'closed section' also included writings by recent Soviet emigres. Some authors (in particular, Trotsky and Solzhenitsyn) had been subject to a 'double prohibition' and could be consulted only with the greatest difficulty. All in all, according to this article, the 'closed section' of the Lenin Library contained over 30,000 book titles, more than 560,000 periodicals and at least a million newspapers.

4. An elaborate system for the jamming of foreign broadcasts, originally installed in 1939 and selectively operated between the late 1940s and December 1988. Coordination of jamming in the Moscow area had been conducted from the tower of the Taganka theatre. (All this was revealed in a *Pravda* interview which appeared in mid-March 1989 with one of those responsible for the jamming operation.)

The system of control over information and the media could not, however, be reduced to a set of rules. Much of it had been dictated, not by security needs, but by the need to conceal the falsification of Soviet history by Stalin, following the collectivisation and political purges of the 1930s. In the end the 'schoolmaster state' concept of propaganda became eclipsed by other considerations. In practice the party hierarchy acquired an essentially arbitrary power to decide what could or could not be divulged. For example, Khrushchev's son-in-law Alexei Adzhubei had been forbidden, after Khrushchev's dismissal in 1964, to publish anything under his own name. (This was revealed in 1991 in the memoirs of Yegor Ligachev.) Academician Tatyana Zaslavskaya has described how members of the public were commonly denied access to newspapers which were more than three years old. There was at one time a ruling that the gravestones of Soviet soldiers killed in Afghanistan and taken home for burial must not refer to the circumstances of their death. (On 5 August 1987, *Pravda* published a letter complaining about this.) The list of similar examples could be greatly extended.

When drawing attention to the scale of past Soviet censorship, it would be incorrect to give the impression of a changeless society consisting only of grey uniformity until 1985. For one thing, the tradition of 'criticism and self-criticism' had long been emphasised by Soviet leaders, not least by Stalin himself. Its function had, it is true, been severely limited. The unwritten rule had been expressed in the formula 'Criticise but do not generalise'; that is, it is all right to find fault in particular situations, but do not write general conclusions because that is politically dangerous. In practice, the press during the late Brezhnev era had begun to erode this rule. Thus the campaign against corruption can be traced at least as far back as New Year's Day 1979, when the Moscow weekly, *Literaturnaya gazeta*, started a feature on the theme of 'Economics and morality'. Furthermore the Brezhnev era, despite its many repressive features, was not character-ised by mass terror as the Stalin era had been; and it coincided with a notable decline of fear among ordinary Russians. Even at that time a number of new ideas were discreetly ventilated in the official press – among them the idea of *glasnost'*, of which Brezhnev himself had sometimes spoken. The notion of pluralism had been mentioned in an article on 'Public opinion' in the *Large Soviet Encyclopedia* as far back as 1974. Though such ideas produced few results at the time, their eventual impact was to be far-reaching.

Glasnost' after 1985: Its Origins and Meaning

This then was the system of media controls which Mikhail Gorbachev inherited on coming to power in March 1985. During the period after that, when the word *glasnost'* began to be popularised, it encoun-tered widespread scepticism among Western observers. Most of them were inclined to dismiss it as nothing more than (1) an attempt to strengthen the Communist Party's hold on power or (2) a largely cosmetic or public relations exercise, or even (3) a deliberate attempt of hoodwink the West. The latter explanation ceased to find favour after the opening of the Berlin Wall in 1989. But the other two both contained a certain element of truth. The reason was that *glasnost'* meant different things to different people within the Soviet establish-ment; and also that its meaning changed radically over time.

Before 1985 the Soviet media had had an appalling public relations record. The extent of secrecy (illustrated by the traditional ban on the reporting of crime or accidents) went far beyond what rational security considerations would have required; as a result, Soviet citizens were ceasing to trust their own media and were increasingly tuning in to foreign broadcasts. Besides that, the prolonged official silences about the last illnesses of Brezhnev, Andropov and Chernenko between 1982 and 1985 must have caused acute embarrassment to Soviet diplomats abroad, besieged by questions from foreign journalists. This inability to handle news was becoming highly unprestigious for a great power. Therefore the call for less secrecy and better public relations may well have been supported by many Soviet leaders who were not liberals.

The claim that *glasnost'* was an attempt to strengthen the Communist Party was also, in a sense, true; although it could be argued that liberals and conservatives within the Soviet hierarchy gradually evolved radically different notions as to what kind of a Communist Party and Soviet system they wanted. By 1989 and 1990, as the movement for political pluralism gathered force, these differences increasingly came out into the open and *glasnost'* gradually became equated with, and finally superseded by, the notion of freedom of speech.

Although the eventual consequences of *glasnost'* have been discussed many times, the meaning and origins of the term have received rather less attention. Nevertheless its origins are highly important – if only because of the light this throws on the thinking of Gorbachev. For it was he who decided which interpretation of the term was to prevail. The word itself was never given an official dictionary definition, although a Communist Party resolution 'On *glasnost''* adopted in July 1988 said that it arose from a public need for 'full and objective information about everything that is going on in society'; and that it was a 'developing process' which must not, however, be used 'to the detriment of the interests of the Soviet state or society'. However the term itself, as we have already noted, was not new. Article 9 of the 1977 Soviet Constitution had expressly called for, among other things, 'the extension of *glasnost''* as well as 'constant responsiveness to public opinion'. It is not entirely clear what Brezhnev understood by *glasnost'*: he apparently meant that the authorities should inform the public about decisions which they had already taken. Thus as far back as 29 March 1968, Brezhnev had said in a speech that '*Glasnost'*, the informing of the party masses and of all working people about the activity of the party, is a principle of our party life and we firmly follow this principle.' Few people at the time paid much attention to these remarks; it seemed reasonable to assume that the word was just one more cliché which signified no change whatever in the Soviet system.

The important point here is, however, that the expression *glasnost'* was already firmly entrenched in the Soviet vocabulary well before Gorbachev became leader. Therefore, when he began to emphasise its importance, no one could accuse him of ideological heresy. In fact he began to use the word at least as early as December 1984 (that is, during the last weeks of Konstantin Chernenko's leadership). Gorbachev then described *glasnost'* as 'an integral part of socialist democracy and norm of all public life', adding that 'Extensive, timely and frank information is evidence of trust in people, of respect for . . . their ability to interpret events for themselves.' On the face of it, this differed in no way from what Brezhnev had said many years before: yet Gorbachev's way of putting it had an altogether more convincing air. He mentioned *glasnost'* yet again in his speech on becoming leader on 11 March 1985. From that time onwards, the Soviet media began steadily to popularise the term. Thus, on 27 March, a *Pravda* leading article said that *glasnost'* was important for, among other things, 'the further improvement of the moral–political climate in our society'.

Then, in a major speech reported on 24 April 1985, Gorbachev began to hint at the more fundamental significance of this newly-popularised expression. He criticised what he called 'the inability to talk to people in the language of truth' and added that 'it sometimes happens that a man hears one thing, but sees something else in life. The question is a serious one, not only from the educational, but from the political point of view.' It was a question, so some might argue, which went to the very root of the problem. The discrepancy between the then ideology (with its professions of 'internationalism', 'democracy' and 'equality') and the observed reality of Soviet society arguably represented the basic flaw of the entire system. Gorbachev's aim, so it appears, was to try, with the help of *glasnost'*, to bridge this gap.

If that analysis is right, then it does point to a certain intellectual coherence in Gorbachev's notion of *glasnost'*; and it strongly suggests that it formed part of a long-term strategy and was not merely a piece of improvisation. This does not of course mean that all the reforms stemming from *glasnost'* were preplanned; on the contrary, the policy of openness led to a whole number of unforeseen and unintended results. Gorbachev's own views clearly changed: one has only to recall his claim (in an interview published in *Pravda* on 8 February 1986) that Stalinism was 'a concept invented by the enemies of communism'. Nevertheless his public support for *glasnost'*, as well as for some form of socialism (which continued even after the failed coup of 1991), represented two unchanging themes in all that he said. To that extent there was, over the years, an undeniable consistency in his position.

For more than a year after Gorbachev's accession to power his top priority was not political reform but so-called 'acceleration' of the economy: that is, getting the economy out of the doldrums. In this context, *glasnost'* or 'openness' was mainly directed towards the exposure of inefficiency (as well as corruption). This, it could have been argued, was intended to strengthen and not to weaken the power base of the Communist Party; and it might have seemed to differ little from the traditional practice of 'criticism and self-criticism' to which all past Soviet leaders had paid lip-service.

But in the summer of 1986, Gorbachev's interpretation of *glasnost'* began to assume a much wider meaning – and became openly aimed at political reform. It is hard to say exactly when the change occurred, although it seems certain that the disaster at the Chernobyl nuclear power station on 26 April 1986 was one of the turning points. That disaster exposed Soviet secrecy at its worst. The accident was first detected by monitoring stations in Sweden; and the first, very brief, Soviet report came only a full two days after the event. Only on 14 May – more than a fortnight later – did Gorbachev finally go on Soviet television and elevate the accident to the level of headline news. By then, however, the damage, both political and physical, had been done, and millions of people in the affected area had been put at risk through not having been warned in good time of the need to evacuate their homes.

The next crucial piece of evidence as to Gorbachev's thinking about *glasnost'* comes from a report (unofficial but apparently authentic) of a meeting he had with a group of Soviet writers on 19 June 1986. It was then that Gorbachev, apparently for the first time, identified democratisation as a top priority, arguing that this was what the enemies of the USSR were most afraid of. ('They are worried by one thing: if democracy develops under us, if that happens, then we will win.') It was also on this occasion that *glasnost'* was, for the first time, presented as one of the key instruments in democratisation: 'We don't have an opposition. How then can we monitor ourselves? Only through criticism and self-criticism. And most of all through *glasnost'*'. He then added a note of caution: 'There can be no implementation of democracy without *glasnost'*. But at the same time, democracy without limits is anarchy. That's why it's complicated.' Furthermore Gorbachev at that time was against immediately delving into the Soviet past: 'If we start trying to deal with the past, we'll lose all our energy. It would be like hitting the people over the head . . . We'll sort out the past. We'll put everything in its place. But right now we have to direct our energy forward.'

The account just quoted appeared in the Italian newspapers *L'Unità* and *La Repubblica* on 7 October 1986 and the *Report on the USSR*, published in Munich by Radio Liberty later the same month. The fact that the report was contemporaneous adds to its credibility. It provides further evidence that the policy of *glasnost'* was launched for strategic, and not just tactical reasons. Gorbachev's stated aim of 'democracy' without 'anarchy' does help to explain his later zigzags, which many saw as pure opportunism. Furthermore his wish to postpone the public discussion of the Soviet past shows that he foresaw – even though he underrated – the risks to the system which this would entail. But his emphasis on *glasnost'* becomes even easier to understand in the light of his own position in 1986. At that time, Gorbachev's power base was far from secure; it derived not from the semi-democratic Soviet parliament (as it later did) but from the conservative-dominated Communist Party hierarchy, which was well-placed to obstruct him, or even to depose him outright, as it had deposed Nikita Khrushchev in 1964. In these circumstances the power to relax censorship was one of the few effective weapons which Gorbachev had at his disposal. The release of information in order to undermine conservative opponents of reform proved a highly effective instrument of policy. Indeed the whole history of *glasnost'* after 1985 might be treated as a case-study in the use of information as a lever for political change.

Soon after this writers' meeting, Gorbachev made a number of public speeches in much the same vein. In a speech delivered in Khabarovsk and broadcast on 31 July 1986 he again emphasised the need for *glasnost'* in the absence of an opposition. But this was a sensitive point: the reference to an opposition was deleted from the otherwise largely verbatim newspaper reports of the speech. The autumn of 1986 saw further significant developments. In September plans were published for a major programme of legislation over the following four years, including a law on referendums, a law on state security and a law on 'the press and information' (which was originally scheduled for preparation in draft by the end of 1986, though the deadline was not met). Meanwhile, on 20 October, Gorbachev had spoken of what he called 'the primacy of all-human values over the goals of one or other class', which seemed like a clear departure from the traditional Bolshevik view (even though Gorbachev sought to justify it by reference to Lenin). On 11 December he expressly renounced any claim by the Soviet Communist Party to absolute infallibility: he told a Yugoslav communist delegation in Moscow that 'no party possesses a certificate to the absolute truth'.

At that time no political reforms had been implemented; but anyone familiar with the traditional ideology could have noticed that there was, so to speak, 'something new on the radar screen'. Practical changes soon followed. In December 1986, Academician Andrei Sakharov was released from exile and allowed to return to Moscow. He was the first avowedly non-communist public figure to be accorded a legitimate status in the Soviet Union, at least since the

1920s. In January 1987, Gorbachev, in a speech to a plenary meeting of the party Central Committee, took another practical step forwards by proposing an end to one-candidate elections; the first experiment along these lines took place the following June. Then, in September, Gorbachev for the first time publicly enunciated a new doctrine of what he called 'socialist pluralism'. Under this doctrine, anti-socialist views were still denied legitimacy, but the previous dogma of a 'unanimous' public opinion was finally ended. Henceforward there was to be no single official point of view; and public debate on current issues was gradually to become a normal occurrence.

Glasnost' in Action, 1986–90

The ensuing political reforms – which led to multicandidate parliamentary elections in 1989 and then, in the spring of 1990, to the abolition of the Communist Party's entrenched position under the Soviet Constitution – lie outside the scope of this chapter (see pp. 92–8, 104, 159–70). So far as the media were concerned, a fundamentally important change gradually came about. Although freedom of expression did not become absolute, there was nevertheless a revolution in the intellectual climate, which might not unreasonably be described as 'de-Orwellianisation'. The old assumption amongst foreign observers that nothing in Soviet politics could be accepted at face value was effectively overturned. There was an entirely new kind of sincerity in the media, since journalists and writers became far freer to voice their personal convictions and were no longer obliged, as in the past, to justify the current official line. The media also became far more truthful, following the release of an enormous amount of hitherto secret information relating to Soviet society, both past and present.

Media freedom in the USSR did not become total; and it is only right to point out some of the limitations. A number of important events certainly received less than complete coverage during the years of *glasnost'*. For example, the reporting of the conflict which erupted in 1988 between Armenia and Azerbaijan over the disputed territory of Nagorno-Karabakh was distinctly patchy. The Soviet media published hardly any criticism of the former communist regimes in Eastern Europe prior to their downfall in the autumn of 1989. Boris Yeltsin had difficulty in getting access to Soviet television prior to his election as Chairman of the Russian parliament in May 1990. And there were certain occasions when it seemed that an attempt was being made to put the clock back. Soviet liberals were particularly alarmed by a now famous article which appeared in the daily paper,

Sovetskaya Rossiya, on 13 March 1988, whose author Nina Andreeva seemed to be advocating a return to neo-Stalinism. What disturbed the liberals most of all was the ban on any press criticism of the article, until a rebuttal appeared in *Pravda* some three weeks later. (It later became clear that the Andreeva article had been inspired by Gorbachev's conservative opponents when he was abroad.) Then, in the autumn of 1989, Gorbachev himself seemed to be trying to curb the press: he demanded the resignation of the editor of the mass-circulation weekly, *Argumenty i fakty*, whose fault consisted in having published an item which showed that Gorbachev was not the most popular of all Soviet parliamentarians and also in publishing a letter of protest at the building of a luxurious residence for party officials in Moscow. However the editor refused to resign and nothing further happened. Again in May 1990 (following anti-communist demonstrations during the May Day parade on Red Square) the Soviet parliament approved a law which made it an offence publicly to insult or slander the President of the USSR (the law applied only to deliberate insults 'expressed in an unseemly form' or to 'fabrications . . . known to be false'). Only one person, however, is known to have even been charged under this law: the accused (Valeriya Novodvorskaya) was later found guilty of a different offence and was freed from prison following the failed coup of August 1991.

The list of actual or attempted restrictions on media freedom could be extended. Yet it would be impossible to deny that the gains for freedom of speech far outweighed the setbacks. Certainly by 1990 it had become permissible to demand Gorbachev's resignation; to suggest that the Bolshevik revolution had been a mistake (the magazine *Dialog* had published an opinion survey on this subject in July 1990); or to attack the KGB (this was highlighted by the case of the former KGB general Oleg Kalugin, who attacked his former employers in a speech in June of that year and went on, in the following September, to win a seat in the Soviet parliament). It could be argued that the decisive threshold of free expression was crossed in July 1989 when the prestigious Moscow literary journal, *Novyi mir*, began to serialise Alexander Solzhenitsyn's *Gulag Archipelago*, perhaps the most famous and comprehensive account yet published of Stalin's labour camps. If that could be passed for publication, it was hard to imagine what could be deemed politically unacceptable.

The movement towards freedom of expression was by that time rapidly accelerating. The first, hesitant, signs of change in the media had, however, begun to be visible more than three years earlier. As early as 13 February 1986, *Pravda* had caused a minor sensation by publishing a letter referring to the special canteens reserved for party workers. On 7 May of the same year, an article in *Literaturnaya gazeta* had for the first time mentioned the fact that judges sometimes received telephoned instructions from 'influential people' as to what verdicts they should reach. On 13 August 1986, the same paper carried a further article which asked why the courts hardly ever brought in verdicts of acquittal and posed the further questions: 'Why does the public not know the statistics of crime – and isn't there a hidden desire . . . to misinform public opinion about the true state of affairs?' Those familiar with traditional Soviet journalism could immediately detect something new. Here at last was 'generalised criticism' of the kind which had previously been forbidden; it was criticism aimed at the system itself and not just at particular misdemeanours by minor officials.

The impact of *glasnost'* on literature and the cinema falls outside our scope, though mention should nevertheless be made of Tengiz Abuladze's film 'Repentance' (*Pokayanie*), originally made in 1984 and first shown two years later. The film, which was seen by 700,000 Muscovites, centred on a tyrant in Georgia and was a thinly fictionalised indictment of Stalinism. Another literary landmark was the publication in early 1988 of Pasternak's *Doctor Zhivago* (which had been publicly demanded at the Soviet writers' congress as early as July 1986). In the light of all the revelations that were soon to follow, Soviet readers may well have wondered why they had been prevented from reading the book for so long.

From 1987, the traditional taboos began to fall away in all directions. For one thing, Soviet citizens were for almost the first time allowed access to the uncensored views of foreigners. On 31 March 1987, Soviet television broadcast in its entirely an interview with Mrs Thatcher, then on a visit to Moscow. In October that year, during a live television link-up by satellite between Moscow and Washington, Senator Daniel Moynihan informed his Soviet audience that they lived in a 'human rights hell' in which restrictions on emigration and press freedom were worse than those imposed under the tsars. The programme was seen by an estimated 150 million Soviet viewers. In that same month, a short review article in *Novyi mir* apparently for the first time broached the subject of whether the USSR had ever made any foreign policy mistakes: 'Foreign policy is, as it were, exempted *a priori* from mistakes and miscalculations. But is this so in real life?' In the following year, not only the Soviet invasion of Afghanistan, but the even more sensitive issue of the 1939 Molotov–Ribbentrop pact with its secret protocol assigning the Baltic states to the Soviet sphere of influence were thrown wide open to debate in the Soviet media.

The end of 1987 also saw the first signs of openness about Soviet history, which had been virtually out of bounds for discussion since the mid-1960s. It then became known that a biography of Stalin by Professor Dmitrii Volkogonov was in preparation. (The biography eventually appeared in four volumes in Moscow in 1989.) The rehabilitation in 1988 of the victims of Stalin's show trials – beginning with Nikolai Bukharin, who in February of that year was formally exonerated of the charges levelled against him half a century earlier – finally prepared the ground for an open reassessment of the Stalin period. In May 1988, Soviet television replayed a 1930s newsreel of one of the notorious show trials and of a speech delivered by Stalin's most notorious prosecutor, Andrei Vyshinsky. Not long afterwards it became known that all history examinations in Soviet schools were being cancelled, pending the preparation of an entirely new history textbook. In 1990, when this new *History of the USSR* appeared (it was described as 'transitional' but was printed in an edition of 2,905,000 copies), it was found to contain information not only about the GULAG camp complex and the failings of Soviet leaders from Stalin onwards: it even included excerpts from a letter sent to the Soviet leadership by Andrei Sakharov in the early 1970s. It was yet another sign that the repudiation of a large part of the Soviet past had become official policy.

Soviet history was probably the most painful of all the issues which *glasnost'* helped to uncover. But the new openness also played a vital part in releasing fresh information about the present. The study of public opinion was one case in point. It had previously been subject to crippling constraints, largely because of the wide range of topics that were off-limits to researchers. The spring of 1988, however, saw the foundation in Moscow of an All-Union Centre for the Study of Public Opinion (known by its Russian initials as VTsIOM), soon followed by the appearance of other polling organisations. At the same time sociological and statistical information relating to such subjects as abortion, crime, suicides, drug addiction and accidents, became much more freely available. Information of this kind had been generally unavailable at least since the 1920s. When it began to reappear, it often showed the Soviet Union in an unfavourable light compared with the countries of the West.

One could go on at far greater length about the new media freedom which *glasnost'* brought. Yet the overall picture is clear enough. By the summer of 1991 – that is, the eve of the failed coup – the media in the USSR were more open than at any time in Soviet or Russian history. To grasp that fact one had only to go round the newspaper kiosks or to the unofficial newspaper sellers in Moscow. Publications covering a whole spectrum, from hard-line communist to anti-communist views, were freely on sale – as were a whole number of others, including those of astrologers and anti-semites. Pornography also made its appearance: this led to the setting up of an 'anti-pornography commission' by the USSR Supreme Soviet in December 1990. The translations of foreign books during this time also testify to the widening of media freedom. Thus 1988 saw the publication of Arthur Koestler's *Darkness at Noon*, and George Orwell's *1984* was published the following year. Foreign books either published or planned for publication in 1990 and 1991 included Friedrich Hayek's *The Road to Serfdom*, Winston Churchill's *The Second World War*, the selected speeches of Ronald Reagan, articles and speeches by Pope Paul II, and Milovan Djilas on *The Face of Totalitarianism*. This latter period also saw an entirely new body of translated literature on the themes of entrepreneurship and the market. In 1991, planned translations from English into Russian included such titles as *How to Become Enterprising and Rich – with American Methods*, *Self-confidence on the Road to Business Success*, *How to Settle the Problems of Marketing*, a *Commercial Dictionary* and much else of a similar kind. All the books just mentioned had been published or planned for publication before, and not after, the coup of 1991; that is, they were products of the Gorbachev era.

These examples should be enough in themselves to demonstrate the headway which media freedom had made since 1985. By the summer of 1991 it would have been impossible, in any meaningful sense, to describe the USSR as a 'totalitarian' state. And indeed the failure of the August coup was, to an important extent, the result of this. Neither Soviet journalists nor the Soviet public were any longer prepared passively to accept a return to the old order. Even during the two days that the plotters were in power they did not have it all their own way with the press. *Pravda*, for example, carried an item on 20 August which referred to Yeltsin's call for a general strike; and *Izvestiya* on the same day printed an extra edition with extensive reporting of the opposition to the coup. The very fact of this reaction was eloquent testimony in itself to the effect that *glasnost'* had produced on Soviet public opinion.

The Media Legislation of 1990

Until the summer of 1990, although *de facto* media freedom had largely arrived, there was no legal framework to guarantee this freedom and prevent it from being reversed. As far back as 1968 Academician Andrei Sakharov had rejected the mere liberalisation of the censorship as an adequate reform and suggested a law which, as he put it, 'would clearly and convincingly define what can and what cannot be printed'. That proposal was not implemented until 1

August 1990, when a Soviet law 'On the press and other media of mass information' finally came into effect. Following the demise of the USSR, the law itself seems to have lapsed. Nevertheless it remains important, not only as a historical watershed but as a benchmark for the future. (Specifically Russian media legislation, on similar lines, was adopted in December 1991 after extensive debate and the modification of some of its original provisions; its full implications lie outside the scope of this chapter.)

The 1990 law (which applied to what were called 'information media', that is, films, radio, television and periodicals, but not, apparently, to books) ran to seven chapters and broke new ground in several important ways. It effectively legitimised the voicing of anti-communist views and officially removed the media from Communist Party supervision. It gave a role for the first time to the courts in settling disputes over the law's interpretation. Finally the sanctions which it laid down for breaking the law did not include imprisonment.

Article 1 of the law said that censorship of the mass media was impermissible. The only limits to free expression were those laid down in Article 5, which forbade the disclosure of state or other legally protected secrets, appeals for the overthrow or forcible change of the existing state or social system, the propaganda of war, violence or racial, national or religious intolerance, the spreading of pornography or the use of the media in the furtherance of acts punishable under the criminal law. Article 5 also included guarantees against the defamation of individuals or the infringement of their privacy.

The second part of the law provided that newspapers (or broadcasting stations or other 'information media' as the case might be) could be set up not only by organisations but by individual Soviet citizens above the age of 18 (Article 7). One of the law's key provisions was that 'information media' had as a rule to be registered with a specified all-Union or local authority (Article 8). However registration was not necessary in the case of material intended for private circulation only, or in the case of publications with a print-run of less than 1,000 copies (Article 10). This dispensation was of great importance, since it effectively legalised *samizdat*. Registration, that is permission to publish, could be refused only on three grounds: (1) that the title or editorial aims of the publication appeared to run counter to the restrictions on free expression laid down in Article 5 and summarised above; (2) that another publication had already been registered under the same name; or (3) that a decision to terminate the particular publication had already been made and had come into force within the previous year (Article 11).

So far as the banning of newspapers and other outlets was concerned, the 1990 law provided that a publication or 'information medium' could be closed down against its will where, for the second time within a year, it contravened the restrictions on free expression in Article 5 (Article 13). However Article 14 gave a right of appeal to a court against both a refusal to register a publication and a decision to close it down. The illegal publication of unregistered material could be punished by a fine of up to 500 rubles, imposed by a court, together with the destruction of the print-run. A repetition of the offence could be punished by a fine of up to 1,000 rubles and by confiscation of the offender's printing press or other equipment. However, as already stated, imprisonment was not one of the sanctions.

Another innovation of the 1990 law was that it set out to define the rights and mutual obligations of founders of publications, editors and journalists. Founders, for example, were given the right to decide the 'basic principles' of activity, while editors were given 'professional autonomy' in implementing these principles (Article 15). A journalist had certain specific duties, such as the duty to check the accuracy of the information supplied to him (Article 32). He also acquired certain new rights; in particular he could refuse to let his name be used in any material which in his opinion had been distorted in the course of editing (Article 30). Considering the record of the Soviet media before 1985, this right appeared to be far from trivial.

Another innovation of the 1990 law was that it gave individuals or organisations a right to reply to inaccurate information which cast a slur on their 'honour and dignity' (Article 26). If the offending publication refused to publish a correction within a month, they could take the publishers to court (Article 27). This provision was put to the test very soon after its enactment when a member of the Congress of People's Deputies, Galina Starovoitova, sued both *Pravda* and TASS for falsely reporting that she had advocated 'physical reprisals' against political opponents. On 4 February 1991 a Moscow court found in her favour and ordered the defendants to apologise. They do not appear to have obeyed the court order, but successful litigation in a Soviet court against *Pravda* and TASS was itself unprecedented.

A further change in the law which broke entirely new ground was to be found in Article 33, which gave Soviet citizens a 'right of access to information from foreign sources, including direct television broadcasting, radio and the press'. The apparent effect of this was to make the jamming of foreign broadcasts illegal, besides removing the traditional ban on the circulation of foreign newspaper and books. It would be difficult to imagine a more complete reversal of earlier Soviet policy.

The law just described was, certainly until the coup of August

1991, the main Soviet statute governing freedom of expression. Admittedly it suffered from certain limitations. In particular, although Article 5 forbade the disclosure of state and other secrets, it did not define what constituted a state secret. (The then Supreme Soviet had originally declared its intention to provide the necessary definition, but this intention was never fulfilled.) Another limitation arose from the power of both the President and the Supreme Soviet to declare a state of emergency under certain conditions; and this power included a right to impose controls over the media. Nevertheless – and this was perhaps its most important feature – the law completely eliminated the arbitrary control over information which the party hierarchy had previously exercised. For the very first time a set of rules, however imperfect, was drawn up to define media freedom.

Problems of the Media Law, 1990–1

How then did the law operate in practice? It unquestionably ran into problems, some although not all of which have now passed into history. But it was already clear that the advent of openness or media freedom had, in some ways at least, become irreversible.

The first set of problems largely arose, as we can now see, from the impending disintegration of the Soviet Union. This in itself imposed strains on the media, above all on Soviet television. The year 1990 had seen a rash of declarations of sovereignty, or in some cases of outright independence, by the newly elected parliaments of the republics – who then insisted that their own laws took precedence over Soviet laws. Boris Yeltsin's election as Chairman of the Russian parliament on 29 May in that year was followed by a prolonged confrontation between him and Mikhail Gorbachev. In the winter of 1990–1, Gorbachev moved visibly towards the conservatives, evidently in an effort to halt the break-up of the USSR. He appointed a new head of Soviet television, Leonid Kravchenko, who imposed tight editorial controls. (Kravchenko was eventually sacked following the August 1991 coup for cooperating with the plotters.) Complaints that the freedom of television was being curtailed reached a peak after the shootings by Soviet troops in Vilnius on 13 January 1991. On that day, and for some time afterwards, the main Moscow television news programme, *Vremya*, reported that Soviet troops had not been the first to open fire – a claim which was flatly contradicted by the evidence of a number of foreign journalists on the spot. Gorbachev for a time seemed to support the official story; then, on 16 January, he made a suggestion in parliament (which he almost immediately withdrew) that the 1990 media law should be temporarily suspended. In the end the operation of the law was referred to one of the committees of the USSR Supreme Soviet and little ensued.

There were also some fears among Soviet journalists that press freedom was in danger. This was particularly reflected in a conflict between the editor of *Izvestiya* and his staff (the paper was at that time the organ of the Presidium of the USSR Supreme Soviet: it became independent after the August coup). It should be added, however, that a number of Soviet newspapers (notably *Moscow News* and *Literaturnaya gazeta*) as well as the newly-founded Russian radio station, *Radio Rossii*, put out reports openly contradicting the official account of the Vilnius shootings. Indeed the Soviet press was one of the main sources of information about attempts to reimpose censorship. Finally, on 13 May 1991, following a rapprochement between Gorbachev and Yeltsin, the Russian Republic was finally given its own television channel – a six-and-a-half-hour daily programme including a news bulletin (known as *Vesti*) whose political slant differed markedly from that of all-Union Soviet television. Media pluralism had finally arrived.

Now that the break-up of the Soviet Union is an accomplished fact, the problems just described are a thing of the past. But a second problem for the media, which is unlikely to disappear so quickly, is that of the transition to market conditions. The full shock of this transition hit Russia as a whole only on 2 January 1992, when prices were finally decontrolled. It is of course too early to predict how this will eventually affect the country's media. However the first effects of the transition to the market had been felt by the Soviet press a year earlier. From the start of 1991 the price of newsprint began to rise steeply (according to *Pravda*, it went up more than threefold, from 424 to 1,300 rubles a ton) and the rise in price has continued. Charges for the postal distribution of newspapers also rose, having apparently been unchanged since 1939; and, for the first time in living memory, Soviet readers had to do without Sunday newspapers. The prices of *Pravda* and *Izvestiya* doubled, having been virtually unaltered since the 1920s.

From the start of 1991 the newsprint allocation and print-run of a newspaper depended on the scale of readers' subscriptions, with the result that Communist Party publications began to lose revenue and independent ones gained. (In the past, Soviet newspapers had been heavily subsidised – and newspapers had relatively little need to cater for readers' tastes, since party members were under a semi-official obligation to subscribe to party newspapers.) However, in the new situation of soaring costs, even the independent publications sometimes suffered. The mass-circulation weekly, *Argumenty i fakty*, had to quadruple its price at the start of 1991 and because of the resulting loss of readers it had to reduce its print-run from over 33 million copies at the end of 1990 to just over 24 million at the start of the following year. The paper noted that, 'in exchange for the censorship which has vanished into the past, economic sanctions have arrived'. There is no sign that these 'economic sanctions' are about to end.

A third problem for the media, which has still finally to be resolved, concerns the disposal of the Communist Party's assets, which were confiscated after the failure of the August 1991 coup. Even before the coup, the question of these assets had been a subject of heated debate. One of the main complaints of the then opposition in Russia about the 1990 media law was that, despite its guarantees of free expression, it left the ownership of media facilities largely in the same hands as before; that is, in the hands of the Communist Party. Therefore, so the opposition then argued, the authorities still retained an overwhelming economic leverage against newspapers seeking political independence.

Communist Party control over the media had been axiomatic until 1990. The party itself, at its final, 28th Congress in July 1990, admitted to owning 144 publishing houses and to providing printing facilities for 406 newspapers and 286 journals. But this almost certainly understated the full extent of its power over the media, because the party had until then controlled virtually all the 8,000 or more newspapers throughout the country; it had in many cases exercised control in nominal partnership with local soviets, and the question of ownership had often been unclear. The value of the party's undoubtedly enormous assets had been semi-officially given – by Arkadii Volsky, a one-time adviser to Gorbachev – as approximately four billion rubles in August 1991. But, even assuming that this was a fair estimate, valuation is likely to be difficult. One can only guess what price the buildings or their contents would fetch, assuming that there were willing buyers on a hypothetical free market. And it would be even harder to ascertain what proportion of those assets was legitimate (for example, derived from membership dues) and what proportion had been unfairly acquired (remembering that, for over 70 years, party premises had been used without payment of rent or taxes). In the event, the question was summarily decided by government action. The Russian Communist Party was suspended on Russian territory on 23 August 1991, just after the coup, and the Soviet Communist Party was permanently dissolved in Russia on 6 November. The legality of this ban is open to doubt, since under the law on 'public associations' a political party could be dissolved against its will only by the decision of a court – which the authorities did not attempt to obtain. It remains to be seen whether the party does eventually reemerge. But, as of 1991, the Communist Party was deprived of its assets.

Immediately after the coup, on 23 August 1991, Yeltsin issued a decree suspending *Pravda* and five other newspapers accused of supporting the coup. This decree was cancelled on 10 September, but the Communist Party lost its right to publish. *Pravda*, on the initiative of its staff, was reregistered under the 1990 media law as an independent newspaper: it came back onto the streets on 31 August, after a gap of only eight days. Other former party newspapers reregistered in a similar way, under non-communist auspices. However *Pravda*, in particular, lost its security of tenure over the premises from which it operated; as early as September 1991, it complained that it no longer owned even the desks on which its journalists wrote, and by December 1991 it found itself obliged to share its accommodation with other occupants. By the end of the year the paper's own prospects of survival were in some doubt. What was already clear, however, was that the former Communist Party publishing houses – and much of the power that went with them – had effectively been placed under the control of the post-coup Russian leadership. It remains to be seen whether they are eventually parcelled out among newspapers of genuinely different points of view. Whether this happens will of course be of crucial importance in determining whether Russia gets a genuinely pluralistic press in the future.

Glasnost': The Historical Perspective

The end of 1991, which saw the resignation of Mikhail Gorbachev, the dissolution of the USSR and the beginning of 'post-communist' rule in Russia, marked the end of a whole chapter in the country's history. No attempt will be made here to speculate on what will happen to the Russian media in these entirely new conditions. One need only point out the rather obvious fact that the main threat to media freedom in the former USSR comes not from local difficulties but from the threat of the country's total economic collapse. Economic collapse would threaten media freedom for the simple reason that it would endanger the country's embryonic democracy. One might note that even during the Gorbachev era freedom of speech, for all its enormous benefits, did have disturbing side-effects. The advent of free information after more than 70 years undermined not only dictatorship but also authority in general. It produced revelations about the Soviet past which came as a severe shock to many Russians; and it played a major part in activating nationalism among the country's non-Russian peoples. (The most dramatic example of this was the rise of Baltic separatism following the publication of the secret protocols to the Nazi–Soviet Pact of 1939 which had assigned the Baltic states to the Soviet sphere of influence.) One undoubted effect of *glasnost'* was to unleash forces which were not merely pluralistic but centrifugal. That in turn aggravated the economic paralysis and contributed to the general decline in public morale. All in all, it is not difficult to see why the Gorbachev reforms were so much more admired abroad than they were at home. For the average Soviet citizen, *glasnost'* meant little more than an unprecedented freedom to complain about an almost unprecedented drop in living standards, as well as a particularly tyrannical history.

But when viewed in a historical perspective, *glasnost'* may well appear in a much more positive light. We may sum up the main conclusions of this chapter as follows:

1. *Glasnost'* was not merely a piece of improvisation. In 1986, it was launched quite deliberately from the top (and not under pressure from below) as a lever for democratic political reform.
2. It was not of itself synonymous with either democracy or with free speech. But it was a crucially important *bridge* to these things. The strategy of extending freedom of information in order to exert pressure on conservative opponents of reform was one of the distinctive features of Gorbachev's style of government. It was one of the main reasons why the dismantling of the old system occurred in such a relatively bloodless way.
3. The foundations for media freedom had already been laid by the summer of 1991, well before the August coup. The achievement therefore belongs to the Gorbachev era and not to the era of his successors.
4. Finally, *glasnost'* has, in important ways, almost certainly become irreversible. The danger of authoritarian control over the media admittedly cannot be ruled out in the years ahead. It is conceivable that future Russian leaders may be less committed to free expression than Gorbachev was. The threat to freedom as a result of economic crisis has already been pointed out. And it should also be remembered that capitalist ownership of the media is not, of itself, an invariable safeguard against dictatorship – as the experience of Latin America and many other third-world countries has shown. Indeed government harassment and the threat of financial ruin for privately owned newspapers which persistently fall foul of the authorities can be highly effective weapons in the hands of dictators.

But what is unlikely in the extreme is any return of the former Soviet Union to the pre-1985 'totalitarian' stereotype, where the authorities maintained the fiction of a 'unanimous' public opinion and imposed a positive duty on journalists to praise government policies. No future Russian regime would have very much rational incentive to go back to that earlier system, because it would lack all credibility with its own public. Today, as a result of *glasnost'*, the awareness of millions of citizens in the former USSR has been transformed beyond recognition. That is a fact which can no longer be reversed. In this sense, it is already too late to undo the consequences of *glasnost'*.

PART THREE

Patterns of Public Policy

10

Economic Crisis and Reform

PETER RUTLAND

Six years after Gorbachev took office, his programme of economic reform had clearly been overtaken by political and economic disintegration. On 18 December 1990, shortly before his resignation, Prime Minister Nikolai Ryzhkov bluntly stated that 'In the form originally conceived, *perestroika* has failed.' The attempted coup of August 1991 was a reaction to this political and economic collapse, and to the failure of Gorbachev's policies. The coup itself accelerated these centrifugal forces, and it is too early to judge what sort of new political and economic order will emerge from the wreckage.

What is clear, however, is the magnitude of the task facing the new leadership. The system of central planning which Stalin imposed in the 1930s, at tremendous human cost, ground on for five decades and totally reshaped the economy of the USSR in all its aspects: geography, institutions, social structure and psychology. After 1985, the old system started to break down. The power of central planners steadily eroded, with enterprises and republics behaving in an increasingly independent manner. From 1988, the previous macroeconomic and foreign trade balance of the Soviet economy also broke down. These processes have left the post-Soviet economy in an institutional vacuum: it is neither a market nor a planned economy, but a curious hybrid whose laws of operation are as yet unclear.

The Origins of the Soviet Economic System

How was it possible that the world's second superpower, capable of conquering space and building a formidable arsenal of nuclear weapons, was unable to feed its own people and provide them with the basic necessities of modern urban life? In order to grasp the paradoxes of the Soviet economy, it is necessary to view it in its historical context.

After the 1930s the USSR operated under a centrally planned economy (CPE). This was a highly distinctive form of economic organisation in which the conventional laws of supply and demand, taken for granted in the West, did not apply. The CPE was a result of a violent political struggle, a 'revolution from above', in which *property rights* were taken away from social classes and vested in the state.

Stalin tried to establish a state monopoly over all forms of economic activity. Private ownership of productive assets (stores, workshops, farms, tools and factories) was abolished, to the maximum feasible extent. All such assets became the property of the state, managed by centrally appointed directors. No capitalist economy has ever approached the level of state monopoly found in the USSR, where the state exercised ownership rights over more than 97 per cent of legally permitted economic activity.

There were of necessity some exceptions to this state monopolisation. For example, labour itself remained the property of the individual, although at times up to 20 per cent of the labour force were in camps or in exile and thus in effect state property. Also laws requiring all adults to work and exercising close control over personal mobility restricted individuals' property rights over their own bodies.

The CPE model had its roots in Marx's vision of a unified economy which would run itself like a giant factory, free from the anarchy of the capitalist market. Lenin was impressed by the achievements of central planning in the German economy during the First World War, but his scattered writings on economics added little of substance to Marx's vision. The New Economic Policy (NEP) which Lenin persuaded the Communist Party to accept in 1921 was a retreat from the utopian Marxist vision. NEP replaced state food requisitioning with a market in grain and thus recognised the need for the state and private sectors to coexist (at least in the short run).

In 1928, Stalin abandoned NEP and set out to construct an economic system which would guarantee the CPSU's monopoly of political power and enable him to impose his development goals on the economy. He wanted to break the peasants' control over resource allocation decisions – by refusing to sell grain to the towns if consumer goods were overpriced, for example. Stalin drove the peasants into collective farms (*kolkhozy*) at a cost of several million lives. The *kolkhozy* were nominally run as cooperatives but in reality were closely controlled by local party officials, and were obliged to meet state grain requisition quotas. Before the 1950s peasants rarely received any income from the *kolkhoz* and sustained themselves from the small private plots that they were allowed to retain.

During the first five year plan (1928–32) Stalin launched the USSR on the path of 'extensive' growth, pumping capital and labour out of agriculture and consumer goods production and pouring it into heavy industry. Developing a network of coalmines, steel mills and power stations was seen as the key to economic accumulation – and to military preparedness. 'Intensive' growth (expansion of production, thanks to the more efficient use of resources) made only a marginal contribution to Soviet economic development. But with the vast natural and human resources of the USSR, an extensive growth strategy could produce impressive results. By 1940 it is estimated that the defence sector accounted for 40 per cent of Soviet economic activity, and the USSR went into the Second World War with more tanks, artillery and aircraft than Nazi Germany, all produced from her own factories.

Stalin's industrialisation strategy turned the USSR into the world's second largest economy, but Soviet citizens saw precious few of the benefits. Real living standards halved during the 1930s, and only regained the 1928 level by the late 1950s. By 1960 it was clear to the Soviet leadership that the scope for further extensive growth was exhausted. Capital accumulation was at maximum levels and the labour reserves of the country were fully mobilised. The decline of the rural economy meant that the USSR became a net importer of food in 1963, despite the fact that 30 per cent of the population still worked the land. Popular pressure for improved living conditions was mounting, as shown by the riots in Novocherkassk in southern Russia in 1962. Attention turned to reforms designed to shift the Soviet economy onto a path of intensive growth.

Through the 1960s and 1970s, however, things continued pretty much as before. The annual growth rate slowly declined, from a respectable 6.5 per cent in 1961–5 to 2 per cent in 1976–85, with the bulk of this modest growth *still* coming from extensive sources. At least during the Brezhnev era (1964–82) consumers saw their living standards start to improve. A steady 3–4 per cent annual rise meant a rough doubling of living standards between 1960 and 1980. Most families acquired a television and refrigerator, although only one in twenty owned a car.

Economic Performance

The economic stability of the USSR during the Brezhnev years was misleading: the USSR was living on borrowed time. Resources were

poured into maintaining high output levels in heavy industry and
defence plants, while investment in the social and economic infrastructure was neglected. For example, the shortage of storage capacity and poor roads meant that 20–30 per cent of the harvest was lost
between field and market.

Even in heavy industry, the most obvious beneficiary of the
Stalinist growth model, the capital stock was outdated and in need of
replacement. Despite the fact that 40 per cent of GNP was being
ploughed back into investment, the average Soviet machine tool was
seventeen years old, as opposed to eight years in the USA.

Soviet economic achievements, in other words, were a house built
on sand. The crunch came in the late 1970s, with crises in agriculture,
transport and energy. The exhaustion of easily accessible coal and oil
deposits led Brezhnev to launch hugely expensive projects in oil, gas,
coal and hydroelectric and atomic power. At the same time, Brezhnev and his allies in the big-spending ministries and regional party
organisations forged ahead with costly prestige projects such as the
Baikal–Amur railway and the 1982 'Food Programme'. Squeezed to
the limit by these massive and unproductive investments, the economy stalled (see Table 10.1). There was probably zero overall
growth between 1980 and 1985 (although this was disguised in the
official statistics). After 1978 rationing of key food items was introduced in many outlying regions.

By the time Gorbachev came to power, it was clear that the sorry
state of the economy threatened the status of the USSR as a

TABLE 10.1 *Soviet economic performance, 1971–88 (average annual rates
of growth, percentages)*

	1971–75	1976–80	1981–85	1986	1987	1988
GNP	3.2	2.2	1.9	4.0	1.3	1.5
Industry	5.6	2.4	2.0	2.7	2.9	2.4
Agriculture	−0.1	1.6	2.1	8.3	−3.1	−3.1
Consumption per capita	3.0	2.0	0.8	−1.5	1.0	1.5
Investment	7.8	3.4	3.5	8.3	4.7	n.a.
Labour productivity	1.4	1.0	1.4	2.3	3.2	3.1

Sources: These data are CIA estimates, taken from *The Soviet Economy in 1988*:
Gorbachev Changes Course, a paper presented to the National Security Economic
Subcommittees of the Joint Economic Committee, US Congress, 14 April 1989.
Figures for agriculture 1971–80 are taken from *Narodnoe khozyaistvo SSSR v 1987g.*
(Moscow: Finansy i statistika, 1988).

superpower. By 1980 the USSR had lost its claim to be the world's second largest economy, having been overtaken by Japan (with half the population and none of the USSR's vast natural resources). As measured by crude output figures, by 1986 the USSR occupied first place in the world league table only in the production of oil, steel, iron ore, potatoes and sugar – hardly the sinews of a twenty-first century superpower. It occupied sixth place in the production of radios (just behind Singapore) and of passenger cars (behind Italy and France). Given what is known about poor product quality, false plan reporting and the general unreliability of Soviet statistics, the real situation was much worse than these raw figures suggested.

The flood of information since *glasnost'* has provided a clear picture of the plight of the Soviet consumer. Purchasing power comparisons show the average Soviet citizen's living standard to be roughly 25 per cent of that prevailing in the developed capitalist economies. One has to go to a country such as Turkey or Mexico to find a comparison favourable to the USSR. Despite official propaganda to the contrary, this low level of personal consumption was not compensated by the social welfare benefits provided by the state. Health care spending was only 4 per cent of GNP (compared to 8–10 per cent in the West) and the USSR occupied fiftieth place in the world in terms of infant mortality, just behind Barbados. Income distribution was seriously skewed, with 40 per cent of the population living at or below the official poverty line (which comes out at $100 at the official exchange rate or $5 at the rate prevailing in currency auctions).

Basic items such as meat, butter, sugar, coffee, soap and toothpaste have continued to be in short supply, and are rationed in many areas. In late 1990, Ukraine introduced ration books for food. By October 1991 meat was rationed in 56 of Russia's 72 regions and bread in 18. The deficit of consumer durables during the 1970s meant that consumers accumulated 280 billion rubles in savings accounts, up from 47 billion in 1970. This sum is equivalent to seven months' retail spending, and is clearly a major cause of the persistent goods 'famine'.

Yet another bombshell hit the Soviet public in October 1988, when the Finance Minister revealed that the government was running a 36 billion ruble budget deficit on a 500 billion ruble budget, a sum equal to 7.3 per cent of Soviet GNP. If an army marches on its stomach, then a state marches on its budget. A breakdown in budgetary balance can radically undermine the capacity of any system of government to survive. Just such a budgetary breakdown seems to have been an important causal factor in the collapse of Soviet communism. Why did it occur?

Previously, one of the few advantages of the CPE had been tight control over the government budget. This central discipline eroded after 1985, largely as a result of increasingly erratic behaviour by the political leadership, who subjected the bureaucracies to a series of bewildering reorganisations. Also production costs were steadily rising, while prices were held constant. The gap was filled with government subsidies (for example, food subsidies rose from two billion rubles in 1965 to 73 billion rubles in 1990). In 1988, for example, in the wake of a relaxation of wages policy, average pay shot up by 7 per cent, while output rose only 1.5 per cent.

After 1985 these structural imbalances were compounded by a series of exogenous shocks. The exchequer lost 40 billion rubles in revenue as a result of falling world oil prices and 36 billion rubles because of cutbacks in alcohol production. Cleaning up after Chernobyl and the Armenian earthquake cost another 20 billion rubles. The Rand Corporation estimates that subsidies to Soviet client states doubled in the early 1980s, costing 37 billion rubles (5 per cent of Soviet GNP) between 1980 and 1983.

It was clear, however, that the Soviet economy was not merely suffering from poor political leadership. Nor was it facing a cyclical crisis that would clear up on its own accord after a few years. The economy had experienced a long-run, secular decline in economic efficiency, which in turn was the product of deep-seated contradictions within the CPE system. These forces brought the economy to the point of collapse, yet also created a complex pattern of economic interdependence, in which all the major economic actors had a vested interest in trying to maintain the *status quo*.

The System of Central Planning

At the centre of the CPE stood the State Planning Committee, Gosplan, which coordinated the work of the 60 economic ministries. The ministries allocated production targets to enterprises in the form of an annual plan. (The famous five year plan was little more than a forecasting exercise.)

This system of central planning was incredibly complicated and difficult to manage. Over time, however, it evolved certain rules of the game which enable it to operate in a predictable fashion. Planners behaved incrementally, making marginal adjustments to the previous year's plans.

Parallel to the economic bureaucracies were a network of political agencies through which the national leadership tried to enforce its priorities. The Communist Party had units in every farm and factory, and regional party officials used their political muscle to play a trouble-shooting role in the local economy: helping a factory acquire scarce supplies, persuading factory directors to help with the harvest, and so forth. Generally speaking, territorial coordination was poor, since the ministries' monopoly of material and financial resources enabled them to override the wishes of local soviets.

The huge quantity of information flowing through the planning system had to be simplified and made manageable. The planners relied on crude, physical measures of output (thousands of cars, tons of coal) and managers knew that output targets had to be met first, even if it was at the expense of other goals set by their ministry (such as introducing new products or conserving energy). Crude physical targets may have been suitable in the 1930s, when the economy revolved around a few simple products (coal, oil and steel), but they were grossly inappropriate for a modern economy.

Money played virtually no role in the CPE. Prices were fixed by planners and bore little relation to production costs. For example, retail prices covered only about one-third of the cost of producing food. Managers faced what Hungarian economist Janos Kornai has termed a 'soft budget constraint': they knew that, if their firm failed to make a profit at the end of the year, the ministry would transfer funds to cover their notional losses.

The biggest headache facing Soviet managers on a daily basis was the unreliability of supplies. The Soviet economy seemed to operate under conditions of 'permanent shortage' and any interruption in deliveries could halt production. Factories worked according to a bizarre rhythm, speeding up to fever pitch during the last month of the year when the supply deliveries finally arrived.

While the USSR enjoyed some spectacular technological successes such as Sputnik, in general it lagged six to ten years behind the USA and Japan in leading-edge electronics and computer technology. Managers had few financial incentives to introduce a new product or production technique, and were discouraged by the need to get all innovations approved through a cumbersome bureaucratic procedure which could drag on for years.

The CPE suited some economic sectors better than others. Mining and heavy manufacturing industries did not fare too badly, because production activity was fairly simple and repetitive, and thus easy to plan. However sectors such as agriculture, construction and consumer goods and services, which required flexibility and adaptability to local conditions, were all severely deformed. In the Soviet economy producers were 'sovereign' and consumer interests were virtually ignored. So few household goods were produced that consumers were glad to get what they could, whatever its quality. Because prices were artificially low, goods were swept off the shelves as soon as they appeared.

Reform Attempts before Gorbachev

Economic reform did not appear on the national agenda for the first time with Gorbachev's arrival in office in 1985. On the contrary, the structural failings of the CPE had been analysed fairly openly in Soviet economics journals and in the popular press since the early 1960s.

Khrushchev experimented with a broad range of reforms, the most ambitious being an attempt to decentralise power from the national ministries to 102 regional economic councils. Such reforms were hasty and poorly designed, and were reversed after his fall from power in 1964. In 1965, Prime Minister Kosygin tried to increase enterprise independence by replacing output targets with a number of financial indicators, such as profits. Brezhnev was lukewarm in his support of the reform, however, and the measure was killed at the implementation stage by ministry bureaucrats hostile to the changes.

The next major reform came in 1973, with the grouping of enterprises into broader industrial associations, resembling capitalist firms, with the idea again being to reduce ministerial interference in factory life. In practice the reform merely served to complicate the chain of command without breaking the planners' addiction to output targets. Other reforms followed, such as the attempt to introduce value-added planning in 1979, without any visible impact on economic efficiency.

What changed with the arrival of Gorbachev was not, therefore, a new diagnosis of the USSR's economic ills, nor a new set of prescriptions about how to cure them. Rather Gorbachev's confident style initially persuaded people that this time around the reform measures would actually be implemented. Khrushchev's reform style was wilful and eccentric. Brezhnev's reforms avoided sensitive issues in order to preserve political stability and were abandoned at the first signs of bureaucratic resistance. Gorbachev gave the impression that, unlike his predecessors, he would be able to take tough decisions and overcome vested interests.

Gorbachev's Economic Reforms

The Learning Phase, 1985–6

Gorbachev's six-year struggle to reform the Soviet political and economic system seems to have ended in failure. His reforms led, not to the revival of the Soviet system, but to its disintegration. Among the reasons for this lack of success must surely be Gorbachev's failure to embark upon serious economic reform.

Gorbachev chose to begin with political rather than economic reform – in marked contrast to the strategy followed by the Chinese leadership since 1978. While his political liberalisation spiralled beyond his control, his economic reforms never really materialised. As time wore on, Gorbachev became more resolute in his verbal commitment to radical economic reform. By 1988 he was using the taboo word 'market', although until 1990 it was invariably qualified by terms like 'planned' or 'regulated'. Unfortunately Gorbachev proved unable or unwilling to persuade the all-Union Supreme Soviet, and later the leadership of the republics, to implement his economic plans.

Historians will argue over whether *perestroika* was doomed to failure because the obstacles to its success were too great or whether Gorbachev himself can be blamed for failing to grasp the enormity of the changes required. Now that Gorbachev has failed, both sides can claim victory. His detractors will say that this proves *perestroika* was unworkable, while his defenders will argue that he did not have enough time to succeed.

When Gorbachev took office in March 1985, it seems clear from his early speeches that he did *not* think a radical overhaul of the system of central planning was required. His initial strategy was to redouble efforts behind the 'acceleration' of economic growth, by shifting investment resources from costly irrigation projects into the machine tool sector. Thus Gorbachev's initial approach to reform was traditional, with campaigns launched and monitored from the centre. Shortly after taking office in 1985 he launched discipline campaigns against alcoholism and corruption. These measures had Stalinist overtones, but Gorbachev preserved a liberal image with his rhetorical invocation of the 'human factor'. The alcohol drive was a typical Brezhnevite campaign. It relied on massive publicity and police measures (2.7 million moonshiners arrested) and involved great haste and disruption (vineyards torn up, shops closed down). These campaigns succeeded in arresting thousands of officials and slashing alcohol sales by 40 per cent, but had no discernible impact on economic efficiency.

Another innovation typical of Gorbachev's centralist approach was the introduction of a new system of quality control, *Gospriemka*, in 1987. Teams of outside inspectors were placed in factories and told to rigorously apply state quality control standards, rejecting defective output and cutting performance bonuses. Previously factory inspectors were internally recruited and in no position to go against their directors and fellow workers. However the *Gospriemka* system was quietly abandoned, as managers and workers complained that they were doing the best they could with the resources made available to them. *Gospriemka* was another top-down, administrative response to a problem whose solution must lie in managers being answerable to their customers, and not to inspectors appointed from Moscow.

By mid-1986, in the wake of the Chernobyl catastrophe, Gorbachev started to acknowledge that some sort of radical restructuring (*perestroika*) of the economic mechanism was in order. The main thrust of the reform programme which emerged in an *ad hoc* fashion lay in three directions: decentralising decision making within the planning system; promoting new forms of ownership; and increasing reliance on international economic integration. Rather than abandon the CPE model entirely, the idea was to make it work more effectively by casting aside ideological dogmas and introducing greater flexibility in the design of institutions. Market-type forces were to be allowed a place within the CPE, but not until 1990 did Gorbachev start to talk openly about the need for a market economy.

Towards a New Planning System

The centrepiece of Gorbachev's plans for a reformed economy was the new Law on the State Enterprise, introduced in June 1987. This was a complex and contradictory measure, whose broad aim was to reduce ministerial interference and increase managerial freedom. Four years and a dozen supplementary decrees later, it is still not clear how much autonomy firms actually won under the new statute. The main elements can be summarised as follows:

1. Planners were to issue indirect guidelines and not detailed operational instructions. The State Planning Committee, Gosplan, would concentrate on strategic forecasting and planners would steer economic activity by setting rules for budget payments, wage allocation, taxation, contract penalties and credit. Investment was to be generated from ploughed-back profits and repayable credits, and new independent banks were to be created. Only projects involving brand-new products would be financed by central allocation of capital.
2. Enterprises would produce according to customer contracts and ministries would no longer issue output targets. However a new system of 'state orders' (*goszakazy*) was introduced. These were supposed to be reserved for priority commodities, but spread rapidly to cover 85 per cent of industrial output. Procurement targets continued to be set for farms.

3. Some prices would be centrally set, but others would be set by producers to reflect the laws of supply and demand ('contract prices' for industrial inputs and 'commercial prices' for consumer durables). Prices would have to rise, since current price levels did not reflect production costs. The idea of retail price increases proved to be politically controversial, however, and was not implemented.

4. Enterprises were to be granted real financial independence and in principle should become self-financing. Rules regarding payments into the ministry budget would be fixed in advance and firms would be left free to plough back profits into new equipment, social projects or bonuses.

5. The new law expanded the role of 'Work Collective Councils', giving them the right to elect the factory director. This was part of Gorbachev's general goal of democratising Soviet society, but led to many disputes between ministries and work collectives. A 1990 amendment to the law revoked the right to elect directors.

6. Central allocation of supplies was to be replaced by a system of wholesale trade, with firms free to purchase inputs from other firms or territorial supply agencies. By 1990 the agency concerned, *Gossnab*, had cut the number of centrally allocated products from 10,000 to 610.

7. The new system would need fewer bureaucrats, so the staff of the central ministries was cut by roughly one-third in 1988. In July 1989, the number of ministries was pruned from 80 to 60 (and only ten of the newly-appointed ministers had been in office before 1985). The sectoral departments through which CPSU Central Committee officials monitored ministries were abolished, as were the equivalent departments in regional and district party organisations.

The transition to the new system did not go smoothly. In fact with the benefit of hindsight one can say that the reform was a complete failure. Why were the results so negative? First, there was a problem of *timing*. The reforms were launched at the worst possible time, in the depths of an economic and fiscal crisis. (Cynics would argue that it is only in such a crisis that politicians summon up the courage to undertake reforms.) After ten years of virtually zero growth, the USSR was hit by a series of additional economic shocks – falling oil prices, Chernobyl, the Armenian earthquake, the alcohol campaign. Given the economic crisis, the Soviet leadership did not want to let the introduction of economic reform disrupt current production. They insisted on firms meeting their targets for the twelfth five year plan (1986–90), now enforced through the *goszakaz* system. This completely undermined the increased autonomy for firms which was supposed to be the keystone of the economic reform.

Second, the new system suffered from some serious *design flaws*. Several crucial issues, such as bankruptcy, unemployment and price reform, were fudged or ignored. There was no clear mechanism for winding up loss-making operations, and it is estimated that one in three farms and one in seven factories ran at a loss. (In fact, even by the end of 1991, there was no bankruptcy mechanism in place.) Ministries had little choice but to subsidise loss-making plants with funds taken from their more successful counterparts, robbing Peter to pay Paul. Similarly, few systematic measures (such as retraining programmes or public works schemes) were introduced to facilitate lay-offs of surplus workers.

It made no sense to try to give managers more freedom without a radical liberalisation of prices. This would mean increases of 200–300 per cent for virtually all commodities, to eliminate subsidies and make prices reflect production costs. For whatever reason (lack of economic understanding or lack of political courage) between 1985 and 1989 Gorbachev repeatedly postponed the promised price reform.

Promoting New Forms of Ownership

In 1987, new laws on cooperatives and 'individual labour activity' were introduced, designed to provide opportunities for hard work and initiative and to meet the pent-up demand for consumer goods and services. Private and cooperative cafés, boutiques, taxis and repair shops flourished, and by December 1988 they employed 787,000 (out of a workforce of 135 million).

This was a novel development for the USSR, but it was a far cry from the restoration of capitalism. While the cooperatives made the lot of the Soviet consumer a little easier, they remained hedged in by bureaucratic restrictions, such as price controls, strict licensing requirements and limitations on hiring labour. For example, only cooperatives, and not individuals, were allowed to run restaurants. Very few cooperatives were allowed to engage in manufacturing. In May 1988, the USSR Supreme Soviet made the first independent decision in its history, rejecting a proposed 90 per cent tax on cooperative profits. After that, some restrictions were relaxed, but others were subsequently reimposed (for example, on printing and medical cooperatives).

There was considerable opposition to the new entrepreneurs, both from state managers who did not appreciate the competition, and from citizens who saw the cooperatives as profiteering from shortages and as being fronts for laundering black-market fortunes. The cooperatives only really took root in the Baltic republics, Moscow and Leningrad. In most provinces, local officials were able to strangle the nascent cooperative movement in its cradle. The official trade unions, searching for a new role, leapt onto the anti-cooperative bandwagon, denouncing high prices and sending teams to monitor the distribution of food and consumer goods.

It was unlikely that the small 'private' sector which emerged under *perestroika* could grow independently into the kernel of an invading market economy. The successful cooperatives were those that found a niche within the interstices of the CPE. Some 80 per cent of cooperatives worked in construction or industrial supplies, and not in the consumer sector, and typically developed close, symbiotic ties with the state enterprise they serviced. By mid-1991, there were 4.5 million people working as private individuals, and another 4.5 million working in 255,000 cooperatives (plus two million part-time workers). This amounted to eleven million employees, or 8 per cent of the labour force, up from 2 per cent in 1988. This is a dramatic change for the USSR, but in a comparative context is not that remarkable: the CPEs of Poland, East Germany and Hungary had maintained a similar-sized private sector since the 1950s.

In marked contrast to the Chinese reform model, the new system of decentralised planning in the USSR left agricultural management virtually unchanged. Farms were still obliged to meet centrally allocated procurement quotas at fixed prices – although since 1990 they have been allowed to sell up to 30 per cent of the procurement quota in the free market.

In late 1988, Gorbachev started to push the idea of leasing land to individual farmers. The lease team, typically a family, was granted use of a plot of land for a given period (50 years according to August 1988 rules, for life under March 1989 proposals). Even as late as the Legislation on Land issued in February 1990, however, full private ownership of land was not allowed. Lease teams had to make fixed payments in kind to the leasing farm, but could then sell at free prices whatever they chose to grow. Such experiments dated back 40 years and demonstrated dramatic improvements in agricultural productivity. They had been stopped in the late 1960s because of opposition from party officials and farm directors. Gorbachev too found it hard to convince regional officials to press ahead with leasing. By 1989, 40 per cent of farms claimed to have some lease teams, but most of these existed only on paper. There were many ways in which farm managers could make life difficult for leaseholders, by denying them access to equipment, transport and fertiliser. Most peasants seemed wary of making a commitment to private farming, since they feared that the political wind could blow in the opposite direction a few years later.

Leasing of industrial units to teams of workers began in 1988, in emulation of Hungarian experience, and a legal framework was provided in 1989. Leaseholders tood advantage of lower tax rates and slacker wage norms to boost average wages, usually improving productivity in the process (but at a rate that lagged behind the wage increases). As with the cooperatives, it was very hard to tell whether leasing was really the shoots of the new sprouting from within the old, or whether it was just a new twist by factory managers, manoeuvring for autonomy within the disintegrating CPE.

Increased International Integration

The problems of economic reform seemed so daunting that several leading Soviet economists (such as Nikolai Shmelev) persuaded Gorbachev that the task could *only* be tackled with outside help. International factors could assist the reform process in a variety of ways. First, a transfusion of Western imports (from consumer goods to machine tools) would help keep the Soviet economy going through the dislocations which would accompany reform, and would provide incentives for managers and workers to embrace the new methods. Second, the monopolistic structure of Soviet industry made it difficult for planners to come up with fair and realistic prices. Making the ruble partially convertible and taking world prices as a benchmark would help shorten the adjustment period. Third, expanding cooperation with Western businesses should promote an influx of technology and know-how, and encourage Soviet firms to strive for the efficiency levels prevailing in global industry. In mid-1987, new liberal regulations were issued on joint ventures and a complete overhaul of the foreign trade system began in January 1988, breaking the former monopoly of the Ministry of Foreign Trade and allowing many Soviet firms to trade directly with Western partners. By early 1989 roughly one-third of all foreign trade was being conducted directly by enterprises.

These developments, encouraging though they were, ran into severe problems. Internationalisation was not a magic wand which could rescue the Soviet economy from its plight, which had been decades in the making. The Soviet economy was highly autarchic: only 10 per cent of GNP was traded, and two-thirds of that was with the former socialist bloc (the members of the Council of Mutual Economic Assistance, or CMEA). An abrupt change in this situation was unlikely, as Soviet export capacities were limited. The USSR ran a trade deficit in three of the four years 1987–90 and accumulated debts of $68 billion by 1991, up from $25 billion in 1985. It was doing all it could with its core exports (oil, gold and weapons accounted for 70 per cent of the total), but Soviet manufactures were not competitive in the West because of their low quality. Consumer goods imports were cut back in 1987, but in response to growing social unrest in 1989 a sum of 37 billion rubles, equivalent to 10 per cent of retail turnover, was allocated for the purchase of such items as soap, razors, cassettes and ladies' boots overseas.

The shortage of hard currency was also a problem for joint ventures, since they relied on reexports to generate their own hard currency earnings. Joint ventures also experienced difficulties with poor transport access, slack work discipline, unreliable supplies and bureaucratic obstacles, all of which make it harder to do business in the USSR than in Mexico or Thailand (where labour costs are lower too). Nevertheless the number of joint ventures rose from 23 in 1987 to 3,400 in April 1991, of which 948 were actually operating, with 117,000 employees and total capital of 7 billion rubles.

Unfortunately the liberalisation of foreign trade only worsened the situation. Joint ventures, for example, imported twice as much as they exported in the first quarter of 1991. A series of well-publicised scandals revealed that firms were exporting scarce materials (such as metals and fertiliser) from the state sector at bargain prices and importing consumer goods, computers and so forth in return.

Another way in which international developments could aid economic restructuring was in military affairs. In his speech to the United Nations in December 1988, Gorbachev announced unilateral cuts of 500,000 in the 3.2 million armed forces. In May 1989, he talked of a 15 per cent cut in defence spending, but not until December 1990 was a formal plan approved for the systematic *conversion* of defence plants to civilian production. The plan which emerged was extremely conservative, calling for vast additional investments to retool the factories according to centrally managed programmes (30 billion rubles over five years). Despite the promises to cut defence spending, even in 1991 there were few signs of serious cuts in the funding for defence plants, and civilian production at these plants merely crept up from 43 per cent in 1988 to 54 per cent in 1991.

The Struggle for Market Reform

The Perils of Perestroika

As *perestroika* unfolded, clear contradictions emerged between the political elements of the programme – *glasnost'* and democratisation – and the economic reforms. It was *not* a good idea to try to democratise a political system, while simultaneously launching a reform programme, in the middle of an economic crisis.

Glasnost' increased the opportunities for people to express their discontent with the economic situation. Investigative journalists filled the papers with articles showing people just how badly off they really were. They even turned up problems, such as infant mortality, which the public had not been aware of because of the suppression of official data. Gorbachev's own 'meet the people' tours, beginning with a visit to Krasnoyarsk in September 1988, brought him face to face with some very dissatisfied consumers, and presumably convinced him of the explosive situation in Soviet society.

The elections of March 1989 and 1990 saw humiliating defeats for Communist Party candidates, with 'anti-establishment' candidates capitalising on popular discontent with meat rationing, poor housing, pollution and corruption. In several Russian provinces and in the Baltic and Caucasian republics democratic and nationalist groups took control of local legislatures and even executive agencies, and were no longer prepared to do Gorbachev's bidding.

By 1989 it was clear that *perestroika* was not producing the hoped-for burst in economic growth. On the contrary, shortages of such basic items as sugar, meat, cheese, soap, washing powder, matches and cigarettes were spreading, as one after another they fell prey to panic buying and disappeared from the shops. In the summer of 1989, the deteriorating economic situation triggered a wave of strikes by some 500,000 coalminers. The government, acutely aware of its lack of popular authority, immediately capitulated to the miners' demands for improved pay and benefits. Strike threats from oil and steel workers won similar concessions in 1990. The main beneficiary of this wave of popular unrest was Boris Yeltsin, who managed to get himself elected as Chairman of the Russian parliament in May 1990, despite intense opposition from Gorbachev.

Thus, by pursuing *glasnost'* and democratisation, Gorbachev sowed a field of dragon's teeth for his *perestroika* programme. His political manoeuvrings were perhaps necessary for the consolidation of his own personal power, but they sharply reduced the leadership's ability to modify its economic policy. Political liberalisation made it far more difficult to take tough decisions that would hurt the interests of certain industrial sectors or social groups.

Gorbachev's vision of *perestroika* was of a carefully managed, step-by-step process, with himself playing a pivotal role, balancing the conflicting demands of the democratic left and the conservative right. As time wore on, Gorbachev found it increasingly difficult to maintain this balance, and his policy started to lurch violently from one side to the other.

The period 1989–90 saw a bewildering parade of economic reform proposals. Some were considered too radical, some not radical enough, but none found a consensus for action among the old and new political elites. Gorbachev became more vocal in his advocacy of reform, but repeatedly backed down in the face of conservative opposition.

The Battle of the Programmes

In July 1989, Gorbachev brought in Leonid Abalkin, a reform-minded economist, as Deputy Prime Minister to head a State Commission on Economic Reform. By November Abalkin's team had come up with a 'radical–moderate' plan to dismantle the central planning system and lift price controls (with compensation for consumers). However Prime Minister Nikolai Ryzhkov advanced his own programme, which was rejected in November 1989 by the USSR Supreme Soviet as too conservative.

In spring 1990, Gorbachev appointed several pro-reform economists to his inner circle, most notably Stanislav Shatalin, who joined the new Presidential Council. In his inaugural address as President on 15 March Gorbachev renewed his commitment to radical economic reform, and the same month a new Law on Ownership put state and collective ownership on an equal footing and opened the door to small-scale private enterprises.

The Abalkin team published a new, more ambitious plan in March, entitled 'Basic propositions for turning the economy into one based on market relations'. Ryzhkov again rejected Abalkin's proposals, and in May 1990 presented an alternative plan for a gradual transition to a 'regulated market economy'. Ryzhkov's main concern was to stem the growing budget deficit. He intended to cut food subsidies from 130 billion to 45 billion rubles by tripling the price of bread on 1 July, and raising other food prices by 100–200 per cent on 1 January 1991. Consumers would be compensated with a 15 per cent salary rise, or a grant of 40 rubles a month. This macro stabilisation programme would not, however, be accompanied by an immediate liberalisation of the planning system: the system of *goszakazy* was to be maintained until 1992. The USSR Supreme Soviet rejected the Ryzhkov plan on 14 June 1990, on the grounds that it was Polish-style 'shock therapy' without any real structural reform to sweeten the pill. This humiliating defeat made it clear that the Ryzhkov government had lost its political credibility.

Over the summer, Soviet and Western economists set to work on a programme capable of meeting the various conflicting demands being made on Gorbachev. At one point six different teams of economists were closeted in various dachas working on draft programmes, under the auspices of different government agencies.

Gorbachev's rhetoric shifted in favour of radical reform. He told the 28th Party Congress on 10 July that 'The old approach brought the country to the brink of bankruptcy', and 'All the world's experience has shown the advantages of the market.' In a speech to military leaders on 17 August he used the word 'privatisation' for the first time.

Shatalin now headed a group working for Boris Yeltsin, Gorbachev's bitter political rival, and he worked up a new version of a '400 days' plan prepared by radical economist Grigorii Yavlinsky. In June, Shatalin presented to the Russian parliament his '500 days' plan, officially entitled 'Transition to the market: Conception and programme'. Key elements of the Shatalin plan were as follows:

Days 1–100   – abolish ministries and plan targets;
             – abolish all subsidies to loss-making enterprises;
             – encourage private farming;
             – create an independent central bank along the lines of the federal reserve system;
             – move towards a unified ruble exchange rate;
             – cut spending on defence (10 per cent), KGB (20 per cent) and foreign aid (75 per cent);
             – preserve a unified, open market across the USSR.
Days 101–250 – create joint-stock companies;
             – privatise half the shops and cafes;
             – phase out price controls, while indexing wages;
             – give republics taxation power and the right to sell their natural resources.
Days 251–500 – privatise some 10 per cent of the assets in the joint-stock companies (100–150 billion rubles);
             – introduce a convertible ruble.

Shatalin's plan was politically appealing. It offered a clear break with the socialist past and recognised the new political realities by calling for an 'Economic Union of Sovereign Republics'. However one may question its viability on economic grounds. It promised not to allow any further fall in living standards, which was clearly unrealistic. It is hard to see how subsidies to firms could be cut in the first stage although retail price increases would be postponed until the second stage. The plan argued, unconvincingly, that sales of apartments and shops could close the gap in the state budget. Initial experiments indicated that most tenants were unwilling to buy their flats, given that they could continue living in them at heavily subsidised rents (estimated at one-sixth of the real cost).

In late July 1990, Gorbachev and Yeltsin entered into talks to seek a compromise programme, and a joint team was formed under Shatalin's direction. Prime Minister Ryzhkov refused to participate, however, and drew up his own programme. Gorbachev commissioned a *third* plan, from Abel Aganbegyan, combining elements of the Ryzhkov and Shatalin plans. In mid-September the USSR Supreme Soviet asked Gorbachev to merge the three plans, and granted him extraordinary presidential powers to run the economy in the interim.

On 1 October 1990, the Russian parliament decided to press ahead on its own with the Shatalin plan. Meanwhile most of the other republics were unhappy with the Gorbachev *and* Shatalin plans, since both seemed to them to leave too much central control in Moscow. In the case of the Shatalin plan, for example, they objected to reliance on a single currency issued by a federal reserve bank in Moscow.

On 16 October Gorbachev countered with his own programme, 'For the stabilisation of the economy and the transition to a market economy', which emphasised the urgency of stabilisation and offered no specific timetable for the dismantling of central planning. Gorbachev's own former economic advisers, Shatalin and Petrakov, denounced his plan on 4 November, as did most of the republics. Throughout the autumn Yeltsin played a game of bluff and counter-bluff with Gorbachev. Many of Yeltsin's economic advisers resigned, among them Yavlinsky, unsure whether Yeltsin was really prepared to break with Gorbachev.

Amid a growing sense of panic and open talk of an authoritarian 'Jaruzelski variant' among party officials, Gorbachev won additional powers from the Supreme Soviet to rule by decree. Yeltsinites were convinced that Gorbachev had abandoned his commitment to reform and turned to the right, and the public seemed to agree. Polls showed that Gorbachev's popularity 'rating' had collapsed from 52 per cent in December 1989 to 21 per cent in October 1990.

In November, Gorbachev used his presidential powers to raise the price of luxury goods and impose a 40 per cent tax on the dollar earnings of Soviet enterprises. (This merely served to accelerate the collapse of Soviet exports in 1991.) On 14 December he issued a decree imposing the same output targets on enterprises for 1991 as for 1990.

On 18 December Ryzhkov suffered a heart attack; he was replaced as USSR Prime Minister, in January 1991, by Valentin Pavlov, formerly Finance Minister. According to reports, there was at this time a stormy meeting between Gorbachev and several hundred leading industrial directors, many from defence plants, who warned him of impending economic catastrophe unless strong steps were taken.

In January 1991, key industrial input prices were raised by 50 per cent, and all 50- and 100-ruble notes were abruptly withdrawn from circulation in a bid to cut back on the monetary overhang. (In fact the withdrawn notes amounted to less than 3 per cent of the total.) There was a new crackdown on 'economic crime', with an enhanced role for the KGB in the struggle against 'speculation'. In March retail prices were raised by 60 per cent, while consumers were compensated for 85 per cent of the increase. Apart from a brief general strike in Minsk, the Belorussian capital, the public response to the price increases was surprisingly muted.

The Emerging Post-Soviet Economy

The economic system of the former Soviet Union is currently in turmoil. The familiar structure of the CPE has been destroyed, but the transition process is not following anyone's blueprint for reform. Rather it is a product of complex political and economy struggles, with an unknown outcome.

The future economy will almost certainly be one in which market forces play a major role. Equally it could well be an economy whose factories and farms remain under the control of local political officials. However, rather than being locked into a vertical chain of command obeying Moscow's orders, the regions and republics will be interacting independently, through a mixture of political dealing and market trading. Four major themes have emerged during the first stages of this transition process.

The Breakdown of Central Planning

From 1988 on, the central ministries progressively lost control and the economy fragmented into a confusing crazy quilt of autonomous enterprises and regional authorities. Firms changed themselves into new types of organisation, often of a type not covered by existing laws. By January 1991, there were 1,420 'associations', 126 'concerns', 156 'intersectoral associations', 102 'consortiums' and 1,200 joint-stock companies. These firms felt, as one director put it, 'like a dog who has lost his master' and began grouping together into new voluntary associations, such as the Scientific-Production Union (founded in June 1990).

The emergence of joint-stock companies was perhaps the most interesting development. In June 1990, a new law was passed allowing state enterprises to convert themselves into joint-stock companies. The giant Kama truck plant, with 120,000 workers, became the first such company. Most of the new joint-stock companies are in fact controlled by their managers and amount to '*nomenklatura* privatisation' of the sort witnessed in Hungary. Most shares are held by other firms, usually the suppliers and customers of the firm in question. Share trading is usually forbidden and shareholder rights are limited.

The other side to destatisation was the continued growth of the non-state sector. By mid-1991, out of a 135 million strong labour force, roughly 15.3 million were employed outside the state sector; 4.5 million were self-employed, 6.5 million were in cooperatives and 4.2 million in leased industrial units. It is not clear to what extent the shadow economy was able to expand to make up for the slump in state sector output. According to official data on the black market, now being gathered for the first time, it amounted to 100 billion rubles in 1991, or about 8 per cent of GNP. Most of this sum was accounted for by moonshining, resale of state goods and bribes to state shop assistants.

Leasing was much slower to develop in agriculture. The number of independent farmers was a mere 47,000 by mid-1991, mostly to be found in the Baltic and Caucasus. At that time there were only 9,000 in Russia and 218 in Ukraine. On the other hand a Russian republic programme gave one million hectares of land to individuals for allotments or housebuilding. Thus plans were well advanced before the coup to carry out a radical 'destatisation' of the Soviet economy. Under USSR legislation introduced in February 1991, the state sector was expected to shrink from 90 to 30 per cent in five years. These laws have now been superseded by republican privatisation legislation. For example, Russia and Kazakhstan passed such laws in July and August 1991, and local State Property Committees started valuing state assets. Auctioning of shops and apartments began during the summer on an experimental basis in cities in several republics, including Russia.

Popular savings are only 700 billion rubles, while the total asset value is three to four trillion rubles, so privatisation will have to proceed through some sort of free distribution, probably using a variant of the Czechoslovak voucher method. Workers are to be given the opportunity to buy shares in their own firm at a discount, and it is likely that most privatisations will take the form of worker/manager buy-outs.

This decentralisation coincided with a massive slump in output in

TABLE 10.2 *Soviet economic performance, 1986–91 (average annual rates of growth, percentages)*

	1986–90 average (plan)	1986	1987	1988	1989	1990	1991
National income produced	4.2	2.3	1.6	4.4	2.4	−4.0	−15.0
Industrial output	4.6	4.4	3.8	3.9	1.7	−1.2	−7.8
Agricultural output	2.7	5.3	−0.6	1.7	1.3	−2.3	−7.0

Sources: *Narodnoe khozyaistvo SSSR v 1989g.* (Moscow: Finansy i statistika, 1990) pp. 8–9; *Ekonomika i zhizn'*, 1991, no. 5, p. 9, and 1992, no. 6, pp. 13–16.

virtually all sectors (see Table 10.2). In the first nine months of 1991, GNP fell 12 per cent, consumption fell 17 per cent and investment 20 per cent. Food output fell 8 per cent and the procurement of food items through the state and cooperative sector fell by 16 per cent for meat, 19 per cent for cheese and 12 per cent for sugar. Industrial output fell 6.4 per cent, with falls of 20 per cent in soap, 11 per cent in clothing and shoes, 10 per cent in oil and 11 per cent in coal.

Ironically many firms saw increased profits in 1991, as they took advantage of greater laxity in price setting. By mid-1991, 45 per cent of industrial products and 60 per cent of consumer goods manufactures were sold at 'free' prices (set by the producer) or 'contract' prices (agreed between producer and customer enterprises). In the first nine months of 1991 the prices of industrial goods rose at an annual rate of 164 per cent, while retail prices rose by 103 per cent and agricultural procurement prices rose 56 per cent.

The one sector of the economy where producers were not enjoying significantly increased autonomy was agriculture, where farmers found themselves caught in a price scissors – between rising industrial prices and fixed state procurement prices. In 1990, fruit and vegetables were taken off the state procurement system, with the worrying result that output fell while prices rose 40 per cent. Farms responded to the 1991 price scissors by refusing to sell grain to the state, instead storing it in the hope that they would be allowed to get a better price as the winter of 1991 progressed.

As industrial firms struck out for independence from the central planning system, they moved quickly to set up banking and trading networks to start to take over the coordination functions abandoned by the centre. In 1990, the old sectoral state banks were abolished and more than 2,000 aggressive new 'commercial' banks sprang up, mostly controlled by industrial enterprises and specialising in inter-firm lending. As a result credit issues rose 36 per cent, to 496 billion rubles, in 1991. Before long 'bank wars' broke out as the USSR State Bank and Russian Central Bank struggled to rein in the commercial banks.

The same year saw the emergence of over a hundred commodity exchanges, where everything from oil to passenger cars to dollars was traded, at free prices. Large state enterprises also dominate the trading exchanges, although a new breed of aggressive entrepreneurs have emerged as brokers in these exchanges.

Monetary and Fiscal Crisis

In 1991 there was further deterioration in the country's financial balances. Retail spending was down 24 per cent in physical volume but up 66 per cent in money terms. By mid-1991, the population held 422 billion rubles in savings accounts and 150 billion rubles in cash, and unsatisfied demand was estimated to be up 44 per cent on 1990.

In the first nine months of 1991 federal spending was 150 billion rubles, only 69 per cent of the planned level. This had catastrophic implications for the funding of federal services, from the armed forces to health services. (Some 62 billion rubles were reportedly spent on the military.) Worse still, federal receipts totalled only 74 billion rubles – 40 per cent of the expected level – owing to the withholding of funds by republican governments. Yawning budget deficits also opened up at republican and local level, and by July 1991 the combined union and republican deficit was running at an annual rate of 200 billion rubles (compared to a projected total personal income of 710 billion rubles). Hyperinflation will almost certainly result. The churning printing presses led to a collapse of faith in the ruble. By the end of 1991, while the 'official' commercial rate was 1.6 rubles to the dollar, the tourist rate was 42 rubles and the rate on dollar auctions was reaching 90 rubles. In December 1991, the State Bank was forced to abandon the official rates altogether.

In retrospect one can see that the budget imbalance was exacerbated by the 1987 Law on the State Enterprise, since after the measure was introduced budget remittances fell while retained profits and waged jumped sharply. Sheer economic incompetence by government leaders also played a part. However the 1991 inflation was also a product of years of suppressed inflation. The old price structure became increasingly unrealistic, with black market prices rising 100 per cent in 1991 and standing at three to five times official prices for the same goods (not that they are available in state stores).

Measures introduced in 1990 and 1991 with a view to strengthening the social safety net were an additional burden on the federal budget. A set of measures in August 1990 increased transfer payments for pensioners and low-income families, and 1991 saw a 49 billion ruble compensation package accompanying the retail price increases. Another 160 billion rubles were allocated to compensate savings account holders, payable in instalments. These were very large sums for a government facing a yawning budget deficit. There were also other selective wage increases: for example, the coalminers' strike won them a 25 per cent wage increase in April 1991. Food subsidies continued to be a crushing burden, amounting to 160 billion rubles in 1991 (more than half the production cost).

The International Debt Crisis

By the end of 1991, the USSR was close to defaulting on its $58 billion hard currency debt (not to mention its $17 billion debt with former CMEA members and other soft currency partners). By the end of 1992, $22 billion was due in interest and capital repayments and there was little chance that the former members of the USSR could find such a sum. It even turned out that Soviet gold reserves had been run down, with 1,100 million tonnes sold since 1989 and only 240 million tonnes (worth three to four billion dollars) left in the vaults.

Foreign trade in the first half of 1991 was 37 per cent lower than in the same period in 1990. The collapse of CMEA and the shift to hard currency payments from January 1991 (at Moscow's insistence) caused a catastrophic 50 per cent drop in trade with East Europe. Trade with capitalist countries also fell 33 per cent, largely because of the disruptive reorganisation of foreign trade and a 10 per cent contraction in domestic oil production in both 1990 and 1991. In 1991, food imports rose; they could reach 49 million tonnes of grain (one-quarter of consumption needs) over 1991–2. Imports of all other types of goods, from industrial spare parts to consumer electronics, were radically cut back, by 30–60 per cent. These ruthless economies enabled the USSR to post a $3 billion surplus for the first half of 1991, but this was still far short of the sums needed to avoid a default on its foreign debt.

The looming crisis stimulated urgent calls for emergency assistance from the West, the most celebrated being the economic programme written by Graham Allison and Grigorii Yavlinsky, entitled 'Window of Opportunity'. This proposed a new Marshall Plan to finance the transition to capitalism in the USSR, with Soviet officials requesting

$14 billion aid and Allison talking of Russia as 'possibly the Klondike of the late twentieth century'. However, in July 1991, the G7 meeting in London turned down such proposals on the grounds that the political chaos in the USSR meant it was unrealistic to expect *any* transition plan to be implemented. Germany, responsible for two-thirds of all the lending to the USSR, was understandably the most reluctant to contemplate writing off some of the Soviet debts.

The Break-up of the Union

In 1991, the political cohesion of the USSR collapsed, and with it what was left of the old structures of central planning. The catalyst for this process was the independence movements in the Baltics, subsequently emulated by other republics (see Chapter 7). Beginning with Estonia in September 1987, a series of republics proclaimed their economic self-management, challenging the legal status of Union enterprises and moving to take control over their own taxation and foreign trade. The Baltic republics were granted formal 'economic independence' in a USSR law in November 1989, but their demands escalated as the centre weakened.

One republic after another declared political sovereignty, beginning with Lithuania in March 1990, and Gorbachev found five republics refusing to accept the new draft Union Treaty he proposed in December 1990. Instead of Gorbachev's formula of 'a strong centre and strong republics', they wanted a horizontal union of equals. In 1991, a 'war of laws' broke out between republican and all-Union authorities, wreaking havoc in the economy. More and more firms withdrew from participation in the Union economy, ignoring output plans and refusing to pay taxes. Most enterprises in Russia chose to pay their turnover tax to the republican government and not to the Union authorities (Yeltsin set the Russian tax at 38 per cent, below the 45 per cent Union rate). Within Russia and Ukraine, regional soviets emulated the Baltics by banning the 'export' of food and consumer goods to other regions. In December 1990, the Russian Republic passed a law allowing private ownership of land – something not permitted in the Union Law on Land of February 1990.

Gorbachev struggled to find a consensus among republic leaders for a new Union. On 23 April the 'nine-plus-one' agreement was concluded, committing the signatories to approve a new Union Treaty by the end of the year. In July 1991, a joint anti-crisis stabilisation programme was adopted by Moscow and ten republics. A series of meetings over the summer resulted in a new draft Union Treaty, due for signature on 20 August. The central theme of all these negotiations was the preservation of a common 'economic space', while recognising the right of the republics to sovereign control over property, natural resources and taxation. The same ideas were carried forward into the new Economic Treaty, signed in Alma Ata in October 1991 by eight republics (with Ukraine an awkward absentee).

All sides recognised that after 70 years of joint development the abrupt severing of economic links between factories in different republics would have a catastrophic impact. (An estimated 20 per cent of Soviet GNP in 1990 consisted of interrepublican flows.) An equally pressing constraint was the fact that the republics were saddled with the foreign debt accumulated by the old regime and the West would not offer any further assistance until there were guarantees that the republics would collectively strive to meet these obligations. The republics were aware that only Russia, with its vast natural resources, was capable of running a positive foreign trade balance in the immediate future. They were fearful of Russian threats to raise the price of oil from its current level of 70 rubles per tonne (two dollars) to the world market price of 140 dollars.

Despite these powerful arguments in favour of cooperation, there are many obstacles to the emergence of a viable economic union. Will all the former Union enterprises become the property of the republics, without compensation for past investment? How much will the republics contribute to the budget of the central institutions that are left? Can the ruble be salvaged as a currency and a reliable central emission bank be created?

The post-coup events left no authoritative central political institutions which could find a consensus on these questions. In fact economic problems have been manipulated by republican politicians as part of an internal and external struggle for political power. Commitment to a separate national currency became a symbolic test of one's commitment to sovereignty. This was most blatant in Ukraine, where former communist leader Leonid Kravchuk seized upon the independence issue in response to the electoral challenge from the nationalists. More worrying still, there are doubts whether any of the republican governments have the ability to enforce their own decisions within their own borders: the 'war of laws' has been replaced by a legal vacuum. It will fall upon Russia, as the largest state, to take the lead and cajole the other republics into line. Unfortunately the Russian government itself is deeply divided over economic and political issues, and until it gets its own house in order will be unable to play a leading role.

In late 1991, a new Interrepublican Economic Council was set up to hammer out a new economic system, and in the meantime Ivan Silaev headed the Committee for Operational Management of the Economy, which partly took over the role of the old Council (renamed Cabinet) of Ministers. Most of the individual Union ministries were converted into independent 'associations' of dubious legality; others were seized by the Russian government. Silaev tried to orchestrate a network of interrepublican trade agreements to salvage what he could from the centrally planned economy. For example, in late September a majority of the republics agreed to enforce a common customs policy.

However the republics distrusted Gorbachev's efforts to preserve what he could of the old USSR. In October 1991, Yeltsin began to adopt independent policies, in an apparent attempt to outflank the Silaev 'government' and bypass Gorbachev's protracted negotiations over a new Union Treaty. Yeltsin took over as Russian Prime Minister in addition to his position as President, and announced his intention to abolish all price controls and move rapidly towards a market economy. At an historic meeting in Brest on 7–8 December, Yeltsin's independent line received support from presidents Kravchuk of Ukraine and Shushkevich of Belorussia, when they joined together to announce a new Commonwealth of Independent States based upon a 'common economic space' as well as other forms of coordination. It was in turn these new republican leaders, with their counterparts from other Commonwealth states, who began to carry out the transition to a fully-fledged market system in the early 1990s; the first results of their endeavours, with rising prices and a continued fall in production, made it clear why Gorbachev had been reluctant to take this step although (like him) the republican leaders insisted there was 'no alternative'.

11

Social Change and Social Policy

MARY BUCKLEY

The coup of August 1991 provoked a revolutionary response which speeded up the pace of political change. Independence for the Baltic states ensured that, in future, social policies would not be decided in Moscow. The same applied in republics such as Georgia, which was unwilling to consider coordinating its economic and social policies with the eight republics that signed, on 18 October 1991, the treaty establishing a new economic community. Georgia also remained outside the new Commonwealth of Independent States. These and other processes of devolution and fragmentation meant that, henceforth, discussions of new social issues would increasingly be shaped by local concerns and pressures. This chapter does not speculate about forthcoming developments of this kind; rather it provides discussion of the historical context out of which future social policies and 'new' issues will emerge and against which they may react.

The Legacy of *Perestroika* and *Glasnost'*

At the 27th Party Congress in 1986, Gorbachev announced that, during the years 1986–2000, the CPSU would 'raise the people's well-being to a qualitatively new level'. Owing to *perestroika*, a 'decisive turning point' had been reached, which meant faster and more effective problem solving and a reexamination of social policy. But by 1989 few citizens believed that in the short term their lives would improve. Economic crisis, looming unemployment and political chaos suggested the opposite. Gorbachev's promise at the 28th Party

Congress in 1990 to protect the people in the 'difficult transition' to 'new forms of economic life' met a cool reception. To his critics, rationing in 1989 and sharp price increases in April 1991 indicated otherwise. Likewise Gorbachev's call in October 1990 for 'a market-driven economy' that enjoyed 'socialist choice' seemed either contradictory or half-hearted. Bolder commitment to a market at the Central Committee Plenum in July 1991 enhanced fears of unemployment and an uncertain future.

Perestroika had required policy makers to rethink the goals of social policy by tailoring them to economic changes. A coherent social policy did not result, however. Confusion over the direction of economic reform, topped by budget deficits, fiscal crisis, the passage of contradictory laws and by the failure to determine a precise division of administrative responsibility for local soviets, city soviets and Supreme Soviets, resulted in, at best, *ad hoc*, changes. By the early 1990s, in a climate of growing despair and social depression, many citizens cursed the poor qality of state medical care and paid for private treatment, simultaneously criticising the cooperative sector for its dishonest sharks and high prices.

In the late 1980s, *glasnost'* had facilitated debate about social issues. 'Old' issues, such as housing shortages and queues for kindergarten places, which had been examined in some depth in the 1970s, received more widespread and critical exposure. 'New' issues which were taboo under Stalin, Khrushchev and Brezhnev, such as how to combat murder, drug addiction, prostitution and the self-immolation of Muslim women, were aired, often in heated exchanges. Democratisation invited citizens to listen to experts express competing views in round-table discussions and welcomed their reactions.

Exhilaration about freer debate began to wane in 1989. Exposure, discussion and criticism, many lamented, had not brought positive changes. Instead a 'moral panic' about crime and the disintegration of the social fabric gripped many citizens. Fresh knowledge about violence, theft and underworld rackets created fear, disorientation and a sense of hopelessness about social collapse. The certainties and stabilities of the past had gone. Few believed that the government could cope with the extent of social problems or that a clear social policy could develop without economic success.

The prospect of progress seemed still more distant to many in 1992, after massive price increases and further inflation. Promises of a better future, but not in the short term, made those weary of the strains and stresses of everyday life wonder if they could even afford to eat properly. It was now the turn of Yeltsin's popularity to decline and, in January 1992, he was jeered on the streets of St Petersburg by discontented shoppers.

The Making of Social Policies

The formulation and implementation of social policy is affected by historical context, ideology, economic needs and pressures, political actors and social attitudes. But what was ideologically desirable in the past, such as full employment and widespread kindergarten provision, was often historically difficult owing to economic constraints. Immediately after the revolution of 1917, for example, meagre resources in a politically fragile state could not meet many basic needs. Communists had taken power in a predominantly agricultural country characterised by widespread illiteracy and rudimentary medical care. Pressing social issues included how to provide enough food to prevent starvation, how to teach citizens to read and write, and how to combat smallpox, cholera, typhoid and syphilis. Progress in many areas, such as the setting up of kindergartens and the provision of restaurants, was inevitably slow. The early Soviet state was unable to offer its workers and peasants generous pensions, spacious housing or excellent medical care. The tasks for social policy were enormous and dependent upon successful economic growth.

Economic resources limit the supply of goods and services that can be distributed. But political choices about the nature of production influence the pace at which resources will be channelled into consumer goods and social services. For example, Stalin's priorities of electrification and the production of steel and coal meant the subordination of light industry to heavy industry. The main goal after 1928 was to build a socialist economy through central planning and thereby to guarantee long-term welfare provision. Heavy industry was the 'means' to the communist 'end'. In the meantime there were serious constraints on welfare policies.

Leaders change, however, and so may their priorities. Khrushchev stepped up housing construction, expanded the welfare state and attempted to boost food production by cultivating more land; Brezhnev presided over the building of high-rise flats, wage increases, larger maternity benefits and general improvements in the standard of living. The commitment of subsequent leaders, such as Gorbachev, Yeltsin, Sobchak and Popov, to developing a market economy carried broad implications for employment patterns, mobility, wage inequalities and personal security. The concerns of a given leadership, as well as historical context and economic resources, affect the content of social policies.

Competing pressures on policy makers from different institutions and different professions also influence policy formulation and implementation. For example, leaders of the Soviet Women's Committee in 1990 and in early 1991 pressed for measures to limit women's

unemployment, but demographers stressed the advantages for population growth of laying women off first. In the fight against drug
abuse, law enforcement institutions pushed for an end to the poppy
crop, while associations which process plants for medicinal purposes
objected. Institutions with competing interests may clash over ways
to tackle different issues. The implementation of social policy can
also vary across regions, influenced by different social attitudes.
Although, since 1917, the state was committed to an expanding
system of child care, Tajikistan and Uzbekistan opened kindergartens
with much less enthusiasm than many non-Muslim republics because
their customs encouraged women to stay at home and rear large
families.

Resources are another important factor. By the 1980s, the Soviet
state, as an advanced industrial superpower, enjoyed the 'material–
technical base' that it had lacked in the 1920s and 1930s. Yet,
although leaders and citizens were eager to close the gap in living
standards between themselves and the West, awareness in 1990 of a
deep-seated economic and political crisis resulted in pessimism about
the likelihood of future successes. Although increases in the quantity
and quality of consumer goods had been among the official goals of
perestroika, it had not delivered them. Similarly, although Gorbachev had also argued that the 'human factor' in economic production should not be neglected because an efficient economy needed a
contented workforce, many workers by 1990 were more disgruntled
than before. Striking miners, in particular, in 1989 and 1991, doubted
Gorbachev's commitment to them. In January 1992, they again
threatened strike action in protest against the results of Yeltsin's huge
price increases.

From Social Justice to Social Protection

According to the official ideology of the Soviet past, 'the full and free
development of every individual forms the ruling principle' of socialist society. The overthrow of capitalist property relations made this
'free development' possible; and the ownership of property by the
socialist state in the name of the working class ensured 'socially just,
public aims', through the 'planned development of the economy'.
Ideologists contended that scientific planning had 'a socially purpose-
ful orientation' because it was linked to the principle of 'from each
according to their abilities, to each according to their work'. Under
communism, this principle would become 'from each according to
their abilities to each according to their needs'. Socialist society

exhibited high morality since it gave 'a new content to the problems of humanism' (Mchedlov, 1987, pp. 14–19).

The promotion of social justice was officially described as a process which established the political, social and economic quality of social groups. 'Deliberate policies' aimed to 'promote the levelling of social conditions' irrespective of family status or level of pay. The right to work, rising real incomes and extensive welfare rights, including the constitutional right to housing, were cited as evidence of the system's 'democratic nature' (Mchedlov, 1987, p. 26). In keeping with this, at the 27th Party Congress, Gorbachev declared that Soviet social policy 'clearly demonstrates the humanistic nature of socialist construction, its qualitative difference from capitalism'.

Since 1986, consistent with condemnations of Brezhnev's 'years of stagnation', it became fashionable to argue that in 'the last ten years' the tendency to destroy social justice intensified as a result of 'formalism' and 'a braking of socialist democracy'. Leaders concerned with their own job security and party privileges caused disaffection, demoralisation and cynicism among the people. Social malaise resulted and, in turn, provoked irresponsible behaviour. Some citizens coped with empty lives through use of alcohol; others, alienated in their public lives, failed to take the initiative at work and became passive cogs in an inert system which they hesitated to criticise openly; still others who worked illegally on black markets profited from immoral 'unearned incomes'.

Because social justice was being undermined under Brezhnev, a 'restructuring' of society and of social attitudes became vital. According to early supporters of *perestroika*, social policies had to struggle against bribery, corruption, unearned income and alcoholism; and to encourage a 'new psychology', 'initiative' and 'social responsibility' among citizens so that they would learn to solve problems independently and actively. According to Gorbachev's book *Perestroika*, published in 1987, socialism had nothing to do with equalising. Social justice referred to the granting of benefits and privileges 'on the basis of the quantity and quality of socially useful work'. By contrast, equalising was 'one of the prime deformities in the past few decades', resulting in 'the development of attitudes of dependence, consumerism and a narrow-minded philosophy of the type: "It is none of our business, let the bosses have the headache"'.

The 27th Party Congress, as well as Central Committee meetings in 1985 and 1987, called for the adoption of the principle of 'socialist social justice' as one of the most important tasks of *perestroika*. The social scientist Tatyana Zaslavskaya even argued that, because different groups made different contributions to socioeconomic development, there should be a 'differentiated approach to social policy' which ensured a 'differentiated growth of the well-being of population groups'. Those who contributed most to the economy should receive a higher standard of living (Zaslavskaya, 1988, pp. 116–17).

By the 28th Party Congress in 1990, a more central place was given to an undefined 'transition to the market'. References to 'socialist social justice' were few. Instead, Gorbachev talked about 'the most complicated task of this period – to work out and realise a complex of special measures of social protection, especially for needy citizens'. 'Socialist social justice' was quietly replaced by 'social protection'. This was prompted by the increasing unpopularity of the word 'socialist' and also by deep fears of the hardships that a market economy would inflict. Citizens badly needed reassurances that they would be protected.

Welfare Provision

Successive Soviet leaders have been committed to a welfare state, arguing that its services and benefits enabled citizens to develop their abilities in similar fashion. This section looks at current social problems and social policies in the selected areas of employment, housing and health care.

Employment

The Soviet state was forged in the name of proletarian revolution to end the exploitation of the working class and poor peasantry. In 1917, a 'dictatorship of the proletariat' championed the liberation of workers who, according to the 1977 Constitution, became the 'leading force' in promoting the 'sociopolitical and ideological unity of Soviet society'. The consolidated alliance of the working class, collective farm peasantry and people's intelligentsia resulted in a replacement of the dictatorship of the proletariat by 'a state of the whole people'.

According to the 1977 Constitution, citizens enjoyed 'the right to work' and 'the right to maintenance in old age, in sickness and in the event of complete or partial disability'. These rights became central principles of Soviet ideology. Labour, consistent with Marxist theory, was the only source of value. Everyone was expected to work, and to do otherwise was to be parasitic on others. Until the 1990s, ideology and consistently portrayed unemployment as an integral part of capitalism, alien to socialism. The new socialist state, however, had been unable to guarantee jobs for all and unemployment was a problem throughout the 1920s. Unemployment and sickness benefits were formally available, but limited resources made payment difficult. It was not until Stalin's policy of industrialisation that the demand for labour significantly increased and unemployment fell.

At the end of the 1980s, many feared that, if *perestroika* were successful, its efficiency and streamlining would result in a return to the unemployment of the 1920s. When *khozraschet* (cost-accounting) was introduced in 1988, 400,000 workers were dismissed in three months and a temporary unemployment benefit was introduced. The logic of *khozraschet* made surplus labour expendable. The encouragement of higher wage differentials in order to reward initiative and skill reinforced the need to shed workers so that higher wage bills could be met.

In July 1991, the youth paper, *Moskovskii Komsomolets*, reported that unemployment had officially reached eight million and might soon be 32 million. *Moscow News* of the same month predicted that by the end of 1991 there would be 300,000 jobless in the capital. Unemployment was now recognised as a permanent feature of the Soviet economy, destined to grow. Transition to a market economy made this inevitable. Labour exchanges were set up to handle job placement and retraining, and to offer help with setting up small businesses. Unemployment benefits would be granted according to past employment records and current circumstances. Then, in August 1991, the television news programme, *Vremya*, informed viewers that the unemployed would receive 70 per cent of their previous earnings for their first three months without work, falling to 60 per cent in the subsequent three months, then to 45 per cent for the rest of one year, by which time they were expected to have new jobs or to be retraining. Women, it revealed, made up the bulk of the unemployed.

Entrepreneurial labour activity began to be encouraged in 1987. The aim had been to provide better goods and services, thereby improving the standard of living. But prices in the cooperative sector were often prohibitive and provoked resentment among citizens who could not afford them. Expensive restaurants, for example, were out of reach for low-paid nurses and unskilled cleaners. Economic cooperatives were consistent with Gorbachev's aim to reward effort and to encourage initiative, but they quickly led to criticisms of excessive prices. The large increases in prices which took place in April 1991 further stunned citizens. Since the 1930s the metro had cost five kopeks. A rise to fifteen kopeks at the same time as steep increases in food prices (with official ceilings of 200 per cent on meat, 100 per cent on eggs and 130 per cent on milk) caused a serious social depression. 'I am in despair' was a common remark in the spring of

1991. Anxiety about price increases was not reduced by the three monthly payments of 'compensation' designed by the government to ease their impact. Neither did citizens consider that simultaneous salary increases decreed to be 'not less than 60 rubles a month' helped sufficiently.

With *glasnost'*, poverty had already been acknowledged; but hardships from price increases, especially for those on low incomes, became an additional issue in 1991. In June 1988, the paper *Sotsialisticheskaya industriya* had estimated that one-fifth of the population was near the official poverty line, especially pensioners, young couples with children and single mothers. Two million people had second jobs, according to *Izvestiya* in October 1988, in order to subsist. At the end of 1990, *Izvestiya* reported that 40 million lived below the official poverty line of 78 rubles a month. By early 1992, with further inflation, the poverty line was 1000 rubles and up to 90 per cent of families were below it.

Emboldened by democratisation, some workers turned wages, output norms, bonuses, economic decision making and pollution into political issues. In March 1989, *Izvestiya* reported that miners were staying underground in protest against excessive output norms, low pay and unpaid bonuses. Their 'just' demands were subsequently met. By July 1989, about 100,000 miners were on strike for similar reasons. Thousands demonstrated in their support and, according to *Trud*, factories stopped work in solidarity. While there was occasional labour unrest in the late 1970s and early 1980s, it lacked the widespread publicity and enormous ripple effect that *glasnost'* triggered. Labour militancy resumed once more in 1990 and 1991, increasingly linked to more political demands, such as the resignation of President Gorbachev and the dissolution of the Congress of People's Deputies. In March 1991, between 280,000 and 300,000 miners were on strike, halting work at 165 mines. They readily struck again in response to Yeltsin's call for a general strike against the coup of August 1991.

An extension of the right to work has always been the right to a pension. Pensions were first introduced after the Civil War, even though resources to provide them were scarce. Pensions did not increase significantly until after Stalin's death when Brezhnev, in particular, paid attention to daily needs. Because the population is aging, pensions are a growing strain on budgets. Over the past 50 years the proportion of elderly people has doubled. Whereas, in 1939, citizens over 60 accounted for 6.7 per cent of the population, by 1987 they made up 13.5 per cent, projected to increase to 17.5 per cent by 2002.

On 1 January 1988, the minimum old-age pension was set at 40 rubles a month, but this was criticised as too low in discussions of the

Draft USSR Law on Working People's Pensions, due to come into effect in January 1991. The same law of March 1991 which put ceilings on price rises decreed an increase in pensions to 65 rubles a month. Critics again responded that this was inadequate.

The relevance of socialist social justice for jobs, wages, bonuses and pensions was that they be allocated according to merit. Training and performance were seen as necessary criteria for the distribution of rewards. Critics in 1987, 1988 and 1989 worried that traditional socialist values were being compromised and that certain social groups, such as women with large families and low levels of training, would be disadvantaged. They objected in stronger terms in 1991, when transition to a market economy seemed inevitable, then again in 1992. Issues of 'social protection' will be thorny ones for future parliaments.

Housing

In 1986, the CPSU declared the housing problem to be one 'of special significance' in need of 'an accelerated solution' so that by the year 2000 'each Soviet family will have separate housing – a flat or a house'. In comparison with the West, the housing situation was grave. Stalin's emphasis on heavy industry meant that investment in housing fell; then, during the Great Patriotic War, about one-quarter of Soviet housing was destroyed. Khrushchev and Brezhnev made tackling these shortages a priority with the result that between 1956 and 1985 about 66 million flats were built, amounting to three-quarters of all housing built under Soviet power.

Despite commitment to massive housing construction, competing pressures on a declining economy have resulted in a reduction in the share of capital investment allocated to housing, from 23.2 per cent under Khrushchev to 12 per cent under Gorbachev. Doubts were soon raised about whether the CPSU would meet its optimistic housing target for the year 2000.

The main problems for policy makers is that housing supply does not meet demand. Newlyweds, for instance, often begin married life by living with one set of parents and it is common for the lounge to be transformed into a bedroom at night. Overcrowding is particularly acute in the old communal flats, shared by several families. Each family has one room in which to live; the kitchen and bathroom is shared with other families. One-quarter of urban dwellers still live this way.

Overcrowding means little privacy and contributes to emotional stress, alcoholism and divorce. Journalistic accounts about the implications of cramped conditions for quality of life and work performances are now frequent. For example, in January 1989, *Izvestiya* reported the case of a 30 year-old pilot who lived in one room of 9.6 square metres with his wife and two children. The young baby cried a great deal, which made rest in non-working hours difficult. Overstressed nerves meant that it was hard to maintain 'flight safety and a high level of service'. The article noted that most pilots in the north lived in this way.

Pressure on scarce housing drastically increased after the 1989 revolutions in Eastern Europe. Soon after, 500,000 Soviet troops returning home needed housing. This figure is expected to rise to two million in the near future. Refugees from trouble spots such as Nagorno-Karabakh also needed shelter. And hundreds of thousands need resettlement from areas of ecological disaster, such as the dried-up Aral Sea.

The quality of housing varies across republics. In September 1988, *Izvestiya* reported that in Tallinn there were 11.8 square metres of living space per person. This was one square metre more than in Moscow, Riga and Leningrad and two square metres more than in Kiev, Vilnius and Tbilisi. Rock bottom space was found at 6.8 square metres per person in Ashkhabad and 7.5 square metres in Dushanbe and Yerevan. The official minimum standard is 9 square metres per person. Although this is often not met, housing space has increased from 4.7 square metres per person in 1950 to an average of 8.6 square metres in the late 1980s.

Since the late 1950s, an average of 2–2.2 million flats have been built each year, but waiting lists remain long. Even in Tallinn, 16 per cent of all families are on housing waiting lists. Figures range from 12 per cent in Moscow to 32 per cent in Kishinev. Aided by *glasnost'*, national and local newspapers address the problem in increasing detail. In November 1988, *Bakinskii Rabochii* reported that 133,000 families in Azerbaijan were on waiting lists. Of these, 20,000, including invalids and war veterans, had been waiting for over ten years and lived in ill-equipped buildings and hostels.

Waiting lists were not eased by corruption. In October 1987, *Pravda* exposed management personnel for illegally allocating housing 'in exchange for various services'. Apparently 'Frunze City Soviet Executive Committee circumvented the existing waiting lists to satisfy requests from the business managers of Kirgizia's Communist Party Central Committee and Council of Ministers'. It was revealed that 78 flats were illegally set aside for them. *Pravda* added that flats were frequently kept vacant just in case a special request was made by party officials.

Shoddily built flats which were thrown up in the 1950s and 1960s aggravated matters because resources had to be channelled into their renovation. The quality of building work has implications for the longevity of housing stock as well as for living standards. In 1986, projects began in six cities to renovate 20-year-old five-storey blocks of flats. According to *Izvestiya* in October 1986, this work was essential because residents were 'plagued by poor sound and heat insulation' and 'constant leaks and freezes'.

Even harsher conditions are found in shanty towns in Kolyma, in the north east, where 'unplanned structures' are built from crates. The case of a man who ran wild with a gun in the city of Susuman drew attention to these conditions. In August 1988, *Izvestiya* commented: 'Arkady Buchuk grew up not only in a troubled family but also in Kolyma's worst slum'. Susuman had 600 'unplanned structures' with several thousand inhabitants. The town of Magadan had a further 8,000. Before *glasnost'*, slums and homelessness were depicted by ideologists as problems of the capitalist West. Now both are recognised as domestic social problems too.

Population growth and migration from rural areas into cities have exacerbated housing problems. According to the 1989 census, between 1970 and 1989 the Soviet population increased from 241.7 million to 286.7 million. But the rural population fell from 105.7 million to 97.9 million over the same period. Admittedly over 200 new towns were created, but this did not sufficiently meet the growing demand for housing.

State housing had predominated, although groups of citizens could form housing cooperatives and, with help from their employer, trade union or the state, pay for a block of flats to be built. Residents of state flats still pay extremely low rents and bills by Western standards – some 4–5 per cent of an average family income – while owners of cooperative flats pay back much larger amounts over 25 years, similar to mortgage repayments. Factories also assume some responsibility for housing workers in hostels, but conditions are criticised as inadequate. As privatisation proceeds, citizens will be increasingly encouraged to purchase their state flats, as happened under Conservative governments in Britain. And energy prices, initially very low, were set to rise substantially in 1992.

The quality of housing is repeatedly linked to medical, demographic, and employment problems, such as sickness, life expectancy, birth rates and work performance. Experts writing in *Izvestiya* in September 1988 claimed that the probability of a child falling ill 'decreases with each extra square metre'. They also argued that couples with an average of 9 square metres per person 'will have a second child 50 per cent more often than those who have 7 square metres per person'. Demographers who are keen for birth rates to increase, particularly in republics where one-child families are the norm in urban areas, view housing policy as a contributory factor to population structure. The profile of different age cohorts, in turn, affects the changing size of the workforce and the proportion of different nationalities in the overall population. The extent of over-crowding endured by workers influences physical and mental health and hence job performance. Thus housing policy is indirectly relevant to employment policy, nationality policy and health care.

Health Care

'Strengthening the health of the Soviet people' and 'increasing life expectancy' were the main goals for health care adopted under Gorbachev. The CPSU aimed to meet them by providing town and country 'with all forms of highly qualified medical services' of increasing quality. New emphasis on entrepreneurship, particularly after 1988, meant that private medicine was encouraged more than ever before. Charity, too, became acceptable again, resulting in a mushrooming of local groups committed to philanthropic purposes.

After the revolution, the Soviet state pledged support for free medical care for its workers. The number of doctors per 10,000 population increased from one in 1917 to four in 1928, 7.9 in 1940, 20 in 1960, 27.4 in 1970, 37.5 in 1980 and 44.4 in 1989. The number of hospital beds per 10,000 people climbed from 40 in 1940 to 132.9 in 1989. Average life expectancy increased by 26 years between 1926 and 1972, but dropped again in 1985 to 69 (73 for women and 64 for men). It increased fractionally in 1989 to 74.0 for women and 64.6 for men.

When ill, citizens visit polyclinics in the workplace or near their home. Medical care is free, but prescriptions are not and many drugs are hard to obtain. Paid private visits to doctors for faster and better care are common. A visit in 1990 to a dentist working in a coopera-tive, for instance, cost 15 rubles. Small payments to hospital person-nel also make a patient's stay more comfortable. The second econ-omy is neatly embedded in the running of many hospitals. This often entails payment for the privilege of receiving anaesthetic (as much as 500 rubles in 1990 for an appendectomy).

Consistent with *perestroika*, hospitals were encouraged to run efficiently and from January 1989 were supposed to adopt *khozras-chet* or cost-accounting methods. Detailed reports on how this pro-ceeded were not forthcoming, but reports on the problems of health care were numerous. *Glasnost'* triggered criticisms of unsanitary conditions, poorly qualified doctors and a lack of equipment. It also

TABLE 11.1 *Infant mortality rates in the Russian Federation and Turk-menia (number of children dying up to one year of age, per 1,000 births)*

	1975	1980	1981	1982	1983	1984	1985	1986	1987	1988
Russia										
Total										
population	23.7	22.1	21.5	20.4	20.1	20.9	20.7	19.3	19.4	18.9
urban	22.5	21.2	20.3	19.5	19.2	19.9	19.8	18.8	18.8	18.2
rural	26.2	24.0	24.3	22.4	22.4	23.4	22.8	20.4	21.0	20.4
Turkmenia										
Total										
population	56.5	53.6	55.9	52.5	53.2	51.2	52.4	58.2	56.4	53.3
urban	55.4	57.4	55.7	54.7	55.3	49.1	49.0	56.5	56.2	52.5
rural	58.0	51.0	56.1	50.9	51.8	52.6	54.7	59.3	56.5	45.2

Source: Goskomstat. *Naselenie SSSR 1988: Statisticheskii sbornik*. (Moscow: Finansy i statistika, 1989) pp. 474–6.

led to the publication of infant mortality rates and abortion statistics, which caused alarm. Particularly high death rates of children up to one year of age in Turkmenia, Tajikistan, Uzbekistan, Azerbaijan and Kirgizia prompted discussions about reasons behind them. The highest infant mortality rates are found in Turkmenia where, unlike the situation in other republics, differences between urban and rural rates are negligible. In 1988, in Turkmenian towns, there were 52.5 deaths per 1,000 births up to the age of one, and 52.4 in the countryside. Particularly worrying was the fact that Turkmenia's rates had been worsening, as Table 11.1 shows, with a miniscule (and perhaps fictitious) improvement in 1988. Even in republics where improvements were more steady, like the Russian Federation, they were slight. Urban rates in Russia fell from 22.5 deaths per 1,000 births in 1975 to 18.2 in 1988, and rural rates decreased from 26.2 to 20.4. But official statistics may be deceptive. In April 1987, the weekly paper *Nedelya* admitted that case histories were often falsified; thus infant mortality rates were previously higher than stated: 'Frequently, when an infant has died or has experienced a severe birth trauma, the mechanism for "correcting" mistakes promptly swings into action: the case history of the birth is rewritten (or, to be more precise, faked) to conceal the mistake or other incorrect actions'.

Since 1987 there has been official recognition that infant mortality rates are worse in the USSR than in advanced capitalist countries. Comparative figures in Table 11.2 show that, although Soviet rates are, on average, worse than Japan, Canada, USA, the UK and

TABLE 11.2 *Infant mortality rates in selected countries*

Year	Country	Deaths per 1,000 births
1985–90	Angola	137.0
1988	Australia	9.2
1987	Burma	70.2
1987	Canada	7.3
1988	France	7.7
1987	India	95.0
1987	Japan	5.0
1985–90	Mexico	47.0
1987	UK (England and Wales)	8.1
	(Scotland)	8.5
1988	USA	9.9
1987	USSR	25.4
1985–90	Vietnam	64.3

Sources: Statistical Yearbook 1987 (New York: United Nations, 1990)
pp. 64–73; *Demographic Yearbook 1988* (New York: United Nations,
1990) pp. 396–404.

France, they do not fall as low as lesser developed nations such as
India, Vietnam, Angola, Burma and Mexico. Nevertheless Soviet
commentators find these figures embarrassing for an advanced
industrial superpower and are keen to reduce them.

The reasons for such high rates include poor conditions in maternity homes and inadequate prenatal care. In August 1987, *Pravda*
reported that in Turkmenia over 60 per cent of maternity clinics,
maternity wards and children's hospitals lacked hot water. There was
no running water in 127 hospitals and two-thirds of these lacked pipes
for sewerage. In the summer epidemics, such as viral hepatitis,
jaundice and intestinal infections, were common.

Many pregnant women are also unhealthy. In February 1987,
Izvestiya pointed out that anaemia among Muslim women, not eased
by frequent births, contributes to infant mortality. In August 1987,
Pravda noted that women agricultural workers are exposed to high
levels of nitrates in fertilisers. A growing sensitivity to ecological
issues has made the link between the 'abuse' of inorganic fertilisers
and infant mortality easier to draw. Pre-natal care is not improved by
overworked gynaecologists. There is general agreement that a reduction in infant mortality rates requires higher standards of hygiene in
hospitals, more medical equipment, available oxygen and hot water,
improved prenatal care and better working conditions for pregnant
women.

Recently published abortion statistics also prompted articles on why they are so high. In 1985, there were 100.3 legal abortions for every 1,000 women between the ages of 15 and 49, falling in 1988 to 82.3. This compared with 28 legal abortions per 1,000 women in the USA and 12.4 in England and Wales. The Soviet average is exceeded in the Russian Federation, reaching, in 1988, 105.2 abortions per 1,000 women. Apparently only 15–18 per cent of women in this republic have never had an abortion. Lower figures in Uzbekistan, Azerbaijan, Tajikistan and Turkemenia of 50.8, 22.4, 38.6 and 43.1 per 1,000 women respectively are due to the high value placed on large families by Muslim cultures.

Abortion was first legalised in 1920 as a necessary evil, banned in 1936, and made legal again in 1955. Many Soviet women endure six or more abortions in a lifetime. Writing in *Pravda International* in 1989, Professor Kulakov lamented, 'The Soviet Union holds a sad record: the highest number of abortions in the world. Every year, 23,000 teenage girls (under 17 years of age) have an abortion. Every year, for each 5.6 million births, there are 6.8 million abortions.' In the USA there are 425 abortions for every 1,000 live births.

According to women's reports, the abortion system is harsh. Patients experience disrespect from medical workers, queues for treatment and filthy bed linen. The operation is performed without anaesthetic and little sympathy is given for the pain and ill-health that results. The topic of abortion was shrouded in silence until 1987, even though it was legal. Apart from a chilling description of the procedure in *samizdat* by Vera Golubeva, little was written about it (Golubeva, 1980).

Glasnost' drew attention to a further problem. Although abortions were legal, some women sought illegal ones because they did not wish those working in official channels to be aware that they needed one. Others did so because pregnancy had gone beyond the legal limits for abortion. In order to try to reduce the number of 'late' backstreet abortions, the USSR Ministry of Health extended the legal termination date to 28 weeks. This contrasted with the situation in the UK and USA. British conservative MPs had been pressing for reductions in the time limit for legal abortions and US Supreme Court judges in 1989 issued a ruling that made it easier for states to restrict their availability. In March 1991, however, *Moskovskii Komsomolets* printed a call for readers to sign a petition to the European Parliament declaring abortion in the Soviet Union to be an 'evil'. As has happened in Poland, anti-abortion sentiments are now being openly expressed.

The main reason for high abortion rates is a dearth of contraceptives. Published abortion statistics, coupled with fears about the spread of AIDS, have led to criticisms of the lack of protective condoms. According to a 1988 edition of the medical paper, *Meditsinskaya gazeta*, just 220 million condoms are produced every year – clearly not enough in a population of over 281 million which lacks choice about contraceptive methods. Professor Kulakov describes the supply as laughable: 'Each male citizen in our country can count on four condoms per year!' Letters to the press complained that shops did not stock them and regretted that a black market in condoms had developed, on which prices had rocketed one hundredfold. By 1991, condoms were more readily available in Moscow.

Articles in the press generally concurred that improvements in the health of citizens called for upgraded hospital facilities, better trained and less overworked doctors, higher-quality medical equipment, regular supplies of drugs, easy access to contraception and fewer abortions. The link between good health and a less polluted environment is increasingly made.

New Social Issues

Social policies go beyond the provision of shelter, health care and social services to address 'social problems' whose existence was only recently acknowledged. These include taboo subjects of the past, such as crime, drug addiction and suicide. Other 'new' issues, such as prostitution and abortion, were discussed in the 1920s, but thereafter cloaked in silence. As a result of *glasnost'*, new social problems were given more media coverage between 1987 and 1990 than they had enjoyed in the entire half-century from 1930 to 1980. By 1991 and 1992, however, citizens were increasingly blasé about new revelations and keen for problems to be solved rather than endlessly discussed.

Crime

Until recently, citizens were unaware of the extent of Soviet crime because statistics were not released. But by April 1989 journalists were allowed to report that 'In the first quarter of the year, 509,000 crimes had been registered in the country, which is 31 per cent up on the same period last year. The crime rate among minors rose by nearly 25 per cent.' Thereafter increases were reported each year. Given the unreliability of crime statistics worldwide, it is hard to interpret these. The result, however, was increased fear and anxiety in society about mugging, theft and rape.

In April 1988, the Central Committee passed a resolution 'On the

Status of the Struggle Against Crime in the Country and Additional Measures to Prevent Lawbreaking'. Party committees were criticised for their lack of vigilance and urged to step up 'law and order'. Gorbachev returned to the issue of crime at the Central Committee meeting plenum of April 1989, when he called for 'an uncompromising struggle against criminal elements'. In 1990, concern about rising crime led to the argument that the army should help the militia to maintain order. In February 1991, this became reality. A presidential decree of the same month on dangerous and organised crime provided for expanded resources.

In their early coverage of crime, journalists highlighted murder and kidnapping. In January 1988, *Pravda* regretted that the number of premeditated murders was increasing. Reporters revealed that, in Central Asia and in the Caucasus, the kidnapping of young children was on the rise and one-third of those kidnapped were killed. In exchange for their victims, kidnappers demand money, authorisations for flats and places in institutes for unqualified students.

According to *Nedelya*, in January 1988, criminal codes did not deal adequately with kidnapping. No clause covered it in the Georgian Code, even though Georgia suffered the highest incidence of kidnapping. The Russian Criminal Code called for 'deprivation of freedom' for up to seven years if the act was committed 'for mercenary purposes or from other base motives', and a one-year sentence in the absence of motives. Yet many commentators considered the Russian law too lax and criticised redrafted criminal codes for leaving the law 'virtually unchanged'.

Press coverage of thefts by criminal gangs of state and private property also increased, particularly in *Pravda*, as did the reporting of bribery, abuse of office and fights between gangs of youths. Rape (generally gang rape) and child abuse were rarely discussed until 1990. The prevalence of crime was initially linked to 'the years of stagnation' which gave rise to parasites, black marketeers, drunkards, home brewers and drug abusers. By 1990, it was portrayed as part of 'the crisis'; and it had doubled under *perestroika*.

Drugs

While marijuana, speed and acid were easily available in the 1960s and 1970s on student campuses in North America and Britain, they were largely unknown in Soviet universities. When discussions about the pleasures and dangers of drugs were commonplace in the West, they were unheard of in Brezhnev's Soviet Union. As heroine addiction spread through Western states, the Soviet Union prided itself on not having this blight. Drug addiction was characteristic of capitalism's moral decay.

By the 1980s that moral decay was part of Soviet society too, but initially hushed up. Once the growing strength of *glasnost'* forced it into the open, it became, according to two writers in *Izvestiya* in November 1987, 'an evil that experts acknowledge is growing around the world'. Three months later, in *Izvestiya*, the same writers (Illesh and Shestinsky) quoted the Head of Criminal Investigations, V. Pankin, to the effect that, at the beginning of 1988, 131,000 people were on record for having tried drugs at least once. Of these, 50,000 were put on the medical register as drug addicts. By mid-1990, *Izvestiya* reported that over 117,000 were on the register.

According to Illesh and Shestinsky, the authorities draw a distinction between 'classical drug abuse' and 'vulgar drug abuse'. The former refers to plant substances, such as marijuana; the latter includes 'new, home-made narcotic substances . . . produced by processing preparations of various kinds . . . similar to those that are produced industrially for medical purposes'. The distinction is similar to Western categories of 'soft' and 'hard' drugs. Whereas in 1984 'vulgar drug abuse' accounted for 2 per cent of all drugs used, in 1986 the figure climbed to 12–16 per cent, and in 1987 exceeded 30 per cent. Hard drugs are particularly popular in the Baltic states, central Russia and the cities of Moscow and St Petersburg.

Medical treatment and punishment are the two main responses to heroin addiction. In 1987, 77 per cent of registered addicts underwent medical treatment, allegedly voluntarily. Of these, 15,000 broke their habit, 21,600 suffered administrative disciplinary action and 4,000 failed to complete their treatment and so were sent to 'treatment and labour centres'. The troubleshooting magazine *Ogonek* criticised, in February 1988, the quality of care available to addicts, questioned the success rate of treatment and pointed out that the authorities often lost track of discharged addicts.

The punishment of addicts was harsh in 1986 and 1987, when 30,000 drug users faced criminal proceedings and some were imprisoned for first-time possession of small amounts. Reports by Illesh and Shestinsky suggest that Criminal Codes are now more lenient. Addicts who do not involve others in their addiction are viewed as ill, rather than as criminals, and small-scale possession no longer results in imprisonment. But they also point out that addicts are regularly convicted for related criminal acts, such as forged prescriptions and domestic theft. In 1987, there were 35 recorded cases of addicts attempting to acquire drugs with forged prescriptions. Chemists were also broken into, with the result that 96 per cent of them now have burglar alarms. An estimated 35 per cent of illegal drugs in cities 'leak' from hospitals and, in the first ten months of 1987, 73 medical employees faced related charges. By the end of 1987, 50 drug dealers had also been arrested because police campaigns were being stepped up. As in the West, burglary, robbery and murder are crimes performed by hardened addicts.

Institutions other than hospitals, chemists, the police and courts have been drawn into the battle against drugs. For example, the Ministry of the Medical and Microbiological Industry and the Agro-Industrial Complex (before it was disbanded) agreed that the planting of poppies should cease. However the decision was taken reluctantly, since oil-bearing poppies supply the needs of the All-Union Association for the Production, Procurement and Processing of Medical Plants, the Ministry of Grain Products, the Ministry of Trade and the Agro-Industrial Complex. Pressure for the proposal to end planting came from the Department for Combatting the Embezzlement of Socialist Property and Speculation since it was spending a great deal of money on guarding the poppy harvest with police and dogs. According to *Izvestiya* of 6 October 1987, 'Chases, night ambushes and the apprehension of addicts, often armed with knives and sawn-off guns' were common.

The destruction of some crops, however, has proved difficult. Experts admit that they do not know how to destroy areas growing marijuana plants without destroying other crops with herbicides as well. Advice has been sought from the United States. The international fight against drug trafficking also requires collaboration with other states.

Prostitution

Like drugs, prostitution was rarely mentioned in the press until 1986. The official line was that under Soviet socialism prostitution did not exist. Instead prostitution was characteristic of capitalist systems where the right to work was not guaranteed and where unemployed women were 'forced' into prostitution in order to eat. Then, beginning in 1986, and escalating in 1987, newspaper articles on prostitution admitted its existence, deplored its extent and provided descriptions of the lives of prostitutes and their pimps.

Sensational stories were printed in *Literaturnaya gazeta*, *Komsomolskaya pravda*, *Nedelya* and *Sovetskaya Rossiya* with explicit moral messages. Under-age schoolgirls who performed sexual favours in cars and then blackmailed their clients were examples of the depravity of youth. Young women who 'worked' hotels in tourist spots in Sochi, soliciting foreigners, were an insult to society. Madames who lured young women to work in brothels, taking advantage of their lack of residence permits and their poverty, were corrupt. Pimps who demanded 70 rubles a day 'protection' money, and who beat up prostitutes if they did not get it, were violent parasites. These early articles focused on moral degradation, deception, crime, violence and venereal disease.

By late 1987, more systematic analyses of why women turn to prostitution were being published in the sociological journal *Sotsio-logicheskie issledovaniya*. Studies of prostitutes in Georgia found that women saw discrepancies between the lives they dreamed of and everyday reality. Images of elegant and successful women in the media underlined the mediocrity of their lives. Unable to afford boots at 120 rubles a pair, some women found prostitution attractive as a supplementary income.

Recommendations for combating prostitution have varied. One argument voiced in *Komsomolskaya pravda* in October 1986 held that 'this immoral business' can best be tackled by 'pooling the efforts of the police and the Komsomol'. Together they could rid society 'of this dirt'. A similar position put forward in the paper *Sovetskaya Kirgiziya* in May 1987 called for a 'war' against prostitution, arguing that non-resistance 'is the same as giving it one's blessing'. Another view expressed in *Trud* in July 1987 argued that prostitution should be made a criminal offence, with sterner punishments than the administrative measures already taken. Prostitutes could be issued with a warning and a fine up to 100 rubles in the first instance and up to 200 rubles if the offence was repeated within the year. Critics questioned whether this was an adequate deterrent: 'Can you really stop these increasingly brazen women with a 100-ruble fine?' In fact prostitutes are generally picked up by the militia for reasons other than prostitution; loitering in hotels results in arrest for violation of hotel regulations. A more enlightened approach taken by *Sovetskaya Rossiya* in March 1987 pointed out that legislation alone could not deter prostitution. Young girls, especially those who left their jobs and families, needed to be educated away from it.

Systematic data on prostitution has not been gathered, but selected articles draw attention to its extent in particular cities. According to *Sovetskaya Rossiya*, the files of one Moscow police chief covering the last fifteen years provide a record of 3,500 prostitutes, aged from 14 to 70. Academics have called for futher research into prostitution to discover more precisely its extent, sources and problems, so that sensible policy recommendations can be made. One problem which makes deterrence pressing is the spread of AIDS. Although by October 1990 there were 1,104 known AIDS carriers in the USSR (of these 553 were Soviet citizens), modest in contrast with Western statistics, there is recognition that far more cases exist and anxiety that prostitution may be a major means of transmission.

Conclusion

Before August 1991, many citizens had become uneasy about the prospect of transition to a market economy. They knew that some of the old guarantees of security would be removed, despite Gorbachev's insistence that the people would be protected. The threat of unemployment took away the certainty of an income and price increases led many to fear that they could not make ends meet. Unemployment benefits and wage increases did not sufficiently cover increased expenditures. The new stress on efficiency meant that many workplaces did not automatically pay out decreed 'compensation' for the price increases of April 1991 since they lacked the money. In addition, cutbacks in funding had put a question mark over the availability of already existing services. Some put their hope in an expansion of private health care, charities, joint ventures and a growing service sector. All, however, were beset with difficulties.

Problems intensified after August 1991 as inflation soared, the value of the ruble against the dollar continued to plummet and the worst grain harvest since 1981 was announced. Food shortages worsened and supply lines became even more unpredictable. A serious fiscal crisis demanded attention. In the first half of 1991, money supply had grown by 40 per cent. Thus, in the view of many economists, it was imperative to control the printing of money, to hold wages down, to allow prices to rise and to reduce subsidies. But Russian trade unions demanded 'market wages' for 'market prices'. Yeltsin pointed out that 'market wages' demanded 'market productivity', which was certainly lacking. In November 1991, the new popular slogan circulating in Moscow was 'free prices – free money'. Again despondency, gloom and despair had set in about rising prices.

From March 1985 to August 1991, three overwhelming problems had faced social policy makers. Established services needed substantial investment in order to improve health care, housing and the general quality of life. Simultaneously, problems long neglected, such as the provision of a basic network of old people's homes, needed to be addressed rather than ignored. And pressing new social problems, such as AIDS, homeless refugees and the results of ecological disasters, needed solutions. All three required increased budgetary allocations at a time of deficits, cutbacks and economic uncertainty. This did not mean that all social policies automatically suffered or that resources never increased. It did mean, however, that at a time of increased awareness about the extent of social problems, policy makers were constrained by budgetary limitations.

In this context anxieties grew. Many working women wondered whether kindergarten provision would be drastically cut back, or its real cost passed on to consumers if subsidies ended. After price increases in April 1991, then again in January 1992, many citizens were horrified that guaranteed protections of the past were over and that prices could even rise again. As the dollar increasingly penetrated the Soviet economy, those without access to it felt deprived of the benefits it could bring. 'Socialist social justice' had ushered in the legitimation of wage differentials and differential access to services and pensions; then 'social protection' seemed to indicate an inadequate safety net for the unemployed and the poor; and in 1992 it was unclear what 'social protection' there really was. So many felt vulnerable to forces beyond their understanding or control. Rumours of revolts by the starving whipped up fears and anxieties. Talk of another coup circulated, this time with the warning that it would not be opposed by barricades.

Economic problems limited the scope of social policies. Although there was space for initiatives to be taken by the private sector, charities and foreign help, their combined efforts barely touched the surface of social problems. In addition unresolved issues of political responsibility and accountability meant that many social policies could not, before 1992, be adequately redefined. It was necessary for relationships between republics and centre, and different administrative levels within republics, to be sorted out. Those living in areas of ecological disaster or nationalist ferment were especially affected.

Although the results of a market economy were feared, there was a growing belief among reformers that, since the socialist experiment had failed, 'the market' was the only salvation. Its short-term results would not be pleasant, but its long-term promise was seductive. Striking miners and some industrial workers, in 1991, welcomed radical economic reform and threatened further disruption if it did not come. But Leninists who criticised *Gorbastroika* as 'bourgeois restoration' and as a 'drift towards fascism' believed that socialism was being betrayed. They continued to feel this way after August 1991 and viewed the price increases of January 1992 with horror, as did the miners who had initially called for reform. Even if pensioners were now to receive 200 rubles a month, with sausage priced at over 60 rubles a kilo and butter at 132 a kilo, how could they survive? Socialist morality had gone. Worsening poverty was the unavoidable result. *Pravda* of 10 January 1992 characterised 'shock price therapy' as among the 'sad omens of our time'. Barter became, for many, the new mode of exchange, although those with hard currency (now one dollar was officially worth 110 rubles) were comfortable. More cynical youth hoped to escape altogether by finding jobs in the West. *Izvestiya* captured this intensified desire in a cartoon printed on its front page at the end of December 1991. True to Russian black humour, it showed a mother walking with a pram. The baby inside pulled a gun on her and demanded, 'Push me to Sweden.'

After the 'revolution' of 1991, it quickly became clear that answers to some problems of centre–republic relations would be found much sooner than expected, however chaotically. Newly independent states would, in future, be formulating their own social policies. But the same social problems remained, still requiring economic resources. Policies to tackle them would, in part, be increasingly linked to the nature of future markets. These markets might ease some social problems, such as the availability of medicines, but exacerbate others, such as unemployment, crime, drug abuse and the spread of pornography. Social inequalities, too, would widen. And economic aid packages, loans and investments from Western states would mean that important aspects of life would be affected by decisions taken outside domestic borders, whether people liked it or not (and many proud Russians disliked food parcels, just as they had a year earlier). Harder to gauge, and highly complex in its likely results, the individualism required by, and resulting from, markets would clash with a multitude of behaviour patterns, deeply ingrained in the collectivism of Russian culture and in the patriarchal practices of the Central Asian republics.

12

The Politics of Foreign Policy

ALEX PRAVDA

Issues of national security and foreign policy penetrated Soviet domestic politics more narrowly than is generally the case in capitalist states. Traditionally the political reach of international issues was restricted both in terms of the groups able to influence the development of external policy and in the range of its domestic ripple effect. The number of actors involved in making international policy has been smaller than in democratic states. Soviet policy making in general was highly secretive and centralised: this was especially the case in defence and foreign policy, fields universally associated with closed decision making. The political reach of external policy was also restricted inasmuch as the USSR remained relatively cut off from the international political and economic system. International contacts certainly grew in the post-Stalin period, yet the country remained relatively closed. As a result the spectrum of domestic issues affected by external policy, and thus the range of domestic constituencies with strong vested interests in foreign policy, has remained quite narrow.

In the course of the last six years the traditional involvement of foreign and security policy in Soviet politics showed signs of moving in the direction of Western patterns. There was some broadening of participation in the formulation of external policy, part of a wider effort to bring a greater variety of ideas to bear on policy making in general. At the same time the political reach of international issues in domestic politics widened and deepened. The unprecedented expansion of international links, especially moves to increase economic interaction with the capitalist world, expanded the number of institutions with a role in external relations. Moves towards more open exchange with the West have paralleled steps to decentralise control over their conduct. This multiplication of foreign policy interest has of course been accelerated by the disintegration of the USSR. This has meant the republicanisation of foreign and to some extent security policy. The external policies of the newly independent successor states are in large part concerned with relations within the old Soviet area. The internationalisation of what were previously domestic issues, coupled with the efforts to economise and democratise external relations, has produced a radical politicisation of security and foreign policy.

This chapter attempts to set these *perestroika* and post-*perestroika* patterns of politicisation within the context of the overall connections linking security and foreign policy with domestic politics. To do this and bring out the remarkable changes that have recently emerged, we first outline the ways in which external policy was embedded in Soviet priorities, then consider the institutions and processes involved in security and foreign policy making, and finally examine the way in which external policy issues figure in the domestic political arena.

Why and How Security and Foreign Policy Matter

In Soviet politics, defence and foreign policy were traditionally made critical by the sheer scale of security concerns and the salience of the ideological dimension of international policy. Security anxieties have always loomed large in Russia and the Soviet Union and will undoubtedly continue to do so in any association or commonwealth of ex-Soviet states. Historical memories of invasions, distant and long-lasting, such as the Mongol or, more recent and brief, such as the French and German, have fed a preoccupation with defence against threats from East and West. Geopolitical facts make the task of defending the country a daunting one, as the Soviet and the new post-Soviet Union has the world's longest frontier (37,000 miles) bordering on no fewer than fourteen states. What is more, security has dimensions within and beyond national borders. The fact that the USSR was the last great land empire continues to make national security far more complex and sensitive a domestic political issue than in most other states. Tensions between the various nationalities, and particularly between the centre and the Union republics (by definition located in border areas), traditionally increased Moscow's concern to maintain very high levels of military vigilance against external 'threats'. On occasion concern to prevent such perceived threats from destabilising vulnerable border areas contributed to the use of force beyond areas of established Soviet dominance – the invasion of Afghanistan in 1979 provides the most graphic recent example.

More often concern about the stability of the 'inner empire' of republics played a part in prompting direct or indirect Soviet action in the 'outer empire' of Eastern Europe. The existence of what was long an external empire of dependent states extended both the logistical and political range of Soviet security policy. It involved a major commitment of forces (almost half a million Soviet troops were stationed in the region) and the maintenance of the Warsaw Pact. An additional extension of security concerns came with the acquisition in the 1960s and 1970s of a global military presence and capability, notably in the third world.

The fact that Soviet superpower status depended so heavily – some would argue exclusively – on military capability, lent security policy even greater political importance than in the USA, whose world standing has rested far more evenly on political and economic as well as military resources. The relative economic weakness of the Soviet Union, coupled with its extensive military commitments, also gave security policy great weight in domestic priorities. Soviet military expenditure, according to the most widely accepted US estimates, amounted to approximately 15–17 per cent of GNP in the 1970s and 1980s. Recent official estimates from Moscow have raised this proportion to 20–25 per cent and some, including Gorbachev, have talked of defence absorbing as much as 40 per cent of resources. Whatever the exact size of the defence burden, the immensity of the military sector and its permeation of the entire economy has made security issues central to domestic priorities.

Many security commitments reflected the ideological content of Soviet external concerns and relations. The ideological dimension of Soviet foreign policy affected the manner in which external events impinged on internal politics in two main ways: by complicating defence tasks and by providing an additional link between domestic and international developments. The Marxist–Leninist ideology officially espoused by the Soviet authorities compounded and strengthened the divisions which had traditionally separated the USSR from the non-socialist world. For 70 years after the revolution of October 1917, the international image of the Soviet Union was coloured by its avowed commitment to exploiting the weaknesses of capitalism and helping promote the spread of world socialism. However pragmatic and prudent Soviet leaders proved to be in practice when pursuing their 'revolutionary' objectives, their continued profession of a global ideologically-based mission challenging the *status quo* helped to magnify the perceived Soviet 'threat'. The ideological aspect of this threat helped foster an ideological rationale in responding to it militarily, thus fuelling an action–reaction arms spiral which increased Soviet security problems and the weight of defence in domestic developments.

As well as magnifying the security challenges facing Soviet policy makers, the ideological dimension long gave external policy a prominent domestic profile by linking regime performance and even legitimacy at home to the way the Soviet cause fared abroad. Links of this kind exist in all states, since all governments seek not merely to secure borders but also to defend and promote national interests and values. The self-image of states or, more exactly, of their political and strategic elites, invariably includes a picture of their place in the international order. Efforts to advance that image are often closely connected with the advancement of values at home. The Falklands War illustrated the tight connection at that time in British politics between the projections of values at home and abroad. In most states such linkages are strong only occasionally, in exceptional circumstances. In the case of the Soviet Union these linkages had a more pervasive presence because of the peculiar role played by ideology in sustaining regime legitimacy.

The communist party monopoly on Marxism–Leninism was traditionally an element in its claim to legitimacy. Recent events have underscored the far greater importance of customary authority and economic performance in determining levels of legitimacy and governance. Nonetheless acceptance of official ideology, however cosmetic, was a factor in sustaining the regime, just as official de-ideologisation helped accelerate its demise. Ideological and value factors were and continue to be particularly important for the elites. Soviet international performance, the advancement of its global mission, may well have affected the popular legitimacy and image of the regime. It probably figured more prominently among the elites as a yardstick of the success, dynamism and even legitimacy of the Soviet system. The concept of the 'correlation of forces' between world socialism and capitalism embodied and reinforced the sense of direct competition between the Soviet system and the West. Successes and setbacks in the progress of socialism throughout the world were seen to redound on the image and even legitimacy of the domestic regime. Whatever role the ideological, psychological and material elements played in this notion of competition, comparisons between the Soviet and capitalist systems figured prominently in elite thinking. It was as much through such comparisons as through the actual impact of international economic, military and political developments on the Soviet Union that external factors affected domestic politics. Publics are especially leaders tended to gauge the health of the domestic system partly in terms of global comparisons.

Concern with poor relative, as well as absolute, performance was a major element in forming the Gorbachev leadership's early judgement that the country was in a crisis that required radical change. As he recalled in his December 1991 resignation speech as President, he had been struck by the fact that, despite all the Soviet Union's natural and human resources, its people 'were living so much worse than the developed countries and were slipping further and further behind them'.

As well as helping to highlight international comparisons of performance, ideology in a broad sense has long provided a link between strategies of foreign and domestic development. The connection here goes back further than Marxism–Leninism: it involved theories of the proper orientation of Russian, not just Soviet development. The last 70 years have echoed many of the debates under tsarism between those like the Slavophils, who advocated Russocentric paths of evolution, and the Westernisers who favoured borrowing from and often copying West European experience. Bolshevism initially represented a strongly westernising strategy, which under Lenin rested on a gradualist path to socialism and peaceful coexistence with capitalism. Stalin brought a reversion to a more introverted strategy under the slogan 'socialism in one country', with class struggle in the international arena being paralleled by class conflict at home. Khrushchev, in this sense, was a Westerniser, but under Brezhnev there was growing closure and immobilism.

Gorbachev and Foreign Policy

To counter the stagnation of the Brezhnev years Gorbachev embarked on a strategy of economic and political modernisation. Critically important for our analysis is the fact that Gorbachev conceived and deployed this strategy as one of *open* modernisation. To a greater extent than any other Soviet leader he sought radically to restructure the economic and political system in a Western orientation by exposing the country to greater international influence and involvement. The *perestroika* and post-*perestroika* periods have seen not merely congruence but symbiosis between open strategies at home and abroad. Opening up in the international arena, where radical change made early progress, helped advances towards domestic openness. Defusing the tensions of the second Cold War period of the early 1980s contributed to a more favourable climate for domestic democratisation. This in turn increased the credibility of the new Soviet policy of cooperation with the international community pursued by Gorbachev and Shevardnadze.

Mutually reinforcing though the external and internal open strategies have proved over the last six years, domestic priorities have clearly provided the driving force. Domestic priorities have generally held sway over international ones, as indeed they have usually done in most states. Even in the brief early period of revolutionary internationalism, the security of the new Soviet state took precedence over spreading socialism abroad, a priority exemplified by the Treaty of Brest Litovsk (1918). Stalin's doctrine of 'socialism in one country' set a seal on the dominance of domestic concerns. Khrushchev on occasion seemed to place the promotion of global influence almost on a par with considerations of domestic security. His attempt to pursue simultaneously ambitious domestic and foreign policy change helped to bring about his political downfall. Brezhnev moved more cautiously and generally placed maintenance of the domestic *status quo* first. He tried, however unsuccessfully, to adjust the aperture of foreign policy to conservative domestic ends.

What distinguished Gorbachev from his predecessors was not so much that he placed domestic priorities first, even if he repeatedly claimed that he did so to a greater extent than ever before. The real distinction of Gorbachev's strategy lay in the fact that he radically realigned foreign policy to facilitate rather than avoid domestic change and sustained this radical international realignment to help drive fundamental transformation at home. The new foreign policy, codified in 'new political thinking', was an intrinsic part of the *perestroika* strategy of open modernisation. In this sense foreign and security policy over the last six years has served domestic objectives and constituted an integral part of politics to a greater extent than in the course of the previous seven decades.

Two major strands of the new foreign and security policy, demilitarisation and de-ideologisation, stand out in the pattern of domestic developments. Both strands, more accurately processes, played a key role in undermining the Soviet regime at home and abroad and continue to be salient in post-Soviet development. Demilitarisation appeared as an early feature of Gorbachev's security policy in the form of a commitment to arms control and disarmament. The priority given to disarmament plainly had a strong domestic as well as international rationale. Demilitarisation as disarmament was a policy pursued to lighten the economic weight of the defence burden as well as to improve the climate of East–West relations. So compelling was this combined rationale that Gorbachev proved willing to sign the asymmetrical agreement on intermediate nuclear forces in December 1987 and offer unilateral conventional cuts a year later. These cuts, together with the conventional reductions agreed under the Conventional Forces in Europe (CFE) treaty in 1990, had a major impact on the domestic scene. Nuclear agreements fuelled a campaign for conversion of defence production to consumer output. Ambitious timetables included in the conventional treaties had less positive repercussions. Lack of adequate provision for housing for troops returning from Eastern Europe resulted in the accommodation of over 250,000 soldiers in makeshift tent cities in 1991. Nonetheless the momentum to cut the size of the military establishment continues to influence the policy of the successor states. Russia intends to make further inroads into the armed forces to create a smaller and increasingly professional force. The other states similarly aim to have leaner contingents. If, however, all states establish sizeable national guards and some, like Ukraine, create large armed forces, the total under arms in the new Commonwealth could exceed the limits envisaged under the CFE.

As well as driving and legitimating arms reductions, demilitarisation has had broader policy connotations, in the sense of curtailing the role of force in international and domestic politics. The decision to withdraw Soviet forces from Afghanistan reflected and reinforced a policy shift away from seeing the military as a prominent instrument of foreign policy towards looking for political means to resolve conflict. First applied to third-world regional disputes, this disinclination to use force was extended in 1986–7 to cover Eastern Europe. Even if this principle was not transferred in any automatic sense to domestic issues, its enunciation and implementation abroad had important political echoes at home. Republican nationalist leaders may have seen official statements denouncing the use of force as significant policy signals. That Gorbachev was reluctant to use force to retain control of the republics became evident in the rather half-hearted coercion employed in the Baltic in January 1991. Demilitarisation in both its guises – curtailment of military capabilities and, especially, of their political use – has thus been an important strand running through international and domestic politics.

The other strand, de-ideologisation, has figured as importantly, if more diffusely. It has involved the rejection of traditional stereotyped ideological thinking which constrained foreign and domestic policy. The mould of such thinking was first clearly broken in the international sphere, with the official elevation in 1986–7 of all-human interests and values above those of class. This basic principle of 'new political thinking' was used to legitimate the new rapprochement with capitalism, with its emphasis on mutuality, interdependence and codevelopment rather than mere coexistence. It justified not only disarmament but new policies to open up the Soviet Union to capitalist investment and the international economy.

The primacy of universal human values was part of a revolutionary acceptance of the fact that norms previously associated with capitalism had general validity for socialism. Repeated references to the need to adhere to 'civilised' ways of conducting international relations had important domestic ramifications. Such references, as well as those to the need to become part of a European Common Home, formed part of a deliberate effort to use international criteria as leverage points to catalyse domestic change. Civilised political practices, including a willingness to settle conflict through compromise, had to be followed at home as well as abroad. Other principles which stemmed from de-ideologisation of international perspectives also had an important domestic dimension. Notable among these was strong endorsement from 1987 of the principles of self-determination and freedom of choice for all states, including those in the socialist community. The fact that Moscow allowed freedom of choice in Eastern Europe encouraged those leading national movements in the Baltic and later in other Soviet republics. If Gorbachev proved reluctant to apply these principles within the USSR, Yeltsin made them central to his policy and they are fundamental to the new Commonwealth of Independent States established in December 1991.

In addition to such revolutionary effects on the substance of traditional Soviet foreign and domestic policy, de-ideologisation has also had a major impact on policy process. A major thrust has been to substitute realism and pragmatism for dogmatic blinkers and incompetence. This has involved encouraging a pluralism of approaches and opinions in the resolution of problems and the formulation of policy. The 'secularisation' of foreign policy making reflected and helped accelerate the freeing of domestic policy making from traditional constraints.

In both domestic and international spheres, secularisation has opened up greater scope for policy input from a wider range of institutions and specialists. This has not necessarily produced expert or democratic policy making, as executives have continued to dominate the process, especially with the development of presidential power since 1990. At the same time policy making over the last three years has become more open and susceptible to a wider range of institutions and views.

Policy Institutions and Processes

Perestroika has a twofold effect on the structure and making of foreign and security policy. First, its general overhaul of party and government institutions shook up traditional structures, procedures and appointment systems. Second, the shift towards a more pragmatic and flexible external policy generated calls for a more imaginative and pluralistic approach to solving policy problems.

To set recent and current changes into context, let us briefly review the bodies and processes involved in the traditional Soviet system of foreign and security policy making. The revolutionary origins of the Soviet state left their imprint on the structure of the foreign policy institutional establishment. For a few months after the revolution of 1917 the Bolsheviks believed that they could dispense with the traditional trappings of 'bourgeois' diplomacy, including the foreign ministry. As in other areas, so particularly in relations with the outside world, Soviet leaders soon found they had to use old as well as new policy instruments. Foreign minister Chicherin laid the foundations of a traditional foreign and diplomatic corps in the 1920s. This was engaged in formulating and running normal, what were called 'technical diplomatic', state-to-state relations. At the same time Moscow used the Comintern (the Communist International), its postwar successor Cominform and subsequently the CPSU International Department, to build links with other communist parties and help them advance the cause of socialism in a way that suited Soviet national interests.

This dual foreign policy was conducted by two parallel institutional machines: the state diplomatic, headed by the Ministry of Foreign Affairs; and the party-ideological, run by the CPSU international apparatus. In theory the two operated in tandem, closely coordinating policies. In practice, party/government dualism, here as in other areas, generated overlapping jurisdictions and inconsistent policy.

The International Department of the Central Committee, while notionally limited to relations with communist and other 'progressive' parties, typically exercised the major influence over the formulation of the CPSU's overall foreign strategy. In certain spheres this party foreign ministry exercised all-important influence, notably in relations with ruling communist parties and many third-world states. Together with the Socialist Countries Department (which had an independent existence from 1957–88), the International Department shaped policy towards Eastern Europe, China and many third-world states. Even in regions such as Western Europe the International Department exercised considerable influence on Soviet strategy. The Department's long-time first deputy head, Vadim Zagladin, had a key say in overall policy towards the region, especially West Germany, a role continued by Valentin Falin, its last head (1988–91).

The tendency of the Central Committee to try and extend its reach in international policy long generated rivalry with the Ministry of Foreign Affairs. To be sure, government and party bodies usually worked within the same strategic framework, yet each had a distinct focus and perspective on priorities. The International Department was particularly concerned with dimensions of policy relating to other countries' domestic politics, public opinion, propaganda and 'progressive' movements. The Ministry tended to look at issues and options from more traditional state and diplomatic vantage points.

For most of the postwar period, the International Department managed to exercise the greater influence on the formulation of general foreign policy strategy, often via Mikhail Suslov, the Central Committee secretary in overall charge of international and ideological affairs. The Ministry, headed for almost 30 years (1959–85) by Andrei Gromyko, typically played more of an executive role, influencing strategy more through interpretation and implementation. After the mid-1970s, with Gromyko a full Politburo member, the policy influence and authority of the Ministry increased. With Suslov and Brezhnev in physical decline and then interim leaders in office, Gromyko really ran much of Soviet foreign policy from the late 1970s until his replacement by Eduard Shevardnadze in July 1985.

During his time in office (1985–90 and November–December 1991) Shevardnadze gave the Ministry the greatest policy influence and the most thorough overhaul of its political life. Started in late 1985 and accelerated through 1986, this overhaul involved organisational rationalisation as well as a shake-up of personnel policy. Such reforms were long overdue since the Ministry, in common with other Soviet bodies, had been allowed to lie fallow with outdated structures and inefficient practices over the previous 20 years. Shevardnadze oversaw an organisational rationalisation which established new sectoral departments, notably for arms control and economic affairs. Headed by Viktor Karpov, an official with long experience in the arms control field, the department gave the Ministry greater input into the formulation of negotiating positions. Setting up an economic affairs department was part of Shevardnadze's campaign for a more vigorous economic diplomacy, something the Ministry had traditionally neglected. This campaign had limited success and the reorganisation of November 1991 sought to further the 'economisation' drive by merging the Foreign Ministry with the Ministry for External Economic Relations to form the short-lived Ministry of External Relations.

Alongside these campaigns Shevardnadze launched a series of broadsides in 1986–7 against the Ministry's traditional work practices and, particularly, its established system of appointments. In tones sharper than those used by leaders when complaining about other ministries (and certainly more hard-hitting than any published

speeches by reforming heads of Western foreign ministries) Shevardnadze railed against the Foreign Ministry's 'stale atmosphere of
protection, nepotism, money-grubbing and narrow-mindedness'. A
former party official was brought in as personnel head and, between
1986 and 1989, all nine deputy ministers and three out of four of the
senior officials were replaced. As Shevardnadze recounts in his
memoirs, making inroads into such a settled establishment proved
difficult and he often found himself facing a conservative ministry
bureaucracy. Even if the changes he introduced did not produce the
new-generation 'diplomatic technology' he wanted, they brought to
bear an array of diplomatic talent which surprised and impressed the
West, particularly during the 1986–9 period.

Similar if less draconian changes affected the Central Committee
International Department under *perestroika*. In June 1986, Boris
Ponomarev, who had headed the Department for over 30 years, was
replaced by Anatolii Dobrynin, the doyen of Soviet diplomacy, who
had served as ambassador in Washington for more than two decades.
He brought with him other professional diplomats to fill key posts
previously held by men from ideology, propaganda and international
communist organisation backgrounds. This 'diplomatisation' of the
Department reflected the wider effort to de-ideologise Soviet foreign
policy. Dobrynin reportedly proved disappointing as a generator of
new ideas and was replaced in September 1988 by Valentin Falin, a
German specialist with a mixed party and diplomatic background.
Under his leadership the Department continued to deal with a wide
range of diplomatic issues beyond the traditional brief of party-to-
party relations. Falin sought to retain institutional predominance for
the Department in formulating the strategic ideas for Soviet foreign
policy. He had to contend with the growing stature of the Foreign
Ministry, enhanced by the influence of Shevardnadze in the inner
leadership core. The International Department had less effective
direct access to decision making through Alexander Yakovlev, who
was in overall charge of the party's external policy and headed the
Central Committee Commission on International Policy. Established
in 1988 as part of the overhaul of the Central Committee structure,
the Commission notionally had the potential to act as an inter-agency
body to coordinate external policy. In the event it met infrequently
and its composition, including a large group of regional party
officials, was inappropriate for any effective coordinating function.

Between 1988 and 1991 foreign policy continued to run along
parallel and often cross-cutting and even discordant lines. The International Department, under pressure from Gorbachev's shift towards
state institutions, took a somewhat conservative line on Eastern
Europe and Germany yet continued to exercise influence through its

expertise, especially on the socialist states. Falin criticised Gorbachev and Shevardnadze for their concessions in Europe in 1989–90 and contributed to the campaign that prompted the Foreign Minister to resign in December 1990. The resignation brought a decline in the political influence of the Ministry, headed as it was from this time by a career diplomat, Alexander Bessmertnykh. The International Department tried to reassert its traditional leading role in East European policy in early 1991.

Both Falin and Bessmertnykh, however, chose the wrong side in the August coup whose aftermath engulfed the International Department, along with all CPSU bodies, thus leaving the Foreign Ministry in sole institutional charge of policy. It was politically handicapped in taking full advantage of its new position by the lack of political influence of the new minister, Boris Pankin, who, after three months in office, gave way to Shevardnadze. Returning to take charge of adjusting the all-Union Ministry in its new relationship with republican bodies, Shevardnadze found himself presiding over the Ministry's unexpectedly brief demise. After a month as the new Ministry of External Relations, it was effectively superseded in December 1991 by the Russian Ministry of Foreign Affairs. Having brought an end to the old institutional party–state dualism, post-Soviet politics have created the basis for a new foreign policy dualism between Commonwealth and state bodies (see below, pp. 272–5).

Security Policy

Under the Soviet system, the military exercised firm control over the formulation as well as the implementation of defence policy. They did so largely by dint of their monopoly of data and expert analysis indispensable for the formulation and evaluation of policy alternatives. The Ministry of Defence, wholly staffed by career officers, gathered and processed technical information relating to security policy. Some processing and the most important analysis on strategy and weapons systems was done by the General Staff of the armed forces. Data on the economic aspects of defence were the province of the Military–Industrial Commission which, until its demise in late 1991, oversaw and coordinated the production of the various defence ministries.

All these bodies jealously guarded their monopoly of military information, to which even the KGB had limited access. The areas of weapons development, military doctrine and strategy as well as arms control traditionally exemplified the general tendency in the Soviet policy process to compartmentalisation. In arms control negotiations in the 1970s, for instance, military members of the Soviet team were reluctant to share what they considered sensitive data on Soviet capabilities with their civilian colleagues, even though the American side already possessed equivalent information.

Gorbachev made determined efforts to break down such compartmentalisation of security information, symptomatic of 'departmentalism' in this as in other policy areas. In the key sphere of arms control, early steps were taken to weaken the military's monopoly of information and assessment by encouraging the multiplication of civilian centres of expertise. The Foreign Ministry and the International Department both established special units which employed retired military officers as well as civilian specialists. They were able to give civilian specialists better access to information and decision makers. Civilian arms controllers had been able, even in the 1970s, to offer alternative analyses to those produced by the military, yet they had made relatively little impression on official policy. Under *perestroika* their ideas, cull.d mainly from Western strategic thinking, made an incomparably greater impact on Soviet arms control approaches and policy. They effectively shaped the security component of 'new thinking', introducing innovative concepts such as 'reasonable sufficiency' and 'defensive defence'.

This civilian influence partly reflected the fact that their recommendations coincided with the demilitarising thrust of Gorbachev's overall priorities. At the same time they had themselves helped to foster this line of reasoning, making a much greater impact on the Gorbachev leadership than on their predecessors. Gorbachev sought out and accepted civilian rather than military proposals on key arms control moves, such as asymmetrical INF reductions and unilateral conventional cuts. He no doubt did so for political as well as substantive policy reasons, but this does not alter the fact that civilians have come to exercise a remarkable influence not just on arms control policy but also, on occasion, on military doctrine.

Not surprisingly this intrusion of civilian expertise into military domains has caused considerable resentment among the Ministry of Defence and General Staff professionals. Some of the more conservative-minded have resorted to their control over the technical implementation of agreements to exercise policy influence. Circumvention of the Conventional Forces in Europe agreement through diversion of large amounts of tanks and other equipment beyond the Urals is the most notable example of some of the military using implementation powers to compensate for loss of influence over policy making.

A similar if less spectacular recent broadening of specialist policy influence has been evident in foreign policy as a whole. It has been less spectacular because specialists outside the main policy institutions contributed importantly to foreign policy thinking before the changes of the mid-1980s. Under *perestroika*, however, many more members of the various academic think-tanks gained access to policy makers and several rose to prominent office within the Foreign Ministry and the International Department. A few rose to the highest levels, becoming, like Georgii Shakhnazarov, key aides to Gorbachev or, like Alexander Yakovlev and Yevgenii Primakov, members of top decision-making executives.

Interlocking executive bodies in Russia and the Soviet Union have long exercised decision-making power over all aspects of security and foreign policy more tightly than in most other political systems. The party Politburo, the cabinet-like executive which ruled the country until 1990, often devolved policy- and decision-making or security issues to the Defence Council. Formally a state body, the Defence Council included the party leader, the Foreign Minister, the Minister of Defence and top defence industry officials. The Chief of the General Staff was also a member and provided the Council's secretariat. If under Brezhnev the Council was dominated by the military and met sporadically, Gorbachev placed it under closer civilian control and used it more regularly to make key defence decisions. With the formation of a presidential system in 1990, the Council's role was assumed by the Security Council.

The Defence Council had no foreign policy equivalent in the Soviet system. External policy issues were of course regularly discussed at Politburo meetings, though, predictably, the foreign and defence ministers, the head of the KGB and the Central Committee secretary in charge of ideology tended to dominate. The party general secretary tended to play a key role in all security and foreign policy decisions and was frequently identified with particular initiatives. Along with a kitchen cabinet of core colleagues, it was the leader who took key decisions, without consulting and even without notifying other members of the Politburo, as happened in 1979 when Soviet troops were sent into Afghanistan.

The Afghanistan decision was cited by Shevardnadze and Gorbachev as the most telling example of the way secret and closed decision making led to grave policy errors. They called for greater transparency in policy making and greater accountability of those who made decisions in all areas of government, but particularly where national security was at stake. To this end an attempt was made to introduce something like the US War Powers Act and the Supreme Soviet acquired the right of final approval of executive decisions to send troops overseas. As part of its efforts to operate like a real parliament, the Supreme Soviet began in 1989 to vet ministerial nominees. It refused to sanction the reappointment of a foreign trade minister and approved the defence minister, Yazov, only after a rough ride. Ratifying state treaties became an increasingly serious matter and debates aired critical views, especially on INF and the German settlement.

While parliamentary debate marked a step forward in accountability, scrutiny of foreign and security policy was the responsibility of new standing committees. The committees, one on International Affairs and one on Defence and State Security, had extensive remits and aspired to the kind of influence exercised by their US counterparts. Both understandably experienced a serious lack of organisational resources, established processes and a powerful parliamentary base. The International Affairs Committee had a conservative chairman who used his position to criticise progressive moves and bid for Shevardnadze's job. The Defence and State Security Committee performed rather better but became absorbed in tussling with the Ministry of Defence on issues relating to military reform, leaving it little time for international security issues. The committees made a start towards involving deputies in scrutinising and influencing the specifics of international policy, but were constrained by working within a politically polarised context in which policy power remained highly concentrated within executives.

For all the willingness of the Gorbachev leadership to listen to a wider range of policy opinion and to have issues aired in parliamentary and other circles, key decisions remained firmly in the hands of a small executive group and particularly in those of the General Secretary and later President himself. Gorbachev, together with Shevardnadze, played a crucial role in many of the foreign policy initiatives that were launched up to 1991. After the August coup, the growing domestic power and international status of Russian President Boris Yeltsin expanded until in December 1991 he eclipsed Gorbachev altogether. Since Yeltsin seems to exert as dominant an influence over Russian external policy as Gorbachev previously exercised over the Soviet, and a similar situation seems to exist in the other successor states, the traditionally tight executive control over decision making in this area appears to be largely intact. Policy making and the policy performance, however, have become increasingly subject to critical political debate.

Political Concerns and Debates

Security and foreign policy issues have in one sense become more politically salient over the last six years, and in another less so.

Measured by the yardstick of the pre-*perestroika* decades, external policy has, by virtue of its own transformation and the opening up of domestic politics, become far more visible and discussed. In the context of the extraordinary domestic political changes of the *perestroika* and post-*perestroika* periods, foreign policy has perhaps lost salience in relative terms.

Neither the salience nor role of external policy has remained constant over the last six years. These can be divided into two main phases which correspond to the headway made on the international front and, especially, to the changing domestic political scene. The first phase, 1986–8, was one of relative foreign policy success and consensus. In the second phase, 1989–91, both declined: international performance deteriorated and attracted increasing criticism in a climate of growing political polarisation. The collapse of the August 1991 coup restored most of the consensus for an open foreign policy, though defining new external policy priorities remains high on the agenda of the successor states.

These shifts in the political role of security and foreign policy were evident at the level of public opinion and, especially, of elite and leadership politics. Public awareness and discussion of international issues developed more slowly than on the domestic front. Informed media analysis of foreign affairs lagged behind *glasnost'* on internal issues. Only in 1988 did the first critical articles appear and then they largely focused on past rather than current policy. They reappraised Stalin's conduct of the war, the Katyn massacre of 1943 and the Molotov–Ribbentrop pact, as well as some key Brezhnev decisions, notably the deployment of SS20 missiles in Europe and the invasion of Afghanistan, both 'soft' targets as their criticism coincided with the Gorbachev foreign policy line.

Criticism reflected and fuelled growing public dissatisfaction with the Afghan war, which helped both to legitimate and to influence the decision to bring Soviet involvement to an end. This key decision helped to create overwhelming public support for the new foreign policy. In polls some expressed concern at the sudden decision to lower the country's military guard and doubts about the feasibility of complete nuclear disarmament. However, with its emphasis on expending fewer domestic resources on ideological global mission and military might, the 'new thinking' had obvious popular appeal. Polls showed that the great majority wanted a rapid end to 'aid' for the third world and cuts in the defence budget deeper than the 14 per cent announced in early 1989 and closer to the rather greater level of reductions favoured in 1990–1.

Even in the second phase, when foreign policy gains became less evident and hurried withdrawal from Eastern Europe was seen by

critics as decreasing security, the public still backed the new conciliatory line. Few thought that the West presented any real threat and
few condoned the use of force to keep erstwhile socialist 'allies' from
breaking with the Warsaw Pact. Even where Germany was concerned,
the great majority rejected the use of force to maintain the *status quo*.
A minority of the public expressed wariness rather than fear of a
united Germany. As for the loss of Moscow's global might, there was
little public regret. If some may have been disappointed by the
quiescent role played during the Gulf crisis, the prevailing sentiment
was against any involvement of Soviet forces, a product of what came
to be known as the Afghan syndrome. This reinforced public opposition to any further expenditure on behalf of third-world allies who
were seen to have embroiled the USSR in costly conflict with the
West. In the public mind, the West became seen increasingly as part
of the solution rather than part of the problem, a view encouraged
and reflected by the leadership's foreign policy line.

On the public opinion front, then, foreign policy performance, in
sharp contrast to domestic policy, has been largely well received.
Active endorsement of Gorbachev's energetic new diplomacy did of
course wane after 1989. This was partly in response to the scale and
speed of troop withdrawal, partly because the leadership appeared to
be paying excessive attention to international affairs to what many
saw as the detriment of more pressing problems at home. Nonetheless over the whole six-year period, foreign policy proved to be a
political asset.

On balance the same may be said about the role of foreign policy in
high politics. However, if we consider how external issues figured in
debates among policy elites and political leaders, this broad-brush
generalisation needs considerable qualification. Given the radical
changes it introduced, the new foreign and security policy was
obviously controversial from the outset. More interesting is the fact
that it was less contested politically than its controversial content may
seem to have warranted. The new external policy aroused more
debate than political challenge.

Three sets of factors may help to account for the relatively weak
contestation of the new foreign and security policy (in large part they
apply also to other policy areas). First, traditional structures and
customs of hierarchy, associated with democratic centralism, worked
strongly in favour of leadership policy. Institutional groups with most
at stake were not in a position to mount an effective political
challenge on foreign policy grounds. The Foreign Ministry bureaucracy was politically weak and, as we noted, was soon managed by
new senior officials. Many in the KGB, at least in the early phase,
were generally supportive of *perestroika* as a form of modernisation

led from the top. Some KGB officials attempted to hamper the progress of new relations with the West (the Daniloff affair in late 1986 was one such instance) but, under the new security chief Kryuchkov, such obstructionism subsequently declined until the reassertion of the right in 1990–1. The military, the group with the greatest vested interest in the area and potentially the most powerful muscle, were constrained by their traditional subordination to the political leadership. Hierarchical subordination applied less of course to the top political leadership. But here Gorbachev managed very rapidly to eliminate conservative opposition. Those who remained critical of *perestroika* focused on domestic rather than international issues because these were closer to their own interests and more open to attack.

The greater political immunity of foreign policy stemmed from more impressive performance and from presentation. The way in which 'new thinking' presented and justified foreign and security policy departures took full advantage of the hierarchical and ideological culture of Soviet politics. In breaking with the old ideology, 'new thinking', its de-ideologisation claims notwithstanding, sought to establish a new orthodoxy and a new line. Apart from having the inbuilt advantage of coming from above, this line was deliberately all-embracing, promoting values such as peace, common sense and economic realism, all difficult targets to criticise. Critics were left with questioning specific moves on disarmament, an area where traditional values supported Gorbachev's moves and where technical expertise remained restricted. Alternatively they could try and challenge 'new thinking' at a higher, ideological level, where they were left with defending class-based concepts while the reformers held the moral and practical high ground, able to point to the wisdom and actual advantage – particularly in lowering military tension – of their policies. Couched in general terms and claiming 'moral enlightenment', 'new thinking' proved quite effective as a political instrument, particularly when critical opinion remained divided.

Divisions within the ranks of potential opposition to the new foreign policy constituted the third and most important factor vitiating effective contestation. The major institutional elites involved in international policy were far from united in principled opposition to what Gorbachev and Shevardnadze were doing abroad. When, late in the second phase, their criticism became vocal, it was piecemeal and offered no coherent alternative strategy. In this sense, the weakness of opposition here was similar to that on economic issues. Many conservative-minded politicians favoured the thrust of foreign policy reform, insofar as it meant a more vigorous diplomacy, lower East–West tension and greater attention to economic questions. What objections they had focused mainly on the degree and speed, rather than the direction, of change.

Opinions differed, of course, within all the policy groups. Among members of the senior security apparatus the turn towards external openness plainly caused concern, especially when it started to affect internal controls. Yet many of the most active and able members of the KGB sympathised with the objectives of *perestroika*, some of which stemmed from Andropovian ideas. For a time improved relations with the West created a favourable climate for many KGB operations, especially in the technological field. When change on international and domestic fronts began to threaten KGB positions opinion still remained divided as to the best way forward, as was evident from the split institutional loyalties during the attempted coup.

The military, the institutional group with the greatest vested interest in security and foreign policy continuity, were also divided throughout these years. Many senior commanders, particularly those of the Second World War generation, remained wary of any precipitate withdrawal from what they saw as hard-won positions. They were concerned about the tendency of politicians and their civilian advisers to underrate the external threat and lower the Soviet defence guard too far and too fast. At the same time, even many of these older officers recognised the costly nature of military overinsurance produced by traditional notions of absolute security. They saw the need for some cuts in order to make better use of scarce resources. This was a strategy actively supported by some senior, middle-level and younger officers, particularly those in technologically dependent sectors. They appreciated the importance of freeing resources for the technological modernisation necessary to generate and sustain a competitive position in new types of conventional weaponry. To compete militarily they accepted that there was urgent need to create a modern and vigorous economy through radical reforms which also embraced the polity. It was on the depth of those reforms, and especially their impact on the size, weight and prestige of the military establishment, that opinion split more evenly, running particularly along generational lines. It was the damage done to the military – public deprecation and hurried troop withdrawals, without adequate rehousing provision – rather than to the Soviet global role that made many senior military officers critical of *perestroika* in 1990–1. Indeed, in the case of all these key groups, it was domestic issues, often closely linked to international ones, rather than foreign policy questions alone, that shaped their political stance through both phases of political debate.

During the first phase of debate, 1986–8, 'new thinking' and the new foreign policy prospered in terms both of success abroad and support at home. Much of the domestic political success reflected not just Gorbachev's ability to override conservative criticism: it was also due to effective use of the new Afghan policy as a political battering ram to break the foreign and security policy mould. Rather than attacking what was an obviously popular decision, approved even by most of the military, conservatives focused on the ideological lynch-pin of the 'new thinking': the elevation of human values above those of class in international politics and Soviet foreign policy. Conservative politicians, such as Yegor Ligachev, engaged rather ineffectively in heated public debates in the summer of 1988 with reform leaders, notably Alexander Yakovlev, on issues of this kind.

Somewhat less polarised yet politically more important debates surrounded leadership efforts to redefine security in mutual and less military terms and introduce new concepts into defence thinking. Many felt uneasy about the key notion of 'reasonable sufficiency': even Gorbachev appointees such as Defence Minister Yazov preferred the term 'defence sufficiency'. Others insisted on referring to the need for 'reliable defence'. Most were prepared to subscribe to a more defensive military doctrine but insisted that the armed forces retain counter-offensive capabilities.

Such criticism had echoes in differences over arms control policy. If the thrust of arms control and disarmament encountered little opposition, its speed and unfavourable asymmetries prompted concern, particularly in military circles. The fact that Shevardnadze and Gorbachev in December 1988 pushed through a decision to cut 500,000 men unilaterally, rather than following military proposals for reciprocal reductions, contributed to the resignation of the Chief of the General Staff, Marshal Sergei Akhromeev.

From 1989 to 1991 Akhromeev and other senior military figures grew increasingly unhappy about the ever more reactive nature of Soviet foreign policy, the ease and scale of concessions made, and the fragmentation of security and political structures that these were precipitating, not just in Eastern Europe but within the USSR itself. The emergence in 1989 of Gorbachev's serious intent to transform rather than improve the power system activated conservative criticism levelled at foreign as well as domestic *perestroika* as strands of a single strategy, something Ligachev made clear when he linked the dangers of market reform with those of appeasing Germany.

The threat of a united Germany was the strongest card in the hand of the many who upbraided the leadership for 'losing' Eastern Europe and thereby opening the USSR to revanchist pressures. Attacks on these foreign policy 'failures' gathered strength as Gorbachev's moves in early 1990 to disestablish the party's leading role galvanised the conservative political establishment to counterattack. The first half of 1990 saw a mounting chorus of criticism, voiced most notably at the February Central Committee plenum, the Congress of People's Deputies, the Russian Communist Party Congress and the 28th CPSU Congress in July.

These broadsides against foreign and security policy fell into two overlapping types: those levelled by politicians accusing the leadership of betraying and humiliating the Soviet Union abroad and those, fired mainly by the military, that censured Gorbachev and Shevardnadze for undermining national security. The politicians concentrated on policy 'failures' in Eastern Europe, contending that Moscow had betrayed fraternal parties and connived at German unification and absorption into NATO. The leadership had thus wasted the sacrifices of the Second World War and thrown away all the gains of Soviet foreign policy in Europe. Further afield, criticism was more muted, though cooperation with the USA in regional conflicts and especially in the Gulf drew charges of letting down allies and kowtowing to those who remained basically hostile towards socialism. Critics such as Brovikov, the ambassador to Warsaw, gave a dismal picture of the achievements of international and domestic *perestroika* which had changed the Soviet Union 'from a power admired in the world into a state with a mistaken past, a joyless present and an uncertain future'. Such charges, Shevardnadze retorted repeatedly, reflected outdated thinking which had in fact weakened Soviet security and ill served its people's interests. Far better, he argued, to settle for a more modest, safer international role in keeping with the country's economic capabilities.

More telling and difficult to counter were the criticisms that focused on insecurity and were vigorously put mainly by representatives of the military and the defence complex. They charged the leadership with being cavalier about security needs, questioned the practicability of 'reasonable sufficiency' and stressed the need to maintain parity with the US. Akhromeev, Yazov and the new Chief of the General Staff, Moiseev, all considered that the civilians minimised the Western threat and remained unimpressed with Shevardnadze's claim that the new security and foreign policy had already created a secure international environment. Upbraiding the leadership for losing socialist allies and allowing the absorption of East Germany into NATO, Admiral Khvatov put the 'insecurity' case in its stark terms at the 28th Party Congress: 'We have no allies in the West. We have no allies in the East. We are therefore back where we were in 1939.'

Such fears were reinforced by the Gulf war, which demonstrated to the Soviet military the inferiority of some of their equipment and the technical efficiency of the American forces. The war confirmed the worst fears of those conservative military officers who had shortly before tried to compensate for what they saw as excessive security concessions by circumventing the Conventional Forces in Europe treaty. The leader most affronted by this circumvention, and most often charged with rendering the USSR less secure and betraying its interests, was Eduard Shevardnadze. Under mounting attack from the military, especially the 'black colonels' of the Soyuz group, on Eastern Europe, Germany, CFE and the Gulf – to which he vehemently denied planning to send troops – Shevardnadze resigned as Foreign Minister in December 1990.

His resignation underscored the close connection between criticisms of foreign and domestic *perestroika*. While attacks on him concentrated on foreign policy, he resigned mainly in protest against Gorbachev's continued drift to the right and in an attempt to draw dramatic attention to the danger of a reactionary takeover. Late 1990 and early 1991 highlighted the tight linkage between the political fortunes of internal and external policy. Just as the autumns of 1986 and 1988, when domestic political opposition was weakened, were associated with foreign policy advances, so the winter of 1990–1 saw a hardening of Moscow's stance abroad. The spring and summer of 1991 brought sharper fire against the Gorbachev leadership, who were accused of paying more attention to foreign than to Soviet interests. Pavlov focused on the dangers of economic openness and tried to shift some of the blame for Soviet economic ills onto foreign exploiters who were taking advantage of corruption and crisis. Pavlov was a member of the coup leadership whose 'Appeal to the Soviet People' included several references to the external threat of 'revanchism' to which Gorbachev's policies had exposed the country. *Perestroika*, it declared, had humiliatingly reduced Soviet people to second-rank citizens.

If the failure of the coup eliminated this kind of extreme criticism, with its stress on insecurity and humiliation, it has not in any sense created an unqualified consensus favouring external openness. Most accept that Western economic aid is vital to their recovery, yet some remain ambivalent about the country, whether the USSR or now Russia and the other states, going cap in hand to foreign institutions. Such is the depth of economic crisis that feelings of humiliation and fears of exploitation are subordinated to eagerness for help through closer interaction with the developed capitalist countries. Such interaction now forms the most important element in the policy of the successor states towards the outside world.

It is likely to be sustained as such not merely by economic need but also by the pressure of the fast-growing number of groups and institutions with vested interests in its expansion. Those involved in joint ventures – over 3,000 registered by late 1991 – or in foreign trade will become lobbies for maintaining an open external policy in a climate in which foreign policy is likely to be subject to considerable debate and influence from an ever-wider array of actors with international policy concerns.

Republicanisation

By far the most important new actors in the external policy arena over the last six years have patently been the republican successor states. The republicanisation of security and foreign policy represents only one dimension of the general transformation of Union republics into sovereign states which Zvi Gitelman discusses in detail in Chapter 7. The international dimension of the metamorphosis of the USSR into the Commonwealth of Independent States (CIS) has two overlapping facets. The first is the external aspect of the nationality problem, of the republics' journey to independence; the second is their developing security and foreign policy role.

One of the most direct political benefits of Gorbachev's new conciliatory foreign policy was its moderating effect on Western attitudes towards Moscow's handling of ethnic problems in general and republican bids for autonomy in particular. There was little reaction to the repression of protest in Tbilisi in spring 1989 and rather less response to the pressure tactics employed against the Baltic states than might have been expected, given that the West had never recognised their incorporation into the Soviet Union: its response to the overt use of force in January 1991 and the subsequent attempt to impose an economic blockade was one of tempered moral outrage rather than action. Not until the Baltic states had effectively won independence from Moscow did the West extend recognition, and then with the proviso that their illegal incorporation made them a special case. Similarly little was done to encourage later Ukrainian demands for independence and there was great caution about condoning Russian sovereignty and giving Yeltsin the international status he claimed.

Western reluctance to support, let alone actively encourage, the republican drive for sovereignty was in part the result of their goodwill towards Gorbachev and their gratitude for his ending of Cold War tensions (in 1991 he was even elected 'German of the year' for his services to reunification). In part, too, it was the product of a natural conservatism, one that associated Gorbachev and a Soviet

Union of some kind with international stability and saw only danger in its fragmentation.

Western caution and prudence meant that the international factor did not play a powerful proactive role in the process of republicanisation. At the same time this process was not simply an internal matter; it clearly had important international ramifications. If the ethnic conflicts in the Caucasus merely led to some outside concern about the stability of *perestroika*, the assertiveness of Azeris in violating their border with Iran in January 1990 alerted authorities in Tehran and in Western capitals to the far-reaching international implications of growing autonomy among the Muslim population of the USSR. Widespread unease in some of the Muslim republics about Soviet passivity during the Gulf crisis may have contributed to the efforts, unsuccessful though they were, to pursue a more active role.

The international factor figured most prominently in the efforts the republics themselves made to strengthen their case for independence by winning international recognition and support. The Baltic states understandably gave greatest prominence to their international campaign as their illegal incorporation gave them claim on the sympathy of the world community. Even if the response they encountered was cautious, they deployed a very active diplomatic campaign from 1990, focused on the large Western powers and especially on the Nordic countries. While Sweden, Norway and Finland followed a cautious line, Denmark and Iceland did give the Baltic states public support in their demands for participation in the Conference on Security and Cooperation in Europe (CSCE) meeting at Paris in December 1990, though ultimately to no avail. The Nordic states, however, were vocal in their protests against the use of force in January 1991. The very fact that Lithuanian, Latvian and Estonian leaders were received in Washington and Paris gave them and their nationalist movements greater confidence. When similar efforts were made from mid-1990 by Ukraine, the security and economic weight of the republic gave its international contacts, with the USA and Germany in particular, greater salience in its overall campaign to exercise leverage on Moscow. Russia itself concentrated on building economic ties, again especially with Germany, to raise its international profile.

Any discussion of the substance of republics' activities abroad brings us to the second facet of the international dimension: the evolution and arrangements for their growing foreign policy role. The Union republics had formal rights to conduct their own external policy even under the pseudo-federal arrangements of the old USSR. Each had nominal foreign ministries, though even Ukraine, which along with Belorussia had a seat in the United Nations, had no more than a score or two of diplomats working in Kiev. Republican foreign policy, whether in the UN or other bodies, was indistinguishable from that of the USSR.

Calls for the distinctive and independent external policies soon became part of the nationalist platform in most of the republics, starting with the Baltic and emerging in 1989 and especially 1990 in the Caucasus, Belorussia and Ukraine. The Ukrainian declaration of sovereignty in July 1990 included provisions for an independent foreign and security policy and neutral and non-aligned status. Republics activated their moribund diplomatic machines and started rapidly to build bilateral political and economic contacts, particularly with neighbouring states, independently of Moscow. Quite apart from the Baltic efforts to draw closer to the Nordic countries, Azerbaijan developed ties with Turkey, Kazakhstan with South Korea, and Ukraine with East European neighbours as well as with Germany. Kiev also started to make independent use of its UN membership, voting in January 1991 against Moscow in condemning the use of force against Lithuania. More importantly, the Russian Republic began in mid-1990 to conduct its own policy, signing bilateral accords with Poland and Germany and challenging the Union's policy on critical issues such as the Kurile Islands. In the sphere of external economic relations, Russia questioned the Union's right to trade in resources, notably gold and energy, taken from its territory.

To try and make the growing autonomy of republican external policy complementary, rather than a challenge, to Union diplomacy, Moscow sought to establish new coordinating mechanisms. These proved as ineffective as other attempts to turn the USSR into something more akin to a real federation. Shevardnadze spoke out from 1988 in favour of more active republican diplomacy and in late 1989 created a new department at the Foreign Ministry to liaise with its republican counterparts. Early 1991 saw the establishment of a Council of Foreign Ministers to increase consultation. This proved wholly inadequate in meeting the demands of self-declared sovereign republics. After the failed coup, Russia led a campaign to decimate the Soviet Foreign Ministry. For a brief period in November 1991 it appeared that the all-Union ministry would survive as the new Ministry of External Relations (merged with the former Ministry of Foreign Economic Relations) with Shevardnadze at its head. After the Alma Ata agreement on the Commonwealth of Independent States (CIS) in December, however, Yeltsin took the Ministry over for the Russian Federation, making Andrei Kozyrev (the Russian Foreign Minister) the only foreign minister in Moscow.

In international organisations the same substitution occurred, with the Russian Federation assuming the USSR's permanent seat in the

UN Security Council. Nevertheless there was still talk of a small body in Minsk coordinating some general aspects of CIS foreign policy. Exactly how such coordination would operate remained unclear even after the Minsk summit at the end of December 1991. Key decisions in this, as in other areas, will presumably be taken by the heads of state council, policy coordination having taken place between the foreign ministers. Much remains to be settled, not just in terms of procedure, but also on matters such as embassy property and representation.

Similar and arguably more pressing problems exist in the sphere of security and military resources. National armed forces are clearly vital not just to the conduct of an independent foreign policy; they are fundamental to the very sovereignty of the nation state. That is why the issue was such a contentious one from 1989, when national movements tacitly and later openly supported those joining national guards instead of the Soviet army. At the end of 1991, the situation within the CIS remained rather uncertain. The Russian Federation, Ukraine, Belorussia and Kazakhstan, the four nuclear members of the CIS, had agreed on joint nuclear decision-making rights, though Yeltsin held the necessary codes and therefore had an effective whip-hand. All agreed, in very general terms, on joint command of strategic forces (including air force, air defence and navy). However, even here, and certainly where ground forces were involved, the situation was confused. Russia favoured the CIS as a single defence space, with state control of very small national guards and joint control of all other ground and strategic forces exercised through a council of defence ministers. Ukraine, Belorussia, Azerbaijan and Moldavia, however, made clear that they envisaged creating substantial armed forces of their own. Financial considerations may help moderate demands for wholly national armed forces, yet the growth of an important measure of military independence seems likely as all are keenly aware of the dangers of Russia hegemony within the CIS.

In this context, Russian Foreign Minister Andrei Kozyrev's statement in January 1992 that 'the chief priority for Russian diplomacy is to shape the Commonwealth of Independent States' may seem as ominous as it is realistic. Whatever the final shape of the CIS, the contours of which remained sketchy at the end of 1991, the foreign and security policy of its states will focus on relations with fellow Commonwealth members. The combination of such Commonwealth introversion with the openness of individual successor states to the rest of the world will further increase the domestic salience and politicisation of security and foreign policy.

PART FOUR

Perspectives on Soviet and Post-Soviet Politics

13

Post-*Perestroika*: Revolution from Above v. Revolution from Below

DAVID MANDEL

The political changes that have occurred in the Soviet Union since the elections of the early spring of 1990 to local and republican soviets, and which were greatly accelerated by the failed conservative coup of 19–21 August, have brought to a close the '*perestroika* chapter' of Soviet history initiated by Mikhail Gorbachev. It is no longer a question of 'restructuring' the old economic system but of replacing it wholesale by what is termed a 'normal', that is, capitalist, economy. Those in power no longer go by the name of communists – the party has been banned by executive decree – but call themselves 'democrats'.

Despite these momentous changes, no less striking are the elements of continuity that link the two periods. The most important of these is the absence of democracy in the discussion and promulgation of the economic reform, reform that is intended to remake the very fabric of the society and determine its path of development for decades to come. The official reform project, which has evolved radically since 1990, continues to be presented as the only possible one. The idea of an alternative that would be neither capitalist nor 'command-administrative' (bureaucratic) is derisively and unanimously dismissed as utopian and pernicious by politicians, 'prominent intellectuals' and journalists, who tirelessly cite the experience – real or imagined – of the 'civilised' world to support their position. Yet, not long ago, many of these same people with no less self-assurance painted the capitalist world in the bleakest of colours and portrayed Soviet reality as the successful realisation of 'scientific socialist theory'.

Though the Western media and politicians persist in regarding democracy and 'market reform' (a euphemism for capitalism) as virtually synonymous, many of their Soviet counterparts have long since concluded that the transformation of their economy along liberal lines requires a 'strong independent executive regime' capable of imposing 'harsh and unpopular measures'. The tendency today is increasingly towards the reintroduction of authoritarian political structures and practices that the 'democrats' now at the helm of the state vigorously condemned when the 'communists' occupied the halls of power and they stood on the outside looking in.

Liberal luminary Anatolii Sobchak, mayor of St Petersburg, fulminates against those 'who hinder our work', although not so long ago he himself stood at the head of the 'hinderers'. The slogan 'All power to the soviets', upon which many liberals rode into elected office in the spring of 1990, has since been declared by Ilya Zaslavsky, former chairman of the October district soviet in Moscow, to have lost its progressive content. In accordance with this revelation, Yeltsin and his allies have moved to appoint prefects and governors, effectively transforming the soviets into appendages of uncontrolled administrative power. As for Zaslavsky, he was ousted from his post at the head of the October district soviet in the spring of 1991 by the soviet's deputies for abuse of office: he, together with some other members of the soviet and its executive, had been involved in transferring the district's real estate holdings to companies in which they were office holders. Gavriil Popov, liberal mayor of Moscow, subsequently dissolved Moscow's district soviets by executive decree (the deputies in the October district barricaded themselves inside when the police came to remove furniture and documents) and is lobbying for Zaslavsky's appointment as chief prosecutor of Moscow.

'Revolution from Above' v. 'Revolution from Below'

This continuity amidst change can best be understood in terms of a 'revolution from above'. The historical role of such transformations is to preserve the power and privilege of at least a part of the old dominant class, in this case the party-state bureaucracy or *nomenklatura*. (In fact it is more a social stratum than an historical class; indeed it is now seeking at last to transform itself into a *bona fide* propertied class.) Such transitions are initiated by the more farsighted elements of the old class, who have realised that the old mode of domination has exhausted itself and that to persist in defending it would invite revolution from below; that is, a popular, genuinely democratic uprising.

Although the situation has evolved far beyond what the initiators of *perestroika* originally envisioned (a rationalised bureaucratic system still based predominantly upon state-owned property), its basic character as an anti-popular 'revolution from above' remains. Large segments of the old bureaucratic stratum have shifted into the burgeoning private sector or have been integrated into the 'democratic' state structures. At the same time new elements, recruited mainly from the former 'shadow (illegal) economy' and from the well-connected, 'enterprising' segment of the intelligentsia, have also moved into open, more or less legal positions of power and wealth. But although this 'revolution from above' has made impressive progress, it is far from completed, and its ultimate success is by no means assured. A popular revolution, one from below, cannot be ruled out, though it today exists only in potential. In the shorter term, a more likely development is a political stalemate in which popular forces block the 'revolution from above' without, however, being capable of effecting a democratic transformation corresponding to their own interests. Such an impasse could last for several years.

The aim of this chapter is to analyse the main sociopolitical interests and forces at work within the framework of these contending revolutions from above and below. It by no means pretends to offer a complete portrait of the society in this turbulent period of transition. Limitations of space as well as of knowledge rule this out. In particular there is no analysis of the very important national issue. The focus is mainly on the Russian Republic, though in its basic outlines the analysis can be applied throughout the territories of the former Soviet Union. Despite the above limitations, the proposed framework is an important tool for making sense of the seemingly chaotic succession of events.

In the Soviet context, 'revolution from below' would signify the mobilisation of the popular classes, of workers, peasants and the basic mass of the intelligentsia; that is, of those today without political power and effective ownership of the means of production, with the aim of placing both the state and economy under democratic control. It would also mean a voluntary, democratic union of nationalities and ethnic groups with a commitment to social and political equality among them. A successful popular revolution would, in essence, amount to the transformation of the old bureaucratic system in a socialist direction.

If the concept 'revolution from below' is relatively straightforward (this, of course, is not to minimise the difficulties and unresolved problems facing its practical realisation), the use of the term 'revolution' to characterise the programme of the currently dominant sociopolitical forces in the former Soviet Union is admittedly dubious. It is used here for convenience's sake, without any pretence of scientific precision. Revolution, at least in Marxist usage, is a qualitative, progressive, sociopolitical transformation that results in increased human freedom. There is no doubt that, compared with what preceded it, *perestroika* and post-*perestroika*, so far at least, have had a number of progressive aspects, especially in the political sphere. At the same time, the socioeconomic situation of the mass of the population has deteriorated and will continue to do so for the foreseeable future, if the forces of the 'revolution from above' remain dominant.

A parallel from Russia's own history is the emancipation of the serfs in 1861. In its conception, it was an anti-popular response to the crisis of the old order, an avowed effort to avoid revolution from below. Nevertheless, despite its contradictory and limited nature, it did immediately improve the situation of a large part of the peasantry (they themselves referred to Alexander II as the 'Tsar Liberator'), though ultimately this 'revolution from above' contributed directly to the popular revolutions of 1905 and 1917.

Perestroika or the 'Socialist' Phase of the 'Revolution from Above'

At the end of 1987, a visiting Central Committee secretary told a gathering in the southern Russian town of Shakhty that, if the party had not announced *perestroika* in time, the people would have taken to the streets. While it is difficult to judge the immediacy of the threat at that time, there is no doubt that by 1985 the depth of popular discontent with stagnant living standards and with the corruption that infected all levels of government had finally convinced a majority of the political leadership that the system Brezhnev had bequeathed them was no longer capable of maintaining either the internal stability of their regime or its great power status (the first consideration being by far the weightier).

The roots of this crisis lay in the contradictory nature of the bureaucracy itself, a ruling stratum whose interests are in conflict with the very logic of the socioeconomic system it administers. The Soviet bureaucracy did not make the October revolution of 1917. It was its product, and its rise to power was an unintended consequence of the backwardness of Russian society and of the socialist revolution's isolation in a hostile capitalist world. But the extreme deformation that the revolution underwent in the 1920s and 1930s under the bureaucracy's leadership did not lead to the restoration of capitalism.

It led rather to the establishment of the 'command economy' and to the totalitarian attempt to control all aspects of social life. The problem with such a regime is that, once established, it tends to be an inherently conservative and wasteful manager and itself to divide along functional, regional and mafia-type, 'clan' lines, as each group pursues its narrow interests at the expense of national goals. Moreover a regime whose basis lies in the usurpation of power and illegitimate appropriation of material privileges finds it very difficult to keep corruption and abuse of office within 'acceptable' limits, as functionaries constantly seek to draw additional benefits from the spheres entrusted to them.

The unfettered pursuit of their interests by the members of the bureacracy thus leads, paradoxically, to the undermining of bureaucratic power. The survival of this system calls for a strong leader to protect the bureaucracy from itself. Stalin kept the bureaucracy – and society – in line through a terror apparatus that he personally controlled. Khrushchev used non-terroristic measures to maintain the bureaucracy in a state of insecurity, while he tried to build an independent political base through a mixture of populist politics and improvements in mass living standards. This strategy failed, and the bureaucracy replaced him with their own man, Brezhnev, who was content to let matters drift, taking as his slogan *'après moi, le déluge'*. His regime led to the profound systemic crisis of the late 1970s. Andropov at the start of the 1980s attempted to reimpose discipline without fundamentally changing the nature of the system. He, however, died soon after coming to power and his regime was succeeded by the even more short-lived reign of Chernenko, a Brezhnev disciple.

When Gorbachev was chosen General Secretary of the CPSU in 1985 by the handful of old men that made up the Politburo (officially he was elected by the several hundred members of the Central Committee, a largely honorific gathering of the elite of the bureaucracy), they saw his task as one of merely pursuing the unfinished work of Andropov. Gorbachev accordingly launched anti-corruption and disciplinary campaigns as well as a programme of industrial restructuring ('acceleration') focused on the engineering branch as the lever of rapid technological and economic modernisation. The relatively modest nature of these initial efforts was dictated by the interests of the bureaucracy, which was, after all, Gorbachev's social base as well as the instrument of his reforms. As such, they were probably foredoomed, in much the same way as the five-year plans of the past three decades had all failed to achieve their principal goals. Although the economic performance indicators of 1986 were relatively good, this was largely a consequence of the popular enthusiasm evoked by the promise of change, by Gorbachev's more populist and forthright leadership style, as well as by the initial fright that his campaigns instilled in the bureaucracy. But the effect was necessarily short-lived and, by the following year, the signs of stagnation reappeared.

Although as late as the summer of 1987 Gorbachev was still reassuring the Central Committee that there would be no market reform, he had already decided that more fundamental change was needed, in fact a 'revolution from above'. And market reform appeared to be the only path that held out some hope of success. Back in the 1960s, such a reform had been openly discussed in the Soviet Union, and a very timid version of it was even initiated until a conservative bureaucratic reaction cut it short. Market reform was also the path taken by all the reform regimes in Eastern Europe and by China in the 1970s. In the Soviet Union many 'closet marketeers' remained in the social science institutes and, once *glasnost'* and *perestroika* became official policy, they quickly moved to occupy government advisory positions and to popularise their ideas in the mass media.

The guiding principle of *perestroika*'s market reform was the replacement of the centralised 'command economy', which in theory (though practice was far from this) treated the economy as a single giant enterprise, with one in which relations among enterprises would no longer be based on administrative orders from above but on freely concluded contracts. Vertical coordination by the huge party-state bureaucracies would give way to horizontal economic coordination through the market. Overall planning and regulation would be achieved mainly by means of indirect economic levers, such as interest rates and taxation, which would set the parameters within which autonomous, competing enterprises would make decisions. The central state's economic role would be limited to regulation of the market and long-term planning as well as to managing those sectors, such as defence, health and education, that could not be left to the regulated market.

Official rhetoric about a 'socialist market' apart, it soon became clear that this reform concept meant a retreat from the traditional socialist vision (again practice had always been rather different, though the ideology was not entirely without a basis in reality) of an increasingly egalitarian society with firm socioeconomic guarantees for all its members. The ideologues of *perestroika* declared such ideas to be outmoded and condemned them as the main source of the inefficiency of the old 'command' system. 'Levelling' tendencies, they argued, had to be abandoned if enterprises and individuals were to have the incentive to produce efficiently goods and services that society valued. And the market was proclaimed the only proven mechanism through which society could effectively express such judgements. At the same time restrictions were lifted on private economic activity by self-employed individuals and cooperatives. These were to help fill the gaping holes left by the state sector in the provision of consumer goods and services.

Bureaucratic Resistance to *Perestroika*

Apart from the purely economic and technical problems posed by this reform, it faced a major political obstacle in that it lacked significant support in society. One of its central contradictions was that the bureaucracy that was called upon to administer the reform was in its mass hostile to this effort by Gorbachev to 'save it from itself'. There were good reasons for this hostility. On the most general level, structural reforms are risky undertakings whose consequences can never be fully predicted. The limited political liberalisation under *glasnost'* quickly revealed the depth and extent of popular hostility toward the 'bureaucratic parasites'. The reform could well lead to a direct threat to bureaucratic power itself, as had occurred in Czechoslovakia in 1968. Nor was it evident that the risk was justified by the contribution that improved economic performance could eventually make to political stability. Although market reform in other Soviet-type societies had initially produced rapid growth, by the second half of the 1980s most of them were mired in foreign debt, high inflation and a renewed tendency towards stagnation.

The establishment of the 'command economy' in the late 1920s was the bureaucracy's response to the crisis of the mixed economy of NEP (the New Economic Policy). Thereafter administration of the 'command economy' became the main *raison d'être* of the huge party and ministerial apparatuses, estimated by some at eighteen million people in 1987. The market reform as officially conceived confronted them with the prospect of losing much of this economic power. Moroever entire administrators, hundreds of thousands of positions, would be abolished. The available jobs in industry and services offered neither the status, conditions nor remuneration comparable to those that were being lost.

But even for those whose positions were not directly threatened, *perestroika* opened a period of heightened insecurity. Gorbachev's early purges were undoubtedly welcomed by middle-aged and younger members of the bureaucracy, who had found their careers blocked by Brezhnev's gerontocracy. (Brezhnev's hallmark had been 'respect for cadres'.) But functionaries would not be functionaries if they did not yearn for job security. *Perestroika* was directed against this fundamental interest. It was to make job tenure dependent upon strict, regular evaluations of job performance. What was even more distressing was that these evaluations were no longer to be made only by administrative superiors but also by rank-and-file workers and employees. Even the most honest and competent Soviet administrators felt that public scrutiny and control only complicated an already difficult job.

In fact, competent and honest administrators were few and far between. The system, especially as it had evolved under Brezhnev, was very efficient in breaking down such administrators or, failing that, in weeding them out. Moreover even those privileges of administrative office sanctioned from above – special access to housing, to scarce and/or high-quality services at low prices – were, as far as the population was concerned, a form of corruption. This became abundantly clear in letters and exposés published in the liberalised press. The sad fact was that, unlike the bourgeoisie in developed capitalist societies, the bureaucracies of the Soviet-type systems, forced to pose as the heirs and guardians of the socialist revolution, had been unable to legitimate their power and privilege. They, therefore, could not help but feel uneasy about any relaxation of bureaucratic control over society.

The same basic attitudes and interests were shared by functionaries in the repressive agencies of the state, the police, army and KGB. The army, in particular, was due for major cutbacks, as was military industry. Gorbachev's 'new thinking' de-emphasised the role of military power in foreign policy. Moreover, in practice, it often amounted to unilateral concessions to the United States and its allies. Public criticism of the army was leading to a decline in its prestige (very high under Brezhnev), especially among the youth, among whom draft dodging soon became a serious problem. As for the KGB, it was a hated institution that was being deprived of one of its key functions – repression of political and cultural dissent. Officers in both organisations were deeply alarmed by the decline in the Soviet Union's great-power status and by the threat to its territorial integrity from the rising national movements.

Genuine, active support in the bureaucracy for *perestroika* was, therefore, very thin. There were, of course, competent, energetic and enlightened elements in all branches of the party-state apparatus that understood the necessity of far-reaching reform and welcomed the challenge. But nowhere were they a majority. Not even enterprise managers, who were to be freed from bureaucratic tutelage, were always enthusiastic about the reforms. Those who had been success-ful in the past owed much of their success to relations they had developed with superiors in the state and party bureaucracies. A consistent market reform would have made these irrelevant and demanded very different talents. It was also necessary now to deal with the workers, who were losing their deference and fear of management. Even if the promised workers' self-management, which administrators abhorred, never materialised (in this area, the man-agement lobby was eventually able to get Gorbachev's ear), the workforce was sure to be much less malleable than before.

Formally all elements of the bureaucracy were enthusiastic suppor-ters of *perestroika*. As a social stratum, the bureaucracy is organised hierarchically and so it could not openly challenge the more or less unified leadership that existed in the first phases of *perestroika*. But opposition did express itself in passive resistance and in behind-the-scenes pressure that resulted in inconsistent or toothless laws and measures. Eventually, however, open political challenges to Gor-bachev were mounted at various top party gatherings as well as in the Supreme Soviet. These were generally preceded by a flurry of media reports alerting the public to a grave conservative threat. But in each case these offensives, half-hearted affairs in any case, were easily beaten back by Gorbachev. The conservatives did not dare to remove Gorbachev, in whom they still saw a bulwark against the liberals and the people. Nevertheless each failed counter-offensive had the effect of strengthening the 'radicals', mostly intellectuals but already joined by some bureaucratic defectors, who were moving in an increasingly open liberal direction.

The bureaucracy thus revealed its extreme political weakness. Deeply divided along sectoral and regional lines, it was unable to act on its own without a strong, decisive leadership at the top. But the main sources of its weakness were its lack of any positive programme to get the country out of the deepening crisis and its almost complete social isolation: it and its system had been totally discredited among the vast majority of the population by the 'period of stagnation'. Already in the second and third years of *perestroika*, and especially after the fall of the Communist regimes in Eastern Europe, the most clearsighted and self-assured elements of the bureaucracy, epit-omised by people like Boris Yeltsin and Ivan Silaev (a life-long functionary who headed Yeltsin's first cabinet), realised that the system was doomed and hitched their stars to the introduction of a market system based predominantly upon full-fledged private prop-erty. Significant numbers of the functionaries and former functionar-ies began themselves to participate in the process of 'primitive accumulation' of capital.

Popular Resistance to *Perestroika*

Despite the initial upsurge of popular enthusiasm evoked by the prospect of positive change after the stifling 'regime of stagnation', reaction to *perestroika* among the general population was cool and mistrustful. Soviet social scientists and journalists attributed this to workers' alleged penchant for the easy life they enjoyed under the old regime. In fact real wages, modest to begin with, had stagnated over the previous eighteen years; health and safety conditions were abysmal; and the reigning chaos in production wreaked havoc with workers' lives, alternating periods of enforced idleness with 'storming' and massive overtime at the end of the quarters, including frequent 'black' Saturdays and holidays. Trade unions were the obedient tools of management, leaving workers with little effective recourse against arbitrary management decisions. Worst of all, perhaps, was the demoralising daily experience of the incredible waste and irrationality of a system that deprived workers even of the satisfaction of doing good, useful work.

Soviet workers had a healthy mistrust of reforms from above, based upon bitter historical experience: bureaucratic campaigns, launched without genuine popular consultation or open debate, had tended to fail miserably, with the workers forced to assume the costs. Moreover, from the workers' point of view, there were many negative sides to the reform Gorbachev was proposing. They were being told that to have a better life they would have to give up key social rights. Most important among these was the *de facto* job security. Subjected to market discipline, enterprises would be forced to shed excess manpower and also run the risk of bankruptcy. Although Soviet enterprises were clearly overstaffed and economic restructuring required a sectoral redistribution of the labour force, in the absence of democratic trade unions or real self-management workers would have no protection against managerial abuses.

More generally the ending of job security and the threat of unemployment would radically alter the correlation of forces in the enterprise, giving management effective new means to enforce its will. Even if there was little immediate threat of an overall labour surplus, the threat of being made redundant would be a real lever in management's hands, since most of the available jobs would be in unattractive sectors (especially services) and regions. In addition many social benefits, for example one's place in the queue for housing, are related to length of service at the enterprise. Despite official denials, many economists were quite frank about the utility of 'a small reserve army of labour' for enforcing discipline. If this army is to play its assigned role well, life within its ranks cannot be too comfortable. The slowness with which the Gorbachev regime moved to establish a job placement and retraining system spoke loudly of the low priority assigned to so important an issue for workers.

The reform would also eliminate the *de facto* guaranteed wage, since wages were to be made dependent upon enterprise profitability. At the same time the 'social wage' (free or subsidised housing, health care, public transport and education, as well as subsidised basic goods), which made up a significant part of workers' income, was to be cut in an effort to increase the incentive role of the individual wage. A significant rise in inequality became official policy, as income 'levelling' (which had never affected the bureaucracy) was condemned as a major obstacle to efficiency. Moreover wages were to be made dependent upon enterprise profitability over which workers had virtually no real control.

It was not reform as such that made workers uneasy. They were at least as disgusted with the old regime as were the intelligentsia. What worried them was the specific nature of the proposed reform which asked them to give up important social rights (even if these were enjoyed at a mediocre level) in return for the mere promise of a higher living standard at some time in the future. Workers knew well the real value of such promises. Gorbachev seemed to understand this. The originality of *perestroika*, when compared with earlier efforts at market reform by Soviet-type regimes, was to link openly economic with political reform. Market reforms elsewhere had been conceived largely as a means to forestall threats to bureaucratic dictatorship. But Gorbachev declared that 'democratisation', on both the state and enterprise levels, was an integral part of the economic reform. This was, at least formally, an offer of popular control over the reform process and, as such, it was intended to win support for the economic reform among a population that in its mass was mistrustful, all the more so as the economic situation in the country began to deteriorate. Similarly enterprise self-management was designed to win workers' acceptance of the far-reaching changes in relations within the enterprise that the economic reform would bring about. It was also a precondition for workers assuming responsibility for the enterprise's market performance, which was to become the principal determinant of their incomes.

'Democratisation' was also intended to mobilise popular hostility to the bureaucracy as a means of neutralising the latter's resistance to reform. Open, legal pressure from below would serve as a counterbalance to bureaucratic conservatism and inertia. In this area, Gorbachev was following in Khrushchev's footsteps, only much more boldly, in an effort to free himself from the conservative embrace of his bureaucratic base. He also understood that open debate and criticism were essential elements of efficient policy making. However 'democratisation' was never intended to go further than limited political liberalisation and the establishment of a circumscribed parliamentary system that would leave the ultimate levers of power in the hands of what was still essentially a bureaucratic elite headed by Gorbachev. Genuine democracy would have entered into direct conflict with *perestroika*'s real goal – 'revolution from above' – whose task it was to prevent a popular, democratic revolution. This was a central contradiction of *perestroika*.

Nowhere was the limited nature of the political reforms more evident than in the area of the economic reform, whose every phase was decided 'on high' behind closed doors and only subsequently submitted to 'popular consultation', where at best minor details could be changed. For example, in March 1990, Gorbachev told a meeting of workers in the Urals, a centre of heavy and military industry, that 'your cries of alarm have reached us', that he had come to 'verify together with the toilers . . . the course of the ship of state before the major choice that lies ahead'. Yet again he pledged to 'consult the working class on all major elements of the reform'. But he also made it clear that there would be no retreat from the basic conception of the reform as he conceived it: 'Let us think about how, when and what to do, to what to give priority, from what to begin. . . . But as concerns the strategic choice, the direction of our policy, no one has yet proposed anything else serious, fundamental.' He failed only to mention that he alone was the arbiter of what was 'serious and fundamental' and that his own 'strategic conception', the 'only serious one', had itself fundamentally changed more than once since he told a Central Committee meeting that there would be no market reform.

Even the self-management reform in the enterprises was parachuted from above without any real consultation with the workers. And nothing concrete was done to help the workers free themselves from the very significant powers that the enterprise administration still wielded. For example, there was no move to eliminate the wide-spread practice of piecework, a highly reactionary and divisive wage system. Nor was there any attempt to provide effective legal protection for elected trade union officials, who remained highly vulnerable to management pressure. This ensured that self-management, with rare exceptions, remained a dead letter. Moreover, since the economic structures standing above the enterprise remained intact and beyond democratic control, the entire operation appeared to the workers as a trap to lure them into assuming responsibility for a declining economic situation over which they had no control.

Perestroika Collapses under its Own Contradictions

This half-hearted 'democratisation' was unable to win active popular support for the economic reform, especially as the economic situation began to decline. A temporary halt in growth and some decline is to be expected in the course of major economic restructuring. People might have accepted this if they had had any faith that the burdens were being shared equally and that their sacrifices would not be in vain. But none of this was the case. Bureaucratic privilege remained essentially intact and was now joined by the fantastic profits of yesterday's 'shadow businessmen' turned 'cooperators', who were making their profits mainly through the purchase or theft and resale at high prices of cheap goods produced in the state sector. Moreover the economic decline was not the result of a genuine economic restructuring that held out the promise of renewed expansion on a qualitatively new basis. It was rather the direct consequence of a flawed reform programme.

The aim of the 'cost-accounting' (*khozraschet*) reform introduced in 1987 was to reduce the role of centralised economic administration and regulation and to increase the autonomy of the enterprises with a view to activating their market-oriented activity. However this ignored the fact that the highly concentrated Soviet economy was (and remains) dominated by monopolistic structures in the form of branch ministries and giant enterprises that are often the sole producers of particular goods. These in turn were often linked with shadowy, mafia-like structures that permeated the distribution sector. Over the preceding decades, and especially under Brezhnev's regime of bureaucratic *laissez-faire*, the central government had increasingly lost its ability to impose national goals on these bureaucratic fiefdoms and clans. Indeed this had been a basic underlying cause of the stagnation.

Now, in the name of market reform, Gorbachev weakened even further what remained of political control of the economy and gave a major new impulse to the existing tendencies. Ignoring formal restrictions and contract obligations, enterprises exploited their monopolistic positions quite 'rationally', using their expanded autonomy to raise prices, even as they cut back on production. The main effect of the legalisation of private enterprise, the so-called 'cooperatives', was to drain an even larger share of production from the state commercial network, where prices were controlled and accessible to the average consumer. As one analyst put it in 1990, 'Although we often say in anger that nothing has changed over the past four years, nevertheless, our economy is different. It is capable of beating back directive attacks from the centre, of subordinating any laws to group egoism.'

Gorbachev's government found itself in the contradictory position of decrying the 'group egoism' of enterprises and local governments, while at the same time condemning 'ministerial dictates' and exhorting enterprises to fight for their autonomy, as promised by the 1987 Law on the State Enterprise, to retain a greater part of their 'cost-accounting' income. The centre was fast losing what had remained of its power to growing centrifugal, regional and corporatist tendencies. Although on one level this might appear as the consequence of a series of policy errors and half-baked measures, on another level it was *the inevitable result of an attempt to reform the economy without democratising the central institutions of power*. This was a policy ultimately dictated by the interests of the 'revolution from above', whose social basis was the reformist wing of the bureaucracy in loose alliance with the liberal intelligentsia and the growing private sector.

The 'radicals', who had themselves vociferously promoted the 'cost-accounting reform', now exploited the deepening economic crisis to push for an even further weakening of central regulation of the economy, arguing that the crisis was the result of the fact that the economic reforms were half-hearted and failed to create a 'real' market, as if a monopoly-dominated market was somehow less than real. They were silent on the fact that the Polish-style 'shock therapy' they demanded would lead to an even swifter economic decline and immiseration of the mass of the population. Exploiting growing popular discontent with the state of the economy, they presented themselves as the most consistent democrats, opponents of the authoritarian, hypercentralised, bureaucratic regime, and the market as the magic antidote, the only solution to the crisis of the administered economy that was collapsing before the people's eyes.

The liberals' appeals found a strong resonance in the profound anti-bureaucratic sentiments of the population. Their anti-bureaucratic appeals and soft-pedalling of their social programmes enabled them to win a number of key positions in the spring of 1990 and to push Gorbachev towards increasingly liberal statements. Yet the majority of the Soviet people, and the workers first of all, while on the whole supporting an expanded role for market relations (about which they generally have only the vaguest and often very confused understanding) did not, and do not, in practice, favour the liberals' project, which was intended to subordinate the economy to market forces. As liberal publicist Igor Klyamkin ruefully noted in 1989, the people wanted efficiency as well as social justice, including economic security, full employment, price stability, a guaranteed decent minimum living standard for all and strict limits to socioeconomic inequality. This implied a strong democratic central economic power capable of subordinating the market mechanism to these social goals.

Although the original conception of *perestroika* was some sort of 'planned market economy', Gorbachev, under pressure from the 'radicals', eventually concluded that was an impossible combination. This conclusion was not in the nature of things but flowed directly from his refusal to entertain genuine democratisation of central state power. As long as the centre that planned and regulated remained undemocratic, its directives and regulations would necessarily be perceived as oppressive and exploitative by the producers who would resist them. The centre's inability to motivate economic actors at the various levels to behave in a manner consistent with centrally set goals had always been the fundamental contradiction of the bureaucratic economy. The introduction of market relations into such a bureaucratic context, as the Yugoslav and other 'market socialist' experiences showed, merely strengthened existing centrifugal tendencies.

Ultimately the only way to overcome this contradiction without riding roughshod over popular interests and democratic process would be to combine democratisation at the enterprise and local levels with democratisation of the central power; that is, to create a self-management system *at all levels* of economic and political decision making. This is not in itself a magic formula for a workable balance between centralisation and decentralisation, between administrative regulation and enterprise autonomy, but it does provide a real basis upon which a solution corresponding to popular interests can be sought. The point is that the liberals' answer to the crisis of the Soviet economy is by no means, as they claim, the only possible one, all the rest being 'merely more experiments'. The real 'experiment', one in true Stalinist tradition, is to impose upon a reluctant population a reform that takes into account neither their interests nor the real, objective socioeconomic conditions of the society. Certainly the experiences so far of Poland and other former Soviet-type societies, which have gone much further that the Soviet Union in their attempts to 'build capitalism', are not at all encouraging, at least from the point of view of the vast majority of the population.

The Advent of the Post-*Perestroika* Phase of the 'Revolution from Above'

Soviet liberals were generally quite candid in admitting that the last thing they wanted was a popular revolution. They often pointed to the October revolution, which they considered a national tragedy. (This did not prevent them at the same time from portraying the October revolution as the opposite of a popular revolution, a military putsch directed against the people.) In an article at the end of 1990, Gavriil Popov made this position very clear: the worst scenario, in his view, would be for the liberals to come to power on a wave of popular mobilisation directed against the ruling bureaucracy, since this would effectively make the liberals prisoners of popular prejudices, left-overs from the old system. (Like other liberals, he refused to entertain the possibility that these 'prejudices' might in fact be quite rational class interests. The Stalinist nature of his argumentation is especially striking here.) In particular, values of social justice were still firmly anchored in popular consciousness and, if given effective political expression, they would constitute insurmountable obstacles to the liberal project. He argued, therefore, for a 'strong independent executive regime', free from control by the soviets, whose deputies were too open to the influence of popular moods. The best political basis for the liberals' project of 'democratic' transformation was, therefore, not genuine democracy at all, but an alliance of 'market democrats' with reformist bureaucrats. Excluded from the coalition would be not only conservative bureaucrats, but 'populist democrats', those who took democracy too literally.

Put more simply, the liberals' project, like that of Gorbachev and the reformist wing of the bureaucratic elite, was also 'revolution from above', but a more radical, openly capitalist one that required a fundamental change in property relations, from state to private ownership. The liberals' strategy seemed to be bearing fruit when, in the summer of 1990, Gorbachev reached an accord with Yeltsin on the introduction of a 'radical market reform'. There was no longer any pretence of it being 'socialist' or retaining any element of planning. However, in the later months of that year, Gorbachev appeared to have second thoughts. He rejected the liberal 'shock therapy' in the form of the '500-day Plan' and, without renouncing market reform, announced a period of economic stabilisation. He appointed conservative figures from the army, KGB and trade union apparatus to his cabinet, attempted to reinforce central economic regulation and made some feeble attempts to rein in *glasnost'*.

The reasons for this retreat are still not entirely clear, but it appears that Gorbachev came under pressure from conservative forces (the threat of a coup?) who were reacting particularly against the danger of the dissolution of the Union. Gorbachev, as president of the USSR, obviously shared an interest in maintaining the country's integrity. Moreover any minimally sober evaluation of the '500-day Plan' revealed it to be an adventurist project with predominantly political goals – the swift creation of *faits accomplis* in the area of price liberalisation and property relations – that would very likely have provided the spark for the long-predicted and much feared 'social explosion'.

After much hesitation, and with his popularity declining, Yeltsin, who had become the recognised leader of the liberal camp, finally 'declared war' on Gorbachev in February 1991, demanding his resignation. In March and April a wave of strikes in the coal regions, as well as in Belorussia and elsewhere, demanded the resignation of the central government and the Supreme Soviet of the USSR. The strikers put forward no social programme of their own, but their political motives were quite straightforward and justified: the central government and parliament had not been democratically elected; they did not enjoy popular confidence, having led the country into an unprecedented crisis for which they could offer no solution; they should be replaced through new democratic elections. These motives, however, were not shared by Yeltsin and his liberal colleagues, who exploited this popular movement (which at the same time they feared) to pressure Gorbachev into renewing the alliance he had broken off with the liberals, bringing along with him the bureaucratic forces that he commanded.

The liberal strategy succeeded when, at the end of April, Gorbachev, Yeltsin and the heads of eight other republics signed a protocol that gave greatly reinforced powers to the republics and provided for a new constitution. The reaction among the miners, who had been kept in the dark about these negotiations, was one of having been betrayed. Yeltsin tried to placate the Russian miners by arranging the transfer of their mines to Russian jurisdiction and promising them that a greater share of the coal output would be left at their disposal. But this apparently did not make much of an impression. In the Kuzbass, the largest Russian coalfield, where Yeltsin had been very popular, he received only 23 per cent of the ballots cast in the June 1991 Russian presidential elections, while Tuleev, chairman of the regional soviet, who had opposed the spring strikes, won over half. Pressure from Yeltsin later forced Tuleev's resignation.

Since Gorbachev had made common cause with the liberals, he lost his usefulness for the conservative elements of the bureaucracy as a bulwark against the liberal version of the 'revolution from above' or against revolution from below. It was in this context that they handed the liberals a final victory beyond their boldest dreams. Many unanswered questions remain about the abortive coup of 19–21 August, certainly one of the most bizarre and inept attempts to seize power by men already occupying top positions in the state. It is a measure of 'democratisation' that, upon returning to Moscow after the coup's defeat, Gorbachev unashamedly declared that he would never reveal the whole truth. Despite the official version of the coup's defeat as a 'popular revolution', the 'genuine October revolution', popular mobilisation against the putschists was quite limited. Yeltsin's call for a general strike went largely unheeded and he himself took no concrete measures to organise it. The weak popular mobilisation was probably due to many causes, the chief one being that few people saw any reason to act, given the unreal nature of the coup: in most places absolutely nothing had changed and the coup's leaders themselves did everything possible to maintain a facade of legality and normality. But popular indifference also played a role, since many saw the coup as just another squabble among elites, none of which had anything to offer.

The coup collapsed essentially from within, as key elements of the repressive apparatuses (army, KGB, Ministry of Internal Affairs troops) refused to participate in it. Moreover the putschists themselves showed no inclination to use even the force that was available to them. The whole episode was a godsend to the liberals (in particular in Russia) who exploited the failed coup to stage a coup of their own, extending and consolidating their power without any recourse to popular mobilisation. Yeltsin, without any regard for the existing laws and constitution, used the 'emergency situation' legislation (which had already passed) to take over Union ministries, to get control of the repressive apparatuses, to appoint prefects to regions, to remove troublesome local leaders and effectively to usurp the powers of the elected (though, admittedly, ineffective) soviets. In October Yeltsin used his immense presidential power to veto the Russian Supreme Soviet's decision to hold elections in December to the heads of local executives (the Soviet had rejected Yeltsin's request to postpone these elections). The liberal press justified this veto with the interesting argument that 'democrats' would probably lose these elections. The words Bertolt Brecht attributed to the leaders of the former GDR after the popular revolt come to mind: 'The people have lost confidence in the government; it is necessary to choose a new people.'

The coup's defeat also greatly increased the confidence, and accelerated the open political organisation, of the new entrepreneurial class, which consists largely of former and current officials or of people with connections to and the protection of such officials. If most people remained spectators to the coup, Moscow's entrepreneurs at once saw the threat to their interests and sent their large corps of bodyguards to defend the 'White House', which they barricaded with their fleet of cars, and placed large sums of money at Yeltsin's disposal. In the mass media, and particularly radio and television, 'entrepreneurial' themes now occupy the place once assumed by 'communist' propaganda. However the style is strikingly similar: one-sided information, distorted interpretations of Western and Soviet reality, stock phrases and ideas repeated *ad nauseam*. It is only in the printed media that small critical islands remain.

The new entrepreneurs, despite their aggressive self-confidence, are in fact a largely parasitical group, raking in enormous profits from speculative trade in goods produced almost exclusively by the state sector. Seats on the various commodity exchanges are regularly advertised on television at the price of one and a half million rubles. Consumer goods and services accessible to the mass population, needless to say, are not advertised. According to one report, there are more commodity exchanges (which trade anything from rolled steel to tights and sneakers) in Russia than in all the capitalist world combined.

As this chapter is being written, the Russian government stands poised to push through its radical liberal programme of price liberalisation, curtailment of state support for industry, rapid privatisation and opening the economy to the world market. It has made quite clear that only the 'neediest' can expect any measure of protection. The vast majority of the population will have to fend for itself. The 'revolution from above' is moving into high gear.

The Forces of the 'Revolution from Below'

Among workers (less so among white-collar employees and intellectuals) illusions about Yeltsin and the interests he represents are quickly dissipating and are unlikely to withstand even the first stages of the liberal reform. In conversations with the author, leaders of the Independent Miners' Union and worker activists in other sectors made clear their view that the proposed reform programme, which they characterise as little more than a hodgepodge of adventurist measures, will crush the mass of the population like an economic steamroller unless workers are able to organise around a programme of their own.

At the present moment, however, the workers are far from being able to do that. The only mass popular organisations are the Independent Miners' Union (IMU) and the Interrepublican Union of Work Collective Councils (IUWCC). The IMU has approximately 55,000 members, though its real influence among the miners is much broader. Its stand is one of strict independence both from management and from the state. Although formally a trade union organisation, virtually all of the collective actions it has led have been political. Although it had fallen under considerable liberal influence, after the strikes of spring 1991 the IMU leadership concluded that the labour movement must develop its own programme of political and economic transformation if it was not to continue to find itself at the tail end of events, manipulated by alien interests. However this movement has so far not been able to spread outside the mining sector, and the miners' own unity itself faces serious challenges from the divisive forces of the market and national separatism.

The Work Collective Councils (self-management bodies) held their first congress in December 1990. The main goal of the Union that was founded by representatives from enterprises employing some eight million people is to fight for self-management and the transfer of the enterprises to the work collectives, against '*nomenklatura* privatisation'. Despite a promising start, its leadership has been relatively inactive and has apparently been coopted by the Yeltsin forces. This was certainly the impression given by its second congress in October 1991, where most of the time was spent hearing government officials make empty promises. The Union's leaders themselves admitted that the Russian government had already passed a series of laws and resolutions basically hostile to the Union's goals. Silaev, then Yeltsin's Prime Minister, declared in New York in the spring of 1991 that the government was staking Russia's future on the private entrepreneur, not the workers.

With the exception of some trade union locals, individual activists and officials, there are no signs of more than cosmetic change among the 'official' trade unions. Even where these unions have formally adopted an oppositional stance it has been along strictly 'trade unionist' lines; that is, they concede the inevitability of the 'revolution from above' but demand that the population be protected from it, as if the two were really compatible. Moreover these demands are never backed up by serious attempts to encourage rank-and-file mobilisation. As for overtly political organisations, so far none has been able to attract more than a few dozen active members in any major industrial centre. The mass of workers are very cynical about parties, in large part as a reaction to their experience with the CPSU.

There are two principal obstacles to the mobilisation of the forces of the revolution from below. The first is ideological. On concrete issues of living standards, social rights and guarantees, property and power relations, workers are clearly opposed to the liberal programme. But to the degree that the old regime is identified with socialism (and both conservative and liberal propaganda has been at pains to drive this idea home) the rejection of the past becomes a rejection of socialism, and with it of an qualitative alternative to the programme of 'revolution from above'. At the same time workers themselves are increasingly aware that the struggle around partial demands at a time of deepening crisis is futile. The result is demobilising. The other major obstacle is the workers' internal divisions (assiduously maintained by management through the piecework system and other less refined mechanisms) and, concomitantly, their continued dependence on enterprise management. After a brief period at the start of *perestroika*, when the correlation of forces shifted in favour of the workers, management has been able to win back much of the ground lost and even to reinforce its positions. This is due in large part to the deepening economic crisis, which has generally had a dampening effect on shopfloor activism, as well as on the greatly increased dependence of workers over the past two years on the enterprise for consumer goods that are no longer available in state shops. These goods are often doled out in a way calculated to undermine worker solidarity and assertiveness.

There are numerous small exceptions (apart from the major exception of the miners) to this general picture. Scattered about the industrial centres of the former Soviet Union, in virtually every large enterprise, are small groups of activists, often very capable organisers and politically conscious workers. While many of these are relatively isolated, others enjoy the organised support of the workers of their shop or department. In addition small socialist organisations, consisting of workers and intellectuals, exist in virtually every city. Despite tremendous material obstacles they have begun to put out their own weekly or monthly papers and have played roles in conflicts over wages and privatisation in individual enterprises. There is also the recently formed Party of Labour, which has some support from people in the Moscow ('official') Trade Union Federation, and which may play a role in uniting the scattered forces of the left.

Emerging from 70 years of extremely repressive bureaucratic rule that wrapped itself in the banner of 'socialism', and with the bulk of the intelligentsia of a liberal or 'communist' orientation (the latter a small minority) the process of working-class formation was bound to be slow and tortuous. The mass of the population of Eastern Europe has remained a relatively passive spectator to the 'revolution from above'. This is also a possible scenario for the Soviet people, though historically, despite important similarities in social and political structure, Russia's trajectory had always been quite different from that of its more westerly neighbours.

If the revolution from below does succeed in mobilising itself, it will most likely begin by following the path taken by the coalminers: from spontaneous strikes provoked by the liberal reform over issues of wages, prices, social rights and privatisation to the formation of strike committees that become permanent workers' committees;

these soviet-type organisations, at once trade union and political, would then unite on city, regional and finally national levels. The emergence of such a credible organisational and political alternative would provide the conditions for the elaboration, with the help of the now scattered socialist intelligentsia and political activists, of a programmatic alternative corresponding to popular interests. The miners' leadership is already working on such a programme for the labour movement as a whole.

As noted earlier, a more likely scenario for the immediate future is something between the two outlined above: a period of intense social conflict, with popular opposition blocking the most extreme liberal measures but incapable of imposing a solution of its own. Any attempt at more precise prediction would be foolhardy. There are no historical parallels to what is happening today in the territories of the former Soviet Union and in Eastern Europe. What does seem certain, however, is that the liberals' plan for the forced 'building of capitalism' is likely to prove at least as difficult as the attempt at the forced 'construction of socialism' that preceded it.

14

Reconceptualising the Soviet System

T.H. RIGBY

The defeat of the August 1991 *coup d'état* removed any likelihood that the essentials of the old Soviet sociopolitical system would be restored. It still left open, however, what kind of system would eventually replace it; or indeed what kind of *systems*, since we are considering some fifteen (or more) successor states, plus whatever overarching entity may supplant the defunct USSR, and an accelerating process of diversification has been evident since at least 1990. Any assumption that these states are all in transition to variants of a liberal–democratic order with a market economy should therefore be questioned. It is too early to say what they are in transition *to*, and therefore premature for such major studies of the transition process as have been devoted to transitions from non-communist authoritarian to liberal–democratic systems (O'Donnell *et al.*, 1986). Comparative analyses of 'democratic transitions' which include the countries of Eastern Europe are already appearing (Stepan and Linz, forthcoming), and this will be an important theme in the study of 'Soviet' politics in the coming years.

Meanwhile it is not too soon for serious reconsideration of opinions as to what this is a transition *from*. Such a reconsideration is clearly called for in the light of the Soviet Union's role as the pioneer and type case of a kind of sociopolitical order which came to embrace a third of the world's population, and which up to the 1970s was seen by many as offering an alternative, superior or even inevitable path into the future for the whole of humanity. There is nothing like watching something being dismantled to make clear what its essential parts are and how it works. Recent developments in Soviet politics have no more important lesson to teach us than this.

This chapter will review some of the main concepts that have been used to describe and explain the Soviet system, not all of which are well known to younger students, and then offer a few suggestions as to how far and in what respects the process of dismantling it tends to confirm or disconfirm them, while also pointing up the relevance of contemporary Soviet perceptions. The reader is invited to pursue the task further by drawing on the rich material on recent developments offered elsewhere in this volume.

Totalitarian and Post-totalitarian Models

The most influential and controversial model of the Soviet system is of course 'totalitarianism', a term once proudly used of his Fascist regime by the Italian dictator Mussolini, and later extended to other contemporary dictatorial regimes that aspired to unlimited control and direction of all social processes and institutions (economic, political, cultural and so on). This aspiration, it was recognised, was in fact realised only to a modest degree in Fascist Italy, considerably more so in Nazi Germany, and most of all in communist Russia. The key components of totalitarianism were usually taken to be a personal dictator, a single centralised and disciplined party, an official ideology and a powerful political police with wide powers to root out opposition to the dictator, the party and the official ideology. The concept undoubtedly caught what seemed to contemporaries the most salient and distinctive features of these societies and this accounts for its widespread acceptance.

Ironically, it was not until the 1950s, by which time German and Italian 'totalitarianism' were dead and Soviet 'totalitarianism' was beginning to undergo major changes, that serious attempts to construct theoretical models of totalitarianism appeared. The most influential of these were Hannah Arendt's *The Origins of Totalitarianism* (1951), which emphasised the systematic elimination of elements of autonomy in 'intermediate' institutions lying between the dictator and the 'atomised' masses, and Friedrich and Brzezinski's *Totalitarian Dictatorship and Autocracy* (1956), which defined totalitarianism in terms of a 'syndrome' of six interrelated traits. However two assumptions of all these models, namely that after Stalin's death he would sooner or later be succeeded by another dictator, and that mass terroristic use of the political police was an endemic concomitant of 'communist totalitarianism', were not confirmed by events, and by the early 1960s the continued applicability of the totalitarian concept was being questioned among Western Sovietologists. Although Friedrich, Brzezinski and other theorists worked hard to adapt their models to changing realities, many scholars came to share Robert C. Tucker's view of these efforts: the Soviet system becomes, as it were, the definition of totalitarianism, and we are still left with the need to define the nature of the Soviet system.

These intellectual challenges to the totalitarianism concept were reinforced later in the 1960s by political challenges, when with the general questioning of established ideas and institutions which swept the Western world at this time 'totalitarianism' came under fire because of the ideological role it had allegedly assumed since the 'cold war' in generating and maintaining hostility towards the USSR and other communist states and indirectly muting internal criticism within Western countries themselves. The most valuable (though at points difficult) product of this period of debate is the book by Friedrich, Curtis and Barber, *Totalitarianism in Perspective* (Friedrich, 1969). Subsequently 'totalitarianism' was discarded by perhaps the majority of professional students of Soviet history and politics, despite its continued vitality on a more popular level. At the same time few scholars contested that the political leaders of the USSR and other communist countries modelled on it still aspired to unlimited control over all social processes and institutions and had maintained an impressive machinery to this end, that they still ruled through a single, centralised and disciplined party, imposed an official, unchallengeable ideology, and vested their political police with wide powers to suppress all opposition to their party and ideology. This surely amounted to a sociopolitical order qualitatively different from all that had gone before, and some leading scholars therefore argued that totalitarianism was still the best concept for conveying its essential distinguishing features (Schapiro, 1972). Others again disputed this, not so much for the reasons mentioned above, but because they saw the concept as glossing over certain important differences (especially in the economic system) between communist and non-communist 'totalitarianism', while failing to encompass some salient and unique features of the communist 'variant' (Rigby, 1990a, chap. 6).

The partial discrediting of 'totalitarianism' led to a sharpened interest in 'pluralist' elements in Soviet-type systems. Totalitarian models, some alleged, were incapable of accommodating evidence of political conflict arising from competing interests in such systems. This was an exaggeration, and indeed some of the best accounts then available of political conflict motivated by interest and/or policy differences had been written by such protagonists of the totalitarian concept as Schapiro, Conquest and Armstrong. It is also curious that among the new wave of 'pluralist' Sovietologists there was little serious awareness of an earlier pluralist approach, albeit less optimistic than theirs in its implications, which was widely current back in the 1950s. This was the view that power in the Soviet Union was shared among a number of competing elites – the party apparatus, the economic administration, the political police, the army high command and so on, and the top leaders in the Politburo and other such bodies were seen more or less as spokesmen for various elites. A good example of this 'pluralism of elites' approach was Roger Pethybridge's *A Key to Soviet Politics: The Crisis of the Anti-Party Group* (1962). Although most came to agree that this approach did not explain nearly as much as it was claimed to, it did rightly identify one of the levels of political conflict in the USSR.

However the pluralist models that became popular in Soviet studies after the 1960s derived, not from this earlier 'pluralism of elites' approach, but from American interest-group theory. Interest-group theory had a long pedigree in American political science and in its most extreme forms sought to account for almost everything that happens in politics and government – a rather tall order, many would argue, even for a country with such well-organised interests as the United States. The best book exploring the potentialities of the concept in Soviet studies is still the one edited by Skilling and Griffiths and published in 1971, *Interest Groups in Soviet Politics*, although a good deal of research and writing informed by the concept continued for some years after that. The results were partly positive and partly negative. On the one hand, it brought a more widespread sensitivity to competing and conflicting interests in the USSR and a greater awareness of the way they sought to influence the political process. But, on the other hand, research extending into the early 1980s tended further to confirm the centrality of bureaucratic and clientelist politics and the limited applicability of the concept of a pluralism of interest groups in a situation where interests could not be taken up by independent associations capable of canvassing public support to press for specific outcomes (cf. Solomon, 1983). Hough's alternative of a 'pluralism of institutions' carried greater plausibility and ironically harked back to the 'pluralism of elites' of a generation earlier.

It thus transpired that 'pluralism', like 'totalitarianism' before it, came to be seen as inadequate and incomplete as a general organising concept for analysis of the development and character of Soviet-type systems. They both need to be put in a broader theoretical framework that identifies more fundamental and distinctive attributes of these systems. Such a framework is offered by two different (though perhaps complementary) types of model, which I shall term 'class' models and 'bureaucratic' models.

Class Models

Class models rest on Marxist or quasi-Marxist assumptions as to the primacy of ownership or control over economic resources in the structuring of society and the distribution of power and privilege. Here, of course, we find the official Soviet self-definition: a socialist society created by the revolutionary victory of the proletariat led by its Communist Party, a society in which antagonistic and exploitative class relations have been swept away, along with private ownership of the means of production. Of greater interest for our purpose here, too, are the several 'new class' models of Soviet-type societies. Most of these can be viewed as Marxist heresies. Their authors usually share with more orthodox Marxists the assumption that the state is a product of the class struggle and that it normally expresses the interests of the economically dominant class. Most of them started as communists but became disillusioned with the social and political system that resulted from the Russian Revolution and concluded that it could not possibly represent the rule of the proletariat and therefore some other social class or stratum must have usurped power.

However the earliest, and in some ways the most interesting, 'new class' theory was enunciated nearly 20 years before the revolution by the Polish–Russian revolutionary and sociologist Jan Waclaw Machajski (A. Volsky). Machajski was one of the first political thinkers to recognise the political potential in modern society of what he called the 'mental worker' – administrators, managers, technologists and professionals. Although he started as a Marxist, Machajski came to see Marxist socialism as the ideology of those mental workers who resented the role of the bourgeoisie and landlords and who wanted to use industrial workers in order to take power for themselves. If a socialist revolution occurred in Russia it would result, not in a classless society, but in a form of what he called 'state capitalism' in which capital in the form of education would replace capital in the form of money as the basis of power. He warned workers against being misled by socialist intellectuals and urged them to keep a firm grip on their own organisations and conduct a militant struggle for equality in their own way (Parry, 1968).

Machajski's writings made a considerable impact on the Russian socialist movement and were regarded by the Bolsheviks as a dangerous heresy, so much so that as late as the 1920s various opposition groups, from the Workers' Opposition on, who claimed to speak on behalf of the workers against the bureaucrats or intelligentsia were frequently labelled Machajski-ites by those in control of the party-state machine. Trotsky was among the Russian Marxists who, as he testifies in his memoirs, was much impressed with Machajski's 'The

Mental Worker' when it first came out, and he was eventually to come to a 'new class' theory of his own, albeit one based on a different line of analysis, one which preserved much more of Marxism and indeed of Leninism. Trotsky's views on the nature of Soviet society changed over time, but central to them was his notion of the bureaucratic degeneration of the proletarian state. Stalinism, in his view, was the political expression of the dominance of the bureaucracy. He preserved the traditional Marxist belief that capitalism can only be succeeded by socialism. But Russia had got stuck somewhere in between as a result of the attempt to create a socialist society in a country that was not sufficiently developed economically and culturally. This had enabled a bureaucratic stratum to emerge and elbow the proletariat aside, and to rule in the name of the proletariat but in its own interests. This, however, was not a new, distinctive and historically viable form of class rule – just a deformation of proletarian rule, and sooner or later there would have to be either a return to capitalism or an overthrow of the bureaucracy by the proletariat, opening up the path to true socialism (Trotsky, 1937).

James Burnham was one of Trotsky's American followers who came to regard his mentor's analysis of the bureaucratic degeneration of the proletarian state as an increasingly inadequate account of Soviet society and moved beyond it to a more radical break with traditional Marxist assumptions. Burnham came to believe that there was indeed a social revolution under way in the world, but that this was replacing bourgeois rule by the rule, not of the proletariat, but of the salaried management class (Burnham, 1941). The basic shortcoming of traditional Marxism, as he saw it, was to assume that class dominance necessarily involved *ownership* of the means of production, whereas in fact the vital thing was *control* over the means of production. What was going on in all industrialised countries, whether it was the liberal–democratic West, Nazi Germany or Soviet Russia, was that control over the means of production was passing to the salaried managers, and in one form or another they were establishing their dominance of society and employing the power of the state to back up their rule.

Burnham saw the political leadership and the party apparatus in the Soviet Union as something like political agents of the managerial class. This was a point from which a good deal of the criticism of his analysis started. To many people it seemed that the relationship between the managers and the party leaders and apparatus was the exact opposite of the way Burnham saw it. To some extent Burnham guarded himself against this kind of criticism by referring occasionally to the party apparatus, police, state bureaucracy *and* the actual plant managers as if they were all equally part of the managerial class. But if they are, is it not misleading to focus most of one's analysis, as Burnham does, specifically on the actual managers themselves?

In the post-war and post-Stalin period a new view of the 'managerial revolution' emerged, according to which the managers had not yet won power, but were destined sooner or later to replace the party-state bureaucrats as the dominant force in Soviet society. The pioneer of this view was Hermann Achimow, whose book *Die Macht im Hintergrund: Totengräber des Kommunismus.* (The Power in the Background: Gravediggers of Communism) was published in 1950. He later developed a more sophisticated variant of his views, emphasising that it was the technical intelligentsia that he had in mind. During the 1960s similar views enjoyed a certain currency in the United States, where some writers saw contemporary changes and discussions pointing towards some kind of market socialism as promising the emancipation of the managers from their subordination to the party-state bureaucracy. The illusoriness of such expectations was persuasively argued by Jeremy Azrael in his *Managerial Power and Soviet Politics* (1966) and later developments have since borne him out.

These disputes underlined the problem of defining the boundary of the class or stratum which had allegedly asserted its dominance in post-revolutionary Russia and the other countries to which the Soviet system had been transplanted. Milovan Djilas (1957) in some measure evaded the problem of identifying it simply as 'the new class'. Like Trotsky he saw this as being more or less commensurate with the bureaucracy as a whole, but he rejected Trotsky's view that its reign was a local and temporary aberration in the world transition from capitalism to socialism. On the contrary, the reign of the new class was exactly what must be expected if an attempt was made to transform society through the medium of a Communist Party dictatorship. The power of the new class was based on its *collective ownership* of the means of production, and Djilas argued that such collective ownership had been a far more frequent basis of class rule in history than was generally realised. A closer analysis of Djilas's thesis brings to light a number of difficulties, including his frequent identification of the 'new class' simply with the party.

All these quasi-Marxist or post-marxist models raise theoretical questions which are also posed by ruling-class models of power in other societies. Who is rider and who is horse in the relationship between government and class? How great is intergenerational class continuity and what significance do we assign to it? How much weight do we place on the distinction between property-based and status-based social differentiation?

A fresh approach was offered by the Hungarian writers George

Konrád and Ivan Szelenyi in *The Intellectuals on the Road to Class Power* (1979). They defined the so-called socialism of Soviet-type societies as 'rational redistributive society', characterised as follows:

> Modern redistribution replaces the decisions of the market with official administrative decisions which, in the aggregate, call into being a bureaucratic organisation that tends to become highly centralised and monolithic, and to encompass the whole of society. Important political and economic decisions are made on the upper levels of the elite bureaucracy, and these upper-level positions must be occupied by intellectual-officials. Not every intellectual takes part in making important redistributive decisions, but every major decision is made by the intelligentsia of office.

On one level, then, Konrád and Szelenyi seemed to be building on Machajski's prediction of the coming rule of the so-called mental worker. But on another level – like the *nomenklatura* model to be discussed later – they shared ground with the bureaucratic models of Soviet society to which we are about to turn. And they overcame some of the difficulties in other new class models by arguing that the intellectuals were not yet a fully-developed ruling class, but only on the way to becoming one.

Bureaucratic and Other Models

The starting-point for our bureaucratic models (not an ideal term, perhaps, in view of the varying meanings attached to 'bureaucracy') is the indisputable fact, already noted in the passage quoted from Konrád and Szelenyi, that in Soviet-type societies administration replaces the market and market-related procedures as the *main* mechanism for ordering social activities. This engenders what Fehér, Heller and Márkus (1983) have brilliantly termed a 'dictatorship over needs'. This consequence of the effort to create a socialist order was not, incidentally, entirely unexpected, and Max Weber and Robert Michels were among those who had warned that it would bring the triumph of an oppressive and alienating bureaucracy. In these societies all spheres of life came to be directly organised and run by various bureaucracies or hierarchies of officials, and these were bound together and coordinated by the organisational machinery of the party, forming a unified organisational structure embracing the whole of society. This was summed up graphically by Alfred Meyer (1961) in his phrase 'USSR Incorporated'. My own term for this kind of sociopolitical order is the 'mono-organisational society'; Maria

Hirszowicz (1980) prefers the 'bureaucratic Leviathan'. The emphasis in these bureaucratic (or organisåtional) models is on the basic structure of organising social activity rather than, as in the 'new class' models, on social differences of wealth, status and power – although they are certainly interested in the patterns of social differentiation engendered by this kind of system. They share some common ground with 'state socialist' views of the system (Giddens, 1973; Lane, 1976) which, however, take a more Marxian approach to the nature and role of the social classes in these societies.

Space will permit only brief mention of some further concepts which have been infuential in the analysis of Soviet politics and society. The concept of political elites has generated a vast amount of empirical research (for example, Armstrong, 1959; Fischer, 1968; Farrell, 1970; Rigby, 1990b). However, while some of this literature, most notably the earlier accounts of political developments in terms of a 'pluralism of elites', implies an elite model of the sociopolitical order, explicit and systematic models in the elite tradition of Pareto, Mosca and others are hard to find. Research on elites shades into work, on the one hand, on political leadership (for example, Farrell, 1970; Brown, 1989c) and, on the other, on political clientelism (for example, Rigby and Harasymiw, 1983) each of which relates to a different theoretical and comparative literature.

Far more prominent in debates on the nature of the system has been the concept of political culture (Brown and Gray, 1977; White, 1979; Tucker, 1987). Despite robust disagreements over the definition and applicability of the concept, few would now contest that historically evolved and culturally embedded patterns of thinking, feeling and acting can substantially affect the operation of political and social systems and that elements of the resultant 'political culture' may survive profound changes in the institutional order, even such radical ones as a communist-led 'building of socialism'. Many would go further and assert that the differences that evolve among communist-ruled countries are partly explained by differences in their inherited political culture. Since it was Russia that pioneered the 'Soviet-type' system, political culture will perhaps bear a greater burden of explanation there than in countries that copied the system or had it imposed on them. Nevertheless it clearly cannot offer more than a partial account of aspects of the system and certainly not a general model of its structure and operation.

Political legitimation, a concept which likewise focuses on subjective elements in the structure of political and social power, aroused considerable interest in the study of Soviet-type societies in the 1980s. While it has long been recognised that popular compliance with rulers' laws and commands may stem not only from the fear of punishment, expectation of gain or habit, but also from the belief that those laws and commands are legitimate, it was Max Weber who first proposed that the grounds on which legitimacy was claimed and granted might be a major determinant of the structure of power. However, while most writing on political legitimation in Soviet-type systems owes much to Weber's approach, there has been little agreement so far on the character of political legitimation in these countries (see Rigby and Fehér, 1982).

Finally concepts of 'development', 'modernisation' and 'industrial society' (notably Rostow, 1960) also strongly influenced the way some scholars have come to view Soviet-type societies. In Richard Lowenthal's words (in Johnson, 1970), communism constituted 'a special type of politically forced development'. Actual models varied widely, at one extreme positing a 'convergence' between 'Western' and communist systems as the state assumed a greater socioeconomic role in the former and moderated its total power in the latter (see Meyer's chapter in Johnson, 1970). At their most sophisticated, the comparative and historical perspectives offered by modernisation/ development models threw valuable light on Soviet-type societies. Yet there was obviously far more to the latter than a 'strategy of development', and one still had to look elsewhere for an explanatory account of those unique features of these systems which contrasted them so sharply with other 'modernising autocracies'.

It seems, then, that the only general explanatory accounts on offer were those provided by the totalitarian, new class and bureaucratic models. And here we should note that these were not necessarily mutually exclusive; indeed in important respects each implied the other. Just as anatomy, physiology and biochemistry may offer equally valid and complementary descriptions of an organism, so study of a society's structure of power, social differentiation and institutional articulation may offer equally valid and complementary descriptions of that society, *provided*, of course, they conform with ascertainable facts and are mutually consistent. I have already hinted at some implications of this for our models of Soviet society. We cannot have a model of totalitarianism that *requires* a personal dictator and mass terroristic use of the political police or that fails to account for structural conflict and competition. We cannot have a new class model that omits to define its boundaries clearly or to demonstrate the mechanics of its dominance. We cannot have a bureaucratic model that operates with a Weberian 'rational–legal' model of bureaucracy or lacks an account of its integrative mechanisms and its informal as well as formal organisation.

No attempt can be made in this brief account to do justice to the full range and richness of ideas that have been brought to bear on the study of Soviet politics and society in recent decades, let alone to the contributions of many oustanding scholars whose books, and often individual articles and chapters, have sharpened our understanding and advanced the process of theory building. Nor should we forget that our knowledge of the system owes much to the work of political scientists and historians who abjure any overarching theory and are sparing in their use of social science concepts generally. By contrast, some social theorists interested mainly in modern Western societies and/or Marxist ideas and lacking a close knowledge of Soviet society have been ready to offer theoretical accounts of it which have had some resonance. And finally, by further contrast, there is a rigorously behaviouralist literature mostly emphasising the formal testing of hypotheses against quantitative data.

Two other limitations of the present account should also be mentioned. First, despite the wish to suppress bias, it is inevitably coloured by the author's perceptions and judgements; and second, the selection and emphasis reflects our immediate purpose, which is to invite reflection on the most influential models employed in Western accounts of the system in the light of the process of its disintegration and of how it seems in retrospect to 'participant observers' inside the Soviet Union itself. Without repeating details and analysis presented from a variety of viewpoints elsewhere in this volume, a preliminary *post mortem* examination will now be attempted, recalling a number of overlapping phases and aspects of developments since 1985 in order to draw out some observations relevant to this purpose.

The Soviet System: A Retrospective Evaluation

Revolution from Above

Although clearly provoked by objective economic and social problems, action for change was initiated entirely within the crypto-political arena of the Politburo and its penumbra of officials and advisors and was in no significant degree a response to a broader institutionalised political process. The personal role of Gorbachev was crucial, and arguably that of Alexander Yakovlev and certain other Gorbachev advisors was little less so. Even when *perestroika* was pushed beyond within-system (essentially administrative) reforms to such radically heretical measures as legalising cooperatives and other elements of private enterprise, encouraging *glasnost'* and permitting unofficial associations (the *neformaly*), these measures were put in train without any serious public debate or evidence even of organised conflict within the closed circles of the party or the government. Instead there was the muted sniping and bureaucratic foot-dragging that had characterised what had passed for politics since Stalin's day. As late as 1988, when the threat presented by this second stage of *perestroika* to the whole established sociopolitical order was abundantly clear, the conservative forces, now taking their cue from Central Committee Secretary Yegor Ligachev, responded, not with an open challenge to Gorbachev's policies but with the typical Stalin-era device of an indignant *cri de coeur* from an obscure loyal citizen (the Nina Andreeva letter, 'I cannot forgo my principles', *Sovetskaya Rossiya*, 13 March 1988).

It is hard to reconcile this with any 'pluralist' view of Soviet politics that posits a basic similarity with political processes in Western countries, but it is fully consistent with the kind of 'politics' described in totalitarian accounts of the system. As the mayor of St Petersburg, Anatolii Sobchak puts it in his recent book, *Khozhdenie vo vlast* (The Path to Power):

> In countries with a totalitarian regime things are different: there life itself depends on the course of politics, but paradoxical though it be, politics as such does not exist. There is fighting among the courtiers, officials with their bureaucratic games, anything else you like – but not politics. (p. 5)

The Unleashing of Politics

During what I have called the second stage of *perestroika* the Soviet Union acquired a level of freedom of information, public expression, association and assembly unknown since the earliest days of Soviet power. The triggering factor seems to have been Gorbachev's concern to open up new political arenas in which to mobilise support to overcome resistance to his reforms within the party-state power structures, but once a public political process was unleashed it soon began to outrun the General Secretary's capacity to orchestrate and contain it. This became dramatically more obvious in 1989–90, when *perestroika* was pushed to its third stage, that of institutional change: the semi-free elections to the Congress of People's Deputies; the emergence of the latter body and the full-time Supreme Soviet chosen by it as something like a genuine parliament; the CPSU's loss of its constitutional monopoly and 'leading and directing' powers over all governmental and non-governmental bodies; the concurrent creation of an executive presidency and its replacement of the Politburo as the focus of supreme power; the largely free elections in the republics and emergence in several of them of independence-minded regimes; the failure of efforts to get the 28th CPSU Congress to reverse the march of reform; and the proliferation of new political parties. Whatever Gorbachev's original 'hidden agenda' may have been, and despite all his skill in manoeuvring between radicals and conservatives, frightening each with the other in order to secure their often grudging acceptance of his moves, he was himself progressively converted into an instrument of tempestuous forces whose power and trajectory he had evidently not foreseen. Why did Gorbachev's controlled 'revolution from above' develop into such an unplanned and even more uncontrolled 'revolution from below'? To understand this I think we need to note three complementary aspects.

Firstly, *'unleashing' is the appropriate term*. All that was necessary in order to start off this explosive chain process was the easing and progressive abdication between mid-1986 and 1989 of those long-entrenched coercive controls over information, public expression, association and assembly which had been deployed through the party apparatus and various governmental and 'voluntary' agencies, backed by the KGB and its army of informers, a compliant procuracy and judiciary equipped with a package of vaguely worded laws on 'state crimes', and the network of prisons, punitive psychiatric hospitals and 'corrective labour' camps. The profound transformation of Soviet political life that came with the withdrawal of these coercive controls testifies to their fundamental importance in the communist-run political and social system. Obviously this lends further weight to totalitarian images of the nature of that system. Further analysis, however, suggests a more qualified and interesting conclusion.

Secondly, *the 'shadow culture'*. It is one thing to be off the leash, but another to have the will and capacity to run free. The main reason why the public political process, once unleashed, soon outran Gorbachev's control was the pent-up force of the 'shadow culture' which had grown and matured under the carapace of coercive controls since the 1950s. The curbing of Stalin's terroristic police measures against those under the slightest suspicion of 'counter-revolutionary' tendencies had dissolved that 'atomisation' of individuals, which came from their fear to share information, ideas and attitudes even with close friends and family, and perforated the 'Iron Curtain' that had been largely successful in protecting them from external heresies. The KGB still rigorously policed what people said, wrote and did in public, but it was no longer much bothered with monitoring ideological and behavioural peccadillos shared by consenting adults in private, let alone their innermost thoughts. There thus emerged a substantial unofficial social zone within which people interacted with a high level of spontaneity and frankness, and within this zone there grew up a many-sided 'shadow culture' based on information, ideas, attitudes, values and practices (everything from the BBC news, to Solzhenitsyn's novels, to rock music) at odds with those enshrined in the official culture, while the latter remained virtually unchallenged in all public settings.

Social changes in the three post-Stalin decades provided an increasingly hospitable environment for the spread of this shadow culture. Of particular importance were the rapid advance of urbanisation and the training of professionals, who quadrupled in numbers in this period to make up over a third of the urban population. Thus, while the few thousand active dissidents played a vital role, underestimated at the time by many Western Sovietologists, the present author included, there were also millions of outwardly conforming *passive* dissidents who largely shared their values. Furthermore the concern of post-Stalin leaders to broaden and improve the range of information and ideas available to them in making policy choices brought many intellectuals into their entourage who were not only at home in this 'shadow culture' but also, notably in the new policy-oriented think-tanks that flourished under Brezhnev and enjoyed licensed access to heretical writings from abroad and relative freedom of debate within their own professional circles. Several such people were later to serve as assistants or consultants to Gorbachev (Brown, 1989c, pp. 169, 228).

It is the existence of this 'shadow culture' that largely accounts for that great explosion of radical political ideas and activity once the controls were eased, in the media, the 'informal groups' of 1987–8, the election campaigns of 1990–1, the new legislatures and the new political parties. It was thus one of the necessary conditions for the transition to a new sociopolitical order. The fact that it could take root and spread within pre-*perestroika* Soviet society shows that the 'totalitarian' label was misleadingly incomplete, and suggests that Hannah Arendt and many of her contemporaries were right in seeing terror and 'atomisation' as core elements of totalitarianism, at least in the sense that without them the other components of totalitarianism would eventually dissolve. The title of Georgii Arbatov's recent book 'Prolonged Convalescence: 1953–1985' (*Zatyanuvsheesya vyzdorovlenie*, 1991) offers one perspective on this. Another would be to characterise it as a 'crippled totalitarianism'.

What we have been discussing in this section also tells us something about political legitimation in the USSR. The massive coercive controls employed to suppress public heresy confirmed the mutual dependence of the regime's self-legitimating formulas and the structure of power, while the effects of withdrawing those controls showed that they, rather than popular legitimacy, had been the main factor in ensuring mass compliance with the regime's demands.

Thirdly, *political hypocrisy as a time-bomb*. Hypocrisy, 'the homage that vice pays to virtue', can also be a political time-bomb since, while betraying the values and institutions it proclaims, it simultaneously legitimises and preserves them. For decades the constant democratic rhetoric of Soviet political life did indeed clothe an authoritarian–bureaucratic reality, and professedly democratic structures and processes were indeed emptied of democratic content, but the citizens of the 1980s had all been habituated to that rhetoric and inherited structures and processes into which a new democratic content could be poured. Of course hypocrisy can also engender cynicism in its victims, and that was also manifest in the USSR, but there were enough Soviet citizens who had internalised the democratic values and were ready to put them into practice once they found themselves unmuzzled and unleashed.

Without the democratic rhetoric and pseudo-democratic structures and processes the rapid (if far from complete) transition to democracy in the USSR and Eastern Europe could scarcely have happened. This self-fulfilling potential of political hypocrisy has been virtually ignored in scholarly writing on Soviet politics. It points to a further important distinction between a 'totalitarianism' that claims to be something else and one, like German National Socialism under Hitler, which does not.

Ideas, Interests and Classes

The process of disintegration affords only indirect evidence on the importance of interest groups in the communist-run system. While the interests of a large variety of occupational and other groups have been vitally affected, the clubs, associations and parties formed to engage in the emergent public political process have been based mainly on shared ideas and values (civil rights, democracy, ethnic-nationalism, environmental concerns, religion and so on) rather than shared material interests. The balance has begun to shift, as most dramatically instanced by the miners' unions and strike committees, but this reflects the emergence of a new non-communist sociopolitical order. There is little indication that citizens had become habituated to engage in interest-group politics under the old order.

On a more general level, the political force of perceived material interests is reflected in the evident hostility to system change among most (though far from all) senior party, government, military and police officials and widely shared by millions of others privileged by their *nomenklatura* status. Yet it would be unduly cynical to deny the force of ideological and value commitments too among many such opponents of reform, especially commitments to 'socialism' and/or the glory of the Soviet state, often coloured by Russian nationalism. On the other hand, while personal ambition undoubtedly helped to motivate many of those working to change the system, it was their shared ideas and values that made them into a political force. What most deserves note is that this force ultimately prevailed over that potent blend of material and ideal commitments deployed by the conservatives.

There are problems here for most theories of the role of classes in revolutionary change. Few would contest that class or class-like divisions and antagonisms do exist in Soviet-type societies, however sharp the theoretical disagreements about them noted earlier in this chapter. But the revolutionary transformation of these societies cannot plausibly be explained from the Marxist position that class conflict is the engine of history. Although hostility to the *nomenklatura* was undoubtedly an important factor, this hostility was not yoked with the economically-based interests of an emergent dominant class, analogous to the bourgeoisie in the French Revolution. Contrary to the expectations of some theorists, neither the workers nor the managers proved to be the 'gravediggers' of communism (or 'state socialism'). The intelligentsia played a vital role, but it is already obvious that it will not be rewarded with 'class power'. The largest eventual winners may well be the emergent new bourgeoisie, but *they* were not yet present in the womb of the old society when the revolution was maturing.

The topic of this chapter is not the process of revolutionary transformation in itself, but aspects of that process can tell us much about the nature of the society that is being transformed. Once open politics was unleashed in that society, it turned out that the most potent political cleavages were based, not on sectional material interests, but on non-material commitments and concerns. The transformation process also offers several pointers to the role of political culture. Revelations from a number of Central Asian and Transcaucasian republics about the operations of local corrupt party machines, with their strong component of traditional clan, tribal and other traditional obligations, lend further weight to the view that cultural factors engendered significant differences in the sociopolitical order of the various Soviet nations in spite of identical official structures and ideology and constant multichannelled direction from Moscow. On the other hand, the rapidity and extent of further political diversification in the republics as central lines of control frayed and broke testifies to the powerful restraints under the old system on the pressures from indigenous political culture. This parallels the deep-going political diversification in the countries of East–Central Europe since the collapse of communist power in 1989.

In Russia itself it is important to note that the 'shadow culture' which emerged to dominate political discourse since the late 1980s contained several political strands, some of which have deep roots in the pre-communist past. These include both a xenophobic ethno-nationalist strand (the *Pamyat* Society and others), a nationalism of the historic Russian state (the *gosudarstvenniki*), and a liberal–constitutional strand which can be traced back to the early nineteenth century. The latter two, especially, have been important factors in the political struggles both at the Union and Russian Republic levels.

Modernisation, Industrial Society and Convergence

The transformation process suggests a number of observations regarding this cluster of concepts. Firstly, the Soviet Union's radical turn to market economics and liberal democracy can hardly be taken as confirmation of the 'convergence theory'. Far from the 'socialist' and 'capitalist' paths converging, the countries of the Soviet Union and East–Central Europe have been simply abandoning the former and stumbling towards the latter, while simultaneously many Western countries have been distancing their paths even further from socialism.

Those who view current changes in advanced Western countries as amounting to a transition to 'post-industrial' and indeed 'post-modern' society would find it paradoxical that many are now interpreting the transition from communist to Western-type systems in terms of the imperatives of modernisation and industrial society. Yet in important respects such an interpretation is surely valid. Gorbachev would scarcely have managed (or probably wished) to launch his revolution from above had it not been for the Soviet Union's 'pre-crisis situation', embodied first and foremost in the rapid relative decline in Soviet technological and productivity levels *vis-à-vis* those of the capitalist democracies. Lucian Pye has persuasively interpreted this as just one example, albeit a key one, of the failure and abandonment of various kinds of authoritarian modernisation in many parts of the globe, and the incorporation of countries concerned in an ever more integrated world system (Pye, 1990). Earlier we saw how social processes associated with modernisation fostered the growth of that 'shadow culture' which was to assume vital importance in the political transformation of the USSR. Thus there was a positive as well as a negative way in which the pressures of modernisation operated as a necessary condition and partial explanation for the current transformation of the Soviet system, and this is indicative of the importance of such pressures in the operation of that system, although not in its underlying character.

As for the view that the Soviet path was an appropriate modernising strategy in certain historical circumstances, the current evidence is not encouraging. That path seems to lead to a dead end and, while accelerating the growth of certain components of a modern industrial society, it is destructive of others, including the institutions and the skills and attitudes necessary to take the modernisation process further.

The Retrospective View from Within

In the Soviet Union itself the three concepts which have dominated both scholarly and journalistic characterisations of the system being discarded are the command–administrative (or administrative–command) system, the *nomenklatura* and totalitarianism. The term 'command–administrative system' came into prominence in 1988 when it was taken up by Gorbachev and, as subsequently used, signified essentially what the present writer means by 'mono-organisational socialism': all spheres of social life run by a series of hierarchies of administrative command bound together by the command hierarchy of the party apparatus. It was described at first as a deformation of socialism and blamed on Stalin, but later its roots were traced back to 'War Communism' and ultimately, by some, to Marx's blanket rejection of the market mechanism. Theoretically an important breakthrough in anchoring analysis of the system in the basic structures of social action, it also served Gorbachev as a polemical weapon against the administrative powers of the party apparatus, especially in the economic sphere, and was meanwhile used more loosely by reformers as a surrogate for 'totalitarianism', at a time when the latter was still unacceptable in the official media as a label for the Soviet system.

Within the 'shadow culture', however, the system had been commonly seen as totalitarian for at least two decades (in 1973, the author was privately reproved by a leading Moscow historian of ideas for soft-pedalling the concept in my own work) and since 1990 it has been used publicly as virtually axiomatic. Serious theoretical discussions of the concept are as yet few, but its general connotation seems to be a regime seeking to exercise total control over all organised social activity and rigorously suppressing all unauthorised public expression and association perceived as damaging to its monopoly. Indeed such a view may be presented without attaching the label 'totalitarian', for example in Alexander Obolonsky's impressive article, 'The political system we inherited' (Obolonsky, 1990). Obolonsky discusses six 'main institutions' of the old regime, which can be summarily listed as follows: undivided dominance of the single party, whose strictly centralised command system extended to all sectors of society; a leader enjoying prerogatives not subject to formal limitations but in practice hedged about by the apparatus; an extraordinarily powerful machinery of compulsion and potential repression; party monopolisation of ideological life to produce a forced public identity of opinion; a developing bifurcation of the ideology into a facade version for the masses and a genuine version for a narrow elite; and total dependence of the individual on the authorities through a comprehensive system of punishments and privileges.

The *nomenklatura* had been the common designation for the 'new class' among Soviet and East European intellectuals for many years, although Western scholars have generally been hesitant in taking it up. More precisely it denotes that category of the workforce who occupy posts of sufficient significance to be included in the appointments schedule (*nomenklatura*) of one or other CPSU committee, and who consequently share a variety of formal and informal privileges and are bound together by a variety of formal and informal mutual dependencies (Volensky, 1984). The *nomenklatura* consists mostly of persons holding bureaucratic office, but also includes professionals and workers performing politically or ideologically sensitive roles. Its cooptative recruitment pattern ensures considerable intergenerational continuity within '*nomenklatura* families' as well as innumerable channels of social mobility, which help to explain its rootedness in the broader society (Sobchak, 1991, pp. 51–3).

The totalitarian, command–administrative and *nomenklatura* concepts do not function as mutually exclusive models of the Soviet system. They are often seen as complementary and mutually reinforcing. The attempt by the political leadership to exercise total control over society gives rise to the command–administrative system, and since power and privilege depend in that system on access to administrative resources rather than to capital or noble birth, it ensures the political and social dominance of the *nomenklatura* 'class'.

To sum up our main conclusions, it is suggested that both the process of disintegration of the Soviet system and the images of it now dominant in the country itself lend additional weight to the totalitarian, new class and bureaucratic approaches in Western sovietological literature, and suggest how these approaches may be refined and integrated. They also point up the relevance and limitations of interest-group, modernisation, legitimation and political culture approaches. While it seems unlikely that further knowledge and experience will invalidate these conclusions, they must be regarded as to some extent provisional and incomplete at this early stage. The opening of archives, the stream of memoir material, a variety of case-studies, and free theoretical reflection will in time permit a far fuller and more precise understanding of the system, and here scholars from Russia and other ex-communist countries will play a vital role. Further lessons will also be learned as the process of transformation continues, in those (mostly Asian) countries where the Communist Party remains in power as well as those where it has been overthrown. Meanwhile a widespread aspiration towards a liberal–democratic order with the rule of law and a free-market economy coexists with authoritarian pressures stemming, not only from conservatives of various hues, but also from reformist leaders faced with the problems of economic chaos, ethnic strife and social disorder. This will accelerate the trend to diversity in the emergent sociopolitical systems of these countries. Outcomes will be affected by such factors as specific economic and international circumstances, leadership styles (compare Yeltsin in Russia, Nazarbaev in Kazakhstan and Gamsakhurdia in Georgia) and entrenched differences in social mores and political culture.

The study of 'comparative communism' is fast losing its topicality, although it will long retain its absorbing scholarly interest and importance for understanding the experience of human society in the twentieth century. Meanwhile 'comparative *post*-communism' has emerged as a key problem area for the social sciences in this final decade of the second millennium.

Guide to Further Reading

General

All the chapters in this volume are based, to varying extents, on the contemporary Soviet press and other sources. A substantial selection of these sources is available in translation in the *Current Digest of the Soviet Press* (Columbus, Ohio, weekly) and in daily monitoring services such as the American-based *Foreign Broadcast Information Service* and the *BBC Summary of World Broadcasts*. Detailed commentaries on current developments are available in the research reports issued by Radio Liberty in Munich, published since 1992 as the *RFE/RL Research Report*. More extended scholarly commentaries are available in the journals that specialise in Soviet and now post-Soviet affairs, among them *Soviet Studies* (Glasgow, quarterly), *Slavic Review* (Austin, Texas, quarterly), *Problems of Communism* (Washington DC, bimonthly), *Russian Review* (Columbus, Ohio, quarterly), *Soviet Economy* (Silver Springs, Md, quarterly, whose scope is broader than its title might suggest), *Soviet Union* (Irvine, Cal. quarterly) and the *Journal of Communist Studies* (London, quarterly).

An unofficial guide to Soviet and now post-Soviet thinking is *Moscow News*, published weekly in Russian and other languages. *Soviet News*, issued weekly by the Soviet (now Russian) Embassy in London, contains official and other statements. Gorbachev's own speeches and articles are available in a number of collections, among them *Selected Speeches and Articles*, 2nd edn (Moscow: Progress, 1987); *Socialism, Peace and Democracy: Writings, Speeches and Reports by Mikhail Gorbachev* (London and Atlantic Highlands, NJ: Zwan, 1987); *Speeches and Writings*, 2 vols (Oxford and New York: Pergamon, 1986 and 1987) and *Meaning of my Life: Perestroika* (Edinburgh: Aspect, 1990). Gorbachev's best-selling book, *Perestroika: New Thinking for Our Country and the World* (London: Collins, 1987) is available in numerous editions; so too is his account of *The August Coup* (London: HarperCollins, 1991). On Yeltsin a starting-point is an interim biography, John Morrison, *Boris Yeltsin* (London: Penguin, 1991) and the Russian leader's own *Against the Grain* (London: Cape, 1990).

Chapter 1   Towards a Post-Soviet Politics?

For an early assessment of Gorbachev's accession and the prospects as they appeared at that time see Brown (1985). The best biography of Gorbachev is still Medvedev (1988); see also Schmidt-Hauer (1986), Doder and Branson (1990) and Ruge (1991). For the development of the Gorbachev reforms more generally see Lewin (1988), an interpretive essay; Bloomfield (1989), a sympathetic but not uncritical symposium; Joyce *et al.* (1989), a symposium by British and American scholars; Hill and Dellenbrant (1989), a British and Scandinavian symposium; Jowitt (1990), an incisive essay that appeared in the first edition of this book; and Dallin and Lapidus (1991), a comprehensive reader. Sakwa (1990) and White (1991a) provide detailed and analytic accounts of the Gorbachev administration as a whole; on the question of pluralism, public attitudes and 'civil society' more particularly see Grey *et al.* (1990), Hosking (1991), Aage (1991) and Hahn (1991a). A wider view is presented in Saivetz and Jones (1992), from which some of the data cited in this chapter have been drawn.

Chapter 2   The Crisis of Marxism–Leninism

A brief review of the development of Soviet Marxist–Leninist ideology through the Stalin period, furnishing a good introduction to the old orthodoxy, is Carew Hunt (1963). Another valuable piece of background reading, providing crucial insights into the outlook of post-Stalin reformers, is Breslauer (1976). For changes in the official ideology from Khrushchev to Gorbachev see White and Pravda (1988), Thompson (1989) and Woodby and Evans (1990). The Party Programme adopted in 1986 is conveniently available, together with a detailed introduction, in White (1989). Other analyses of Soviet reformist thinking in the Gorbachev years include Moses (1989, 1990), Brown (1989a, 1989b), Lapidus (1989), Evans (1990), Gooding (1990) and Lynch (1989).

Chapter 3   Executive Power and Political Leadership

A number of texts offer useful overviews of the evolving Soviet national leadership and political system in the post-1985 period. Among these, White (1991a) offers an especially detailed treatment, as does Sakwa (1990). Gustafson and Mann (1986, 1987) provide partial discussions of the elite politics of the early Gorbachev period; see also Teague and Mann (1990). Edited volumes by Lane (1988) and Brown (1989c) include a diversity of analyses by leading scholars on political elite and leadership issues. Willerton (1992) offers a comparative study of the Brezhnev and Gorbachev period elite mobility and regime formation norms. A series of articles that appeared in the journal *Soviet Economy* between 1989 and 1991 span a range of perspectives on Gorbachev's leadership style and effectiveness. Especially noteworthy are contributions by Breslauer (1989 and 1990), Brown (1990), Hough (1991) and Reddaway (1990).

For a comprehensive review of the Soviet political leadership prior to the Gorbachev period see Hough and Fainsod (1979). Breslauer (1982) provides a thorough treatment of the policy dilemmas and authority-building efforts of the Khrushchev and Brezhnev regimes. A discussion of Soviet elite generational change and its consequences is found in Bialer (1980) and Breslauer (1984). Two collections of Rigby's work (1990a, 1990b) provide a comprehensive overview of one leading scholar's careful study of the Soviet system and elite.

Among studies of Soviet subnational politics and leadership are Bahry (1987) and Urban (1989). A useful collection of articles on regional and local leadership issues is found in Kaplan (1988). Articles dealing with subnational elite politics include Brovkin (1990a), Gleason (1991) and Willerton and Reisinger (1991).

Chapter 4   The Communist Party and After

For a general account of the CPSU's traditional role and structures, see Hill and Frank (1987). Two standard histories of party development are Rigby (1968) and Schapiro (1970). The Party Programme and Rules, as adopted in 1986, are conveniently available in White (1989); for the Rules since their adoption up to 1986 see Gill (1988). Several recently published volumes contain chapters dealing with the CPSU: see for instance Sakwa (1989), Hill (1989) and Smith (1991). For a selection of more research-oriented studies see, for instance, Potichnyj (1988) and Rigby (1990b), which expertly examine a number of the issues central to the CPSU, its role and performance. Contributions to the CPSU in its changing identity and role include John Miller's two chapters in Miller *et al.* (1987), Hill (1988, 1991a, 1991b), White (1991c) and Millar (1992). A preliminary survey of the emerging multiparty system is Tolz (1990).

Chapter 5   State Institutions in Transition

The Soviet and now post-Soviet state system has been overhauled so frequently and comprehensively that it is essential, for current developments, to consult the periodical literature. Not everything has changed, however, and even where changes have taken place they need to be seen in the context of what preceded them. The theory of the state in Soviet society received attention in Harding (1984). Constitutional change up to the adoption of the 1977 Constitution is considered in Unger (1981), which includes the relevant texts. The workings of the old-style state institutions at the national level are considered in Vanneman (1977) and Siegler (1982). For the local elections that incorporated an 'experimental' element of choice, see White (1988) and Hahn (1988a); for the March 1989 elections, see White (1991b). Other issues of political reform are considered in Urban (1990), Hahn (1991b), Huber and Kelley (1991) and Huskey (1992).

Chapter 6   The Rule of Law and the Legal System

The basic English-language account of the Soviet legal system is Butler (1988), which has been continued as *Russian Law* (Butler, 1992a). For encyclopaedic coverage up to the Gorbachev era, see Feldbrugge (1985). A comprehensive casebook is Hazard *et al.* (1984), also effectively covering the pre-*perestroika* era. *Perestroika* and post-*perestroika* legislation may be found respectively in Butler, *Basic Documents on the Soviet Legal System* (1991) and in Butler, *Basic Legal Documents of the Russian Federation* (1992b). Selected enactments appear in *Soviet Statutes and Decisions* (White Plains, NY, quarterly). For scholarly discussion of these and other matters see the *Review of Socialist Law* (Dordrecht, quarterly) and the *Yearbook on Socialist Legal Systems* (Dobbs Ferry, since 1986).

Chapter 7   Nations, Republics and Commonwealth

There is a large general literature on the national question in what is now the former USSR. See, for instance, Katz (1975); Carrère d'Encausse (1979); Connor (1984), a study that includes other communist-ruled systems; and Wixman (1984), an ethnographic handbook. Karklins (1986) uses interviews with Soviet German émigrés to provide a perspective 'from below'; Motyl (1987) is principally concerned with Ukraine. Kozlov (1988) provides an informed Soviet perspective. For recent developments see Nahajlo and Swoboda (1990), Smith (1990) and Denber (1991), as well as current periodicals.

Chapter 8   Towards a Participatory Politics?

For participation under the traditional regime, see for instance Barghoorn (1966), Friedgut (1979) and Hahn (1988b), as well as Nicholas Lampert's contribution to the first edition of this book (Lampert, 1990). Useful conceptual discussions are available in Dahl (1971) and di Palma (1990). Di Franciesco and Gitelman (1984) is a study of participation conceived as parochial contacting (such as letters to officials and organisations) as well as the use of networks for favour-trading and influence-peddling. This view has been challenged in Bahry and Silver (1990), who argue that there is a greater degree of continuity between Brezhnev-era mass participation and the explosive informal associational activity under Gorbachev than is commonly supposed. There is a comprehensive record of dissent before the Gorbachev years in Alexeeva (1987) and a wide-ranging discussion of informal activity in later years in Brovkin (1990b) and Sedaitis and Butterfield (1991).

Chapter 9 *Glasnost'* and the Media

The pre-1985 background is set out in White (1979) and Benn (1989). More recent developments are surveyed in Nove (1989), Laqueur (1989) and Benn (1992), where much of the more recent information in this chapter can be found with full source references. A detailed survey of the Gorbachev reforms is available in White (1991a), especially Chapter 3 on *'Glasnost'* and public life'. The material on Nazi propaganda quoted in the chapter is taken from Dallin (1981). The best recent discussions of the Soviet and now post-Soviet media are Mickiewicz (1988), which deals with television, and Remington (1988), which gives more emphasis to the printed word. There is, of course, no substitute for a close study of the Soviet and post-Soviet electronic and printed media themselves, many of them now accessible through the translation sources that have already been mentioned (and television and radio through satellite).

Chapter 10 Economic Crisis and Reform

Given the rapid pace of development in recent years, the best sources are journals such as *Soviet Studies*, *Soviet Economy* and the commentaries provided in the Radio Liberty research reports. The best monographs are Hewett (1988), which concentrates upon the longer-term background to current changes, and Aslund (1991), which provides a thorough and critical discussion of the Gorbachev reform programme. Goldman (1991) is a lively survey of 'why *perestroika* had to fail', and an authoritative overview is the three-volume IMF study completed in late 1990 with the cooperation of the Soviet authorities (IMF, 1991). Also useful is the two-volume collection of reprinted articles from the journal, *Soviet Economy* (Hewett and Winston, 1991).

Chapter 11 Social Change and Social Policy

Soviet arguments about *perestroika*, social policy and 'socialist social justice' can be found in Gorbachev (1987), Mchedlov (1987) and Zaslavskaya (1988). A more propagandistic but nonetheless informative tract on how socialism is supposed to increase the people's well-being is provided by Klavdienko (1986). Smith (1991), Chapter 11, offers an up-to-date introductory account of the Soviet welfare state. A more detailed discussion is provided by George and Manning (1980). Employment policies are examined by McAuley (1979) and Lane (1987). Echols (1986) gives a succinct comparative analysis of earnings in East and West. On housing, see Andrusz (1984) and Morton (1974). On health care, see for instance Ryan (1978, 1991), Hyde (1974) and Navarro (1977). Davis and Feshbach look particularly at infant mortality (1980). Feshbach (1991) also links issues of population, health and environment. Pryde (1991) gives an overview of environmental policy. On youth, see

Wilson and Bachkatov (1988), Riordan (1989) and Pilkington (1992). On children's homes, refer to Waters (1992). Up-to-date discussions about crime, prostitution, drug abuse, alcoholism, health care, aging and pollution can be found in Jones, Connor and Powell (1991). A more detailed analysis of prostitution is provided by Waters (1990).

Chapter 12   The Politics of Foreign Policy

An accessible introductory text is Nogee and Donaldson (1990). The standard history is Ulam (1974) and its continuation Ulam (1983). More recent developments are covered in Hasegawa and Pravda (1990) and Laird and Hoffmann (1991). On domestic aspects, consult Bialer (1981) and Valenta and Potter (1984). For security issues, see MccGwire (1991). The changing Soviet theory of international relations, up to and including Gorbachev's 'new thinking', is considered in Light (1988) and Woodby (1989).

Chapter 13   Post-*Perestroika*: Revolution from Above v. Revolution from Below

This chapter is based upon the Soviet central press as well as popular and more specialised social science periodicals. Many of these appear in the translated sources noted at the start of this section, and additionally in *Soviet Sociology*, *Soviet Studies in Philosophy*, *Soviet Review* and *Soviet Studies in History* (all published in Armonk, NY, by M.E. Sharpe). See also *Labour Focus on Eastern Europe* (London), *Critique* (Glasgow) and *Socialist Alternatives* (Montreal and Moscow) for a critical perspective on these issues. A useful interpretive essay is Lewin (1988). An earlier account of some of the issues raised in this chapter, with full citations, is available in Mandel (1988, 1989). A more recent discussion is Ticktin (1992) and the symposium in the 1991 issue of the *Socialist Register* (London, annual); see also the extended treatment in Mandel (1991).

Chapter 14   Reconceptualising the Soviet System

On concepts employed in accounts of the system see Brown (1974), Fleron (1969) and Lane (1976). Apart from the works directly identified in the chapter, look out for reviews of conceptual approaches in more recent textbooks. Post-*perestroika* conceptualisation is just beginning; the reader may find useful ideas in journal review articles and magazines of opinion as well as in more conventional scholarly sources.

Bibliography

This bibliography contains full details of items cited in the chapters or in the Guide to Further Reading section, together with a number of other items that students may be expected to find useful.

Aage, Hans (1991) 'Popular Attitudes and *Perestroika*', *Soviet Studies*, vol. 43, no. 1, pp. 3–26.

Achimov, Hermann (1950) *Die Macht im Hintergrund*, Ulm: Spaten Verlag.

Afanas'ev, Yu. (ed.) (1988) *Inogo ne dano*, Moscow: Progress.

Aganbegyan, Abel (1988) *The Challenge: Economics of Perestroika*, London: Hutchinson.

Alexeyeva, Ludmilla (1987) *Soviet Dissent: Contemporary Movements for National, Religious and Human Rights*, Middletown, CT: Wesleyan University Press.

Almond, Gabriel and Verba, Sidney (1960) *The Civic Culture*, Princeton, NJ: Princeton University Press.

Andrusz, Gregory D. (1984) *Housing and Urban Development in the USSR*, London: Macmillan.

Arbatov, G.A. (1991) *Zatyanuvsheesya vyzdorovlenie*, Moscow: Mezhdunarodnye otnosheniya.

Arendt, Hannah (1951) *The Origins of Totalitarianism*, New York: Harcourt Brace.

Armstrong, John A. (1959) *The Soviet Political Elite: A Case Study of the Ukrainian Apparatus*, New York: Praeger.

Armstrong, John A. (1961) *The Politics of Totalitarianism. The Communist Party of the Soviet Union from 1934 to the Present*, New York: Random House.

Armstrong, John A. (1973) *The European Administrative Elite*, Princeton, NJ: Princeton University Press.

Aslund, Anders (1991) *Gorbachev's Struggle for Economic Reform*, 2nd edn, Ithaca, NY: Cornell University Press.

Azrael, Jeremy R. (1966) *Managerial Power and Soviet Politics*, Cambridge, Mass.: Harvard University Press.

Bahry, Donna (1987) *Outside Moscow: Power, Politics and Budgetary Policy in the Soviet Republics*, New York: Columbia University Press.

Bahry, Donna L. and Moses, Joel C. (eds) (1990) *Political Implications of*

326

Economic Reform in Communist Systems, New York: New York University Press.

Bahry, Donna L. and Silver, Brian D. (1990) 'Soviet Citizen Participation on the Eve of Democratization', *American Political Science Review*, vol. 84, no. 3 (September) pp. 821–48.

Balzer, Harley J. (ed.) (1991) *Five Years that Shook the World*, Boulder, CO: Westview.

Barghoorn, Frederick C. (1966) *Politics in the USSR*, Boston, Mass.: Little, Brown.

Benn, David Wedgwood (1989) *Persuasion and Soviet Politics*, Oxford: Blackwell.

Benn, David Wedgwood (1992) *From Glasnost to Freedom of Speech*: *Soviet Openness and International Relations*, London: Pinter.

Berezkin, A.V. *et al.* (1990) *Vesna 89*: *Geografiya i anatomiya parlamentskikk vyborov*, Moscow: Progress.

Bialer, Seweryn (1980) *Stalin's Successors*, New York: Cambridge University Press.

Bialer, Seweryn (ed.) (1981) *The Domestic Context of Soviet Foreign Policy*, London: Croom Helm.

Bialer, Seweryn (ed.) (1989) *Politics, Society and Nationality inside Gorbachev's Russia*, Boulder, CO: Westview.

Bloomfield, Jon (ed.) (1989) *The Soviet Revolution. Perestroika and the Remaking of Socialism*, London: Lawrence & Wishart.

Breslauer, George (1976) 'Khrushchev Reconsidered', *Problems of Communism*, vol. 25, no. 5 (September–October) pp. 18–33.

Breslauer, George (1978) 'On the Adaptability of Soviet Welfare-state Authoritarianism', in Karl W. Ryavec (ed.), *Soviet Society and the Communist Party*, Amherst: University of Massachusetts Press.

Breslauer, George (1980) 'Political Succession and the Soviet Policy Agenda', *Problems of Communism*, vol. 29, no. 3 (May–June) pp. 34–52.

Breslauer, George (1982) *Khrushchev and Brezhnev as Leaders*: *Building Authority in Soviet Politics*, London: Allen & Unwin.

Breslauer, George (1984) 'Is There a Generation Gap in the Soviet Political Establishment? Demand Articulation by RSFSR Provincial Party First Secretaries', *Soviet Studies*, vol. 36, no. 1 (January) pp. 1–25.

Breslauer, George (1989) 'Evaluating Gorbachev as Leader', *Soviet Economy*, vol. 5, no. 4, pp. 229–340.

Breslauer, George (1990) 'Gorbachev: Diverse Perspectives', *Soviet Economy*, vol. 7, no. 2, pp. 110–20.

Brovkin, Vladimir (1990a) 'First party secretaries: an endangered Soviet species?', *Problems of Communism*, vol. 39, no. 1 (January–February) pp. 15–27.

Brovkin, Vladimir (1990b) 'Revolution from Below: Informal Political Associations in Russia, 1988–1989', *Soviet Studies*, vo. 42, no. 2 (June) pp. 233–58.

Brown, A.H. (1974) *Soviet Politics and Political Science*, London: Macmillan.

Brown, Archie (1984) 'Political Science in the Soviet Union: A New Stage of Development', *Soviet Studies*, vol. 36, no. 3 (July) pp. 317–44.

Brown, Archie (1985) 'Gorbachev: New Man in the Kremlin', *Problems of Communism*, vol. 34, no. 3 (May–June) pp. 1–23.

Brown, Archie (1989a) 'Ideology and political culture', in Bialer (1989).

Brown, Archie (ed.) (1989b) *Political Leadership in the Soviet Union*, London: Macmillan.

Brown, Archie (1989c) 'Political Change in the Soviet Union', *World Policy Journal*, vol. 6, no. 3 (Summer) pp. 469–501.

Brown, Archie (1990) 'Gorbachev's Leadership: Another View', *Soviet Economy*, vol. 6, no. 2, pp. 141–54.

Brown, Archie and Gray, Jack (eds) (1977) *Political Culture and Political Change in Communist States*, New York: Holmes and Meier.

Brzezinski, Zbigniew (1989/90) 'Post-communist Nationalism', *Foreign Affairs*, vol. 68, no. 5 (Winter) pp. 1–25.

Buckley, Mary (ed.) (1992) *Perestroika and Soviet Women*, Cambridge: Cambridge University Press.

Bunce, Valerie (1981) *Do New Leaders Make a Difference? Executive Succession and Public Policy under Capitalism and Socialism*, Princeton, NJ: Princeton University Press.

Bunce, Valerie and Echols, John M. (1980) 'Soviet Politics in the Brezhnev Era: "Pluralism" or "Corporatism"?', in Donald Kelley (ed.), *Soviet Politics in the Brezhnev Era*, New York: Praeger.

Bunce, Valerie and Roeder, Philip G. (1986) 'The Effects of Leadership Succession in the Soviet Union', *American Political Science Review*, vol. 80, no. 1 (March) pp. 215–40.

Burnham, James M. (1941) *The Managerial Revolution*, New York: John Day.

Butler, William E. (1988) *Soviet Law*, 2nd edn, London: Butterworths.

Butler, William E. (ed.) (1991) *Basic Documents on the Soviet Legal System*, 3rd edn, Dobbs Ferry: Oceana.

Butler, William E. (1992a) *Russian Law*, London: Butterworths.

Butler, William E. (ed.) (1992b) *Basic Legal Documents of the Russian Federation*, Dobbs Ferry: Oceana.

Carew Hunt, R.N. (1963) *The Theory and Practice of Communism*, Baltimore, Md: Penguin.

Carr, E.H. (1945) *Nationalism and After*, London: Macmillan.

Carrère d'Encausse, Hélène (1979) *An Empire in Decline*, New York: Newsweek.

Cohen, Stephen F. (1985) *Rethinking the Soviet Experience*, New York: Oxford University Press.

Connor, Walker (1984) *The National Question in Marxist–Leninist Theory and Practice*, Princeton, NJ: Princeton University Press.

Conquest, Robert (1961) *Power and Policy in the USSR*, New York: Macmillan.

Converse, Philip E. (1969) 'Of Time and Partisan Stability', *Comparative Political Studies*, vol. 2, no. 2 (July) pp. 139–71.

Croan, Melvin (1970) 'Is Mexico the Future of East Europe? Institutional Adaptability and Political Change in Comparative Perspective', in Samuel P. Huntington and Clement H. Moore (eds), *Authoritarian Politics in Modern Society*, New York: Basic Books.

Dahl, Robert A. (1971) *Polyarchy: Participation and Opposition*, New Haven, CT: Yale University Press.

Dallin, Alexander (1981) *German Rule in Russia, 1941–1945*, 2nd edn, London: Macmillan.

Dallin, Alexander and Lapidus, Gail W. (eds) (1991) *The Soviet System in Crisis: A Reader of Western and Soviet Views*, Boulder, CO: Westview.

Davis, Christopher and Feshbach, Murray (1980) *Rising Infant Mortality in the USSR in the 1980s*, Washington DC: Bureau of the Census.

Denber, Rachel (ed.) (1991) *The Soviet Nationality Reader: The Crisis in Context*, Boulder, CO: Westview.

Dibb, Paul (1988) *The Soviet Union: The Incomplete Superpower*, 2nd edn, London: Macmillan.

Di Franciesco, Wayne and Gitelman, Zvi (1984) 'Soviet Political Culture and "Covert Participation" in Policy Implementation', *American Political Science Review*, vol. 78, no. 3 (September) pp. 603–21.

Di Palma, Guiseppe (1990) *To Craft Democracies: An Essay on Democratic Transitions*, Berkeley: University of California Press.

Doder, Dusko and Branson, Louise (1990) *Gorbachev: Heretic in the Kremlin*, New York: Viking.

Djilas, Milovan (1957) *The New Class. An Analysis of the Communist System*, London: Thames & Hudson.

Easton, David (1965) *A Systems Analysis of Political Life*, New York: Wiley.

Echols, John M. (1986) 'Does Socialism Mean Greater Equality? A Comparison of East and West along Several Major Dimensions', in Stephen White and Daniel N. Nelson (eds), *Communist Politics: A Reader*, London: Macmillan.

Edmonds, Robin (1983) *Soviet Foreign Policy: The Brezhnev Years*, Oxford, Oxford University Press.

Evans, Alfred B. (1977) 'Developed Socialism in Soviet Ideology', *Soviet Studies*, vol. 29, no. 3 (July), pp. 409–28.

Evans, Alfred B. (1986) 'The Decline of Developed Socialism? Some Trends in Recent Soviet Ideology', *Soviet Studies*, vol. 38, no. 1 (January) pp. 1–23.

Evans, Alfred B., Jr. (1990) 'Economic reward and inequality in the 1986 Program of the Communist Party of the Soviet Union', in Bahry and Moses (1990).

Fainsod, Merle (1958) *Smolensk under Soviet Rule*, Cambridge, Mass.: Harvard University Press.

Fainsod, Merle (1964) *How Russia is Ruled*, 2nd edn, Cambridge, Mass.: Harvard University Press.

Farrell, R. Barry (ed.) (1970) *Political Leadership in Eastern Europe and the Soviet Union*, Chicago: Aldine.

Fehér, Ferenc, Heller, Agnes and Márkus, Gyorgy (1983) *Dictatorship over Needs*, Oxford: Blackwell.

Feldbrugge, F.J.M. (ed.) (1985) *Encyclopedia of Soviet Law*, Dortrecht: Martinus Nijhoff.

Feshbach, Murray (1991) 'Social Change in the USSR under Gorbachev: Population, Health and Environmental Issues', in Balzer (1991).

Fischer, George (1968) *The Soviet System and Modern Society*, New York: Atherton House.

Fleron, Frederick, J., Jr. (ed.) (1969) *Communist Studies and the Social Sciences*, Chicago: Rand McNally.

Friedgut, Theodore (1979) *Political Participation in the USSR*, Princeton, NJ: Princeton University Press.

Friedrich, Carl J (ed.) (1969) *Totalitarianism in Pespective: Three Views*, New York: Praeger.

Friedrich, Carl J. and Brzezinski, Zbigniew (1956) *Totalitarian Dictatorship and Autocracy*, Cambridge, Mass.: Harvard University Press; second edn, New York: Praeger, 1961; revised edn by Carl J. Friedrich, Cambridge, Mass.: Harvard University Press, 1965.

Fukuyama, Francis (1992) *The End of History and the Last Man*, London: Hamish Hamilton.

Gabrichidze, B.N. (1991) 'Sovet, prezidium, ispolkom: sootnoshenie i razgranichenie funktsii', *Sovetskoe gosudarstvo i pravo*, no. 3, pp. 76–86.

George, Vic and Manning, Nick (1980) *Socialism, Social Welfare and the Soviet Union*, London: Routledge.

Getty, J. Arch (1985) *The Origins of the Great Purges. The Soviet Communist Party Reconsidered, 1933–1938*, New York: Cambridge University Press.

Giddens, Anthony (1973) *The Class Structure of the Advanced Societies*, London: Hutchinson.

Gill, Graeme (1987) 'The Single Party as an Agent of Development: Lessons from the Soviet Experience', *World Politics*, vol. 39, no. 4 (July) pp. 566–78.

Gill, Graeme (1988) *The Rules of the Communist Party of the Soviet Union*, London: Macmillan.

Gleason, Gregory (1991) 'Fealty and loyalty: informal authority structures in Soviet Asia', *Soviet Studies*, vol. 43, no. 4, pp. 613–28.

Goble, Paul A. (1991) 'Nationalism, Movement Groups, and Party Formation', in Sedaitis and Butterfield (1991).

Goldman, Marshall I. (1991) *What Went Wrong with Perestroika*, New York and London: Norton.

Golubeva, V. (1980) 'The Other Side of the Medal', in Women in Eastern Europe Group, *Women and Russia: First Feminist Samizdat*, London: Sheba.

Gooding, John (1990) 'Gorbachev and Democracy', *Soviet Studies*, vol. 42, no. 2 (April) pp. 195–231.

Gorbachev, Mikhail (1987) *Perestroika: New Thinking for Our Country and the World*, London: Collins.

Grey, Robert D. *et al.* (1990) 'Soviet Public Opinion and the Gorbachev Reforms', *Slavic Review*, vol. 49, no. 3 (Summer) pp. 261–71.

Grossman, Gregory (1977) 'The "Second Economy" of the USSR', *Problems of Communism*, vol. 26, no. 5 (September–October) pp. 25–40.

Gustafson, Thane and Mann, Dawn (1986) 'Gorbachev's First Year: Building Power and Authority', *Problems of Communism*, vol. 35, no. 3 (May–June) pp. 1–19.

Gustafson, Thane and Mann, Dawn (1987) 'Gorbachev's Gamble', *Problems of Communism*, vol. 36, no. 4 (July–August) pp. 1–20.

Hague, Rod and Harrop, Martin (1987) *Comparative Government and Politics*, 2nd edn, London: Macmillan.

Hahn, Jeffrey W. (1988a) 'An Experiment in Competition: The 1987 Elections to the Local Soviets', *Slavic Review*, vol. 47, no. 2 (Fall) pp. 434–47.

Hahn, Jeffrey W. (1988b) *Soviet Grassroots: Citizen Participation in Local Soviet Government*, Princeton, NJ: Princeton University Press.

Hahn, Jeffrey W. (1989) 'Power to the Soviets?', *Problems of Communism*, vol. 38, no. 1 (January–February) pp. 34–46.

Hahn, Jeffrey W. (1991a) 'Continuity and Change in Russian Political Culture', *British Journal of Political Science*, vol. 21, no. 4 (October) pp. 393–421.

Hahn, Jeffrey W. (1991b) 'Developments in Local Soviet Politics', in Alfred J. Rieber and Alvin Z. Rubinstein (eds), *Perestroika at the Crossroads*, Armonk, NY: M.E. Sharpe.

Hammer, Darrell P. (1986) *USSR: The Politics of Oligarchy*, 2nd edn, Boulder, CO: Westview.

Harasymiw, Bohdan (1984) *Political Elite Recruitment in the Soviet Union*, London: Macmillan.

Harding, Neil (ed.) (1984) *The State in Socialist Society*, London: Macmillan.

Hasegawa, Tsuyoshi and Pravda, Alex (eds) (1990) *Perestroika: Soviet Domestic and Foreign Policies*, London: Sage.

Hazard, John, *et al.* (eds) (1984) *The Soviet Legal System: The Law in the 1980s*, Dobbs Ferry: Oceana.

Hewett, Ed. A. (1988) *Reforming the Soviet Economy*, Washington DC: Brookings.

Hewett, Edward and Winston, Victor (eds) (1991) *Milestones in Glasnost and Perestroyka: The Economy*, 2 vols, Washington DC: Brookings.

Hill, Ronald J. (1988) 'Gorbachev and the CPSU', *Journal of Communist Studies*, vol. 4, no. 4 (December) pp. 18–34.

Hill, Ronald J. (1989) *The Soviet Union: Politics, Economics and Society*, 2nd edn, London: Pinter.

Hill, Ronald J. (1991a) 'The CPSU: from Monolith to Pluralist?', *Soviet Studies*, vol. 43, no. 2, pp. 217–35.

Hill, Ronald J. (1991b) 'The CPSU: Decline and Collapse', *Irish Slavonic Studies*, vol. 12, pp. 97–119.

Hill, Ronald J. and Dellenbrant, Jan Ake (eds) (1989) *Gorbachev and Perestroika*, Aldershot: Edward Elgar.

Hill, Ronald J. and Frank, Peter (1987) *The Soviet Communist Party*, 3rd edn, London: Allen & Unwin.

Hirschman, Albert (1970) *Exit, Voice and Loyalty*, Cambridge, Mass.: Harvard University Press.

Hirszowicz, Maria (1980) *The Bureaucratic Leviathan*, Oxford: Martin Robertson.

Hosking, Geoffrey A. (1991) *The Awakening of the Soviet Union*, rev. edn, London: Mandarin.

Hough, Jerry F. (1971) 'The Apparatchiki', in H.G. Skilling and Franklyn

Griffiths (eds), *Interest Groups in Soviet Politics*, Princeton, NJ: Princeton University Press.

Hough, Jerry F. (1980) *Soviet Leadership in Transition*, Washington DC: Brookings.

Hough, Jerry F. (1991) 'Understanding Gorbachev: the Importance of Politics', *Soviet Economy*, vol. 7, no. 2, pp. 166–84.

Hough, Jerry F. and Fainsod, Merle (1979) *How the Soviet Union is Governed*, Cambridge, Mass.: Harvard University Press.

Huber, Robert T. and Kelley, Donald R. (eds) (1991) *Perestroika-era Politics: The New Soviet Legislature and Gorbachev's Political Reforms*, Boulder, CO: Westview.

Huskey, Eugene (ed.) (1992) *Executive Power and Soviet Politics. The Rise and Fall of the Soviet State*, Boulder, CO: Westview.

Hyde, Gordon (1974) *The Soviet Health Service*, London: Lawrence & Wishart.

IMF (1991) *A Study of the Soviet Economy*, 3 vols, Paris: IMF and World Bank.

Johnson, Chalmers (ed.) (1970) *Change in Communist Systems*, Stanford, Cal.: Stanford University Press.

Jones, Anthony, Connor, Walter D. and Powell, David E. (eds) (1991) *Soviet Social Problems*, Boulder, CO: Westview.

Jones, Ellen (1986) *Red Army and Society. A Sociology of the Soviet Military*, paperback edn, London: Allen & Unwin.

Jowitt, Kenneth (1974) 'An Organizational Approach to the Study of Political Culture in Marxist–Leninist Systems', *American Political Science Review*, vol. 68, no. 3 (September) pp. 1171–9.

Jowitt, Kenneth (1975) 'Inclusion and Mobilization in European Leninist Regimes', *World Politics*, vol. 28, no. 1 (October) pp. 69–96.

Jowitt, Kenneth (1978) *The Leninist Response to National Dependency*, Berkeley: Institute of International Studies.

Jowitt, Kenneth (1983) 'Soviet Neotraditionalism: the Political Corruption of a Leninist Regime', *Soviet Studies*, vol. 35, no. 3 (July) pp. 275–97.

Jowitt, Kenneth (1987) 'Moscow "Centre" ', *East European Politics and Society*, vol. 1, no. 3 (Autumn) pp. 296–348.

Jowitt, Kenneth (1990) 'Gorbachev: Bolshevik or Menshevik?', in White, Pravda and Gitelman (1990).

Joyce, Walter, *et al.* (eds) (1989) *Gorbachev and Gorbachevism*, London: Cass.

Kaplan, Cynthia S. (ed.) (1988) 'Local Party Organizations in the USSR', *Studies in Comparative Communism*, vol. 21, no. 1 (Spring) pp. 3–98.

Karklins, Rasma (1986) *Ethnic Relations in the USSR. The Perspective from Below*, Boston: Allen & Unwin.

Katsenelinboigen, Aron (1976) 'Conflicting Trends in Soviet Economics in the Post-Stalin Era', *Russian Review*, vol. 35, no. 4 (October) pp. 373–99.

Katz, Zev (ed.) (1975) *A Handbook of Major Soviet Nationalities*, New York: Free Press.

Keane, John (ed.) (1988) *Civil Society and the State*, London: Verso.

Klavdienko, V. (1986) *People's Wellbeing in Socialist Society*, Moscow: Progress.

Knight, Amy W. (1988) *The KGB. Police and Politics in the Soviet Union*, Boston: Unwin Hyman.

Konrád, George and Szelenyi, Ivan (1979) *The Intellectuals on the Road to Class Power*, New York and London: Harcourt Brace Janovich.

Kornai, Janos (1980) *Economics of Shortage*, Amsterdam: North-Holland.

Kozlov, V.I. (1988) *The Peoples of the Soviet Union*, London: Hutchinson.

Laird, Robbin F. (ed.) (1987) *Soviet Foreign Policy*, New York: Academy of Political Science.

Laird, Robbin F. and Hoffmann, Erik P. (eds) (1987) *Soviet Foreign Policy in a Changing World*, New York: Aldine.

Laird, Robbin and Hoffmann, Erik P. (eds) (1991) *Contemporary Issues in Soviet Foreign Policy*, New York: Aldine.

Lampert, Nicholas (1985) *Whistleblowing in the Soviet Union: Complaints and Abuses under State Socialism*, London: Macmillan.

Lampert, Nicholas (1990) 'Patterns of Participation', in White, Pravda and Gitelman (1990).

Lane, David (1976) *The Socialist Industrial State. Towards a Political Sociology of State Socialism*, London: Allen & Unwin.

Lane, David (1987) *Soviet Labour and the Ethic of Communism*, Brighton: Harvester.

Lane, David (ed.) (1988) *Elites and Political Power in the USSR*, Aldershot: Edward Elgar.

Lapidus, Gail W. (1989) 'State and Society: Towards the Emergence of Civil Society in the Soviet Union', in Bialer (1989).

Laqueur, Walter (1989) *The Long Road to Freedom: Russia and Glasnost'*, London: Unwin Hyman.

Lewin, Moshe (1988) *The Gorbachev Phenomenon*, Berkeley: University of California Press.

Light, Margot (1988) *The Soviet Theory of International Relations*, Brighton: Wheatsheaf.

Lowenhardt, John (1982) *The Soviet Politburo*, Edinburgh: Canongate.

Lynch, Allen (1989) *Gorbachev's Intellectual Outlook: Intellectual Origins and Political Consequences*, New York: Institute for East–West Security Studies.

Mandel, David (1988) 'Economic Reform and Democracy in the Soviet Union', in Ralph Miliband *et al.* (eds), *The Socialist Register 1988*, London: Merlin Press.

Mandel, David (1989) '"Revolutionary Reform" in Soviet Factories', in Ralph Miliband *et al.* (eds), *The Socialist Register 1989*, London: Merlin Press.

Mandel, David (1991) *Perestroika and Soviet Society: Rebirth of the Soviet Labor Movement*, Montreal: Black Rose Press.

McAuley, Alastair (1979) *Economic Welfare in the Soviet Union*, London: Allen & Unwin.

McCauley, Martin (ed.) (1987) *The Soviet Union under Gorbachev*, London: Macmillan.

MccGwire, Michael (1991) *Perestroika and Soviet National Security*, Washington DC: Brookings.

Mchedlow, M.P. (1987) *Socialist Society: its Social Justice*, Moscow: Progress.

Medvedev, Zhores (1988) *Gorbachev*, rev. edn, Oxford: Blackwell.

Meyer, Alfred G. (1961) 'USSR Incorporated', *Slavic Review*, vol. 20, no. 3 (October) pp. 369–76.

Meyer, Alfred G. (1965) *The Soviet Political System. An Interpretation*, New York: Random House.

Mickiewicz, Ellen (1988) *Split Signals. Television and Politics in the Soviet Union*, New York: Oxford University Press.

Millar, James R. (ed.) (1987) *Politics, Work, and Daily Life in the USSR. A Survey of Former Citizens*, New York: Cambridge University Press.

Millar, James R. (ed.) (1992) *Cracks in the Monolith. Party Power in the Brezhnev Era*, Boulder, CO: Westview.

Miller, John H. *et al.* (eds) (1987) *Gorbachev at the Helm: A New Era in Soviet Politics?*, London: Croom Helm.

Morrison, John (1991) *Boris Yeltsin*, Baltimore Md: Penguin.

Morton, Henry W. (1974) 'What Have the Soviet Leaders Done about the Housing Crisis?', in Henry W. Morton and Rudolf L. Tokes (eds), *Soviet Politics and Society in the 1970s*, New York: Free Press.

Moses, Joel C. (1989) 'Democratic Reform in the Gorbachev Era: Dimensions of Reform in the Soviet Union, 1986–1989', *Russian Review*, vol. 48, no. 3 (July) pp. 235–69.

Moses, Joel C. (1990) 'The Political Implications of New Technology for the Soviet Union', in Bahry and Moses (1990).

Motyl, Alexander J. (1987) *Will the Non-Russians Rebel?*, Ithaca: Cornell University Press.

Nahajlo, Bohdan and Swoboda, Victor (1990) *Soviet Disunion. A History of the Nationalities Problems in the USSR*, London: Hamish Hamilton.

Navarro, Vincente (1977) *Social Security and Medicine in the USSR*, Lexington: Lexington Books.

Nelson, Daniel N. (1988) *Elite–Mass Relations in Communist Systems*, London: Macmillan.

Nogee, Joseph L. and Donaldson, Robert H. (1990) *Soviet Foreign Policy since World War II*, 4th edn, Oxford and New York: Pergamon.

Nove, Alec (1989) *Glasnost' in Action*, Boston: Unwin Hyman.

Obolonsky, A.V. (1990) 'Kakuyu politicheskuyu sistemu my unasledovali (Anatomiya "doaprel'skogo politicheskogo rezhima")', *Sovetskoe gosudarstvo i pravo*, no. 10, pp. 54–71.

O'Donnell, Guillermo, *et al.* (eds) (1986) *Transitions from Authoritarian Rule: Comparative Perspectives*, Baltimore Md: Johns Hopkins University Press.

Parry, Albert (1968) 'Jan Waclaw Machajski. His Life and Work', in A. Volsky, *Umstvennyi rabochii*, New York and Baltimore: Interlanguage Literary Associates.

Pethybridge, Roger (1962) *A Key to Soviet Politics: The Crisis of the Anti-Party Group*, London: Allen & Unwin.

Pilkington, Hilary (1992) 'Going Out "In Style": Girls in Youth Cultural Activity', in Buckley (1992).

Potichnyj, Peter J. (ed.) (1988) *The Soviet Union: Party and Society*. New York: Cambridge University Press.

Pryde, Philip (1991) *Environmental Management in the Soviet Union*, Cambridge: Cambridge University Press.

Pye, Lucian W. (1990) 'Political Science and the Crisis of Authoritarianism', *American Political Science Review*, vol. 84, no. 1 (March) pp. 3–19.

Reddaway, Peter (1990) 'The Quality of Gorbachev's Leadership', *Soviet Economy*, vol. 6, no. 2, pp. 125–40.

Remington, Thomas F. (1988) *The Truth of Authority. Ideology and Communication in the Soviet Union*, Pittsburgh: University of Pittsburgh Press.

Rigby, T.H. (1968) *Communist Party Membership in the Soviet Union 1917–1967*, Princeton, NJ: Princeton University Press.

Rigby, T.H. (1979) *Lenin's Government: Sovnarkom 1917–1922*, New York: Cambridge University Press.

Rigby, T.H. (1990a) *The Changing Soviet System*, Aldershot: Edward Elgar.

Rigby, T.H. (1990b) *Political Elites in the USSR*, Aldershot: Edward Elgar.

Rigby, T.H. and Fehér, Ferenc (eds) (1982) *Political Legitimation in Communist States*, London: Macmillan.

Rigby, T.H. and Harasymiw, Bogdan (eds) (1983) *Leadership Selection and Patron–Client Relations in the USSR and Yugoslavia*, London: Allen & Unwin.

Riordan, James (ed.) (1989) *Soviet Youth Culture*, London: Macmillan.

Roeder, Philip G. (1985) 'Do New Soviet Leaders Really Make a Difference? Rethinking the "Succession Connection"', *American Political Science Review*, vol. 79, no. 4 (December) pp. 958–76.

Rostow, W.W. (1960) *The Stages of Economic Growth: A Non-Communist Manifesto*, Cambridge: Cambridge University Press.

Ruge, Gerd (1991) *Gorbachev: A Biography*, London: Chatto.

Ryan, Michael (1978) *The Organisation of Soviet Medical Care*, Oxford: Blackwell.

Ryan, Michael (1991) 'Policy and Administration in the Soviet Health Service', *Social Policy and Administration*, vol. 25, no. 3 (September) pp. 327–37.

Saivetz, Carol and Jones, Anthony T. (eds) (1992) *The Emergence of Pluralism in the Soviet Union*, Boulder, CO: Westview.

Sakharov, A.D. (1974) *Sakharov Speaks*, New York: Knopf.

Sakwa, Richard (1989) *Soviet Politics: An Introduction*, London: Routledge.

Sakwa, Richard (1990) *Gorbachev and his Reforms 1985–1990*, Englewood Cliffs, NJ: Prentice-Hall.

Scanlan, James P. (1985) *Marxism in the USSR. A Critical Survey of Current Soviet Thought*, Ithaca: Cornell University Press.

Schapiro, Leonard (1970) *The Communist Party of the Soviet Union*, 2nd edn, London: Eyre & Spottiswoode.

Schapiro, Leonard (1972) *Totalitarianism*, London: Pall Mall.

Schmidt-Hauer, Christian (1986) *Gorbachev: The Road to Power*, London: Tauris.

Sedaitis, Judith and Butterfield, Jim (eds) (1991) *Perestroika from Below: Social Movements in the Soviet Union*, Boulder, CO: Westview.

Shevardnadze, Eduard (1991) *The Future Belongs to Freedom*, London: Sinclair-Stevenson.

Shlapentokh, Vladimir (1989) *Public and Private Lives of the Soviet People: Changing Values in Post-Stalin Russia*, New York: Oxford University Press.

Siegler, Robert W. (1982) *The Standing Commissions of the Supreme Soviet*, New York: Praeger.

Skilling, H.G. and Griffiths, Franklyn (eds) (1971) *Interest Groups in Soviet Politics*, Princeton, NJ: Princeton University Press.

Slavin, Boris and Davydov, Valentin (1991) 'Stanovlenie mnogopartiinosti', *Partiinaya zhizn'*, no. 18 (September) pp. 6–16.

Smith, Gordon B. (1991) *Soviet Politics: Struggling with Change*, 2nd edn, London: Macmillan.

Smith, Graham (ed.) (1990) *The Nationalities Question in the Soviet Union*, London: Longman.

Sobchak, Anatolii (1991) *Khozhdenie vo vlast*, Moscow: Novosti.

Solomon, Susan G. (ed.) (1983) *Pluralism in the Soviet Union*, London: Macmillan.

Steele, Jonathan (1985) *The Limits of Soviet Power*, Harmondsworth: Penguin.

Stepan, Alfred and Linz, Juan (eds) (forthcoming) *Democratic Transitions and Consolidation: Eastern Europe, Southern Europe and Latin America*, New Haven, CT: Yale University Press.

Tatu, Michel (1988) 'The 19th Party Conference', *Problems of Communism*, vol. 38, nos 3–4 (May–August) pp. 1–15.

Teague, Elizabeth (1990) 'Soviet Workers Find a Voice', *Report on the USSR*, 13 July, pp. 13–17.

Teague, Elizabeth and Mann, Dawn (1990) 'Gorbachev's Dual Role', *Problems of Communism*, vol. 39, no. 1 (January–February) pp. 1–14.

Thompson, Terry L. (1989) *Ideology and Policy: The Political Uses of Doctrine in the Soviet Union*, Boulder, CO: Westview.

Ticktin, Hillel (1992) *The Origins of the Crisis in the USSR*, Armonk, NY: M.E. Sharpe.

Tolz, Vera (1990) *The USSR's Emerging Party System*, New York: Praeger.

Trotsky, Leon (1937) *The Revolution Betrayed. What is the Soviet Union and Where is it Going?*, London: Faber.

Tsabriya, D.D. (1990) *Sistema upravleniya – k novomu obliku*, Moscow: Politizdat.

Tucker, Robert C. (1987) *Political Culture and Leadership in Soviet Russia*, Brighton: Wheatsheaf.

Ulam, Adam (1974) *Expansion and Coexistence. Soviet Foreign Policy, 1917–1973*, 2nd edn, New York: Praeger.

Ulam, Adam (1983) *Dangerous Relations. The Soviet Union in World Politics, 1970–1982*, New York: Oxford University Press.

Unger, Aryeh L. (1981) *Constitutional Development in the USSR*, London: Methuen.

Urban, Michael E. (1985) 'Conceptualising Political Power in the USSR: Patterns of Binding and Bonding', *Studies in Comparative Communism*, vol. 18, no. 4 (Winter) pp. 207–26.

Urban, Michael E. (1989) *An Algebra of Power: Elite Circulation in the Belorussian Republic 1966–1986*, Cambridge: Cambridge University Press.

Urban, Michael E. (1990) *More Power to the Soviets*, Aldershot: Edward Elgar.

Valenta, Jiri and Potter, William (eds) (1984) *Soviet Decision-making for National Security*, London: Allen & Unwin.

Vanneman, Peter (1977) *The Supreme Soviet: Politics and the Legislative Process in the Soviet Political System*, Durham, NC: Duke University Press.

Voslensky, Michael (1984) *Nomenklatura: The Soviet Ruling Class*, Garden City: Doubleday.

Walker, Rachel (1989) 'Marxism–Leninism as Discourse: the Politics of the Empty Signifier and the Double Bind', *British Journal of Political Science*, vol. 19, no. 2 (April) pp. 161–90.

Waters, Elizabeth (1990) 'Restructuring the "Woman Question": *Perestroika* and Prostitution', *Feminist Review*, no. 33, pp. 3–19.

Waters, Elizabeth (1992) 'Cuckoo Mothers and *Apparatchiki*: *Glasnost'* and Soviet Children's Homes', in Buckley (1992).

White, Stephen (1979) *Political Culture and Soviet Politics*, London: Macmillan.

White, Stephen (1988) 'Reforming the Electoral System', *Journal of Communist Studies*, vol. 4, no. 4 (December) pp. 1–17.

White, Stephen (1989) *Soviet Communism: Programme and Rules*, London: Routledge.

White, Stephen (1990a) *Gorbachev in Power*, Cambridge and New York: Cambridge University Press.

White, Stephen (1990b) "Democratisation" in the USSR', *Soviet Studies*, vol. 42, no. 1 (January) pp. 3–24.

White, Stephen (1991a) *Gorbachev and After*, Cambridge: Cambridge University Press.

White, Stephen (1991b) 'The Soviet Elections of 1989: From Acclamation to Limited Choice', *Coexistence*, vol. 28, no. 4 (December) pp. 513–39.

White, Stephen (1991c) 'Rethinking the CPSU', *Soviet Studies*, vol. 43, no. 3, pp. 405–28.

White, Stephen and Pravda, Alex (eds) (1988) *Ideology and Soviet Politics*, London: Macmillan.

White, Stephen, Pravda, Alex and Gitelman, Zvi (eds) (1990) *Developments in Soviet Politics*, London: Macmillan and Durham, NC: Duke University Press.

Willerton, John P. (1987) 'Patronage Networks and Coalition Building in the Brezhnev Era', *Soviet Studies*, vol. 39, no. 2 (April) pp. 175–204.

Willerton, John P. (1992) *Patronage and Politics in the USSR*, Cambridge: Cambridge University Press.

Willerton, John P. and Reisinger, William M. (1991) 'Troubleshooters,

Political Machines, and Moscow's Regional Control', *Slavic Review*, vol. 50, no. 2 (Summer) pp. 347–58.

Wilson, Andrew and Bachkatov, Nina (1988) *Living with Glasnost'. Youth and Society in a Changing Russia*, Harmondsworth: Penguin.

Wixman, Ronald (1984) *The Peoples of the USSR: An Ethnographic Handbook*, Armonk, NY: Sharpe.

Woodby, Sylvia (1989) *Gorbachev and the Decline of Ideology in Soviet Foreign Policy*, Boulder, CO: Westview.

Woodby, Sylvia and Evans, Alfred B., Jr. (eds) (1990) *Restructuring Soviet Ideology: Gorbachev's New Thinking*, Boulder, CO: Westview.

Zaslavskaya, Tatyana (1988) 'The Human Factor in the Development of the Economy and Social Justice', in Vladimir Gordon (trans.), *Big Changes in the USSR*, Moscow: Progress.

Zaslavsky, Victor and Brym, Robert J. (1978) 'The Functions of Elections in the USSR', *Soviet Studies*, vol. 30, no. 3 (July) pp. 362–71.

Zhuravlev, V.V. *et al.* (1990) *Na poroge krizisa: narastanie zastoinykh yavlenii v partii i obshchestve*, Moscow: Politizdat.

Index